THE ANNUAL DIRECTORY OF

New England
Bed & Breakfasts

1999 Edition

THE ANNUAL DIRECTORY OF

New England
Bed & Breakfasts

1999 Edition

Tracey Menges, *Compiler*

RUTLEDGE HILL PRESS®
NASHVILLE, TENNESSEE

Published in Nashville, Tennessee, by Rutledge Hill Press®, Inc., 211 Seventh Avenue North, Nashville, Tennessee 37219. Distributed in Canada by H. B. Fenn and Company, Ltd., 34 Nixon Road, Bolton, Ontario L7E 1W2. Distributed in Australia by The Five Mile Press Pty. Ltd., 22 Summit Road, Noble Park, Victoria, 3174. Distributed in New Zeland by Tandem Press, 2 Rugby Road, Birkenhead, Auckland 10. Distributed in the United Kingdom by Verulam Publishing, Ltd., 152a Park Street Lane, Park Street, St. Albans, Hertfordshire AL2 2AU.

Cover design and book design by Harriette Bateman
Page composition by Roger A. DeLiso, Nashville, Tennessee

Printed in the United States of America.

1 2 3 4 5 6—02 01 00 99 98

Contents

Introduction

The 1999 edition of *The Annual Directory of New England Bed & Breakfasts* is one of the most comprehensive directories available today. Whether planning your honeymoon, a family vacation or reunion, or a business trip (many bed and breakfasts provide conference facilities), you will find what you are looking for at a bed and breakfast. They are all here just waiting to be discovered.

Once you know your destination, look for it, or one close by, to see what accommodations are available. Each state has a general map with city locations to help you plan your trip efficiently. There are listings for all New England states and the Canadian Provinces of New Brunswick, Nova Scotia, Prince Edward Island, Quebec. Don't be surprised to find a listing in the remote spot you thought only you knew about. Even if your favorite hideaway isn't listed, you're sure to discover a new one.

How to Use This Guide

The sample listing below is typical of the entries in this directory. Each bed and breakfast is listed alphabetically by city and establishment name. The description provides an overview of the bed and breakfast and may include nearby activities and attractions. *Please note that the descriptions have been provided by the hosts. The publisher has not visited these bed and breakfasts and is not responsible for inaccuracies.*

Following the description are notes that have been designed for easy reference. Looking at the sample, a quick glance tells you that this bed and breakfast has four guest rooms, two with private baths (PB) and two that share a bath (SB). The rates are for two people sharing one room. Tax may or may not be included.

GREAT TOWN

Favorite Bed and Breakfast

123 Main Street, 12345
(800) 555-1234

This quaint bed and breakfast is surrounded by five acres of award-winning landscaping and gardens. There are four guest rooms, each individually decorated with antiques. It is close to antique shops, restaurants, and outdoor activities. Breakfast includes homemade specialties and is served in the formal dining room at guests' leisure. Minimum stay of two nights.

Hosts: Sue and Jim Smith
Rooms: 4 (2 PB; 2 SB) $65-80
Full Breakfast
Credit Cards: A, B
Notes: 2, 5, 8, 10, 11, 12, 13

The specifics of "Credit Cards" and "Notes" are listed at the bottom of each page. For example, the letter A means that MasterCard is accepted. The number 10 means that tennis is available on the premises or within 10 to 15 miles.

In many cases, a bed and breakfast is listed with a reservation service that represents several houses in one area. This service is responsible for bookings and can answer other questions you may have. They also inspect each listing and can help you choose the best place for your needs.

Before You Arrive

Now that you have chosen the bed and breakfast that interests you, there are some things you need to find out. You should always make reservations in advance, and while you are doing so you should ask about the local taxes. City taxes can be an unwelcome surprise. Make sure there are accommodations for your children. If you have dietary needs or prefer nonsmoking rooms, find out if these requirements can be met. Ask about check-in times and cancellation policies. Get specific directions. Most bed and breakfasts are readily accessible, but many are a little out of the way.

When You Arrive

In many instances you are visiting someone's home. Be respectful of their property, their schedules, and their requests. Don't smoke if they ask you not to, and don't show up with pets without prior arrangement. Be tidy in shared bathrooms, and be prompt. Most places have small staffs or may be run single-handedly and cannot easily adjust to surprises.

With a little effort and a sense of adventure you will learn firsthand the advantages of bed and breakfast travel. You will rediscover hospitality in a time when kindness seems to have been pushed aside. With the help of this directory, you will find accommodations that are just as exciting as your traveling plans.

We would like to hear from you about any experiences you have had or any inns you wish to recommend. Please write us at the following address:

The Annual Directory of
New England Bed & Breakfasts
211 Seventh Avenue North
Nashville, Tennessee 37219

THE ANNUAL DIRECTORY OF

New England
Bed & Breakfasts

1999 Edition

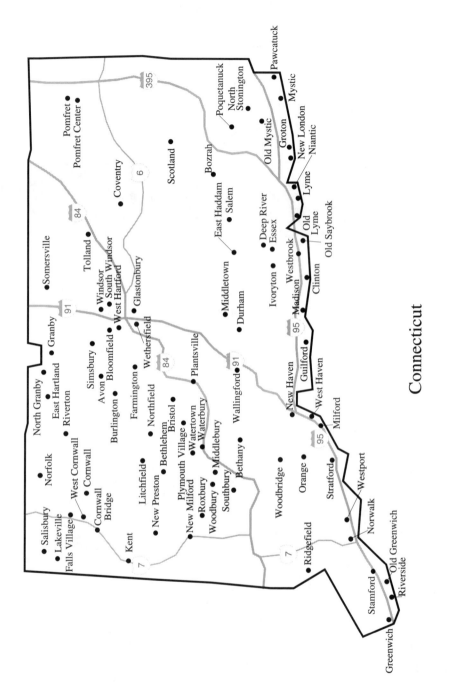

Connecticut

Connecticut

AVON

Nutmeg Bed and Breakfast Agency

P.O. Box 1117, West Hartford, 06127-1117
(860) 236-6698; (800) 727-7592
FAX (860) 232-7680

405. This Colonial farmhouse was built in 1850 and sits on three acres bordering the Farmington River. Lovely screened porch and open deck where guests are welcome to relax and enjoy the scenery. The guest room, on the second floor, is furnished with white wicker. The steps, quite steep, are original, adding to the authenticity of the house. The guest room has a double bed, TV, and air conditioning for the warmer weather. There is an additional small room for a child. Continental breakfast. Children welcome. No smoking. Dog in residence.

BETHANY

Nutmeg Bed and Breakfast Agency

P.O. Box 1117, West Hartford, 06127-1117
(860) 236-6698; (800) 727-7592
FAX (860) 232-7680

204. This stately English-style country manor, built in 1937, has a surprisingly contemporary interior. Convenient to New Haven for Yale functions. Exercise equipment available and there are three guest rooms. The second floor room has twin beds, which can be made into a king-size bed, and private bath. Also on the second floor is a room with a futon and a half-bath. These two rooms would be most suitable for families traveling together. On the third floor is a double bed and private bath. Continental breakfast. Children welcome. No smoking.

BETHLEHEM

Nutmeg Bed and Breakfast Agency

P.O. Box 1117, West Hartford, 06127-1117
(860) 236-6698; (800) 727-7592
FAX (860) 232-7680

310. On a very secluded hillside is one of the oldest New England bed and breakfasts. The building dates back to the 1700s and features three sitting rooms, three dining rooms, and four guest rooms. All are tastefully furnished. One guest room has a fireplace, one of four original to the house. Wide-plank floors and lots of rustic charm inside combine with the beauty of the country outside for an unbeatable getaway experience. Full breakfast. Children welcome. No smoking.

BLOOMFIELD

Nutmeg Bed and Breakfast Agency

P.O. Box 1117, West Hartford, 06127-1117
(860) 236-6698; (800) 727-7592
FAX (860) 232-7680

450. Four guest rooms with private and shared baths. One has connecting playroom with TV and telephone. Another is a full suite with fireplace. Convenient to West Hartford and Hartford and across the road from Penwood State Forest for walking,

NOTES: Credit cards accepted: A MasterCard; B Visa; C American Express; D Discover; E Diner's Club; F Other; 2 Personal checks accepted; 3 Lunch available; 4 Dinner available; 5 Open all year; 6 Pets welcome; 7 No smoking; 8 Children welcome; 9 Social drinking allowed; 10 Tennis nearby; 11 Swimming nearby; 12 Golf nearby; 13 Skiing nearby; 14 May be booked through a travel agent; 15 Handicapped accessible.

jogging, or cross-country skiing. Full breakfast. Children welcome.

BOZRAH

Nutmeg Bed and Breakfast Agency

P.O. Box 1117, West Hartford, 06127-1117
(860) 236-6698; (800) 727-7592
FAX (860) 232-7680

505. Gambral Home circa 1790. Lovely country setting; host grows berries and makes wine; the berries are served in the country breakfast. Twenty minutes from Mystic and Ledyard. The four guest rooms have private baths, TVs, telephones, gas fireplaces, beautiful furnishings, ceiling fans; one bath has jet tub. Breakfast is served in glass-enclosed sunroom and guests have use of several sitting rooms. Guest room wing has its own private entrance. No children. No smoking.

BRISTOL

Chimney Crest Manor

5 Founder Drive, 06010
(860) 582-4219; FAX (860) 584-5903

Experience quiet elegance in this splendid 32-room Tudor mansion. Chimney Crest was built in 1930 in the Federal Hill historic district, just minutes away from the Litchfield Hills, where guests will find antiques, wineries, parks, museums, and restaurants. Stay in the spacious suites for pleasure or on business. Guests are treated with warm, attentive hospitality. Listed in the National Register of Historic Places. Mobil Travel Guide three-star-rated. Closed Christmas Eve and Christmas Day.

Hosts: Don and Cynthia Cimadamore
Rooms: 5 (PB) $75-165
Full Breakfast
Credit Cards: A, B, C
Notes: 2, 7, 9, 10, 11, 12, 13, 14

Nutmeg Bed and Breakfast Agency

P.O. Box 1117, West Hartford, 06127-1117
(860) 236-6698; (800) 727-7592
FAX (860) 232-7680

411. Bright and spacious English Tudor mansion has a grand foyer, large den, elegant formal dining room, sunroom, and back patio overlooking Farmington Valley and the fountains in the large yard. The ballroom suite contains a large living room with double sofa bed, a full eat-in kitchen, bedroom with double bed, and bath. Also five suites on second floor, including one with two bedrooms and a kitchen. All rooms have ceiling fans and TVs. Full breakfast. Smoking in designated areas only. Children welcome.

BURLINGTON

Nutmeg Bed and Breakfast Agency

P.O. Box 1117, West Hartford, 06127-1117
(860) 236-6698; (800) 727-7592
FAX (860) 232-7680

478. This ranch-style home has a screened porch, pool, and lovely gardens. There is a room with a double bed, private bath, living room, porch, and deck for guests' use. Convenient to Avon Old Farms, Miss Porter's, and the University of Connecticut Medical Center. Full breakfast. No children. No smoking. Dog on premises.

CLINTON

Captain Dibbell House

21 Commerce Street, 06413
(860) 669-1646; FAX (860) 669-2300

This 1866 Victorian, on a historic residential street, is two blocks from the harbor and has a century-old, wisteria-covered iron truss bridge. Rooms are furnished with

NOTES: Credit cards accepted: A MasterCard; B Visa; C American Express; D Discover; E Diner's Club; F Other; 2 Personal checks accepted; 3 Lunch available; 4 Dinner available; 5 Open all year; 6 Pets welcome;

a comfortable mix of heirlooms, antiques, auction finds, and a growing collection of original art by New England artists. Bicycles are available. The inn is closed January through March. Children 14 and older are welcome.

Hosts: Helen and Ellis Adams
Rooms: 4 (PB) $85-105
Full Breakfast
Credit Cards: A, B, C
Notes: 2, 7, 9, 10, 11, 12, 13, 14

Nutmeg Bed and Breakfast Agency

P.O. Box 1117, West Hartford, 06127-1117
(860) 236-6698; (800) 727-7592
FAX (860) 232-7680

501. This 1865 Victorian sea captain's home is two blocks from the beach and one block from town. It is furnished with family heirlooms, antiques, and other comfortable pieces. A formal dining room and a grand living room featuring a fireplace, player piano, TV, and games, offering opportunities for conversation and relaxation. Four guest rooms have private baths and ceiling fans. Bicycles, fresh fruits, flowers, bathrobes, and light refreshments are some of the amenities offered. Full breakfast. Smoking permitted in designated areas only. No children.

CORNWALL

Covered Bridge

69 Maple Avenue, Norfolk, 06058
(860) 542-5944; FAX (860) 542-5690

2C. Enjoy warm, quiet hospitality at this custom-designed stone home set on a 64-acre private estate with breathtaking views of the countryside. Hearty full breakfasts are served before the library fireplace or on the terrace. All of the rooms are decorated in antiques. Two guest rooms with private baths. $125.

CORNWALL BRIDGE

Nutmeg Bed and Breakfast Agency

P.O. Box 1117, West Hartford, 06127-1117
(860) 236-6698; (800) 727-7592
FAX (860) 232-7680

344. Recently renovated small inn/motel has five rooms on the second floor of inn; three rooms have private baths, two share and are rented to families or to couples traveling together; also second-floor sitting room with TV, books, and games. Rooms have TVs. Full breakfast included; inn also has restaurant (serving lunch and dinner) and a bar. Children allowed (five and under stay free). Smoking permitted. Dog and cat on premises. Pets welcomed. Checkin 2:00 P.M.; checkout 11:00 A.M.

COVENTRY

Nutmeg Bed and Breakfast Agency

P.O. Box 1117, West Hartford, 06127-1117
(860) 236-6698; (800) 727-7592
FAX (860) 232-7680

457. This Colonial was built in 1731 and operated as a tavern until 1823. It was used as part of the Underground Railroad in the mid-1800s. The two guest rooms have canopied beds, working fireplaces, and a feather mattress for winter warmth. One has a private bath, the other a shared. There is also a cottage with private entrance, sofa bed, private bath, fireplace, and small kitchen. Hostess will prepare a hearth-cooked dinner with advance notice. Full country breakfast on weekends; Continental weekdays. Children 10 and over welcome. No smoking. Cat in residence.

463. Gentleman's farmhouse built in 1731 on three and one-quarter acres with a pool,

7 No smoking; 8 Children welcome; 9 Social drinking allowed; 10 Tennis nearby; 11 Swimming nearby; 12 Golf nearby; 13 Skiing nearby; 14 May be booked through a travel agent; 15 Handicapped accessible.

Jacuzzi, maple trees with hammocks, and three fireplaces. The hosts have carefully added modern amenities so the charm of their original Colonial home is not compromised. Four guest rooms with double beds share one upstairs and one downstairs bath. Rollaway available. Full breakfast. Infants and children over five welcomed. No smoking. Dog in residence.

DEEP RIVER

Riverwind Inn

209 Main Street, 06417
(203) 526-2014

With its eight wonderfully appointed guest rooms, rambling common areas, and informal country atmosphere, Riverwind is more than just a place to stay; it's a destination. Relax, step back in time, and enjoy a stay amid an enchanting collection of New England and southern country antiques. Each morning starts with the inn's complimentary southern buffet breakfast.

Hosts: Barbara Barlow and Bob Bucknall
Rooms: 8 (PB) $105-175
Full Breakfast
Credit Cards: A, B
Notes: 2, 5, 9, 10, 11, 12, 13, 14

DURHAM

Nutmeg Bed and Breakfast Agency

P.O. Box 1117, West Hartford, 06127-1117
(860) 236-6698; (800) 727-7592
FAX (860) 232-7680

509. Georgian Colonial built in 1740 with museum-quality restoration. Furnished with antiques. Two second-floor guest rooms with private baths, one room with twin beds, and one pencil-post double-canopied rope bed. Both bathrooms have beautifully crafted fixtures. Continental

breakfast. No smoking. Charming cat on the premises.

EAST HADDAM

Bishopsgate Inn

7 Norwich Road, 06423
(860) 873-1677; FAX (860) 873-3898

This exceptional 1818 Colonial home welcomes guests seeking gracious hospitality in well-appointed accommodations. Six tastefully furnished guest rooms with private baths. Four have open fireplaces and one a sauna. A short walk to the Goodspeed Opera House and shops, the inn's setting offers seclusion even in the middle of town. Known for its exceptional kitchen. Ample breakfasts are included while picnic lunches to go and candlelight dinners served in guests' rooms can be ordered.

Hosts: The Kagel Family—Colin Sr., Jane, Colin Jr., and Lisa
Rooms: 6 (PB) $95-140
Full Breakfast
Credit Cards: A, B
Notes: 2, 3, 4, 5, 7, 9, 12

EAST HARTLAND

Nutmeg Bed and Breakfast Agency

P.O. Box 1117, West Hartford, 06127-1117
(860) 236-6698; (800) 727-7592
FAX (860) 232-7680

480. Guest house adjacent to Colonial farmhouse built in 1700s. Private entrance to sitting room with working fireplace, double Murphy bed, complete kitchen, full bath, and beautiful setting with horses, stone fences, and hills beyond. Full breakfast served in antique-filled main dining room or in guest house. Only 20 minutes to the airport; hiking, skiing, biking, and fishing minutes away. Children allowed. No smoking. No pets in guest house.

ESSEX

The Griswold Inn
36 Main Street, 06426
(860) 767-1776

More than a country hotel. More than a comfortable bed, an extraordinary meal, or a superb drink. It embodies a spirit understood perhaps only as one warms up to its potbellied stove or is hypnotized by the magic of a crackling log in one of its many fireplaces. It is a kaleidoscope of nostalgic images. There are 29 guest rooms, all with air conditioning, private baths, telephones, and piped-in classical music. Some have fireplaces.

Hosts: Gregory, Douglas, and Geoffrey Paul
Rooms: 28 (PB) $90-185
Continental Breakfast
Credit Cards: A, B, C
Notes: 2, 3, 4, 5, 7, 8, 9, 10, 11, 12

The Griswold Inn

Nutmeg Bed and Breakfast Agency
P.O. Box 1117, West Hartford, 06127-1117
(860) 236-6698; (800) 727-7592
FAX (860) 232-7680

508. If guests are boating enthusiasts, this entertaining hostess, whose family shares the passion, would love to trade some sailing stories. This special home, right on the bank of the Connecticut River, is convenient to many attractions of the area, 20 miles from Mystic, and close to Hammonasset public beach in Madison. Theaters and fine restaurants are nearby. Two rooms have private baths. Full breakfast. Children welcome.

FALLS VILLAGE

Nutmeg Bed and Breakfast Agency
P.O. Box 1117, West Hartford, 06127-1117
(860) 236-6698; (800) 727-7592
FAX (860) 232-7680

307. This elegant Dutch Colonial, circa 1700, is in the northwest corner of the state on the Housatonic River. The house offers three guest rooms. One has a king-size bed, fireplace, and private bath. The second room has a double bed with private bath. The third room has twin beds and a shared bath. This bed and breakfast is on 40 acres. A great getaway with many walking trails. Full breakfast served on weekends. Children welcome. No smoking.

FARMINGTON

The Farmington Inn
827 Farmington Avenue, 06032
(860) 677-2821; (800) 648-9804

In the heart of the unspoiled and scenic Farmington River Valley, one mile off exit 39, I-84 at Routes 4 and 10. Seventy-two charming guest rooms and suites blending antique furnishings, original paintings, and fresh flowers in a setting with historic homes, museums, and prep schools. Exceptional complimentary breakfast and daily newspapers. Unique meeting facilities. Deluxe amenities. Four-star restaurant. Golfing, tennis, canoeing, antiquing, fishing, sunbathing, beach, ballooning, and hiking all nearby. Winter activities.

Rooms: 72 (PB) $99-129
Continental Breakfast
Credit Cards: A, B, C, D, E
Notes: 2, 3, 4, 5, 6, 7, 8, 10, 11, 12, 13, 14

7 No smoking; 8 Children welcome; 9 Social drinking allowed; 10 Tennis nearby; 11 Swimming nearby; 12 Golf nearby; 13 Skiing nearby; 14 May be booked through a travel agent; 15 Handicapped accessible.

Nutmeg Bed and Breakfast Agency

P.O. Box 1117, West Hartford, 06127-1117
(860) 236-6698; (800) 727-7592
FAX (860) 232-7680

402. Small inn has traditional country furnishings. Guest rooms each have private bath, TV, VCR, and telephone. The gracious staff can help arrange a dinner or business meeting in-house or nearby. Children under 12 stay free in same room. Continental breakfast served.

406. This elegant estate is now a gracious small inn with beautifully landscaped grounds, pool, tennis court, conference room, and lounge. There are six rooms with TVs, telephones, and private baths. A short drive from Hartford. Perfect for the business traveler. Continental breakfast served. Children welcome.

415. This is a luxurious new inn with suites complete with kitchens, fireplaces, and bathrooms with all the amenities. Enjoy complimentary racquet club privileges with pools and tennis courts. Continental breakfast. Children welcome.

GLASTONBURY

Butternut Farm

1654 Main Street, 06033
(860) 633-7197; FAX (860) 659-1758

An 18th-century architectural jewel is furnished in museum-quality period antiques. Estate setting has ancient trees, herb gardens, prize dairy goats, barnyard chickens, pigeons, ducks, a llama, and geese. Three Abyssinians inhabit the main house. Enjoy a full breakfast of fresh eggs, milk, and cheese. Ten minutes from Hartford. All of Connecticut is within 90 minutes. Two rooms, two suites, and one apartment, all with private baths. Cancellation policy.

Butternut Farm

Host: Don Reid
Rooms: 5 (PB) $70-90
Full Breakfast
Credit Cards: C
Notes: 2, 5, 7, 8, 9, 10, 11, 12, 13

GRANBY

Nutmeg Bed and Breakfast Agency

P.O. Box 1117, West Hartford, 06127-1117
(860) 236-6698; (800) 727-7592
FAX (860) 232-7680

442. There is a sophisticated country atmosphere to this stone house. The separate guest wing includes a sitting room with TV, and two guest rooms with private baths. Convenient to Bradley International Airport, state parks, historic Old Newgate Prison, and local attractions. Guests enjoy wine, cheese, and crackers in the afternoon. Horses can be boarded for a nominal fee. Continental breakfast. Children welcome. No smoking.

GREENWICH

The Stanton House Inn

76 Maple Avenue, 06830
(203) 869-2110; FAX (203) 629-2116

The Stanton House Inn is a converted mansion that is now a bed and breakfast inn, in the prestigious village of Green-

NOTES: Credit cards accepted: A MasterCard; B Visa; C American Express; D Discover; E Diner's Club; F Other; 2 Personal checks accepted; 3 Lunch available; 4 Dinner available; 5 Open all year; 6 Pets welcome;

wich. The Stanton House Inn offers elegant surroundings, comfortable rooms, and a satisfying Continental breakfast at rates competitive with area hotels. The rooms are bright and cheery, decorated primarily with Laura Ashley-style fabrics, period antiques, and reproductions. Two rooms with working fireplaces. On-site outdoor swimming pool (seasonal).

Hosts: Tog and Doreen Pearson
Rooms: 24 (22 PB; 2 SB) $89-179
Continental Breakfast
Credit Cards: A, B, C, D, E
Notes: 5, 7, 9, 10, 11, 12, 14

GROTON

Bluff Point Bed and Breakfast

26 Fort Hill Road, Route 1, 06340
(860) 445-1314

A restored Colonial bed and breakfast (early 1990s) on U.S. Route 1 and adjacent to Bluff Point State Park Coastal Preserve. Conveniently four miles from the Mystic Seaport Museum. Large common area with shared TV is available to guests. The home is equipped with a central fire sprinkler system. No smoking or pets. "We give warm and friendly service to our guests."

Hosts: Walter and Edna Parfitt
Rooms: 3 (PB) $85-95
Continental Breakfast
Credit Cards: A, B, C
Notes: 2, 5, 7, 10, 11, 12

GUILFORD

Nutmeg Bed and Breakfast Agency

P.O. Box 1117, West Hartford, 06127-1117
(860) 236-6698; (800) 727-7592
FAX (860) 232-7680

510. A contemporary home with lovely grounds awaits the guest who wishes to be near the coast. The two rooms have private baths—one has a king-size bed and the other has twin beds. There is also a private sitting room for guests. Enjoy a short walk to the village green, colonial churches, and shops. Full breakfast. Children welcome. Smoking in designated areas only.

518. This cottage has a private entrance, gardens, and lovely grounds. Inside, guests will find a small sitting room and small dining room with refrigerator and microwave. The bedroom has a private bath. The sitting room can accommodate a third person on a pull-out sofa bed. Continental breakfast. Children welcome. No smoking.

IVORYTON

The Copper Beech Inn

46 Main Street, 06442
(860) 767-0330; www.copperbeechinn.com

Gracious gardens and rustic woodlands set the stage for this handsome inn. A gallery offers antique oriental porcelain, and the dining room is noted for fine country French cuisine. Beautiful countryside, quaint villages, museums, antique shops, theater, and water sports distinguish the area. Two-night minimum stay for weekends and holidays. Closed Christmas and the first week of January. Children over 10 welcome. Dining rooms and first-floor guest rooms in carriage house are handicapped accessible.

Copper Beech Inn

Hosts: Eldon and Sally Senner
Rooms: 13 (PB) $123.20-201.60
Continental Breakfast
Credit Cards: A, B, C, E
Notes: 2, 4, 5, 7, 9, 10, 11, 12

KENT

Nutmeg Bed and Breakfast Agency

P.O. Box 1117, West Hartford, 06127-1117
(860) 236-6698; (800) 727-7592
FAX (860) 232-7680

322. Friendliness awaits guests at this 1860s Colonial home. Unwind in the romantic rose-stenciled room with beamed ceiling or the country Adirondack room with carved Victorian headboard, both with private baths. There is an adjacent cottage with a sitting area, private bath, and kitchen. Relax by the fireplace in the cozy den or walk the lovely grounds and view St. John's Ledges. After a Continental breakfast, visit the antique shop. Near hiking, skiing, canoeing, museums, and fine restaurants. Children over 12 welcome. No smoking.

303. Enjoy the fall foliage from this lovely Colonial, circa 1790. Guests are offered a suite that has a kitchen, living room, private bath, and air conditioning. There is a pull-out sofa bed in the suite's sitting room for extra family members. Two additional guest rooms share a bath. Both have ceiling fans. Continental breakfast served in the guest's room. Children welcome. No smoking. Dog and cat on premises.

LAKEVILLE

Nutmeg Bed and Breakfast Agency

P.O. Box 1117, West Hartford, 06127-1117
(860) 236-6698; (800) 727-7592
FAX (860) 232-7680

328. Set on lovely private acreage, this 15-room turn-of-the-century bed and breakfast is filled with antiques and charm. Guests may choose rooms with a sleigh or a spool bed, each with its own private bath. After a sumptuous Continental breakfast, enjoy some of the area's many attractions: Lime Rock Park, Music Mountain, and Mohawk ski area. Children over eight are welcome. No smoking.

LITCHFIELD

Nutmeg Bed and Breakfast Agency

P.O. Box 1117, West Hartford, 06127-1117
(860) 236-6698; (800) 727-7592
FAX (860) 232-7680

333. On a quiet country road outside the historic village of Litchfield, this bed and breakfast features two guest rooms with private baths. The house is a pre-Revolutionary Colonial, shaded by century-old sugar maples. Horses and sheep graze in the pasture. Guests may enjoy a delicious full breakfast on the stone terrace or the covered porch in warm weather where they can overlook a view of the wooded brook. Children over 12 welcome.

Tollgate Hill Inn and Restaurant

Route 202 and Tollgate Road, P.O. Box 1339,
   06759
(860) 567-4545; FAX (860) 567-8397

This 1745 inn is listed in the National Register of Historic Places and has 20 guest rooms. Air conditioned. Private baths. Direct-dial telephones. Cable TV. Half of the rooms have wood-burning fireplaces. Excellent restaurant on premises. Seasonal and corporate rates are available upon request. Limited handicapped accessibility.

Host: Frederick J. Zivic
Rooms: 20 (PB) $110-175
Continental Breakfast
Credit Cards: A, B, C, D, E
Notes: 2, 3, 4, 5, 6, 8, 9, 10, 11, 12, 13, 14

NOTES: Credit cards accepted: A MasterCard; B Visa; C American Express; D Discover; E Diner's Club; F Other; 2 Personal checks accepted; 3 Lunch available; 4 Dinner available; 5 Open all year; 6 Pets welcome;

LYME

Covered Bridge

69 Maple Avenue, Norfolk, 06058
(860) 542-5944; FAX (860) 542-5690

2LY. European charm and antiques make
this Colonial set on 14 acres a very special
retreat. Several pieces of furniture have
been hand painted by the hostess, reflecting
her Swiss heritage. The three queen-bedded
guest rooms, each with a private bath, have
gorgeous handmade quilts. Full breakfast
served. $95-110.

Nutmeg Bed and Breakfast Agency

P.O. Box 1117, West Hartford, 06127-1117
(860) 236-6698; (800) 727-7592
FAX (860) 232-7680

512. This center-chimney Colonial, built as
a bed and breakfast, is on several acres of
woods and has its own walking trail and
horseshoe court. Three guest rooms with
private baths are accented by family pieces
and European furnishings. Convenient to
the Old Lyme Art Center, all the shoreline
attractions, and many restaurants. Full
breakfast. No smoking allowed.

MADISON

Madison Beach Hotel

94 West Wharf Road, P.O. Box 546, 06443
(203) 245-1404

Built in the early 1800s, the Madison
Beach Hotel is nestled on a private beach
on Long Island Sound, and it is distinctly
Victorian in style and decor. Most hotel
rooms have private balconies overlooking
the water. Antique oak bureaus, wainscoting, wicker and rattan furniture, along with
old-fashioned wallpaper, complete the Vic-

torian feeling. The hotel's restaurant serves
lunch, dinner with entertainment on weekends, and outdoor dining. Closed January
and February.

Hosts: Betty and Henry Cooney;
   Roben and Kathy Bagdasarian
Rooms: 35 (PB) $85-225
Continental Breakfast
Credit Cards: A, B, C, D, E
Notes: 2, 3, 4, 8, 9, 10, 11, 12, 13, 14, 15

Nutmeg Bed and Breakfast Agency

P.O. Box 1117, West Hartford, 06127-1117
(860) 236-6698; (800) 727-7592
FAX (860) 232-7680

520. Tasteful gambrel Colonial with large
living room for guests, gracious dining
room, pool, large eat-in kitchen, fireplace
in family room, pool, patio for breakfast
on nice days; about five minutes from
beach. Two second-floor guest rooms
which share a bath are offered. Continental
breakfast is served. No children. No smoking. No resident pets.

Tidewater Inn

949 Boston Post Road, 06443
(203) 245-8457

Explore coastal Connecticut's boutiques,
antiques, and shoreline restaurants. Relax
at a nearby beach or in the English
garden. Visit Gillette Castle, Yale's
Peabody Museum of Natural History,
Chamard Vineyards, or the Museum of
the Fife and Drum. Tour the area's many
colonial houses and town greens. Nine
guest rooms with private baths. Fireplaces. Full breakfast. Children seven and
older welcome.

Hosts: Jean Foy and Rich Evans
Rooms: 9 (PB) $80-160
Full Breakfast
Credit Cards: A, B, C
Notes: 2, 5, 7, 9, 11

7 No smoking; 8 Children welcome; 9 Social drinking allowed; 10 Tennis nearby; 11 Swimming nearby;
12 Golf nearby; 13 Skiing nearby; 14 May be booked through a travel agent; 15 Handicapped accessible.

MIDDLEBURY

Nutmeg Bed and Breakfast Agency

P.O. Box 1117, West Hartford, 06127-1117
(860) 236-6698; (800) 727-7592
FAX (860) 232-7680

304. This New England Colonial is near the village green and is convenient to Taft School and Westover. There are four guest rooms, two of which share a bath. Enjoy the outdoor activities offered in the area and then relax in this inviting home. Full breakfast. Children welcome. No smoking.

Tucker Hill Inn

96 Tucker Hill Road, 06762
(203) 758-8334

Tucker Hill Inn is a large center-hall Colonial just down from the village green in Middlebury. It was built around 1920 and was a restaurant and catering house for almost 40 years. The period rooms are spacious. Nearby are antiques, country drives, music and theater, golf, tennis, water sports, fishing, hiking, and cross-country skiing. Closed Christmas Day.

Hosts: Richard and Susan Cabalenski
Rooms: 4 (2 PB; 2 SB) $70-125
Full Breakfast
Credit Cards: A, B, C
Notes: 2, 7, 8, 9, 10, 11, 12, 14

MIDDLETOWN

Nutmeg Bed and Breakfast Agency

P.O. Box 1117, West Hartford, 06127-1117
(860) 236-6698; (800) 727-7592
FAX (860) 232-7680

409. Decorated with cheer and good taste is a five-year-old raised ranch with a lower-level suite complete with a fireplace, TV, VCR, and a connecting half-bath. This is a large room with ample sitting area. The full

bath is on the entry level where there is an additional room that can be used by families traveling together. Robes are provided. Continental breakfast weekdays; full breakfast weekends. No smoking.

MILFORD

Nutmeg Bed and Breakfast Agency

P.O. Box 1117, West Hartford, 06127-1117
(860) 236-6698; (800) 727-7592
FAX (860) 232-7680

213. The host calls her home "a seaside bungalow." The house was built in 1910 and overlooks Long Island Sound on a very quiet, peaceful lane. The sunny second-floor guest room with a double bed and an additional room with twin beds share a bath. The room has a water view and a large connecting screened porch for taking in the ocean air. Continental breakfast. Smoking permitted outside only. Cat in residence.

MYSTIC

The Adams House of Mystic

382 Cow Hill Road, 06355
(860) 572-9551

Charming 1750 Colonial home features five rooms with private baths and queen-size beds;

Adams House of Mystic

two rooms have fireplaces. Adjacent garden cottage features two rooms, one with sauna; each with private bath, queen-size bed, and private entrance. Hearty candlelight breakfast served daily with tea in the afternoons. Smoke free. Children welcome in cottage. One and one-half miles to downtown Mystic Seaport and aquarium. Open year-round.

Hosts: Mary Lou and Gregory Peck
Rooms: 7 (PB) $95-165
Full Breakfast
Credit Cards: A, B, C, D
Notes: 2, 5, 7, 8, 11, 12

Comolli's House

36 Bruggeman Place, 06355
(860) 536-8723

Ideal for vacationers touring historic Mystic or the business person who desires a homey respite while traveling. This immaculate home, on a quiet hill overlooking the Mystic Seaport complex, is convenient to Olde Mistick Village and the aquarium. Sightseeing, sporting activities, shopping, and restaurant information are provided by the host. Off-season rates are available.

Host: Dorothy M. Comolli
Rooms: 2 (PB) $75-125
Continental Breakfast
Credit Cards: F
Notes: 2, 9, 10, 11, 12

Covered Bridge

69 Maple Avenue, Norfolk, 06058
(860) 542-5944; FAX (860) 542-5690

1MYCT. This restored 150-year-old Victorian farmhouse is on two acres of lovely landscaped grounds with old stone walls, fruit trees, and an outdoor eating area for the enjoyment of guests. A full breakfast is served in the dining room and a Scottish tea is served in the afternoon. There are six guest rooms, one with fireplace and all with private baths. $125-145.

2MYCT. An 1840s Greek Revival just outside the center of town is beautifully deco-

rated with antiques and offers four exquisitely decorated guest rooms: one with a fireplace and another with a Jacuzzi. A delicious full breakfast is served in the dining room. $95-145.

House of 1833 Bed and Breakfast

72 North Stonington Road, 06355
(860) 536-6325; (800) FOR-1833

This elegant Greek Revival mansion is on three acres just minutes from all Mystic area attractions. The mansion was fully restored in 1994 with romance and comfort in mind. All five guest rooms are elegantly furnished with fireplaces and private baths. Several have canopied beds and whirlpool tubs as well. The estatelike surroundings include a swimming pool or a Har-Tru tennis court. Bicycles are also available for touring the countryside. Breakfast is served with a piano accompaniment.

Hosts: Matt and Carol Nolan
Rooms: 5 (PB) $95-225
Full Breakfast
Credit Cards: A, B
Notes: 2, 5, 7, 9, 10, 11, 12, 14

Nutmeg Bed and Breakfast Agency

P.O. Box 1117, West Hartford, 06127-1117
(860) 236-6698; (800) 727-7592
FAX (860) 232-7680

513. Built in 1837, this large farmhouse is surrounded by fruit trees and strawberry beds. Eight guest rooms have private baths; two have fireplaces. There is also a spacious dining room and a warm family room. The home-cooked full breakfast, with specialty muffins, is amply satisfying. Children welcome. Cat and dog in residence. No smoking.

515. Take a walk back in time in this historic 1771 house. The keeping room was

---

7 No smoking; 8 Children welcome; 9 Social drinking allowed; 10 Tennis nearby; 11 Swimming nearby; 12 Golf nearby; 13 Skiing nearby; 14 May be booked through a travel agent; 15 Handicapped accessible.

once used for open hearth cooking—now it is the sitting room. There are five guest rooms, each with a private bath, a fireplace, and a Jacuzzi in the bath. Continental breakfast. No children. No smoking.

Red Brook Inn

P.O. Box 237, Old Mystic, 06372
(860) 572-0349

Red Brook Inn offers colonial hospitality in two 18th-century buildings. Near Mystic and Foxwoods Casino on seven acres of woods. Most bedrooms are furnished with antique beds, working fireplaces, or whirlpool tubs. The area is tranquil and serene. A country breakfast is served every morning and afternoon refreshments are readily available. Three minutes to downtown, the aquarium, and Mystic Seaport Museum.

Host: Ruth Keyes
Rooms: 10 (PB) $95-189
Full Breakfast
Credit Cards: A, B, C, D
Notes: 2, 5, 7, 8, 9, 10, 11, 12

Steamboat Inn

73 Steamboat Wharf, 06355
(203) 536-8300

On the river, this romantic and luxurious inn is in the heart of downtown Mystic. Ten beautiful rooms, all with antique and custom furnishings, TV, telephones, and individually controlled heat and air conditioning. Six rooms feature wood-burning fireplaces, along with four dock-level demi-suites with double whirlpools. A Continental breakfast is included, featuring home-baked muffins daily. There are many shops, restaurants, and boats all within walking distance.

Host: Diana Stadtmiller
Rooms: 10 (PB) $95-275
Continental Breakfast
Credit Cards: A, B, C, D
Notes: 2, 5, 7, 9, 14, 15

NEW HAVEN

Bed and Breakfast, Ltd.

P.O. Box 216, 06513
(203) 469-3260; e-mail: BandB@aol.com

Bed and Breakfast, Ltd., offers more than 125 listings of bed and breakfasts throughout Connecticut from elegantly simple to simply elegant. The emphasis is on variety of accommodations, gracious hospitality, and very affordable rates. In operation for the 16th year, the service features Victorian, Federal, Greek Revival, Tudor, Italianate, and contemporary homes in every price range. Deluxe and suite rates are slightly higher. Children are welcome at some establishments. Inquire about other amenities listed in notes.

Contact: Jack Argenio
Rooms: 125 plus (80 PB; 45 SB) $55-95
Full and Continental Breakfasts
Credit Cards: A, B
Notes: 2, 5, 9, 10, 11, 12, 13

Nutmeg Bed and Breakfast Agency

P.O. Box 1117, West Hartford, 06127-1117
(860) 236-6698; (800) 727-7592
FAX (860) 232-7680

203. This 1920 Queen Anne with beamed ceilings, fireplace in parlor, eclectic but charming furnishings, gracious hosts. First floor has two rooms that share a bath. Another suite is available on the third floor. Kitchen and breakfast nook on second floor for convenience of guests. Five-minute drive to public beach in West Haven, convenient to Yale, downtown New Haven, airport. Continental breakfast buffet. Children welcome. No smoking. One cat in residence.

205. This turn-of-the-century grand, gracious, large home is in a special residential area. Formal dining room and lovely gardens await visitors. The third floor has a

---

NOTES: Credit cards accepted: A MasterCard; B Visa; C American Express; D Discover; E Diner's Club; F Other; 2 Personal checks accepted; 3 Lunch available; 4 Dinner available; 5 Open all year; 6 Pets welcome;

room with a walk-through full bath shared with a second room. On the second floor, one room has a full private bath and may be used with a room with a single bed. Also there is a lovely suite with a private bath with a tub. The shower is down the hall. First and second floors are air conditioned and the third floor has a large fan. Continental breakfast. Children welcome. No smoking.

208. Catch a game at the Yale Bowl or the bus downtown from this bed and breakfast in the Westville section. This English Tudor has guest rooms with a shared bath. Guests help themselves to Continental breakfast during the week; full breakfast on weekends. Children welcome. Smoking restricted. Dog in residence.

210. Walk to Yale from this gracious Victorian home set in the residential section of New Haven. A newly decorated third-floor suite consists of a bedroom with a large private bath and a smaller bedroom. A guest room is also available on the second floor. Continental breakfast. Children welcome. Cats in residence.

215. This home near Yale is a 1910 Dutch Colonial with a private garden and deck. Two guest rooms are on the second floor. One has a double bed and the other has twin beds; both share a bath. Baby equipment available. The house is just over one block from the bus. Continental breakfast. Infants traveling with parents welcome. No smoking. Dog in residence.

Three Chimneys Inn

1201 Chapel, 06511
(203) 789-1201; (800) 443-1554 (outside CT)
FAX (203) 776-7363
e-mail: chimneysnh@aol.com

Two blocks from Old Main Gate at Yale University and just steps from the renowned

Three Chimneys Inn

Shubert, Yale Repertory, and Palace Theaters; the Yale Center for British Art; Yale Art Gallery; and the Peabody Museum of Natural History, in a vibrantly eclectic little area known as Chapel West, reigns this grand "painted lady." Understated elegance in 10 distinctive guest rooms with full private baths. Fireplaces reflect the Georgian and Federal period furnishings and oakwork of days gone by. The inn offers unique venues for both social and business gatherings. Gourmet breakfast; traditional afternoon tea and sweets; honor bar; guest pantry; catering.

Host: Michael A. Marra
Rooms: 10 (PB) $160
Full Breakfast
Credit Cards: A, B, C, D
Notes: 2, 5, 7, 9, 10, 12, 14, 15

NEW LONDON

Queen Anne Inn

265 Williams Street, 06320
(860) 447-2600; (800) 347-8818

This spectacular turn-of-the-century home features rich oak woodwork and nautical art displayed throughout the inn. Relax by the fire in the parlor, enjoy the wraparound porch, or unwind in the Jacuzzi. Retire to one of the 10 antique-filled rooms with brass, canopied, or four-poster beds. The inn serves a full gourmet breakfast and afternoon tea. Minutes from Mystic, Ocean Beach, Foxwoods and Mohegan Sun Casinos, and antiquing. Convenient access to I-95. No smoking. Children over 12 welcome.

Hosts: Janet and Ed
Rooms: 10 (8 PB; 2 SB) $89-185
Full Breakfast
Credit Cards: A, B, C, D, E
Notes: 2, 5, 7, 10, 11, 12, 14

NEW MILFORD _____

Covered Bridge

69 Maple Avenue, Norfolk, 06058
(860) 542-5944; FAX (860) 542-5690

1NM. Vista for viewing, woods for walking, hills for cross-country skiing, streams for fishing, flower gardens, and a pool are some of the attractions of this sprawling estate three miles outside of town. First-floor guest room with private bath and an upstairs guest room. $60-95.

Heritage Inn

34 Bridge Street, 06776
(860) 354-8883; FAX (860) 350-5543

The Heritage Inn is a country hotel that combines personal comfort with efficiency in a relaxed atmosphere. Here guests will find amenities they expect like a 20-inch color TV with bedside remote control, plus air conditioning, private bath, and a telephone in every room. In addition, guests will receive a newspaper every morning and a full breakfast. Enjoy New Milford's traditional New England charm while staying at the Heritage Inn. Picnic on the town green; shops, boutiques, restaurants, movie theaters, historic attractions, and churches and synagogues are close by.

Host: Fred Berry
Rooms: 20 (PB) $85-100
Full Breakfast
Credit Cards: A, B, C, D
Notes: 2, 5, 6, 7, 8, 10, 11, 12, 13, 14

Nutmeg Bed and Breakfast Agency

P.O. Box 1117, West Hartford, 06127-1117
(860) 236-6698; (800) 727-7592
FAX (860) 232-7680

A charming home built with wood from a reverse wood tobacco barn, this bed and breakfast is delightfully landscaped with a pool. First-floor room with separate entrance to deck has twins or king-size bed and private bath. Second-floor room has twin beds and shared bath. One small bedroom on second floor is suitable for a child. Continental breakfast includes home-grown berries, homemade jams, popovers, and muffins prepared by a former chef. Children welcome. Smoking in designated area only. Dog in residence.

319. This 1850s Colonial-style home with more than three acres of glorious grounds, formal dining room, living room with fireplace, front porch, patio. Two newly decorated rooms on the first floor have private baths, air conditioning, and ceiling fans. One room has a TV and VCR; the other room has a TV. One block from public transportation, convenient to many good restaurants and private schools, and antiquing. Full breakfast. Closed Thanksgiving, Christmas, and New Year's. Children 12 and older welcome. No smoking. No pets in residence.

NEW PRESTON _____

The Birches Inn

233 West Shore Road, 06777
(860) 868-1735; FAX (860) 868-1815
e-mail: birches@ctz.nai.net

Unwind in the quiet beauty of this small European-style inn. The Birches is on the banks of Lake Waramaug, surrounded by the Litchfield Hills. Accommodations are elegant and comfortable. Each guest room is individually decorated with antiques

---

NOTES: Credit cards accepted: A MasterCard; B Visa; C American Express; D Discover; E Diner's Club; F Other; 2 Personal checks accepted; 3 Lunch available; 4 Dinner available; 5 Open all year; 6 Pets welcome;

and fine furnishings, has a private bath, telephone, air conditioning, and cable TV. Several waterfront rooms offer private decks and lake views. The highly acclaimed restaurant features exquisite New American and French cuisine. Dine on the open-air porch overlooking the lake or in the intimacy of the inn's main dining room. Rated Excellent by the *New York Times*.

Hosts: Karen Hamilton and Frederic Faveau
Rooms: 8 (PB) $95-300
Full Breakfast
Credit Cards: A, B, C
Notes: 2, 4, 7, 10, 11, 12, 13, 14, 15

The Boulders Inn

East Shore Road, Route 45, 06777
(860) 868-0541; (800) 55-BOULD(ers)
FAX (860) 868-1925
e-mail: boulders@bouldersinn.com
www.bouldersinn.com

Built in 1895 as a private residence, the Boulders Inn is nestled at the foot of Pinnacle Mountain in the Litchfield Hills, overlooking the beautiful Lake Waramaug. This architecturally striking Victorian home combines mansion-like elegance with the warmth of the country. In the 50 years of its existence as an inn, it has established an outstanding reputation, receiving countless kudos from respected national publications such as the *New York*

The Boulders Inn

Times, *Travel & Leisure* magazine, the *Wine Spectator*, *Country Inn and Bed & Breakfast* magazine, and so forth. The restaurant has been voted one of the top 10 in Connecticut. Please inquire about accommodations for children.

Hosts: Kees and Ulla Adema
Rooms: 17 (PB) $150-325
Full Breakfast
Credit Cards: A, B, C
Notes: 2, 4, 5, 7, 9, 10, 11, 12, 13, 14, 15

NIANTIC

Nutmeg Bed and Breakfast Agency

P.O. Box 1117, West Hartford, 06127-1117
(860) 236-6698; (800) 727-7592
FAX (860) 232-7680

522. Wake up on the water in a completely renovated bed and breakfast with sparkling new interior and exterior. Eight bedrooms with water or marina view; two rooms with balcony. All have ceiling fans. Transient boat slips available at marina. Restaurants, shops, theaters within walking distance. Convenient to Mystic, Foxwoods, Harkness Memorial Park, Westbrook and Clinton shopping outlets. Continental breakfast. Children welcome. No smoking. No pets on premises.

NORFOLK

Covered Bridge

69 Maple Avenue, 06058
(860) 542-5944; FAX (860) 542-5690

2N. Romantic 1880 Victorian on 11 acres of woods, gardens, and a brook is just steps from the village green. All have private baths, two with Jacuzzis, two with fireplaces. A full breakfast is served on one of the lovely porches, in the dining room, or in one of the four enchanting guest rooms. $110-145.

7 No smoking; 8 Children welcome; 9 Social drinking allowed; 10 Tennis nearby; 11 Swimming nearby; 12 Golf nearby; 13 Skiing nearby; 14 May be booked through a travel agent; 15 Handicapped accessible.

Greenwoods Gate
Bed and Breakfast Inn

105 Greenwoods Road East, 06058
(860) 542-5439
www.greenwoodsgate.com

Warm hospitality greets guests in this beautifully restored 1797 Colonial home. Small and elegant, it has four exquisitely appointed guest suites each with private bath, one with a Jacuzzi. Fine antiques, fireplaces, and sumptuous breakfasts indulge guests. *Yankee* magazine calls this "New England's most romantic Bed and Breakfast." *Country Inns Bed and Breakfast* magazine calls it "a Connecticut Jewel." New in 1996: the Lilian/Rose Suite with country elegance. Afternoon tea, early evening refreshments served. Children over 12 are welcome.

Hosts: George and Marian Schumaker
Suites: 4 (PB) $175-245
Full Breakfast
Credit Cards: None
Notes: 2, 5, 7, 9, 10, 11, 12, 13, 14

Manor House

69 Maple Avenue, 06058
(860) 542-5690
www.manorhouse-norfolk.com

Victorian elegance awaits guests at this historic Tudor/Bavarian estate. Antique-decorated guest rooms, several with fireplace; canopies, balconies, a two-person Jacuzzi, and a two-person soaking tub offer a romantic retreat. Enjoy a sumptu-

Manor House

ous breakfast in the Tiffany-windowed dining rooms or be treated to breakfast in bed. Designated "Connecticut's Most Romantic Hideaway" and included in *Fifty Best Bed and Breakfasts in the USA*. Children over 12 welcome.

Hosts: Hank and Diane Tremblay
Rooms: 9 (PB) $125-225
Full Breakfast
Credit Cards: A, B, C, D, E
Notes: 2, 5, 7, 9, 10, 11, 12, 13, 14

Mountain View Inn

Mountain View Inn

Route 272, P.O. Box 467, 06058
(860) 542-6991; FAX (860) 542-5689
e-mail: mvinn@snet.net; www.mvinn.com

Pristine landscapes and gardens, historic homes and winding country roads welcome guests to historic Norfolk and the Mountain View Inn. Norfolk's only full-service country inn offers the perfect location for guests' quiet country respite, romantic weekend, or unique wedding site. Lovingly restored, the inn combines the romance of the small bed and breakfast experience with the privacy and convenience of a full-service property. Dinner available seasonally.

Host: Michele Sloane
Rooms: 8 (6 PB; 2 SB) $60-125
Full Breakfast
Credit Cards: A, B, D
Notes: 2, 5, 6, 9, 10, 11, 12, 13, 14

NOTES: Credit cards accepted: A MasterCard; B Visa; C American Express; D Discover; E Diner's Club; F Other; 2 Personal checks accepted; 3 Lunch available; 4 Dinner available; 5 Open all year; 6 Pets welcome;

Nutmeg Bed and Breakfast Agency
P.O. Box 1117, West Hartford, 06127-1117
(860) 236-6698; (800) 727-7592
FAX (860) 232-7680

302. Visit the northwest hills and stay in an 18th-century inn with Victorian furnishings. The seven guest rooms have private baths. The inn serves dinner Wednesday through Sunday in its spacious dining room with a large fireplace. Full breakfast. Children 10 and older welcome. Smoking permitted.

308. This Colonial inn is in the country on 22 acres, complete with a pool and tennis court. The original main building has four guest rooms with private baths. Some have fireplaces and decks. The carriage house has an additional 16 rooms—some with private and some with shared baths. A full breakfast is served in the inn, where guests can also enjoy a fireplace in the parlor. Children welcome. Smoking permitted outside only.

NORTHFIELD

Covered Bridge
69 Maple Avenue, 06058
(860) 542-5944; FAX (860) 542-5690

A 1755 Colonial farmhouse close to the town of Litchfield offers a two-bedroom suite with a sitting area with a TV and a bath. A full breakfast is served in the dining room with a fireplace which is also open to the living room. $85-125.

Nutmeg Bed and Breakfast Agency
P.O. Box 1117, West Hartford, 06127-1117
(860) 236-6698; (800) 727-7592
FAX (860) 232-7680

311. Just a few minutes from Litchfield is a Colonial built in 1755 on an open setting. Show horses graze on the grounds. The two guest rooms have double beds and share a

bath, although a private bath can be arranged. There is a wonderful living room with a TV for use by the guests. Continental breakfast. Children welcome. Smoking permitted outside only.

NORTH GRANBY

Nutmeg Bed and Breakfast Agency
P.O. Box 1117, West Hartford, 06127-1117
(860) 236-6698; (800) 727-7592
FAX (860) 232-7680

401. A contemporary home on five acres sits near a three-quarter-acre pond. There are many hiking trails, and three bridges span the stream. A guest suite has a bedroom with a queen-size bed, sitting area, private bath with sauna, wood-burning stove, and a deck. The other room has a double Hide-a-Bed and private bath. Continental breakfast. Children welcome. Cat in residence.

NORTH STONINGTON

Antiques and Accommodations
32 Main Street, 06359
(860) 535-1736; (800) 554-7829
FAX (860) 535-2613

Centered among Mystic, Foxwoods Casino, and superb sandy beaches in an enchanting historic village. Browse through the hosts' collection of fine antiques and enjoy the library. Stroll through the lovingly tended English gardens, relax on the porches and patios. Greet the morning with the multi-course candlelight breakfast replete with gleaming silver and sparkling crystal. Luxuriate in blissful bed chambers where canopied beds, fresh flowers, and fireplaces await guests. *Connecticut Magazine*'s Top Three Bed and Breakfasts in Connecticut, November 1996. Cover of *Country Inns*, April 1995.

Hosts: Ann and Tom Gray
Rooms: 6 (PB) $99-229
Full Breakfast

7 No smoking; 8 Children welcome; 9 Social drinking allowed; 10 Tennis nearby; 11 Swimming nearby; 12 Golf nearby; 13 Skiing nearby; 14 May be booked through a travel agent; 15 Handicapped accessible.

Credit Cards: A, B
Notes: 2, 5, 7, 9, 10, 11, 12, 14

Nutmeg Bed and Breakfast Agency

P.O. Box 1117, West Hartford, 06127-1117
(860) 236-6698; (800) 727-7592
FAX (860) 232-7680

511. A 1742 Colonial home on 150-acre horse farm has beautiful pasture views of southeast Connecticut. Enjoy Mystic and Foxwoods Casino. Three guest rooms have queen-size beds and the third room has a king-size or twin beds. All have private baths. Full breakfast. Children welcome. No smoking. Dogs and horses on premises.

NORWALK

The Silvermine Tavern

194 Perry Avenue, 06850
(203) 847-4558; FAX (203) 847-9171

The Silvermine Tavern offers one of the most soothing and serene views in Connecticut and is the perfect romantic getaway. Dining alfresco overlooking the mill pond in the summer or near a cozy fireplace amid the various antiques in winter is all a part of the Silvermine experience. Guest rooms, some with canopied beds or decks overlooking the river, all await guests' arrival to romance and relaxation.

Hosts: Frank and Marsha Whitman
Room: 11 (PB) $95-115
Suite: $165
Continental Breakfast
Credit Cards: A, B, C, E
Notes: 2, 3, 4, 5, 7, 8, 9, 10, 11, 12, 14

OLD GREENWICH

Harbor House Inn

165 Shore Road, 06870
(203) 637-0145; FAX (203) 698-0943

This lovely bed and breakfast is in a quiet New England village. Shopping, beach, and fine restaurants are nearby. Train station is one mile away. New York City is 45 minutes away. There are bikes for guests' use and kitchen facilities available. Each room is equipped with a refrigerator, coffee maker, TV and VCR, and telephone with voice mail. Lunch and dinner available nearby.

Hosts: Dolly Stuttig and Dawn Browne
Rooms: 23 (17 PB; 6 SB) $89-149
Continental Breakfast
Credit Cards: A, B, C
Notes: 5, 7, 10, 11, 12, 13, 14

Nutmeg Bed and Breakfast Agency

P.O. Box 1117, West Hartford, 06127-1117
(860) 236-6698; (800) 727-7592
FAX (860) 232-7680

108. This Victorian inn has 23 guest rooms with a large entry/sitting room. Guests are free to use the kitchen for storing or cooking. Seventeen rooms have private baths and six have shared baths. All rooms have TV, VCR, small refrigerator, and coffee maker. Continental breakfast. Children welcome. Smoking permitted outside only.

OLD LYME

Old Lyme Inn

85 Lyme Street, P.O. Box 787, 06371
(860) 434-2600; (800) 434-5352
FAX (860) 434-5352

Outside, wildflowers bloom all summer; inside, fireplaces burn all winter, beckoning guests to enjoy the romance and charm

Old Lyme Inn

of this 13-room Victorian country inn with an award-winning, three-star *New York Times* dining room. Within easy reach of the state's attractions, it is tucked away in an old New England art colony. Closed first two weeks in January. Nonsmoking rooms available.

Host: Diana Atwood Johnson
Manager: Debbie Capone
Rooms: 13 (PB) $99-158
Continental Breakfast
Credit Cards: A, B, C, D, E
Notes: 2, 3, 4, 6, 8, 9, 10, 11, 12, 14, 15

OLD MYSTIC

Covered Bridge

69 Maple Avenue, Norfolk, 06058
(860) 542-5944; FAX (860) 542-5690

1OMCT. This 1800s Colonial offers a quiet retreat only minutes from the center of Mystic. There is a pleasant living room with a fireplace and a large dining room where a full breakfast is served. There are four guest rooms in the main house, three with fireplaces, and four guest rooms in the carriage house, two with whirlpool tubs. All rooms have queen-size beds and private baths. $115-145.

OLD SAYBROOK

Deacon Timothy Pratt Bed and Breakfast

325 Main Street, 06475
(860) 395-1229

Step back in time and enjoy the splendor of yesteryear in this circa 1746 national historic register home in the heart of the historic district. Guest rooms are romantically furnished in period style with private baths and working fireplaces. Full country breakfast on fine china. Sherry, tea, and snacks always available. Walk to shops, restaurants, movie theaters, town green activities, Hart House museum, and Saybrook Point at the mouth of Connecticut River. Wonderful area for

Deacon Timothy Pratt

walking, biking, boating; beach passes provided. One mile to Long Island Sound.

Host: Shelley Nobile
Rooms: 3 (PB) $95-140
Full Breakfast
Credit Cards: A, B, C
Notes: 2, 5, 7, 8, 9, 10, 11, 12, 13, 14

Nutmeg Bed and Breakfast Agency

P.O. Box 1117, West Hartford, 06127-1117
(860) 236-6698; (800) 727-7592
FAX (860) 232-7680

514. The river and sound meet at this bed and breakfast. The host even has beach passes for her guests. The contemporary home has a lovely deck off the living room facing the Oyster River and two of the three guest rooms have a water view. One room has a private bath. The two additional rooms share a hall bath. Arrangements can be made to have a private bath. Full breakfast. Children welcome. Smoking permitted outside only. Dog in residence.

ORANGE

Nutmeg Bed and Breakfast Agency

P.O. Box 1117, West Hartford, 06127-1117
(860) 236-6698; (800) 727-7592
FAX (860) 232-7680

206. This bright Colonial farmhouse was built in 1725 and has been in the same

---

7 No smoking; 8 Children welcome; 9 Social drinking allowed; 10 Tennis nearby; 11 Swimming nearby; 12 Golf nearby; 13 Skiing nearby; 14 May be booked through a travel agent; 15 Handicapped accessible.

family for 11 generations. It remains a working dairy farm and there is always fresh milk. There are two second-floor guest rooms which share a bath. One room has a double bed, the other twin beds. Continental breakfast. Children are welcome. No smoking permitted. Dog, cows, and horses on premises.

PAWCATUCK

Nutmeg Bed and Breakfast Agency

P.O. Box 1117, West Hartford, 06127-1117
(860) 236-6698; (800) 727-7592
FAX (860) 232-7680

506. This unique single-story house has a beautiful addition for guests. The new wing has a king-size bed that can be made into twin beds, a private bath, and private entrance with a small deck. Enjoy a walk down the street to a spectacular water view. This is close to Mystic Seaport and many beaches. Full breakfast. Children welcome. No smoking. Cats in main part of the house only.

PLANTSVILLE

Nutmeg Bed and Breakfast Agency

P.O. Box 1117, West Hartford, 06127-1117
(860) 236-6698; (800) 727-7592
FAX (860) 232-7680

465. This 11-room central-chimney Colonial, circa 1740, is on a beautifully landscaped acre with a pool and surrounded by centuries-old maple trees. There are four fireplaces and a dutch oven in the great room. The guest room has a king-size bed, private bath, and air conditioning. Full breakfast served. Children welcome. Smoking in designated areas only. Cat and dog on premises.

PLYMOUTH

Nutmeg Bed and Breakfast Agency

P.O. Box 1117, West Hartford, 06127-1117
(860) 236-6698; (800) 727-7592
FAX (860) 232-7680

407. This beautiful 1825 Greek Revival, furnished with antiques, is on three lovely acres enhanced with a perennial garden. There are three guest rooms. They share two baths, and a private bath can be arranged for additional cost. The bed and breakfast is convenient to activities in the northwest hills. Full breakfast. No smoking. No children.

PLYMOUTH VILLAGE

Shelton House Bed and Breakfast

663 Main Street, Route 6, 06782
(860) 283-4616 (phone/FAX)
e-mail: sheltonHBB@aol.com

Enjoy a step back in time with a stay in this historic 1825 Greek Revival, elegantly furnished with antiques and period furniture. Separate guest living room with fireplace and TV. Lovely grounds. Full breakfast served. Afternoon tea. Convenient to Route 8 and I-84. Short distance to

Shelton House

all attractions in the scenic Litchfield Hills. Four guest rooms with private and semiprivate baths.

Hosts: Pat and Bill Doherty
Rooms: 4 (2 PB; 2 SB) $65-90
Full Breakfast
Credit Cards: None
Notes: 2, 5, 7, 10, 11, 12, 13

POMFRET CENTER

Nutmeg Bed and Breakfast Agency

P.O. Box 1117, West Hartford, 06127-1117
(860) 236-6698; (800) 727-7592
FAX (860) 232-7680

421. This Victorian sits on six acres with flower and vegetable gardens. The formal dining room and sitting room have fireplaces. There are two queen-size rooms with private baths, and twin- and queen-size rooms with a shared bath. Full breakfast. No smoking. Children welcome. Dog in residence.

POQUETANUCK

Captain Grant's, 1754

109 Route 2A, 06365
(860) 887-7589; (800) 982-1772
FAX (860) 892-9151
www.bbonline.com/ct/captaingrants

Built in 1754, Captain Grant's is now a national historic home. Colonial ambiance includes canopied beds, fireplaces, a library, keeping room, kitchenette, and three-story deck; all for guests' exclusive use. Modern amenities include all private baths, air conditioning, color cable TV, evening wine, and a full country breakfast. Minutes from Foxwoods, Mystic, Coast Guard Academy, Naval submarine museum, and much more.

Hosts: Ted and Carol
Rooms: 6 (PB) $80-150

Full Breakfast
Credit Cards: A, B, C, D
Notes: 5, 7, 8, 9, 10, 11, 12, 14

RIDGEFIELD

Nutmeg Bed and Breakfast Agency

P.O. Box 1117, West Hartford, 06127-1117
(860) 236-6698; (800) 727-7592
FAX (860) 232-7680

101. Savor a Finnish sauna in a 1945 Cape-style house. The private lower level suite has a queen-size bed and a wonderful luxurious bath. The floor is terra cotta tile; furnishings are tastefully European; and a TV is provided so guests might never want to reappear outside the room, except to enjoy their tasty Continental breakfast. Smoking is not permitted Dog and cats in residence.

102. Originally a private boys' school, this home sits on a hilltop overlooking five pastoral acres with a magnificent view. It is only one hour from Manhattan. Guests enjoy a private suite that includes a large sitting room with fireplace and a private bath. French doors separate the main house from the guest suite. Continental breakfast is served. Smoking is permitted.

West Lane Inn

22 West Lane, Route 35, 06877
(203) 438-7323; FAX (203) 438-7325

The West Lane Inn offers Colonial elegance in overnight accommodations. Special attention is paid to detail and the individual. Also close to shopping, museums, and points of interest.

Hosts: M. M. Mayer and Deborah Prieger
Rooms: 18 (PB) $125-170
Continental Breakfast
Credit Cards: A, B, C, E
Notes: 5, 8, 10, 11, 12, 13, 14

7 No smoking; 8 Children welcome; 9 Social drinking allowed; 10 Tennis nearby; 11 Swimming nearby; 12 Golf nearby; 13 Skiing nearby; 14 May be booked through a travel agent; 15 Handicapped accessible.

RIVERSIDE

Nutmeg Bed and Breakfast Agency

P.O. Box 1117, West Hartford, 06127-1117
(860) 236-6698; (800) 727-7592
FAX (860) 232-7680

105. These active hosts have decided to share this lovely country-style Cape home. Guest room has private bath. New York City is only one hour away. Full breakfast is served. Children are welcome. No smoking.

110. More than 100-years-old, this farmhouse is on three-quarters of an acre. Spacious and bright first-floor room with deck, private bath with shower, contemporary furnishings, TV, small refrigerator, and coffee maker. On weekdays a Continental breakfast served; weekends full breakfast served. House is one-half mile from Riverside Railroad station, close to Greenwich beaches, many antique stores, and other Greenwich attractions. Crib and high chair are available. Smoking is permitted on the deck only.

RIVERTON

Nutmeg Bed and Breakfast Agency

P.O. Box 1117, West Hartford, 06127-1117
(860) 236-6698; (800) 727-7592
FAX (860) 232-7680

305. Close to Lime Rock Park and many of the private schools, this log home is secluded on five acres. Superb place for cross-country skiing, hiking, and stream fishing. Two guest rooms with private baths. The former innkeepers will also prepare a hearty dinner for overnight guests with prior arrangements. Children welcome. Full breakfast. Smoking in designated area only. Cat in residence.

Old Riverton Inn

Route 20, Box 6, 06065
(860) 379-8678; (800) EST-1796
FAX (860) 379-1006

Hospitality for the hungry, thirsty, and sleepy since 1796. Overlooking the designated Wild and Scenic Farmington River and the Hitchcock Chair Factory Store. Listed in the National Register of Historic Places. Serving lunch and dinner Wednesday through Sunday. Originally a stagecoach stop on the Hartford to Albany route. Pets welcome with prior approval.

Hosts: Mark and Pauline Telford
Rooms: 12 (PB) $85-175
Full Breakfast
Credit Cards: A, B, C, D, E
Notes: 3, 4, 5, 7, 8, 9, 10, 11, 12, 13, 14

ROXBURY

Nutmeg Bed and Breakfast Agency

P.O. Box 1117, West Hartford, 06127-1117
(860) 236-6698; (800) 727-7592
FAX (860) 232-7680

301. The main house, built in 1790, has a private guest wing with private entrance and bath, a canopied waterbed with feather mattress. A sitting area has a pull-out sofa bed for children. Guests may use the main house to relax in front of the wood-burning stove. The Shepaug River and hiking trails beckon guests outdoors. Full breakfast. Children welcome. No smoking. Pets on premises.

SALEM

Nutmeg Bed and Breakfast Agency

P.O. Box 1117, West Hartford, 06127-1117
(860) 236-6698; (800) 727-7592
FAX (860) 232-7680

524. A center-chimney Colonial built over 200 years ago has a pastoral view. Close to

---

NOTES: Credit cards accepted: A MasterCard; B Visa; C American Express; D Discover; E Diner's Club; F Other; 2 Personal checks accepted; 3 Lunch available; 4 Dinner available; 5 Open all year; 6 Pets welcome;

Mystic Seaport, Foxwoods Casino, the Connecticut shoreline, and Rhode Island beaches. Six guest rooms, three with private bath and fireplace. Continental breakfast. Children over 12 welcome. No smoking. Dogs, cats, and horses on premises.

Woodbridge Farm

30 Woodbridge Road, 06420
(860) 859-1169; FAX (860) 887-5555
e-mail: wdbgfmbb@aol.com

Open all year. Seven rooms with four private and three shared baths in a 1792 central chimney on 20 wooded and pastoral acres on a hill with views. Horses stabled in barn and roaming pastures. Trails lead from house and connect to other properties. TV in library with TV/VCR, CD, and stereo. Hiking, biking, bird watching, antiquing, art galleries. Children over 12 are welcome.

Host: Mariam Bingham
Rooms: 7 (4 PB; 3 SB) $83-250
Continental Breakfast
Credit Cards: A, B, C
Notes: 5, 7

SALISBURY

Covered Bridge

69 Maple Avenue Norfolk, 06058
(860) 542-5944; FAX (860) 542-5690

1S. This 1810 Colonial is set on two private landscaped acres in the center of town. Large living room with a fireplace and a study with a TV for guests. A full breakfast is served. Two guest rooms. $95.

Nutmeg Bed and Breakfast Agency

P.O. Box 1117, West Hartford, 06127-1117
(860) 236-6698; (800) 727-7592
FAX (860) 232-7680

312. Overlooking the village of Salisbury is an Italianate 1850 historic house. The house is 100 feet above Main Street and is on one and one-half acres. The two guest rooms have queen-size beds and private baths. One room has a fireplace and French doors which lead to a private terrace. A full breakfast is served. Sorry, children are not welcome. Smoking is not permitted. Cat is in residence.

337. This 1813 Colonial is in the historic district of Salisbury, one of Connecticut's most charming villages. Two guest rooms with private baths. Breakfast is served in the dining room or on the stone terrace. Walk to fine restaurants, shops, and antiques. Convenient to Lime Rock. Children are welcome. No smoking. Pets are on premises.

324. A large countrified Colonial built in 1765 lies just outside of town on a lovely lake. The screened porch overlooks the lake and guests can enjoy a swim from the owner's dock. There are five guest rooms, two of which share a bath. The rooms are all on the second floor. Picnic lunches are available by special arrangement. Continental breakfast is served. Smoking is not permitted. Dogs are in residence.

SCOTLAND

Nutmeg Bed and Breakfast Agency

P.O. Box 1117, West Hartford, 06127-1117
(860) 236-6698; (800) 727-7592
FAX (860) 232-7680

454. A 1797 Colonial-style country inn with a large sitting room for guests, keeping room, and kitchen for breakfast. Also a TV room with fireplace, double bedroom, and queen-size bedroom with fireplace. Both share a bath. Full breakfast. Children over 10 welcome. No smoking. Cat on premises.

---

7 No smoking; 8 Children welcome; 9 Social drinking allowed; 10 Tennis nearby; 11 Swimming nearby; 12 Golf nearby; 13 Skiing nearby; 14 May be booked through a travel agent; 15 Handicapped accessible.

SIMSBURY

Nutmeg Bed and Breakfast Agency

P.O. Box 1117, West Hartford, 06127-1117
(860) 236-6698; (800) 727-7592
FAX (860) 232-7680

425. This gracious inn, listed in the National Register of Historic Places, has rooms with private bath, TV, telephone, and amenities. A full-service dining room, wedding and banquet facilities, and a country Continental breakfast make it a perfect spot for business or social functions. Children asre welcome. Smoking is permitted.

SOMERSVILLE

Old Mill Inn Bed and Breakfast

63 Maple Street, 06072
(860) 763-1473 (phone/FAX)

Surrounded by giant maple trees, this spacious old New England home provides romantic lodging and gourmet breakfast. Guests have use of the private beach on the serene Scantic River with hammock, swing, canoe, picnic table, and fishing. Bicycles available for countryside touring and a soothing spa to end a perfect day. Gazebo enhances picturesque settings for intimate weddings, parties, and family reunions.

Rooms: 5 (1 PB; 4 SB) $85-95
Full Breakfast
Credit Cards: None
Notes: 2, 4, 5, 7, 9, 10, 11, 12, 13

SOUTHBURY

Nutmeg Bed and Breakfast Agency

P.O. Box 1117, West Hartford, 06127-1117
(860) 236-6698; (800) 727-7592
FAX (860) 232-7680

320. A Georgian Federal home, circa 1818, has six guest bedrooms, three acres of nicely landscaped grounds with pool, cozy keeping room with fireplace, cable TV, VCR, exercise room. Convenient to antiquing, private schools, horseback riding, hiking, vineyards, fishing, and all outdoor activities. Can be booked for weddings or receptions up to 100 guests. Afternoon high tea. Full breakfast but Continental breakfast is occasionally served with breakfast bar adjacent to guest rooms. Picnic lunches can be arranged. Children 12 and older welcome. No smoking. No pets. Two small dogs in residence.

SOUTH WINDSOR

Nutmeg Bed and Breakfast Agency

P.O. Box 1117, West Hartford, 06127-1117
(860) 236-6698; (800) 727-7592
FAX (860) 232-7680

410. All guest rooms in this large Palladian-style mansion, circa 1788, have fireplaces. The original floor plan is intact, and two rooms have original paper. Convenient to Hartford, Springfield, and many historic sites. Close to bus line. Two rooms on first floor with sitting area, desk, outdoor sitting area, private bath, cable TV. All telephones have data lines; rooms ADA handicapped accessible. Space is available for meetings for up to 10 people. Continental breakfast. Children welcome. No smoking.

STAMFORD

Nutmeg Bed and Breakfast Agency

P.O. Box 1117, West Hartford, 06127-1117
(860) 236-6698; (800) 727-7592
FAX (860) 232-7680

116. This Nantucket Colonial has a water view on a sandy beach. Breakfast is served

NOTES: Credit cards accepted: A MasterCard; B Visa; C American Express; D Discover; E Diner's Club; F Other; 2 Personal checks accepted; 3 Lunch available; 4 Dinner available; 5 Open all year; 6 Pets welcome;

on the sun porch. Two guest rooms, each with a private bath. Full breakfast served. Children are welcome. No smoking.

STRATFORD

Covered Bridge

69 Maple Avenue, Norfolk, 06058
(860) 542-5944; FAX (860) 542-5690

This 1843 Federal Greek Revival farm-house, set on several acres, is in the National Register of Historic Places. Antique-decorated parlor, living room with fireplace, and large sun porch are available for guest use. There are four guest rooms, two with private baths and two available as a suite with a bathroom. Full breakfast is served. $100.

TOLLAND

Nutmeg Bed and Breakfast Agency

P.O. Box 1117, West Hartford, 06127-1117
(860) 236-6698; (800) 727-7592
FAX (860) 232-7680

403. Just east of Hartford is this lovely two-story Colonial, circa 1840, on three acres. The two guest rooms have queen-size beds and private baths. The home is beautifully decorated with English country antiques that have been carefully selected and is a treat to stay in. Full breakfast. Children are welcome. Smoking permitted outside only.

Old Babcock Tavern Bed and Breakfast

484 Mile Hill Road, Route 31, 06084
(860) 875-1239; FAX (860) 870-9544
e-mail: babcockbb@juno.com

One of the finest restored early inns in America today. A complete theme of Early American furnishings is found in every room of this 1720 tavern. The center

chimney is constructed of granite with clay mortar. Three fireplaces and two bake ovens adorn the rooms on the main floor. Early fireplace implements add to the interest. One thousand books, classical music, and a candlelight breakfast will relax guests. This post-and-beam early tavern is in the National Register of Historic Places. Children over 12 are welcome. Cross-country skiing nearby.

Hosts: Barb and Stu Danforth
Rooms: 3 (PB) $70-85
Full Breakfast
Credit Cards: None
Notes: 2, 5, 7, 9, 10, 11, 12, 13

The Tolland Inn

63 Tolland Green, 06084-0717
(860) 872-0800

Built in 1800, the inn stands on Tolland's historic village green, less than one mile north of I-84 exit 68. Seven guest rooms are decorated with antiques and furniture made by the host. Two suites have canopied beds, one with sitting room and fireplace, one with sitting room and hot tub. The first-floor room has a canopied bed, fireplace, and a sunken hot tub. Three beautiful common rooms and a fireplace complete the picture. Convenient to Brimfield Fair, Old Sturbridge, and the University of Connecticut. AAA three-diamond-rated.

Hosts: Susan and Stephen Beeching
Rooms: 7 (PB) $78.40-95.20

7 No smoking; 8 Children welcome; 9 Social drinking allowed; 10 Tennis nearby; 11 Swimming nearby; 12 Golf nearby; 13 Skiing nearby; 14 May be booked through a travel agent; 15 Handicapped accessible.

The Tolland Inn

Suites: $123.20-145.60
Full Breakfast
Credit Cards: A, B, C, D, E
Notes: 2, 5, 7, 9, 10, 11, 12, 14

WALLINGFORD

Nutmeg Bed and Breakfast Agency

P.O. Box 1117, West Hartford, 06127-1117
(860) 236-6698; (800) 727-7592
FAX (860) 232-7680

209. The original part of this center chimney Colonial was built in 1742 as the family homestead, with an addition in 1995. It rests on two handsome acres with a pond at the end of the property. The two guest rooms are in the original part of the house. One room has a double bed; the other has either a king-size bed or twin beds and each has a private bath. The host is an international traveler and a gourmet cook. Full breakfast. Children welcome. No smoking. Dog and cat in residence.

WATERBURY

Nutmeg Bed and Breakfast Agency

P.O. Box 1117, West Hartford, 06127-1117
(860) 236-6698; (800) 727-7592
FAX (860) 232-7680

318. This restored Victorian, in the historic district, is furnished with antiques. It offers three guest rooms on the second floor, two of which share a bath. The other has a private bath. There is also a third-floor suite. A grand city gem, the architecture is the best that New England cities have to offer. Continental breakfast is served. Smoking is not permitted.

WATERTOWN

The Clarks

97 Scott Avenue, 06795
(860) 274-4866

The Clarks is a 1939 Cape-style home three blocks from Taft Preparatory School and convenient for travelers on Routes 8 and 84. Two guest rooms, one with a double bed and one with twin beds, have ceiling fans. Guests are welcome to use the entire house, including porches, barbecue grill, and laundry facilities. The hosts are active in the Lions Club, the community, and the church, and provide a warm family atmosphere. Closed during the months of February and March.

Hosts: Richard and Barbara Clark
Rooms: 2 (SB) $40-45
Continental Breakfast
Credit Cards: None
Notes: 2, 6, 7, 8, 9

WESTBROOK

Covered Bridge

69 Maple Avenue, Norfolk, 06058
(860) 542-5944; FAX (860) 542-5690

Federal Colonial close to the beach offers five guest rooms, three with private baths, all with air conditioning and a TV. A full breakfast is served and on the grounds there are gas grills and picnic tables for guests' use. $80-115.

NOTES: Credit cards accepted: A MasterCard; B Visa; C American Express; D Discover; E Diner's Club; F Other; 2 Personal checks accepted; 3 Lunch available; 4 Dinner available; 5 Open all year; 6 Pets welcome;

Nutmeg Bed and Breakfast Agency

P.O. Box 1117, West Hartford, 06127-1117
(860) 236-6698; (800) 727-7592
FAX (860) 232-7680

516. For the many activities along the Connecticut coast, this house built in 1895 is ideal. There are three guest rooms; one has a private bath and two share a bath. The home is 150 feet from the beach and is furnished with antiques. Full breakfast served. Children are welcome. No smoking.

517. This stately Federal-style house was built in 1880 and is two blocks from the sound. There are three floors and five guest rooms, two of which share a bath. The rooms all have TVs. Full breakfast served. Children 10 and older welcome. No smoking.

521. For lovers of the Victorian era, this house is ideal. Built in 1876, it is close to the beach and downtown. Four rooms have private baths and five rooms have shared baths. The interior is newly decorated in the Victorian period. Full breakfast is served on Sunday; Continental is served the rest of the time. Children welcome. Smoking permitted.

Talcott House Bed and Breakfast

161 Seaside Avenue, P.O. Box 1016, 06498
(860) 399-5020

Beautifully restored 1890 home directly on the shore of Long Island Sound. All four of the spacious guest rooms have ocean views and private baths. Two large fireplaces grace the decor in the living/dining room area. Enjoy the adjacent beach for swimming, sunning, or walking. Many area attractions within easy driving distance including Mystic Seaport, factory outlet malls, and Indian casinos. Off-season rates available.

Host: Don
Rooms: 4 (PB) $135-150
Full Breakfast
Credit Cards: A, B, C
Notes: 2, 5, 7, 9, 11

Welcome Inn Bed and Breakfast

433 Essex Road, 06498
(860) 399-2500

Originally a strawberry farm, the inn was built around 1897 and retains its country charm. Convenient to everything the Connecticut River valley and seashore have to offer. The inn is decorated with antiques, fine reproductions, lace, and heirlooms. Breakfast is served 8:00-9:30 A.M. daily with delicious homemade goodies and special coffee. Relax in the parlor with a crackling fire, a glass of sherry, and a good book, or in the garden. Hosts will be happy to assist guests with arranging restaurant reservations, tours, and other activities.

Hosts: Alison and Robert Bambino
Rooms: 3 (SB) $85-125
Full Breakfast
Credit Cards: A, B
Notes: 2, 5, 7, 9, 10, 11, 12,

WEST CORNWALL

Nutmeg Bed and Breakfast Agency

P.O. Box 1117, West Hartford, 06127-1117
(860) 236-6698; (800) 727-7592
FAX (860) 232-7680

317. A great seasonal getaway spot. Newly renovated streamside studio cottages have working fireplaces, private baths, porches with sitting area, coffee makers in rooms. Hearty Continental breakfast served on porch. Pets accepted. Convenient to Lime Rock, Housatonic River, Kent, and Salisbury, private schools. Fly-fishing guide on premises, canoeing, hiking, kayaking. Good restaurants are nearby. Children are welcome. No smoking.

7 No smoking; 8 Children welcome; 9 Social drinking allowed; 10 Tennis nearby; 11 Swimming nearby; 12 Golf nearby; 13 Skiing nearby; 14 May be booked through a travel agent; 15 Handicapped accessible.

WEST HARTFORD

Nutmeg Bed and Breakfast Agency

P.O. Box 1117, 06127-1117
(860) 236-6698; (800) 727-7592
FAX (860) 232-7680

441. This single-story home is furnished with a blend of modern, traditional, and antique. One guest room with TV has two twins or king-size bed and private bath. Convenient to Hartford, the University of Connecticut, and the University of Hartford. Hungarian spoken. Continental breakfast. Children are welcome. No smoking.

WEST HAVEN

Nutmeg Bed and Breakfast Agency

P.O. Box 1117, West Hartford, 06127-1117
(860) 236-6698; (800) 727-7592
FAX (860) 232-7680

212. A lovely porch wraps around this 80-year-old Victorian not far from Long Island Sound. The accommodations are on the first floor and include a dining room, kitchen, parlor, private bath, private entrance, and a double bed in the bedroom. On the weekends, a candlelight dinner can be arranged. Continental breakfast is served on weekdays; full breakfast is served on weekends. Children over 10 are welcome. No Smoking.

WESTPORT

Nutmeg Bed and Breakfast Agency

P.O. Box 1117, West Hartford, 06127-1117
(860) 236-6698; (800) 727-7592
FAX (860) 232-7680

104. This Georgian Colonial, with pool, has a second-floor guest room with a king-size bed that can be made into twin beds, wicker furnishings, and private bath with shower. Convenient to railroad station. A full breakfast is served. Children are welcome. Smoking is not permitted. Dog in residence.

111. This home combines rural beauty with metropolitan sophistication in a breathtaking setting overlooking Long Island Sound. The private guest wing has its own sitting room, fireplace, and entrance. There are three guest rooms that have either a private or shared bath. Enjoy the beach during summer. Continental breakfast is served. Children are welcome. No smoking. $60.

WETHERSFIELD

Nutmeg Bed and Breakfast Agency

P.O. Box 1117, West Hartford, 06127-1117
(860) 236-6698; (800) 727-7592
FAX (860) 232-7680

408. Nestled in the historic village of Old Wethersfield, this classic Greek Revival brick house has been lovingly restored to provide a warm and gracious New England welcome to all travelers. Built in 1830, it boasts five airy guest rooms furnished with period antiques. Three rooms have private baths; two rooms share a bath. Fresh flowers; cozy living room and parlor. Afternoon tea and elegant full breakfast is served. Children over 11 are welcome.

429. This attractive Colonial home is rich in the history of the town. The hostess, a member of the historical society, offers one guest room with a private bath. A small room suitable for a child is available. Close to a park and safe for walking. Full breakfast is served. Children are welcome. Smoking is permitted in designated areas only.

NOTES: Credit cards accepted: A MasterCard; B Visa; C American Express; D Discover; E Diner's Club; F Other; 2 Personal checks accepted; 3 Lunch available; 4 Dinner available; 5 Open all year; 6 Pets welcome;

WINDSOR

Covered Bridge
69 Maple Avenue, Norfolk, 06058
(860) 542-5944; FAX (860) 542-5690

1WINCT. This 1860 Queen Anne Victorian rests in Connecticut's oldest town and is furnished with exquisite period antiques and William Morris wallpapers. Guests are welcome to relax in the living room or music room with a grand piano and a century-old music box. Three guest rooms with private baths offered. One room has a fireplace. $75-100.

Nutmeg Bed and Breakfast Agency
P.O. Box 1117, West Hartford, 06127-1117
(860) 236-6698; (800) 727-7592
FAX (860) 232-7680

469. Charming Victorian home dating to 1860s, renovated with an addition in 1890. Lovely antique furniture; large front porch; three second-floor bedrooms, two with extra-long double beds, one with extra-long twin beds, and all with private baths. Convenient to airport, University of Hartford, and Loomis Chaffee. Full breakfast. Children over 12 welcome. No smoking. Dog on premises.

WOODBRIDGE

Nutmeg Bed and Breakfast Agency
P.O. Box 1117, West Hartford, 06127-1117
(860) 236-6698; (800) 727-7592
FAX (860) 232-7680

201. This bilevel contemporary home, on two acres, is convenient to New Haven.

Guests may enjoy the suite with a sliding glass door to the patio. The bedroom has a double bed, TV, a sitting room with a fireplace, and a small kitchen. Ideal for longer stays. Continental breakfast is served. Smoking is not permitted

WOODBURY

Covered Bridge
69 Maple Avenue, Norfolk, 06058
(860) 542-5944; FAX (860) 542-5690

1WOCT. This 1789 Colonial, set on four acres, is in a town which has been described as "the Antique Capital of Connecticut." Many of the original features of the house, such as the large covered porch, wide-oak floorboards, and fireplaces, have been preserved. A grand living room with a fireplace and a library are available for guest use. There are five lovely bedrooms and suites. A full country breakfast is served. $105-125.

Nutmeg Bed and Breakfast Agency
P.O. Box 1117, West Hartford, 06127-1117
(860) 236-6698; (800) 727-7592
FAX (860) 232-7680

345. This 1789 Colonial, on three acres, has been carefully restored and tastefully furnished with antiques. Two guest rooms have double beds and shared bath; combined they make a suite. Remaining three guest rooms all have private baths. They have twin, king-, or queen-size beds. Full breakfast is served. Children five and over are welcome. Smoking is not permitted. Resident cat on the premises.

7 No smoking; 8 Children welcome; 9 Social drinking allowed; 10 Tennis nearby; 11 Swimming nearby; 12 Golf nearby; 13 Skiing nearby; 14 May be booked through a travel agent; 15 Handicapped accessible.

Caribou •

Greenville •

Guilford •
Dexter •

Stratton •

Bangor • Holden •
Sullivan
Harbor
West
Gouldsboro

Dixfield •
Rumford Center •
Bethel •

Stockton Springs
Searsport •
Belfast •
Orland •
Brooksville

Eastpor •
Lubec •

Cherryfield

Augusta •
S. Brooksville
Stonington
Rockland •
Thomaston •
Camden •
Waldoboro •

Corea
Winter Harbor
Bar Harbor
Mount Desert Island
Northeast Harbor

Waterford •

Fryeburg •

Bridgton •
Casco
Naples •
Gorham •

Damariscotta
Newcastle
Wiscasset

Vinalhaven
Isle au Haut

Southwest Harbor
Bass Harbor

Brunswick
Freeport •
Portland •

Bath •

Tenants Harbor
Friendship
Round Pond

Saco
Kennebunk
Biddeford Pool

Newagen
Boothbay
Boothbay Harbor

Chamberlain
New Harbor

Kennebunk Beach

Bailey Island
Kennebunkport

Wells •
Eliot •

Ogunquit

Kittery
York,
York Beach,
York Harbor

Maine

Maine

Maple Hill Farm
Bed and Breakfast Inn

Outlet Road, Rural Route 1, Box 1145,
Hallowell, 04347
(207) 622-2708; (800) 622-2708
FAX (207) 622-0655; e-mail: info@MapleBB.com
www.MapleBB.com

"Best of Maine 1997...hands down"—
Maine Times. Unique pampered service for
relaxation or business travel combined with
this inn's barnyard menagerie—llama, pony,
goats, sheep, more! On 130 serene acres of
unspoiled rural beauty, minutes to turnpike,
capitol, national historic district, shopping,
eclectic dining, antiquing. Central to coast,
lakes, mountains. Adjacent to 550-acre
wildlife preserve with pristine pond for
canoeing/hiking. Full breakfast featuring
eggs from farm. Spacious antique-furnished
rooms with air conditioning, telephones, TV.
Private whirlpool available. Liquor license.
Fully accessible guest room available.

Host: Scott Cowger
Rooms: 7 (4 PB; 3 SB) $60-125
Full Breakfast
Credit Cards: A, B, C, D, E
Notes: 2, 4, 5, 7, 8, 9, 11, 12, 13, 14, 15

Captain York House
Bed and Breakfast

Route 24, P.O. Box 298, 04003
(207) 833-6224

Enjoy true island atmosphere on scenic
Bailey Island, in an unspoiled fishing vil-

Captain York House

lage accessible by car over the only crib-
stone bridge in the world. Near Brunswick,
Freeport, and Portland. Former sea captain's home tastefully restored to original
charm, furnished with antiques. Informal,
friendly atmosphere and ocean views from
every room. From the deck, enjoy sights of
local lobstermen hauling traps and sunsets
to remember. Nearby fine dining/summer
nature cruise. Ocean-view apartment rental
also available. Children over 12 welcome.

Hosts: Alan and Jean Thornton
Rooms: 5 (3 PB; 2 SB) $70-95
Full Breakfast
Credit Cards: A, B
Notes: 2, 5, 7, 11, 12, 14

The Lady and the Loon

P.O. Box 98, 04003
(207) 833-6871

Restored 1875 inn on ocean bluff overlooking beautiful Casco Bay. Private baths and
queen-size beds. Panoramic ocean views.
Private rocky Maine beach. Full breakfasts.
Owner paints Celtic mythology on porce-

lain and teaches landscape painting. Rooms decorated in Maine island atmosphere with antiques and original art. Bailey Island offers charming, quiet walks along beaches and bluffs. Delicious dining on island. Three hours from Boston.

Hostess: Gail O'Hara
Rooms: 4 (PB) $80-100
Full Breakfast
Credit Cards: A, B
Notes: 2, 7

BANGOR

Mann Hill Morgans Bed and Breakfast

Rural Route 2, Box 8230, Mann Hill Road,
    East Holden, 04429
(207) 843-5657; e-mail: mannhill@mint.net
www.maineguide.com/bangor/manhill

This lovely and spacious New England Colonial, with private stable, features two beautifully decorated rooms, one with fireplace. Both rooms have private baths. A delightful getaway for those seeking peace and tranquillity. Nestled on a foothill with mountains that surround, it is only two miles from Route 1A. It is the "Maine" route to and from Bar Harbor and Acadia National Park. Ten minutes to Bangor. Fifteen minutes to Bangor International Airport. Forty miles to Bar Harbor.

Hosts: Mary and Larry Winchester
Rooms: 2 (PB) $45-60
Full Breakfast
Credit Cards: A, B
Notes: 2, 5, 7, 8, 9, 10, 11, 12, 13

Mann Hill Morgans

BAR HARBOR

Bar Harbor Tides Bed and Breakfast

119 West Street, 04609
(207) 288-4968; FAX (207) 288-2997
e-mail: thetides@acadia.net
www.barharbortides.com

An 1887 Greek Revival cottage in quiet historic district. One room and three luxurious suites—the suites all have sweeping views of Frenchman's Bay, king- or queen-size beds, and private baths; two have fireplaces. Full gourmet breakfast served on the veranda overlooking the bay, or in the formal dining room with its own grand view of the bay. Very private, nonsmoking.

Hosts: Joe and Judy Losquadro
Rooms: 4 (PB) $150-275
Full Breakfast
Credit Cards: A, B, D
Notes: 5, 7, 10, 12

Black Friar Inn

Black Friar Inn

10 Summer Street, 04609
(207) 288-5091; FAX (207) 288-4197
e-mail: blackfriar@acadia.net
www.blackfriar.com

This comfortably restored and rebuilt Victorian house with antiques is on a quiet side street. Six guest rooms with queen-size beds and private baths, plus a suite with king-size bed, private bath, fireplace, and sofa bed. Rates include delicious full breakfast, late afternoon refreshments, and rainy day teas. Easy access to Acadia National Park. Short walk to waterfront, shops, and restaurants. Ample parking. Two-night minimum mid-June through mid-October. Sorry, no cots or rollaway beds; the six guest rooms can accommodate one or two people only. Children over 11 welcome.

Hosts: Perry and Sharon Risley and Falke
Rooms: 6 (PB) $90-115
Suite: 1 (PB) $140
Full Breakfast
Credit Cards: A, B, D
Notes: 2, 7, 9, 10, 11, 12

Canterbury Cottage Bed and Breakfast

12 Roberts Avenue, 04609
(207) 288-2112; e-mail: canterbury@acadia.net
www.acadia.net/canterbury

Small bed and breakfast with comfortable, tastefully decorated rooms. On a quiet side street within easy walking distance to in-town and harbor activities. Owners share a lifetime of island knowledge with guests while breakfast is served in the dining room. Sorry, not appropriate for children, pets, or smoking. Winter rates available.

Hosts: Armando and Maria Ribeiro
Rooms: 4 (PB) $65-100
Full Breakfast
Credit Cards: A, B
Notes: 2, 5, 7, 10, 12, 14

Castlemaine Inn

39 Holland Avenue, 04609
(207) 288-4563; (800) 338-4563

Castlemaine Inn is nestled on a quiet side street in the village of Bar Harbor, which is surrounded by the magnificent Acadia National Park. The rooms are well appointed, with canopied beds and some whirlpool bathtubs, private balconies, fireplaces. A delightful Continental buffet-style breakfast is served. Air conditioning. Color

Castlemaine Inn

cable TV with VCR. Open May through October. Children over 13 are welcome.

Hosts: Terence O'Connell and Norah O'Brien
Rooms: 15 (PB) $98-168
Continental Breakfast
Credit Cards: A, B
Notes: 2, 9, 10, 11, 12

Cleftstone Manor

92 Eden Street, 04609
(207) 288-4951; e-mail: cleftstone@acadia.net

Cleftstone Manor offers friendly, country inn hospitality in a beautiful 1884 mansion perched on a hillside. Spacious rooms furnished with antiques, all with private baths and air conditioning, some with balconies or fireplaces. Delicious full breakfast, afternoon and evening refreshments. Within walking distance of downtown Bar Harbor and the waterfront. Open May through October.

Hosts: Steve and Kelly Hellmann
Rooms: 16 (PB) $70-185
Full Breakfast
Credit Credit: A, B, D
Notes: 2, 7, 9, 10, 11, 12, 14

Cleftstone Manor

7 No smoking; 8 Children welcome; 9 Social drinking allowed; 10 Tennis nearby; 11 Swimming nearby; 12 Golf nearby; 13 Skiing nearby; 14 May be booked through a travel agent; 15 Handicapped accessible.

Graycote Inn

Graycote Inn

40 Holland Avenue, 04609
(207) 288-3044; e-mail: graycote@acadia.net
www.graycoteinn.com

This light and airy Victorian house is ideal
for a romantic getaway. The day begins
with morning coffee placed outside guests'
room; then enjoy a made-from-scratch
breakfast served on a sunny, enclosed
porch. The inn is on a large lot with trees,
lawns, flower gardens, a croquet court, and
hammocks. Relax in wicker chairs on the
veranda or walk to shops, art and craft galleries, and restaurants. Five minutes to
Acadia National Park.

Hosts: Roger and Pat Samuel
Rooms: 12 (PB) $95-155
Full Breakfast
Credit Cards: A, B, C, D
Notes: 2, 5, 7, 9, 10, 11, 12, 13, 14

Hatfield Bed and Breakfast

20 Roberts Avenue, 04609
(207) 288-9655

Jeff and Sandy Miller invite guests to enjoy
quiet country comfort at Hatfield, on a quiet
side street just a short walk to the waterfront
and town center—a five-minute drive to
Acadia National Park or the ferry to Nova
Scotia. Previously from rural Pennsylvania,
Jeff and Sandy are known for their "country
hospitality" and great breakfasts. Smoking

is permitted outdoors only and seasonal
rates are available. Sorry, no pets.

Hosts: Jeffrey and Sandra Miller
Rooms: 6 (4 PB; 2 SB) $85-110
Full Breakfast
Credit Cards: A, B
Notes: 3, 5, 7, 10, 11, 12, 13

Hearthside

7 High Street, 04609
(207) 288-4533; e-mail: hearth@acadia.net

Built at the turn of the century as the residence for Dr. George Hagerthy, Hearthside
is now a cozy and comfortable bed and
breakfast. Hearthside is on a quiet side
street in Bar Harbor. All of the rooms have
queen-size beds and private baths; some
have private porches, whirlpool tubs, or
working fireplaces. All rooms have air conditioning. Each morning a lavish breakfast
buffet is served, and lemonade and homemade cookies are offered each afternoon.
Off-season rates available.

Hosts: Susan and Barry Schwartz
Rooms: 9 (PB) $90-135
Full Breakfast
Credit Cards: A, B, D
Notes: 2, 5, 7, 9, 10, 11, 12

Hearthside

Holbrook House

74 Mount Desert Street, 04609
(207) 288-4970; (800) 860-7430

A delightful Victorian setting with a light
summer ambiance. A formal breakfast is
served in the beautiful sunroom. Join for

refreshments on the rocker-filled front porch. Ten guest rooms with private baths and cottage suites with two bedrooms each. Off-street parking. Bicycle storage. Non-smoking inn. Open May to October. AAA three-diamond-rated.

Hosts: Bill and Carol Deike
Rooms: 12 (PB) $65-225
Full Breakfast
Credit Cards: A, B
Notes: 2, 7, 9, 10, 11, 12

The Inn at Bay Ledge

1385 Sand Point Road, 04609
(207) 288-4204; FAX (207) 288-5573

Dramatic and peaceful. Overlooking Frenchmen's Bay. All rooms have ocean views. Picked as one of the 12 most romantic hideaways on the East Coast for 1998. At top of an 80-foot cliff with steps leading to private beach. On two acres of tall pines. Five miles to town center, two miles to Acadia National Park main entrance. Open May through October. Two-night minimum, June 15 through October 1. Picnic lunches available.

Hosts: Jack and Jeani Ochtera
Rooms: 10 (PB) $150-250
Full Breakfast
Credit Cards: A, B
Notes: 2, 7, 12,

The Kedge Historic Bed and Breakfast

112 West Street, 04609
(207) 288-5180; (800) 597-8306

The Kedge, built in 1870, has a peaceful beauty that is full of light and comfortable elegance. In town across the street from Frenchman Bay, this bed and breakfast rests on a double lot and has beautiful gardens. The dream room is 18- x 22-feet, has a king-size brass bed, fireplace, and whirlpool tub. In the historic district. Smoke free. Full breakfast. AAA three-diamond rating. Children seven and older welcome.

Rooms: 3 (PB) $65-160
Full Breakfast

Credit Cards: A, B, C
Notes: 2, 5, 7, 9, 10, 11, 12, 13, 14

Manor House Inn

Manor House Inn

106 West Street, 04609
(207) 288-3759; (800) 437-0088

This beautiful 1887 Victorian summer cottage is listed in the National Register of Historic Places. Near Acadia National Park. Within walking distance of downtown Bar Harbor and waterfront. Enjoy the acre of landscaped grounds and gardens. Minimum stay July, August, and holidays is two nights. Closed December through mid-April. Children over 10 welcome.

Host: Mac Noyes
Rooms: 14 (PB) $55-175
Full Breakfast
Credit Cards: A, B
Notes: 2, 7, 9, 10, 11, 12, 14

Mansion at the Atlantic Oakes by-the-Sea

P.O. Box 3, 04609
(800) 33-MAINE; FAX (207) 288-8402

Restored in 1993, this oceanfront "cottage" on the grounds of the Atlantic Oakes Resort offers the ambiance of an elegant inn, full resort amenities, the convenience of a bed and breakfast, stone-walled gardens, splendid ocean views, plus tennis and swimming. Nine lovely guest rooms: two suites, private baths, king- or queen-size beds. Continental

7 No smoking; 8 Children welcome; 9 Social drinking allowed; 10 Tennis nearby; 11 Swimming nearby; 12 Golf nearby; 13 Skiing nearby; 14 May be booked through a travel agent; 15 Handicapped accessible.

Mansion at the Atlantic Oakes by-the-Sea

plus breakfast served in high season. Minutes to Acadia National Park and downtown Bar Harbor.

Rooms: 9 (PB) $67-205
Continental Breakfast
Credit Cards: A, B, C
Notes: 2, 7, 10, 11, 12, 13, 14

The Maples Inn

16 Roberts Avenue, 04609
(207) 288-3443

Built in 1903, this lovely inn is on a quiet tree-lined street, near the downtown area of Bar Harbor and just a short walk to boutiques, intimate restaurants, and the surrounding sea. For the perfect romantic

The Maples Inn

getaway, reserve the White Birch Suite with wood-burning fireplace. Palates will be treated to host's breakfast recipes, some of which have been featured in *Gourmet* and *Bon Appétit* magazines. Just two miles from Acadia National Park.

Host: Tom Palumbo
Rooms: 6 (PB) $60-150
Full Breakfast
Credit Cards: A, B, D
Notes: 2, 7, 9, 11, 12, 13

Mira Monte Inn and Suites

69 Mount Desert Street, 04609
(800) 553-5109; FAX (207) 288-3115
e-mail: mburns@acadia.net

This 1864 Victorian blends antique furnishings with modern amenities—each room has king- or queen-size bed, cable TV, telephone, air conditioning, and a fireplace, balcony, or both. Two-room suites have a kitchen unit and double whirlpool in addition. On a two-acre village estate with exquisite gardens. Common spaces include the library with a piano, parlor, and the formal dining room as well as the porch and terraces. Four-room housekeeping suite by weekly rental.

Host: Marian Burns
Rooms: 13 (PB) $125-200
Suites: 3 (PB)
Full Breakfast
Credit Cards: A, B, C, D, E
Notes: 2, 7, 9, 10, 11, 12, 14, 15

Moseley Cottage Inn

12 Atlantic Avenue, 04609
(207) 288-5548; (800) 458-8644
FAX (207) 288-9406

This guest house is a graciously furnished Victorian summer cottage where old-fashioned comfort has been successfully combined with modern conveniences. All rooms have private baths and cable TVs, while some rooms feature a cozy fireplace and a comfortable porch. A delicious breakfast buffet is served daily in the lovely dining room. Enjoy these amenities and more in a smoke- and pet-free environment set in a quiet in-town neighborhood. Off-season rates available upon request.

Hosts: Joe and Paulette Paluga
Rooms: 8 (PB) $85-140
Continental Breakfast
Credit Cards: A, B, C, D
Notes: 2, 7, 8, 9, 10, 11, 12, 14

The Ridgeway Inn

11 High Street, 04609
(207) 288-9682

Built at the turn of the century, today the Ridgeway Inn offers warm hospitality in a comfortable atmosphere. Set in a quiet in-town location, the inn is just a short walk from the many shops, restaurants, the harbor, and Acadia National Park. The aged stone walls, bright flower-lined yard, and porch with ornamental wrought-iron furniture invites guests inside. Hardwood floors with scatter rugs, fireplaces with ornate mantels, lace curtains set in bay windows, and a sprinkling of antiques, including a working pump organ, provide an intimate and visually pleasing atmosphere. Open year-round with seasonal rates.

Host: Kerry Hartman
Rooms: 5 (PB) $100-150
Full Breakfast
Credit Cards: A, B
Notes: 2, 7, 9, 10, 11, 12

The Ridgeway Inn

Stratford House Inn

Stratford House Inn

45 Mount Desert Street, 04609
(207) 288-5189

Stratford House Inn features English Tudor architecture with a likeness to Queen Elizabeth's summer home. Beautiful bedrooms, each with its own individual decor. Easy walk to stores, restaurants, or the waterfront. Acadia National Park is nearby with beautiful scenery and activities for everyone. Two-night minimum stay on weekends and holidays. Closed October 15 through May 15.

Hosts: Barbara and Norman Moulton
Rooms: 10 (8 PB; 2 SB) $75-150
Continental Breakfast
Credit Cards: A, B, C
Notes: 2, 7, 8, 9, 10, 11, 12

Twin Gables Inn

P.O. Box 282, 04609
(207) 288-3064

Just one-half mile from beautiful Acadia National Park and three miles from downtown Bar Harbor. Guests are provided with a hearty breakfast to fortify them on their hiking, biking, and sightseeing expeditions. After a busy day guests return rest in the casual comfort and charm of this 100-year-old home. "You'll love our ocean views."

Host: Mindy Hill
Rooms: 6 (PB) $39-99
Full Breakfast
Credit Cards: A, B
Notes: 7, 8, 9, 10, 11, 12

7 No smoking; 8 Children welcome; 9 Social drinking allowed; 10 Tennis nearby; 11 Swimming nearby; 12 Golf nearby; 13 Skiing nearby; 14 May be booked through a travel agent; 15 Handicapped accessible.

Willows at Atlantic Oakes-by-the-Sea

119 Eden Street, P.O. Box 3, 04609
(800) 33MAINE

The Willows, circa 1913, is on the grounds of Atlantic Oakes-by-the-Sea and was named after the willow trees beside the entrance drive. There are nine guest rooms. All rooms on the ocean side have ocean views and balconies. Rooms two and three connect via the bath and are rented to one party. Four rooms have king-size beds and the other three rooms have double beds. Continental plus breakfast served in the mansion in season. There are an apartment and penthouse separate from the bed and breakfast available. Not suitable for children. Seasonal rates available. Near Acadia National Park.

Rooms: 9 (7 PB; 2 SB) $70-248
Continental Breakfast
Credit Cards: A, B, C
Notes: 2, 7, 10, 11, 12, 14

Pointy Head Inn

anchor overnight. Haven for photographers and artists. Minutes to lighthouse, trails, restaurants, stores. Children over 10 welcome.

Hosts: Doris and Warren Townsend
Rooms: 6 (2 PB; 4 SB) $60-110
Full Breakfast
Credit Cards: A, B
Notes: 2, 7, 9, 10, 11, 12

BATH

Benjamin F. Packard House

45 Pearl Street, 04530
(207) 443-6069; (800) 516-4578
e-mail: packardhouse@clinic.net
www.mainecoast.com/packardhouse/

The Packard House is in the heart of Bath's historic district. It was built in the 1790s and an eight-room addition was put on in 1844. The decor remains in the Victorian tradition. There are a parlor, formal dining room, and enclosed garden for guests to enjoy.  The midcoast location is perfect for antiquing, historic adventure, oceanfront parks, or shopping in nearby Freeport. Enjoy all of this by making the Packard House one's midcoast home port.

Willows at Atlantic Oakes-by-the-Sea

BASS HARBOR

Pointy Head Inn

Route 102A, HCR 33, Box 2A, 04653
(207) 244-7261

Relax on the quiet side of Mount Desert Island near Acadia National Park in an old sea captain's home. On the shore of a picturesque harbor where schooners

NOTES: Credit cards accepted: A MasterCard; B Visa; C American Express; D Discover; E Diner's Club; F Other; 2 Personal checks accepted; 3 Lunch available; 4 Dinner available; 5 Open all year; 6 Pets welcome;

Hosts: Debby and Bill Hayden
Rooms: 3 (PB) $60-90
Full Breakfast
Credit Cards: A, B, C
Notes: 2, 5, 7, 9, 10, 11, 12, 14

Fairhaven Inn at Bath

North Bath Road, Rural Route 2, Box 85, 04530
(888) 443-4391; FAX (207) 443-6412
e-mail: fairhvn@gwi.net

Where eagles soar, birds sing, and tidal river
meets meadow. This comfortable, quiet
1790 Colonial is renowned for its breakfast
and is the perfect midcoast base from which
to enjoy all that Maine's coast has to offer.
Hiking and cross-country skiing on property. Beaches and Maine Maritime Museum
nearby. Smoking restricted to outside only.

Hosts: Susie and Dave Reed
Rooms: 8 (PB and SB) $80-120
Full Breakfast
Credit Cards: A, B, D
Notes: 2, 5, 7, 8, 9, 11, 12, 13, 14

The Galen C. Moses House

1009 Washington Street, 04530
(207) 442-8771; (888) 442-8771
e-mail: galenmoses@clinic.net
www.bnbcity.com/inns/20028

This Italianate structure, built in 1874, has
been draped in vivid colors to give it the
nickname "the Pink House." The large
rooms are reminiscent of 19th-century Victorian style. There are many surprises
throughout the house, including a full theater on the third floor. The house also contains a number of assuredly friendly spirits,
who make their presence known on a fre-
quent basis. Full gourmet breakfast varies
according to the cook's mood. Coffee,
juices, and muffins are available for early
risers and late sleepers. AAA-rated three
diamonds. Children over 12 welcome.
Check website or call for midweek deals.

Hosts: James Haught and Larry Kieft
Rooms: 4 (PB) $65-99
Full and Continental Breakfast
Credit Cards: A, B
Notes: 2, 5, 7, 9, 10, 11, 12, 13, 14

Small Point

Small Point Bed and Breakfast

312 Small Point Road, Phippsburg, 04562
(207) 389-1716; FAX (207) 389-2005

Enjoy the tradition of bed and breakfast in
this century-old coastal farmhouse. Tasteful
renovations combine today's comforts with
the charm of yesteryear. Choose shared
bath, private bath, or suite. A full country
breakfast is served with good conversation
in the dining room or privately on the wraparound screened porch. Take advantage of
the location amidst hiking, miles of sandy
beach, bird watching, boating, and sailing.
A short drive to Bath will find museums and
shopping, or arrange a charter with Captain
Dave on the hosts' *Rhodes 19* daysailer.
Carriage House also available in July and
August. Pets welcome with prior approval.

Hosts: Captain David and Jan Tingle
Rooms: 3 (1 PB; 2 SB) $48-80
Suite and Carriage House: $95-130.
Full Breakfast
Credit Cards: A, B
Notes: 2, 5, 7, 8, 9, 10, 11, 12, 13

BELFAST

The Alden House Bed and Breakfast

63 Church Street, 04915
(207) 338-2151; e-mail: alden@agate.net
www.bbonline.com/me/alden

USA Today has rated Belfast as "one of the
top five culturally cool small towns in

---

7 No smoking; 8 Children welcome; 9 Social drinking allowed; 10 Tennis nearby; 11 Swimming nearby;
12 Golf nearby; 13 Skiing nearby; 14 May be booked through a travel agent; 15 Handicapped accessible.

America." This midcoastal Maine jewel, which sits on the Penobscot Bay, is home to the Alden House Bed and Breakfast. Featured on the *Oprah Winfrey Show*, the Alden House has been completely renovated for guests' comfort, but retains it Greek Revival beauty of 1840 with imported marble fireplaces and a hand-carved cherry winding staircase. Within minutes one can walk to restaurants, shops, and the waterfront. Guests' stay is ended with a memorable, multi-course breakfast.

Hosts: Jessica Jahnke and Marla Stickle
Rooms: 7 (5 PB; 2 SB) $65-95
Full Breakfast
Credit Cards: A, B, C
Notes: 2, 5, 7, 9, 10, 11, 12, 13, 14

Belhaven Inn Bed and Breakfast

14 John Street, 04915
(207) 338-5435; e-mail: belhaven@ime.net

Stay at this circa 1861 Victorian home. A comfortable, family-oriented inn, a short walk to harbor, shops, and restaurants. Full country breakfast served on columned veranda or in charming dining room with fantastic leaded-glass cupboard and period mantel. Unwind in one of the four common rooms. A circular staircase leads up to four delightful and unique guest rooms. The efficiency guest suite with private entry and sun deck sleeps four. Discounted single, senior, and Canadian rates. "Belhaven—a comfortable haven in Belfast."

Hosts: Anne and Paul Bartels
Rooms: 5 (3 PB; 2 SB) $65-90
Full Breakfast
Credit Cards: A, B
Notes: 2, 5, 6, 8, 9, 10, 11, 12, 13

The Inn on Primrose Hill

212 High Street, 04915
(207) 338-6982; (888) 338-6982 (reservations)
e-mail: primroseh@aol.com

Elegant Greek Revival additions enhance this historic Federal Colonial home built in 1812 on Primrose Hill overlooking Penobscot Bay. Public rooms include twin

The Inn on Primrose Hill

front parlors overlooking the bay and pine-paneled conservatory with vaulted ceilings and French doors to the brick terrace and rose gardens where guests enjoy the splashing fountain. Afternoon tea and gourmet breakfast are graciously served.

Hosts: Linus and Pat Heinz
Rooms: 4 (3 PB; 1 SB) $80-90
Full Breakfast
Credit Cards: None
Notes: 2, 5, 7, 9, 10, 11, 12

The Jeweled Turret Inn

40 Pearl Street, 04915
(207) 338-2304; (800) 696-2304
www.bbonline.com/me/jeweledturret/

Step back into a time when lace, elegant furnishings, and afternoon tea were everyday necessities. The inn is named for the grand staircase that winds up the turret, lighted by stained- and leaded-glass panels with jewel-like embellishments. Lots of

The Jeweled Turret Inn

woodwork, fireplaces, public rooms, and two verandas. Gourmet breakfasts and afternoon tea are available in the dining room or, during summer, on the veranda. In the historic district; shops, restaurants, and waterfront nearby. Smoking restricted.

Hosts: Carl and Cathy Heffentrager
Rooms: 7 (PB) $75-105
Full Breakfast
Credit Cards: A, B
Notes: 2, 5, 9, 10, 11, 12, 13, 14

The Thomas Pitcher House Bed and Breakfast

19 Franklin Street, 04915
(207) 338-6454; (888) 338-6454
e-mail: tpitcher@acadia.net
www.thomaspitcherhouse.com

Indulge oneself in the elegant comfort of this handsome, in-town Victorian built in 1873. Spacious guest rooms and inviting common areas feature original Victorian architecture and are distinctively furnished with antiques and reproduction pieces. Fabulous three-course breakfasts are served in the large Chippendale dining room. Host speaks German and some French. Children over 12 welcome. Recommended by Fodor's, the *Boston Herald*, *Jackson Clarion-Ledger*, *Knoxville News-Sentinel*, *Toronto Sun*, and *Allentown Morning Call* newspapers, and *Bride's* magazine.

Hosts: Fran and Ron Kresge
Rooms: 4 (PB) $70-90
Full Breakfast
Credit Cards: A, B
Notes: 2, 5, 7, 9, 10, 11, 12, 13, 14

BETHEL

Abbott House

170 Walker Mills Road, P.O. Box 933, 04217
(207) 824-7600; (800) 240-2377

The Abbott House offers five rooms with three shared baths in an 18th-century Cape Cod on two and one-half acres. In the winter a hot tub is available. Near Sunday

River skiway and White Mountains. In summer three air-conditioned rooms with private baths are offered. Perennial gardens, murder mystery weekends, golf, hiking, and multiday packages available. Massage therapists are on staff.

Hosts: Joe Cardell; Penny Bohac and Nestlé
Rooms: 5 (2 PB; 3 SB) $50-80
Full Breakfast
Credit Cards: A, B, C, D
Notes: 2, 4, 5, 7, 9, 10, 11, 12, 13

The Chapman Inn

1 Mill Hill Road, 04217
(207) 824-2657; FAX (207) 824-7152
e-mail: Chapman@nxi.com

Great inn in the center of the historic district. Named "the best family inn in New England" by the New England Travel Guide. Walk to shops, restaurants, championship golf. Outstanding skiing at Sunday River, only five minutes away. Seven miles to private beach, fishing, boating. Private saunas and game room. Plenty of parking. A 22-bed dorm available—perfect for large groups. Family units available. Owner is a classically trained chef. Lunch and dinner available upon request. Pets welcome by prior arrangements.

Hosts: Fred and Sandra
Rooms: 8 (4 PB; 4 SB) $55-100
Full Breakfast
Credit Cards: A, B, C, D
Notes: 2, 5, 7, 8, 9, 10, 11, 12, 13, 14, 15

BIDDEFORD POOL

The Lodge

19 Yates Street, 04006
(207) 284-7148

Next to the Yacht Club, on Saco Bay at one of the most pristine settings on the Maine

7 No smoking; 8 Children welcome; 9 Social drinking allowed; 10 Tennis nearby; 11 Swimming nearby; 12 Golf nearby; 13 Skiing nearby; 14 May be booked through a travel agent; 15 Handicapped accessible.

coast, Biddeford Pool offers a private beach, rockbound coast, marsh lands, and much more. Guests can choose golf, tennis, boating, sun bathing, or visit many of the fine shops within 10 miles. Stores and restaurants are all nearby. Warm days, 75 degrees, and cool nights, 60 to 70 degrees, are the average temperature. Smoking permitted outside only. Inquire about accommodations for children.

Host: John Oddy
Rooms: 4 (2 PB; 2 SB) $70-99
Continental Breakfast
Credit Cards: A, B
Notes: 2, 5, 7, 9, 10, 11, 12

BOOTHBAY

Hodgdon Island Inn

Barter's Island Road, Box 492, 04571
(207) 633-7474

A gracious restored sea captain's home, circa 1810, decorated with wicker and antiques, just a five-minute drive to downtown Boothbay Harbor. Relax on the front porch and watch the sunset over the water. Swim in the heated chlorine-free swimming pool. Six tastefully furnished guest rooms, all with private baths. Full breakfast. Afternoon tea in winter, lemonade in summer. Good old-fashioned Down East hospitality at its best. Children over 12 welcome.

Hosts: Sydney and Joseph Klenk
Rooms: 6 (PB) $85-102
Full Breakfast
Credit Cards: None
Notes: 2, 5, 7, 9, 10, 11, 12

Kenniston Hill Inn

Route 27, P.O. Box 125, 04537-0125
(207) 633-2159; (800) 992-2915
FAX (207) 633-2159
e-mail: innkeeper@maine.com

This inn for all seasons is surrounded by large lawns and shady maples. Built in 1786, Kenniston Hill is the most historic inn in Boothbay with 10 antique-filled

Kenniston Hill Inn

guest rooms, private baths, and comfy quilts. When there is a chill in the air, seven working fireplaces warm body and soul. Complimentary full breakfast greets guests. On Route 27, the inn is open all year. Limited handicapped accessibility.

Hosts: Susan and David Straight
Room: 10 (PB) $65-110
Full Breakfast
Credit Cards: A, B, D
Notes: 2, 5, 7, 8, 9, 10, 11, 12, 13, 14

BOOTHBAY HARBOR

Anchor Watch Bed and Breakfast

3 Eames Road, 04538
(207) 633-7565

Islands, fir trees, and lobster boats provide the setting for this cozy bed and breakfast on the prettiest shore of the harbor. Country quilts and stenciling set the style inside. Breakfast features a baked cheese omelet or baked orange French toast. Enjoy a table for two or sit with others at an ocean-view window. Watch sunsets from the private pier. Five-minute walk to shops, boat trips, Monhegan ferry, and fine dining. Open year-round.

Hosts: Diane and Bob Campbell
Rooms: 5 (PB) $80-135
Full Breakfast
Credit Cards: A, B
Notes: 2, 5, 7, 9, 10, 11, 12, 14

NOTES: Credit cards accepted: A MasterCard; B Visa; C American Express; D Discover; E Diner's Club; F Other; 2 Personal checks accepted; 3 Lunch available; 4 Dinner available; 5 Open all year; 6 Pets welcome;

The Atlantic Ark Inn

64 Atlantic Avenue, 04538
(207) 633-5690

An intimate bed and breakfast inn, offering lovely views of the harbor and only a five-minute stroll to town. This 100-year-old Maine home offers wraparound porch, balconies, antiques, oriental rugs, floor-length drapes, poster beds, fresh flowers, and private baths—one with Jacuzzi and another with Greek tub. Each morning celebrate the day with a delicious full gourmet breakfast prepared with the freshest and purest of ingredients. Recommended in *Good Housekeeping* magazine as one of the best places to stay in Boothbay Harbor. Smoking permitted outside only. Children over 12 welcome.

Host: Donna Piggott
Rooms: 6 (PB) $80-149
Full Breakfast
Credit Cards: A, B, C
Notes: 2, 7, 9, 10, 11, 12, 14

Bed and Breakfast Reservations North Shore, Greater Boston, Cape Cod

P.O. Box 600035, Greater Boston Branch,
 Newtonville, MA 02160-0001
(617) 964-1606; (800) 832-2632
FAX (617) 332-8572; e-mail: info@bbreserve.com
www.bbreserve.com

67. This cozy 1850 New England Cape is the perfect place to base while taking easy day trips and enjoying one of the most scenic areas of coastal Maine. Antique and fine wood furniture, hand tooled by the host, are featured. The master guest room has a detached full private bath. A two-room guest suite is perfect for families or small groups (up to four) traveling together. A single room in the suite may be taken at private bath rates. A gourmet full breakfast awaits guests in the morning. Open year-round. Children over 14 welcome. No smoking. $75-95.

1830 Admiral's Quarters Inn

1830 Admiral's Quarters Inn

71 Commercial Street, 04538
(207) 633-2474; FAX (207) 633-5904
e-mail: loon@admiralsquartersinn.com
www.admiralsquartersinn.com

Commanding an unsurpassed view of the harbor, each accommodation has its own deck, separate entrance, and private bath. This 1830 sea captain's home offers charming accommodations, a blend of antiques and white wicker, color-cable TVs and telephones. Hearty homemade buffet breakfast and afternoon refreshments are served in the dining room, the solarium with woodstove, or perhaps on the wraparound porches. Steps away are unique shops and harbor activities. "Way out of the ordinary...but not out of the way." Children 12 and older are welcome.

Hosts: Les and Deb Hallstrom
Rooms: 6 (PB) $75-135
Full Breakfast
Credit Cards: A, B, D
Notes: 2, 5, 7, 10, 11, 12

Five Gables Inn

Murray Hill Road, P.O. Box 75, 335 East Boothbay,
 04544
(207) 633-4551; (800) 451-5048

Five Gables Inn is a completely restored Victorian, circa 1890s, on Linekin Bay. All rooms have an ocean view and private baths and five have fireplaces. A gourmet breakfast is served in the large common

7 No smoking; 8 Children welcome; 9 Social drinking allowed; 10 Tennis nearby; 11 Swimming nearby; 12 Golf nearby; 13 Skiing nearby; 14 May be booked through a travel agent; 15 Handicapped accessible.

Five Gables Inn

room or on the spacious wraparound veranda. Open mid-May to mid-October. Children eight and older are welcome.

Hosts: Mike and De Kennedy
Rooms: 15 (PB) $95-165
Full Breakfast
Credit Cards: A, B
Notes: 2, 7, 9, 10, 11, 12, 14

Harbour Towne Inn on the Waterfront

71 Townsend Avenue, 04538
(207) 633-4300; (800) 722-4240
FAX (207) 633-4300

"The Finest Bed and Breakfast on the waterfront" commands scenic harbor views from outside decks in a quiet location on Boothbay Harbor. All rooms have private baths in this refurbished Victorian townhouse. Also available is a luxury penthouse that will sleep six in absolute privacy. Walk to shops, art galleries, restaurants, churches, library, dinner theaters, boat trips, and fishing. One- to two-hour drive to skiing. Reservations recommended. Special off-season getaway packages. Continental plus breakfast. Inquire about accommodations for children. Limited handicapped accessible.

Host: George Thomas
Rooms: 12 (PB) $69-149
Penthouse: $150-250
Continental Breakfast
Credit Cards: A, B, C, D
Notes: 2, 7, 9, 10, 11, 12, 13, 14

The Howard House Motel Bed and Breakfast

Route 27, 04538
(207) 633-3933; (207) 633-6244

Unique chalet design on 20 wooded acres, quiet setting, beautiful flowers. Each spacious, sparkling, clean room features glass patio door with private balcony, cable TV, and full private bath. Delicious, healthful buffet breakfast. Shopping, sightseeing, boating, island clam bakes, seal and whale watches, and fine restaurants are nearby. AAA three-diamond- and Mobil Travel Guide-approved. Smoking in designated areas only.

Hosts: The Farrins
Rooms: 14 (PB) $66-84
Full Breakfast
Credit Cards: None
Notes: 2, 10, 11, 12, 14, 15

Howard House Motel

BRIDGTON

The Noble House Bed and Breakfast

37 Highland Road, P.O. Box 180, 04009
(207) 647-3733; FAX (207) 647-3733

Stately manor set on a hill across the street from scenic Highland Lake. Secluded lake frontage with canoe, foot-pedal boat, hammock, and barbecue for guests' use. Experience Shaker village, antique and craft shops, museums, and chamber music festival in

The Noble House

summer. One hour inland from Portland, and one hour from the White Mountains. Sumptuous full breakfast. Whirlpool baths and family suites. Open June through October. Winter by advance reservation only. Smoking permitted on porches only.

Hosts: Jane and Dick Starets
Rooms: 8 (5 PB; 3 SB) $78-125
Full Breakfast
Credit Cards: A, B, C
Notes: 2, 8, 10, 11, 12, 13

BROOKSVILLE

Breezemere Farm Inn

Rural Route 1, Box 290, 04617
(207) 326-8628; FAX (207) 326-8912
e-mail: breezemere@acadia.net
www.bbonline.com/me/breezemere

Inn and cottages on a working saltwater farm at the head of Orcutt's Harbor and East Penobscot Bay. Convenient to Acadia National Park, Blue Hill, Castine, and Stonington. Acres of hiking and bicycle trails. Guests are encouraged to try their hand at fishing or clamming in the bay. Open year-round.

Hosts: Laura Johns and Carolyn Heller
Rooms: 14 (9 PB; 5 SB) $55-125
Full Breakfast
Credit Cards: A, B, D
Notes: 2, 4, 5, 6, 7, 8, 10, 11, 12

Eggemoggin Reach Bed and Breakfast

Rural Route 1, Box 33A, Herrick Road, 04617
(207) 359-5073; FAX (207) 359-5074

The inn enjoys a waterfront panorama of the "reach," Pumpkin Island Light, and the Penobscot Bay. Every room is on the water and most are studio efficiencies with kitchenettes, wood stoves, comfortable sitting areas, and screened porches. The inn's shorefront privacy, complete with dock, moorings, and guest boating, make it a perfect getaway headquarters from which to explore Acadia National Park, Deer Isle, Blue Hill, Castine, and the awesome beauty of the Down East coast. Children over 12 welcome.

Hosts: Susie and Michael Canon
Rooms: 10 (PB) $160-175
Full Breakfast
Credit Cards: A, B
Notes: 2, 7, 9, 10, 11, 12, 14

Oakland House's Shore Oaks Seaside Inn

Herrick Road, Rural Route 1, Box 400, 04617
(207) 359-8521; (800) 359-RELAX
www.acadia.net/oaklandhse

Dreamy 1907 oceanfront inn. More like a friend's private home. Tastefully renovated and furnished with original antiques. Its 10 bedrooms, living room with stone fireplace, library, dining room, porch, and gazebo are truly inviting. Explore the beaches and

Oakland House's Shore Oaks Seaside Inn

7 No smoking; 8 Children welcome; 9 Social drinking allowed; 10 Tennis nearby; 11 Swimming nearby; 12 Golf nearby; 13 Skiing nearby; 14 May be booked through a travel agent; 15 Handicapped accessible.

mossy trails. Relax! Breakfast and dinner (in season) are included. Enjoy the dock and rowboats. The villages of Blue Hill, Brooksville, Castine, and Stonington as well as Acadia National Park are nearby.

Hosts: Jim and Sally Littlefield
Rooms: 10 (7 PB; 3 SB)
Full or Continental Breakfast
Credit Cards: Yes
Notes: 2, 3, 4, 5, 7, 9, 11, 12, 14

Rockmeadow Farm Bed and Breakfast
The Herrick Road, 04617
(207) 326-8485

Country charm and setting: a large, sunny back yard and blueberry field, with giant oak shade trees in front. The two downstairs bedrooms feature fireplaces and private entrances with a double and twin bed. Breakfast includes bagels, tea, coffee, juice, and yogurt with homemade muffins and muesli. Conveniently between Blue Hill and Deer Isle; close to several summer camps. Listen to the loons on Walker Pond at night. Open May to October.

Host: Kay Kemper
Rooms: 2 (2 SB) $60-85
Continental Breakfast
Credit Cards: None
Notes: 2, 7, 8

BRUNSWICK

Brunswick Bed and Breakfast
165 Park Row, 04011
(800) 299-4914

The Brunswick Bed and Breakfast is a Greek Revival house overlooking the town green. On the main level, the twin front parlors offer guests the inviting warmth of two fireplaces for wintertime comfort; wraparound front porch for summer leisure. The guest rooms are decorated with antique furnishings, unique accessories, and quilts. Within walking distance of local restaurants, museums, and shops. Convenient,

allowing guests to easily explore midcoast Maine harbors and coastline.

Hosts: Mercie and Steve Normand
Rooms: 8 (PB) $87-125
Full Breakfast
Credit Cards: A, B
Notes: 2, 5, 7, 9, 10, 11, 12

CAMDEN

Castleview by the Sea Bed and Breakfast
59 High Street, 04843
(207) 236-2344; (800) 272-VIEW (8439)

Spectacular glass-walled rooms overlooking Camden's only two castles and the sea, right from your bed! Count the stars across the bay and wake up to inspiring Maine views found nowhere else. Bright and airy charm of classical 1856 Cape architecture, wide pumpkin-pine floors, beamed ceilings, clawfoot tubs, skylights, balconies, ceiling fans, and stained glass. Five-minute walk to harbor. Video and reading libraries. Healthy breakfast. Open May through October.

Host: Bill Butler
Rooms: 4 (PB) $75-175
Full or Continental Breakfast
Credit Cards: A, B
Notes: 2, 7, 8, 9, 10, 11, 12, 13, 14

The Elms Bed and Breakfast
84 Elm Street, 04843
(207) 236-6250; (800) 755-ELMS
FAX (207) 236-7330
e-mail: theelms@midcoast.com

"Let us welcome you to the Elms all year." Experience the casual warmth of this circa 1806 home surrounded by beautiful lighthouse artwork and collectibles. Spend the day hiking, sailing, or browsing the many shops and galleries within walking distance. Tuck oneself into a spacious bed chamber. Awake to the smells of a delightfully prepared and beautifully presented breakfast. Lighthouse boat tours and quiet season packages. Visit the Elms and leave with the

NOTES: Credit cards accepted: A MasterCard; B Visa; C American Express; D Discover; E Diner's Club; F Other; 2 Personal checks accepted; 3 Lunch available; 4 Dinner available; 5 Open all year; 6 Pets welcome;

feeling of having been to visit friends. Children over 10 welcome.

Hosts: Ted and Jo Panayotoff
Rooms: 6 (PB) $65-95
Full Breakfast
Credit Cards: A, B
Notes: 2, 5, 7, 9, 10, 11, 12, 13, 14, 15

The Hartstone Inn

41 Elm Street, 04843
(207) 236-4259; (800) 788-4823
FAX (207) 236-9575
e-mail: hrtstone@midcoast.com

Come fall under the spell of one of Camden's grandest historic homes, in the heart of the village. Each guest room is a unique experience in pampered luxury. The beautifully decorated rooms and suites offer a private bath, sitting area, and designer bedding. Elegant china, fine crystal, and the internationally award-winning chef make the hearty breakfast and gourmet candlelit dinner a truly memorable experience. "We look foward to your visit." Children 12 years welcome.

Hosts: Mary Jo and Michael Salmon
Rooms: 10 (PB) $75-155
Full Breakfast
Credit Cards: A, B, C
Notes: 4, 5, 6, 7, 9, 10, 11, 12, 13

The Hartstone Inn

Hawthorn Inn Bed and Breakfast

9 High Street, 04843
(207) 236-8842

This elegant, turreted Victorian mansion overlooks Camden Harbor with spacious

Hawthorn Inn

grounds, bright and airy rooms, large deck, lovely antiques throughout, full buffet breakfast, and friendly innkeepers. Stroll through back garden to town amphitheater and harbor park. Near shops and restaurants. Carriage house rooms have full harbor views, private decks, double Jacuzzis, fireplaces, and VCRs. Recommended by *Yankee*, *Glamour*, and *Outside* magazines. Featured in *Minneapolis Star Tribune* and *Chicago Tribune*. Children over 12 welcome.

Hosts: Patty and Nick Wharton
Rooms: 10 (PB) $80-195
Full Breakfast
Credit Cards: A, B, C
Notes: 2, 7, 12, 13, 14

A Little Dream

66 High Street, 04843
(207) 236-8742

Sweet dreams and little luxuries abound in this lovely white Victorian with wrap-around porch. Noted for its lovely breakfast, beautiful rooms, and charming atmosphere. A Little Dream's English country-Victorian decor has been featured in *Country Inns* magazine, and in *Glamour*, "40 Best Getaways Across the Country." In the historic district just a few minutes from shops and harbor, it is listed in the National Register of Historic Places. Rooms have either a private deck, view, or fireplace. All have special touches, such as imported soaps and

7 No smoking; 8 Children welcome; 9 Social drinking allowed; 10 Tennis nearby; 11 Swimming nearby; 12 Golf nearby; 13 Skiing nearby; 14 May be booked through a travel agent; 15 Handicapped accessible.

chocolates, and a hostess who will do her very best to please.

Hosts: Joanna Ball and Bill Fontana
Rooms: 7 (PB) $95-195
Full Breakfast
Credit Cards: A, B, C
Notes: 2, 5, 7, 10, 11, 12, 13

Lord Camden Inn

24 Main Street, 04843
(207) 236-4325; (800) 336-4325
FAX (207) 236-7141
e-mail: lordcam@midcoast.com

Lord Camden Inn, housed in a century-old brick building, offers guests the gentle warmth of a seaside inn with all the comforts and service of a modern downtown hotel. In the midst of Camden's fine shops and restaurants, the bustling waterfront, and beautiful parks, Lord Camden Inn offers splendid views of the harbor, Camden Hills, and the village. Amenities include private bath, cable TV, air conditioning, telephones, and elevator service.

Hosts: Stuart and Marianne Smith
Rooms: 31 (PB) $88-178
Continental Breakfast
Credit Cards: A, B
Notes: 2, 5, 8, 9, 10, 11, 12, 13, 14

Maine Stay

22 High Street, 04843
(207) 236-9636; FAX (207) 236-0621
e-mail: mainstay@midcoast.com
www.mainestay.com

A comfortable bed, a hearty breakfast, and three friendly innkeepers will be found in

Maine Stay

this 1802 Colonial home in Camden's historic district. Take a short walk to the harbor, shops, restaurants, and state park. Recommended by the *Bangor Daily News*, *Miami Herald*, *Boston Globe*, *Harper's Bazaar*, *Country Inns*, *Glamour*, *Yankee*, and *Country Living* magazines. Children over eight welcome.

Hosts: Peter and Donny Smith; Diana Robson
Rooms: 8 (6 PB; 2 SB) $75-140
Full Breakfast
Credit Cards: A, B, C
Notes: 2, 5, 7, 9, 10, 11, 12, 13, 14

The Swan House

The Swan House

49 Mountain Street (Route 52), 04843
(207) 236-8275; (800) 207-8275
FAX (207) 236-0906
e-mail: swanhse@midcoast.com
www.swanhouse.com

This fine Victorian home dates from 1870 and has been renovated to offer six spacious guest rooms. Some offer private sitting areas as well. A creative and generous full breakfast is served each morning on the sun porch. Landscaped grounds and a gazebo are available for guests to relax and enjoy. A hiking trail leading to Camden Hills State Park starts right behind the inn. Off busy Route 1, Swan House is a short walk to Camden's beautiful harbor, shops, and restaurants. Seasonal rates. Children over 12 welcome.

Hosts: Lyn and Ken Kohl
Rooms: 6 (PB) $85-125
Full Breakfast
Credit Cards: A, B
Notes: 2, 5, 7, 9, 10, 11, 12, 13

NOTES: Credit cards accepted: A MasterCard; B Visa; C American Express; D Discover; E Diner's Club; F Other; 2 Personal checks accepted; 3 Lunch available; 4 Dinner available; 5 Open all year; 6 Pets welcome;

Windward House

Windward House

6 High Street, 04843
(207) 236-9656; FAX (207) 230-0433
e-mail: b&b@windwardhouse.com
www.windwardhouse.com

A fine example of Victorian architecture with Greek Revival features. The Windward House was built in 1854 by Elijah Glover, a prominent local shipbuilder and lumberman. The eight tastefully appointed guest rooms, all with queen-size beds and private baths, reflect the charm of this historic home. Three bed chambers include gas fireplaces, wingback chairs, CD players, and two have soak tubs. Full service candlelight breakfast. Only minutes' walk to the village, harbor, shops, and restaurants. Children over 12 welcome.

Hosts: Tim and Sandy LaPlante
Rooms: 8 (PB) $105-175
Full Breakfast
Credit Cards: A, B
Notes: 2, 5, 7, 9, 10, 11, 12, 13, 14

CARIBOU

The Old Iron Inn
Bed and Breakfast

155 High Street, 04736
(207) 492-4776; e-mail: oldiron@mfx.net
www.mainerec.com/oldiron

The Old Iron Inn is a European-style bed and breakfast, an intimate establishment run by the owners. Named the Old Iron Inn because it sports a fine collection of antique irons, the collection currently numbering around 250. Two guest rooms have private baths and two rooms share a bath and a half. Books are throughout the house and the reading room stocks 40 different magazine subscriptions. The inn is in downtown Caribou within walking distance to restaurants.

Hosts: Kevin and Kate McCartney
Rooms: 4 (2 PB; 2 SB) $39-49
Full Breakfast
Credit Cards: A, B, C, D, E
Notes: 2, 5, 7, 10, 12, 13

CASCO

Maplewood Inn and Motel

Route 302, Box 627, 04015
(207) 655-7586; FAX (207) 655-5131
e-mail: rdamen1@maine.rr.com

Cozy family inn in the heart of the lakes region (Sebago Lake). Nicely renovated 19th-century house with additional motel units near the outdoor pool. Amenities include cable TV and miniature golf. One mile from Sebago Lake State Park and many fine restaurants just minutes away.

Hosts: René and Youngok Damen
Rooms: 4 (1 PB; 3 S2B) $50-65
Full Breakfast
Credit Cards: A, B, C, D
Notes: 2, 5, 7, 8, 10, 11, 12, 13

Maplewood Inn and Motel

7 No smoking; 8 Children welcome; 9 Social drinking allowed; 10 Tennis nearby; 11 Swimming nearby; 12 Golf nearby; 13 Skiing nearby; 14 May be booked through a travel agent; 15 Handicapped accessible.

CHAMBERLAIN

Ocean Reefs on Long Cove

376 State Route 32, 04541-3901
(207) 677-2386

Watch the waves break over the reefs, lobstermen hauling in traps, or the shoreline between tides. Hike or bicycle on the roads along the rocky coast. Pemaquid Beach, Pemaquid Lighthouse, Fort William Henry, and the boat to Monhegan Island are all within five miles. Two-night minimum stay required during July and August. Closed September 30 through Memorial Day.

Host: John Hahler
Rooms: 4 (PB) $70
Continental Breakfast
Credit Cards: None
Notes: 2, 9, 10, 11, 12

CHERRYFIELD

Ricker House

Park Street, Box 256, 04622
(207) 546-2780

Selected as one of the top 50 inns in America. Comfortable 1802 Federal Colonial, in the National Register of Historic Places, borders the Narraguagus River and offers guests a central place for enjoying the many wonderful activities in Down East Maine, including scenic coastal area, swimming, canoeing, hiking, and fishing. Inquire about

Ricker House

accommodations for pets. Cross-country skiing nearby.

Hosts: William and Jean Conway
Rooms: 3 (SB) $53.50-64.20
Full Breakfast
Credit Cards: None
Notes: 2, 7, 10, 11, 12, 13

COREA

The Black Duck on Corea Harbor

Crowley Island Road, P.O. Box 39, 04624
(207) 963-2689; e-mail: bduck@acadia.net
www.blackduck.com

This restored 1890s house, filled with art and antiques, overlooks Down East lobster harbor and open ocean in a tranquil fishing village. Explore the 12 acres and discover hidden salt marshes and a private bay. Curl up in front of a fireplace to read or find a sunny rock outcrop and watch the gulls soar overhead and maybe spot a bald eagle. Rooms and cottages furnished in antiques of various periods. Children under one and over eight are welcome. Low-fat but elegant breakfast in the antique- and art-filled dining room.

Hosts: Barry Canner and Robert Travers
Rooms: 5 (3 PB; 2 SB) $70-145
Suite: 1 (PB) $145
Full Breakfast
Credit Cards: A, B
Notes: 2, 5, 7, 9, 11, 12, 14

DAMARISCOTTA

Brannon-Bunker Inn

349X State Route 129, Walpole, 04573
(207) 563-5941; (800) 563-9225
e-mail: brbnkinn@lincoln.midcoast.com

Intimate, relaxed, country bed and breakfast in an 1820 Cape, 1880 converted barn, and 1900 carriage house. Seven rooms furnished in themes reflecting the charm of yesterday with the comforts of today. Ten minutes to lighthouse, fort, beach, antiques, and craft shopping. Antique shop on the premises.

NOTES: Credit cards accepted: A MasterCard; B Visa; C American Express; D Discover; E Diner's Club; F Other; 2 Personal checks accepted; 3 Lunch available; 4 Dinner available; 5 Open all year; 6 Pets welcome;

Hosts: Jeanne and Joe Hovance
Rooms: 7 (5 PB; 2 SB) $64.20-80.25
Continental Breakfast
Credit Cards: A, B, C
Notes: 2, 7, 8, 9, 10, 11, 12, 13, 14, 15

Mill Pond Inn

Route 215, Damariscotta Mills
50 Main Street, Nobleboro, 04555 (mailing)
(207) 563-8014
www.virtualcities.com/me/millpondinn.htm

This 1780 home offers an excellent atmosphere to view the wonders of Maine's wildlife. Complimentary canoes can be paddled from the pond in the back yard directly into Damariscotta Lake. Mountain bikes and guided fishing trips available. Nestled in the little 1800s village of Damariscotta Mills, this inn offers guests a unique experience. Boothbay Harbor, Camden Hills, Pemaquid Lighthouse, Bath-Brunswick area, and the rugged coast of midcoast Maine await.

Hosts: Bobby and Sherry Whear
Rooms: 6 (PB) $80
Full Breakfast
Credit Cards: None
Notes: 2, 5, 10, 11, 12, 13

DEXTER

Brewster Inn

37 Zions Hill Road, 04930
(207) 924-3130

Built in the 1930s for Gov. Owen Brewster. Classic but comfortable elegance furnished with antiques and family heirlooms, lots of books, and art. Beautiful gardens. Walk to downtown shopping and lake. One hour from coastal Belfast, one hour to Moosehead Lake, mountains, skiing. On the Maine snowmobile trails. Take exit 39 from I-95, then 15 miles on Route 7. Coffee/tea and cookies all day.

Hosts: Ivy and Michael Brooks
Rooms: 7 (PB) $59-89
Full Breakfast
Credit Cards: A, B
Notes: 2, 3, 4, 5, 7, 8, 9, 10, 11, 12, 13, 14, 15

DIXFIELD

Von Simm's Victorian Inn Bed and Breakfast

Route 2, P.O. Box 645, 04224
(207) 562-4911; (800) 349-4911

Recently renovated home offers guests privacy in a comfortable, homey, and nostalgic atmosphere with beautiful antiques, wood floors, and pretty woodwork. Spacious bedrooms have queen-size beds, period pieces, air conditioning, and an ambiance of elegance. Relax before the parlor fireplace, walk the streets of the quaint New England village, enjoy sitting on the side porch, or in the gazebo overlooking the old-fashioned flower gardens. Breakfast is served family style in the charmingly furnished dining room.

Hosts: Sylvia and Bruce Simmons;
   Dorothy and Mac Vaughn
Rooms: 7 (5 PB; 2 SB)
Full Breakfast
Credit Cards: A, B, C, D
Notes: 2, 3, 4, 5, 7, 8, 9, 10, 11, 12, 13, 14

EASTPORT

Weston House

26 Boynton Street, 04631
(207) 853-2907; (800) 853-2907

This imposing 1810 Federal-style house overlooks Passamaquoddy Bay across to

Weston House

Campobello Island. Listed in the National Register of Historic Places; in a lovely Down East coastal village. Grounds include a lawn suitable for croquet and a flower garden for quiet relaxation. Picnic lunches available.

Hosts: Jett and John Peterson
Rooms: $64.20-80.25
Full Breakfast
Credit Cards: None
Notes: 2, 3, 4, 5, 9, 10

ELIOT (KITTERY)

The Farmstead Bed and Breakfast

379 Goodwin Road, 03903
(207) 439-5033; (207) 748-3145

Come and step back in time and enjoy the hospitality that Farmstead offers its guests. Awake to the aroma of coffee, bacon, sausage, and blueberry pancakes on the griddle. Inspect the 1704 Cape and the "new" floor built in 1896. Explore the two and one-half acres, swing under the pear tree, or have an early morning cup of coffee on the glider after a quiet, restful night. All rooms have private bath, mini-refrigerator, and microwave oven. Picnic facilities and gas grill available.

Hosts: Col. and Mrs. John Lippincott
Rooms: 6 (PB) $54-58
Full Breakfast
Credit Cards: A, B, D
Notes: 2, 5, 6, 7, 8, 9, 10, 12, 14, 15

FREEPORT

Anita's Cottage Street Inn Bed and Breakfast

13 Cottage Street, 04032
(207) 865-0932; (800) 392-7121
FAX (207) 865-0932

A cozy bed and breakfast, nestled in a wonderful wooded area, yet in walking distance to L.L. Bean and 125 village shops. On a dead-end street with cross-country ski trails

in the winter and jogging trails in the summer. Rooms are graciously appointed with Laura Ashley linens and decor. A hearty breakfast welcomes guests in the morning. Hiking, swimming, biking, golf, and tennis nearby. Private baths, cable TV, air-conditioned rooms, and smoke free. AAA three-diamond-rated. Efficiency suite also available.

Hosts: Tom and Anita Willett
Rooms: 3 (PB) $65-150
Suite: 1 (PB)
Full Breakfast
Credit Cards: A, B, C
Notes: 2, 5, 7, 8, 9, 10, 11, 12, 13, 14

The Bagley House

The Bagley House

1290 Royalsborough Road, Durham, 04222
(207) 865-6566; (800) 765-1772

Peace, tranquility, and history abound in this magnificent 1772 country home. Six acres of fields and woods invite nature lovers, hikers, berry pickers, and cross-country skiers. The kitchen's hand-hewn beams and enormous free-standing fireplace with beehive oven inspire mouth-watering breakfasts. A warm welcome awaits guests. Ten minutes from downtown Freeport. Lunch and dinner available by special request.

Hosts: Suzanne O'Connor and Susan Backhouse
Rooms: 7 (PB) $85-125
Suite: $95-135
Full Breakfast
Credit Cards: A, B, C, D, F
Notes: 2, 5, 7, 8, 9, 11, 12, 13, 14, 15

NOTES: Credit cards accepted: A MasterCard; B Visa; C American Express; D Discover; E Diner's Club; F Other; 2 Personal checks accepted; 3 Lunch available; 4 Dinner available; 5 Open all year; 6 Pets welcome;

Brewster House Bed and Breakfast

180 Main Street, 04032
(207) 865-4121; (800) 865-0822
FAX (207) 865-4221
www.members.aol.com/bedandbrk/brewster

Brewster House is a newly renovated 1888 Queen Anne home. Each room is quiet, comfortable, furnished with antiques, and has a full-size private bath. Guests enjoy a delicious full breakfast including home-baked muffins and breads and a variety of main dishes. Just two blocks from L.L. Bean. Park in the lot and walk to Freeport's many outlets, shops, and restaurants. Family suites accommodate up to five people. Air conditioned. AAA-rated three diamonds. Children eight and over welcome.

Hosts: Matthew and Amy Cartmell
Rooms: 5 (PB) $70-105
Full Breakfast
Credit Cards: A, B, D
Notes: 2, 5, 7, 9, 10, 11, 12, 13, 14

Captain Briggs House Bed and Breakfast

8 Maple Avenue, 04032
(207) 865-1868; (800) 217-2477

Welcome to the Captain Briggs House Bed and Breakfast in the heart of the quaint village of Freeport, just a three-minute walk to L.L. Bean and other fine stores and restaurants. The inn has been lovingly restored with modern amenities tastefully added. The hosts offer comfortable, cheerful guest rooms beautifully decorated with either

king-, queen-, full-, or twin-size beds. All rooms have private baths. Relax in the cozy sitting room with cable TV, VCR, and books. A delicious homemade breakfast is served from 8:00 to 9:00 A.M. Nonsmoking inn. AAA three-diamond property.

Hosts: The Frank Family
Rooms: 5 (PB) $66-106
Full Breakfast
Credit Cards: A, B
Notes: 2, 5, 7, 8, 9, 10, 11, 12, 13

Captain Josiah Mitchell House

188 Main Street, 04032
(207) 865-3289

Famous historic ship captain's home, circa 1779. The 1866 miraculous survival-at-sea story of Captain Mitchell of the ship *Hornet* is a classic. Mark Twain, then a young newspaperman, wrote about it. Restored more than 25 years ago by the present owners, the house is filled with antiques. Beautiful grounds and only a five-minute walk to L.L. Bean. Fourteenth year as an inn. Off-season rates available.

Hosts: Alan and Loretta Bradley
Rooms: 6 (PB) $70-95
Full Breakfast
Credit Cards: A, B
Notes: 2, 5, 7, 9, 10, 11, 12, 13, 14

Harraseeket Inn

162 Main Street, 04032
(207) 865-9377; (800) 342-6423
FAX (207) 865-1684

An elegant 84-room country inn two blocks north of L.L. Bean in the village of Freeport. Antiques, 23 fireplaces, Jacuzzi tubs, air conditioning, cable TV, indoor pool, lovely gardens, and two restaurants. Steps from 110 upscale factory outlets; three miles from waterfront. Breakfast and afternoon tea included. AAA four-diamond rating.

Hosts: The Gray Family
Rooms: 84 (PB) $110-235
Full Breakfast
Credit Cards: A, B, C, D, E
Notes: 3, 4, 5, 8, 9, 11, 12, 14, 15

7 No smoking; 8 Children welcome; 9 Social drinking allowed; 10 Tennis nearby; 11 Swimming nearby;
12 Golf nearby; 13 Skiing nearby; 14 May be booked through a travel agent; 15 Handicapped accessible.

181 Main Street Bed and Breakfast

181 Main Street, 04032
(207) 865-1226

Comfortably elegant, antique-filled 1840 Cape. Just a five-minute walk to L.L. Bean and Freeport's luxury outlets. Hosts provide a renowned breakfast, New England hospitality, and information on all that Maine has to offer—on and off the beaten path. In-ground pool; ample parking. Featured in *Country Home* magazine, and ABBA- and AAA-approved.

Rooms: 7 (PB) $85-100
Full Breakfast
Credit Cards: A, B
Notes: 2, 5, 7, 9, 10, 11, 12, 13

White Cedar Inn

White Cedar Inn

178 Main Street, 04032
(207) 865-9099; (800) 853-1269
www.members.aol.com/bedandbrk/cedar

Historic Victorian home stands just two blocks north of L.L. Bean. Spacious and cozy rooms are antique furnished, with private baths. Full country breakfast served in the sunroom overlooking beautifully landscaped grounds. Air conditioned. AAA three-diamond rating.

Hosts: Phil and Carla Kerber
Rooms: 7 (PB) $70-130
Full Breakfast
Credit Cards: A, B, C, D
Notes: 5, 7, 9, 10, 11, 12, 13, 14

FRIENDSHIP

The Outsiders' Inn Bed and Breakfast

Box 521A, Corner of Routes 97 and 220, 04547
(207) 832-5197

The Outsiders' Inn is in the center of the village of Friendship, a short walk from the harbor, the home of historic Friendship sloops and scores of lobster boats. This inn features five comfortable guest rooms with double beds, private and semiprivate baths. Efficiency cottage also available. Full breakfasts served daily. Sea kayak rentals and guided tours available. Sauna on premises. Country furnishings, delicious food, friendly folks. Come enjoy midcoast Maine.

Hosts: Debbie and Bill Michaud
Rooms: 5 (1 PB; 4 SB) $50-65
Full Breakfast
Credit Cards: A, B
Notes: 2, 5, 7, 8, 9, 11, 12

FRYEBURG

Acres of Austria

Rural Route 1, Box 177, 04037
(800) 988-4391; FAX (207) 925-6547

View the Old Saco River, White Mountains, or acres of forest from any room. Enjoy the antique billiard table, German/English library, and on-site canoes. Take advantage of the nearby cog railway, antiquing, and outlet shopping. Indulge in Franz's schnitzel, gulash, spinatnock'n, crêpes, and homemade

Acres of Austria

NOTES: Credit cards accepted: A MasterCard; B Visa; C American Express; D Discover; E Diner's Club; F Other; 2 Personal checks accepted; 3 Lunch available; 4 Dinner available; 5 Open all year; 6 Pets welcome;

breads and pastries. "Come, sit back, relax, and make yourself at home on our 65 acres."

Hosts: Candice and Franz Redl
Rooms: 4 (PB) $65-125
Full Breakfast
Credit Cards: A, B
Notes: 2, 3, 4, 5, 7, 8, 9, 10, 11, 12, 13, 15

Admiral Peary House

9 Elm Street, 04037
(207) 935-3365; (800) 237-8080
e-mail: admpeary@nxi.com

This home, once the residence of Arctic explorer Admiral Robert E. Peary, has been lovingly restored for guests' comfort, with air-conditioned rooms and private bathrooms, country breakfasts, and billiards. The clay tennis court is framed by spacious lawns and perennial gardens. Use one of the bicycles to explore the village and nearby sights. Canoe the Saco River or hike the White Mountains. Top it off with a leisurely soak in the outdoor spa. Snowshoe rentals and trail in winter.

Hosts: Ed and Nancy Greenberg
Rooms: 6 (PB) $70-128
Full Breakfast
Credit Cards: A, B, C
Notes: 2, 5, 7, 8, 9, 10, 11, 12, 13, 14

GORHAM

Pine Crest Bed and Breakfast

91 South Street, 04038
(207) 839-5843; e-mail: pinecrst@aol.com

Just 10 miles west of Portland on Route 114. A gracious 1825 bed and breakfast with lots of privacy. A living room with TV is available for all to enjoy. Private baths and down-home cleanliness. Coffee or tea in rooms, a hearty Continental breakfast in dining room. Close to beaches, mountains, lakes, and shopping. Central location for southern and mid-coast stays. AAA-rated three diamonds. Cross-country skiing nearby.

Hosts: Joseph and Jane Carlozzi
Rooms: 5 (PB) $49-99
Continental Breakfast
Credit Cards: A, B
Notes: 2, 5, 7, 8, 10, 12, 13

GOULDSBORO

Sunset House Bed and Breakfast

Route 186, 04607
(800) 233-7156

This late-Victorian home offers guests a choice of six spacious bedrooms spread over three floors with a selection of ocean and freshwater views. The second floor has three bedrooms with private baths. The third floor includes three bedrooms with shared bath and optional kitchen. Perfect accommodations for reunions and traveling couples. A full country breakfast is served.

Hosts: Carl and Kathy Johnson
Rooms: 6 (3 PB; 3 SB) $69-89
Full Breakfast
Credit Cards: A, B, C, D
Notes: 2, 5, 7, 9, 11, 12

GREATER PORTLAND

Black Point Inn

510 Black Point Road, Scarborough, 04074
(207) 883-4126; (800) 258-0003
FAX (207) 883-9976; e-mail: bpi@nlis.net

The Black Point Inn is a turn-of-the-century beachfront resort. Its oyster gray shingles and striking white trim emulate New England charm. On the exclusive peninsula of Prouts Neck, a summer community of Greater Portland, it is surrounded by miles of white-sand beaches and fragrant balsam forests. Its many amenities include fine dining, miles of sandy beaches, an 18-hole PGA golf course, 14 tennis courts, indoor and outdoor pools, boating, fishing, miles of nature trails, and a full health club with massage room. Breakfast and dinner included in rates. AAA four-diamond-rated.

Hosts: The Black Point Inn Staff
Rooms: 80 (PB) $270-450 MAP
Full Breakfast
Credit Cards: A, B, C, D, E
Notes: 2, 3, 4, 10, 11, 12, 15

7 No smoking; 8 Children welcome; 9 Social drinking allowed; 10 Tennis nearby; 11 Swimming nearby; 12 Golf nearby; 13 Skiing nearby; 14 May be booked through a travel agent; 15 Handicapped accessible.

GREENVILLE _____

Greenville Inn

Norris Street, P.O. Box 1194, 04441
(207) 695-2206 (phone/FAX); (888) 695-6000
e-mail: gvlinn@moosehead.net
www.greenvilleinn.com

This 1895 Victorian lumber baron's mansion is on a hill overlooking Moosehead Lake and Squaw Mountain. A large leaded-glass window decorated with a painted spruce tree is the focal point at the landing of the stairway. Gas lights, embossed wall coverings, carved fireplace mantels, and cherry and oak paneling grace the inn. In the elegantly appointed dining rooms, diners may savor fresh Maine seafood, glazed roast duckling, grilled chops, or steaks. Whether relaxing by a cozy fire or sipping cocktails on the veranda at sunset, the evening hours are most enjoyable.

Hosts: The Schnetzers
Rooms: 12 (PB) $95-205
Continental Breakfast
Credit Cards: A, B, D
Notes: 2, 4, 5, 7, 8, 9, 10, 11, 12, 13, 14

Greenville Inn

GUILFORD _____

The Guilford Bed and Breakfast

Elm Street, P.O. Box 88, 04443
(207) 876-3477; FAX (207) 876-3615

On the Moosehead Trail in central Main. This 1905 post-Victorian offers a perfect location for business and vacation. Public rooms—paneled den with fireplace,

formal living room and dining room. Large guest rooms. Antiques. Gourmet breakfast daily. Lunch, dinner, picnics, afternoon tea upon request. North on I-95, exit 39, north on Route 7 to Dexter, north on Route 23 to Guilford.

Hosts: Harry and Lynn Anderson
Rooms: 6 (2 PB; 4 SB) $50-65
Full Breakfast
Credit Cards: A, B
Notes: 2, 5, 7, 9, 11, 12, 13

HOLDEN _____

Tether's End Bed and Breakfast

50 Church Road, 04429
(207) 989-7886

Tether's End Bed and Breakfast is 10 minutes from downtown Bangor in an 1890s country home with award-winning gardens, and screened porch for guests' enjoyment. The inn offers quiet comfort with warm hospitality and a full country breakfast graciously served. The inn is just off the Bar  Harbor road, 15 minutes from the Bangor Airport, 40 miles from Bar Harbor/Acadia.

Hosts: Harris and Judy Madson
Rooms: 3 (2 PB; 1 SB) $45-60
Full Breakfast
Credit Cards: A, B
Notes: 2, 5, 7, 8, 10, 11, 12

ISLE AU HAUT _____

The Keepers House

P.O. Box 26, 04645
(207) 367-2261

Remote island lighthouse station in the undeveloped wilderness area of Acadia National Park. Guests arrive on the mail boat from Stonington. No telephones, cars, TV, or crowds. Osprey, seal, deer, rugged

trails, spectacular scenery, seclusion, and inspiration. Two-night minimum stay June 16 through October 15. Closed November 1 to April 30. Rates include three elegant meals and bikes.

Hosts: Jeff and Judi Burke
Rooms: 6 (SB) $250-285
Credit Cards: None
Notes: 2, 3, 4, 7, 8, 9, 11

KENNEBUNK

Arundel Meadows Inn

P.O. Box 1129, 04043-1129
(207) 985-3770
www.biddeford.com/arundel_meadows_inn

This 165-year-old farmhouse, two miles north on Route 1 from the center of town, combines the charm of antiques and art with the comfort of seven individually decorated bedrooms with sitting areas. Two of the rooms are suites, three have fireplaces, some have cable TV, and all have private bathrooms and summer air conditioning. Full homemade breakfasts and afternoon teas are prepared by co-owner Mark Bachelder, a professionally trained chef.

Hosts: Mark Bachelder and Murray Yaeger
Rooms: 7 (PB) $75-125
Full Breakfast
Credit Cards: A, B
Notes: 2, 5, 7, 9, 11, 12, 14

Arundel Meadows Inn

The Kennebunk Inn

45 Main Street, 04043
(207) 985-3351; FAX (207) 985-8865

The Kennebunk Inn is a historic 200-year-old building in the center of Main Street in downtown Kennebunk. All 28 rooms and suites have private baths and include a hearty Continental breakfast. Each room has a distinctive personality of its own. Antique claw-foot porcelain baths, four-poster beds, hardwood floors, and cozy quilts are just some of the features guests may find in the great variety of rooms. TVs, and in-room telephones are also available for the person on the go, and don't overlook the several sitting rooms featuring shelves of "good reads" and plenty of games. Skiing one hour away.

Hosts: Kristen and John Martin
Rooms: 28 (PB)
Continental Breakfast
Credit Cards: A, B, C, D
Notes: 2, 4, 5, 6, 7, 8, 9, 10, 11, 12, 14, 15

The Kennebunk Inn

Sundial Inn

211 Beach Avenue, P.O. Box 1147, 04043
(207) 967-3850; FAX (207) 967-4719
e-mail: sundial@gwi.net

The Sundial Inn is a turn-of-the-century seaside inn in the residential section of Kennebunk Beach. The 34 guest rooms have all been renovated to include private

7 No smoking; 8 Children welcome; 9 Social drinking allowed; 10 Tennis nearby; 11 Swimming nearby; 12 Golf nearby; 13 Skiing nearby; 14 May be booked through a travel agent; 15 Handicapped accessible.

baths, telephones, TVs, and air conditioning. Two deluxe oceanfront rooms feature whirlpool bathtubs. The inn has a large sitting room with sofas and wicker chairs and a beautiful ocean view. The Sundial is one and one-half miles from the center of Kennebunkport. There are also several museums, antique stores, wildlife refuges, and golf courses in the area.

Rooms: 34 (PB) $70-170
Continental Breakfast
Credit Cards: A, B, C, D, E
Notes: 5, 7, 9, 10, 11, 12, 15

KENNEBUNK BEACH

The Ocean View

171 Beach Avenue, 04043
(207) 967-2750; FAX (207) 967-5418
e-mail: arena@theoceanview.com
www.theoceanview.com

An intimate oceanfront inn. "The closest you'll find to a bed on the beach." Sights, sounds, and aura of the Atlantic at the doorstep, yet only a scant mile to downtown Kennebunkport. A perfect location! The inn is whimsical and colorful with an eclectic flair. It is a blend of subtle amenities set in an atmosphere of friendliness and helpfulness. It is immaculate and sparkling...a jewel of distinct quality.

Hosts: Carole and Bob Arena
Rooms: 9 (PB) $100-250
Full Breakfast
Credit Cards: A, B, C, D
Notes: 7, 9, 10, 11, 12

KENNEBUNKPORT

Captain Fairfield Inn

8 Pleasant Street, P.O. Box 1308, 04046
(207) 967-4454; (800) 322-1928
FAX (207) 967-8537
e-mail: chefdennis@cybertours.com

A gracious 1813 sea captain's mansion in Kennebunkport's historic district, only steps to the village green and harbor. A delightful walk to sandy beaches, Dock

Captain Fairfield Inn

Square Marina, shops, and excellent restaurants. The bedrooms are beautifully decorated with antiques and period furnishings. Several bedrooms have fireplaces, one with a double whirlpool tub. Relax in the living room, study, or enjoy the tree-shaded grounds and gardens. Wake up to birdsong, fresh sea air, and the aroma of gourmet coffee. Cross-country skiing. Children over six welcome.

Rooms: 9 (PB) $89-225
Full Breakfast
Credit Cards: A, B, C, D, E
Notes: 2, 5, 7, 9, 10, 11, 12, 13, 14

Captain's Hideaway

12 Pleasant Street, P.O. Box 2746, 04046-2746
(207) 967-5711; FAX (207) 967-3843
e-mail: hideaway@cybertours.com
www.gndesigns.com/hideaway

The Captain's Hideaway is a meticulously restored Federal period home with two luxurious guest rooms in Kennebunkport's lovely historic district. Each room features an antique four-poster canopied bed, gas fireplace, whirlpool tub, private telephone, air conditioning, cable TV with VCR, CD/tape deck stereo systems, and a mini-refrigerator stocked with complimentary non-alcoholic beverages. A custom three-course breakfast is served by candlelight each morning. The Hideaway is but a five-minute walk to Dock Square shops, marinas, galleries, and restaurants.

NOTES: Credit cards accepted: A MasterCard; B Visa; C American Express; D Discover; E Diner's Club; F Other; 2 Personal checks accepted; 3 Lunch available; 4 Dinner available; 5 Open all year; 6 Pets welcome;

Hosts: Susan Jackson and Judith Hughes Boulet
Rooms: 2 (PB) $179-279
Full Breakfast
Credit Cards: A, B
Notes: 2, 5, 7, 9, 10, 11, 12, 13, 14

The Captain Jefferds Inn

The Captain Jefferds Inn

5 Pearl Street, P.O. Box 691, 04046
(207) 967-2311; (800) 839-6844
FAX (207) 967-0721
e-mail: captjeff@captainjefferdsinn.com

Enjoy the gracious hospitality in this 1804 Federal-style mansion. Each of the inn's 16 guest rooms is named and designed in the spirit of the hosts' favorite places including Assisi, Italy, Adar, Ireland, Charleston, and Chatham. Six rooms have fireplaces, all have private baths, and are furnished with antiques and period reproductions. Guests are treated to candlelit gourmet breakfasts served on the sunny terrace overlooking the gardens or in front of the warm fire. In the historic district, within easy walking distance of many fine restaurants, shops, and galleries.

Hosts: Pat and Dick Bartholomew
Rooms: 16 (PB) $105-240
Full Breakfast
Credit Cards: A, B
Notes: 2, 5, 6, 7, 9, 10, 11, 12, 13, 14

The Captain Lord Mansion

P.O. Box 800, 04046
(207) 967-3141; FAX (207) 967-3172
www.captainlord.com

The Captain Lord Mansion is an intimate 16-room luxury country inn, at the head of a sweeping lawn, overlooking the Kennebunk River. The inn is famous for its warm, friendly hospitality, attention to cleanliness,

and hearty breakfasts served family style in the big country kitchen. In 1997 and 1998 the inn received a four-star rating from Mobil and is AAA-rated four diamonds. Children over six welcome.

Hosts: Bev Davis and Rick Litchfield
Rooms: 16 (PB)
Full Breakfast
Credit Cards: A, B, D
Notes: 2, 5, 7, 9, 10, 11, 12, 14

Charrid House

2 Arlington Avenue, 04046
(207) 967-5695

Built in 1887, this charming cedar-shingled home started life as a gambling casino for the Kennebunkport River Club. It went through incarnations as a tennis clubhouse and a single-family home before becoming Charrid House in 1986. On a residential street, the Charrid House is one block from the stunning scenery of Ocean Avenue and Colony Beach. Several restaurants and shops are within walking distance and the village itself is one mile south.

Host: Ann M. Dubay
Rooms: 2 (2 S1B) $65
Full Breakfast
Credit Cards: F
Notes: 2, 7, 10, 11, 12

Cove House

11 South Maine Street, 04046
(207) 967-3704

This cozy bed and breakfast is an Early Colonial home in a quiet residential area on a cove with views of the water from the yard. Decorated with antiques and a collection of Flow Blue, it offers charm with authentic bed and breakfast hospitality. A hearty breakfast is served each morning in the dining room. A short walk from the village and beach. An additional $20 for third person.

Hosts: The Jones Family (Kathy, Bob, and Barry)
Rooms: 3 (PB) $75-85
Full Breakfast
Credit Cards: A, B, C
Notes: 2, 5, 7, 8, 9, 10, 11, 12

7 No smoking; 8 Children welcome; 9 Social drinking allowed; 10 Tennis nearby; 11 Swimming nearby; 12 Golf nearby; 13 Skiing nearby; 14 May be booked through a travel agent; 15 Handicapped accessible.

Crosstrees

South Street, Box 1333, 04046-1333
(207) 967-2780; FAX (207) 967-2610
e-mail: crosstrees@cybertours.com
www.crosstrees.com

Tucked into a quiet corner of Kennebunkport's historic district is this beautifully restored 1818 Federal-style inn in the National Register of Historic Places. Surrounded by spacious, shaded grounds, lovely perennial gardens, and a sparkling pond, guests relax and feel refreshed. Inside are four guest rooms decorated individually with antiques and period furniture, private baths, three with fireplaces, plus suite with Jacuzzi. Guests enjoy early morning coffee, a full breakfast, and afternoon refreshments. A short walk from shops, galleries, marinas, restaurants, and the ocean. Children over 12 welcome. Cross-country skiing.

Hosts: Dennis Rafferty and Keith Henley
Rooms: 4 (PB) $115-195
Full Breakfast
Credit Cards: A, B
Notes: 2, 5, 7, 9, 10, 11, 12, 13, 14

Elaine's Bed and Breakfast Selections

4987 Kingston Road, Elbridge, 13060
(315) 689-2082 (after 10 A.M.)

This moderately priced bed and breakfast is on a fine old residential street, just a block from Ocean Avenue and a nice walk to downtown Dock Square. There are four guest rooms with private and shared baths. The living room has a fireplace as well as a wood stove and TV. A fully furnished knotty-pine walled guest cottage sits more privately away from the main house and is ideal for a couple or small family. Weekly rental of the cottage is $575. Daily rates may be available during the off-season.

Rooms: 4 (2 PB; 2 SB) $75-85
Full Breakfast
Credit Cards: A, B
Notes: 2, 5, 7, 8, 9, 10, 11, 12, 14

English Meadows Inn

141 Port Road, Kennebunk, 04043
(207) 967-5766; (800) 272-0698

English Meadows is an 1860 Victorian farmhouse that has been operating as an inn for more than 80 years. Within a five- or ten-minute stroll past interesting shops and galleries to the village of Kennebunkport, English Meadows offers its guests a peaceful taste of country living and the many unique attractions of the area. Antique-appointed guest rooms, deliciously full breakfasts, and convivial hosts add further pleasure for visitors at this wonderful inn. Children welcome.

Hosts: Kathy and Pete Smith
Rooms: 13 (PB) $85-145
Full Breakfast
Credit Cards: A, B, C, D
Notes: 2, 5, 7, 8, 9, 10, 11, 12

The Inn on South Street

South Street, P.O. Box 478A, 04046
(207) 967-5151

Now approaching its 200th birthday, this stately Greek Revival house is in the historic district. There are three beautifully decorated guest rooms and one luxury suite. Private baths, fireplaces, a common room, afternoon refreshments, and early morning coffee. A sumptuous breakfast is

The Inn on South Street

NOTES: Credit cards accepted: A MasterCard; B Visa; C American Express; D Discover; E Diner's Club; F Other; 2 Personal checks accepted; 3 Lunch available; 4 Dinner available; 5 Open all year; 6 Pets welcome;

served in the large country kitchen with views of the river and ocean or, weather permitting, in the garden. On a quiet street within walking distance of restaurants, shops, and the water.

Hosts: Jacques and Eva Downs
Rooms: 3 (PB) $105-149
Suite: 1 (PB) $185-225
Full Breakfast
Credit Cards: A, B
Notes: 2, 7, 10, 11, 12, 13, 14

Kennebunkport Inn

Dock Square, P.O. Box 111, 04046
(207) 967-2621; (800) 248-2621
FAX (207) 967-3705

This large sea captain's home was built in 1899 along the Kennebunk River. Now an inn with a restaurant, known for creative cuisine, classically prepared. Each of the 34 guest rooms offers a private bath, color TV, telephone, and period furnishings. The restaurant lounge with fireplace and swimming pool with patio are popular spots for relaxing. Antique shops, boutiques, galleries, and restaurants are within walking distance. Local theaters, deep sea fishing, golf, and fine beaches are within a short drive. Families welcome. Meeting facilities available. Lunch and dinner available seasonally.

Hosts: Rick and Martha Griffin
Rooms: 35 (PB) $79.50-249
Full and Continental Breakfast
Credit Cards: A, B, C
Notes: 2, 5, 8, 9, 10, 11, 12, 14

King's Port Inn

Corner of Routes 9 & 35, P.O. Box 1172, 04046
(207) 967-4340; (800) 286-5767
FAX (207) 967-4810; e-mail: info@kingsport.com

King's Port Inn has affordable rates with a great location, just a short walk to famous Dock Square and most shops, restaurants, beaches, and area attractions. Guest rooms have two double beds, cable TV, telephone, refrigerator, full private bath, and air conditioning. Five deluxe rooms have king-size

bed, dual shower, and private Jacuzzi. Other amenities include a pantry sideboard breakfast buffet each morning in the cozy fireside parlor, and movie entertainment in the minitheater. Smoking in designated rooms only. Wildlife sanctuaries nearby.

Host: Bill Greer
Rooms: 32 (PB) $49-175
Suite: 1 (PB)
Continental Breakfast
Credit Cards: A, B, C, D
Notes: 2, 5, 8, 9, 10, 11, 12, 13, 14, 15

Lake Brook Bed and Breakfast

P.O. Box 762, 04046
(207) 967-4069

Lake Brook Bed and Breakfast is an appealing turn-of-the-century farmhouse on the edge of the salt marsh and tidal brook. Sit on the porch and relax in comfortable rockers and enjoy the flower gardens and ocean breeze. All rooms are individually decorated and offer private baths and ceiling fans. A full gourmet breakfast is served daily. Coffee is ready by 7:00 A.M. Weekends and holidays two- and three-night minimum stay required in season. Reservations suggested. Seasonal rates available. Cross-country skiing nearby.

Rooms: 4 (PB) $85-120
Continental Breakfast
Credit Cards: A, B
Notes: 2, 5, 7, 8, 9, 10, 11, 12, 13, 14

Maine Stay Inn and Cottages

Box 500A- AD, 04046
(207) 967-2117; (800) 950-2117
FAX (207) 967-8757

A beautiful 1860 Victorian inn distinguished by Queen Anne-period flying staircase, wraparound porch, and bay windows. A variety of accommodations, from charming rooms and suites to delightful one-bedroom cottages, some with fireplaces and double whirlpool tubs. The living room is a comfortable place to sit and meet fellow travelers or enjoy a fire on a cold winter day. The inn

7 No smoking; 8 Children welcome; 9 Social drinking allowed; 10 Tennis nearby; 11 Swimming nearby; 12 Golf nearby; 13 Skiing nearby; 14 May be booked through a travel agent; 15 Handicapped accessible.

is four blocks from the village, allowing guests a leisurely walk to shops, galleries, restaurants, and the harbor.

Hosts: Lindsay and Carol Copeland
Rooms: 17 (PB) $95-225
Full Breakfast
Credit Cards: A, B, C
Notes: 5, 7, 8, 9, 10, 11, 12

Maude's Courtyard Bed and Breakfast

Route 9, Western Avenue, P.O. Box 182, 04046
(207) 967-8433; FAX (207) 967-2858

Cozy, comfortable, and casual…the perfect place to relax and unwind, just one mile from town, beaches, and golf. Bring own bike. Designed for privacy. Ideal for couples travel-ing together and families with older children.  Two bedrooms upstairs and a first-floor suite. Large sunny rooms fur-nished with favorite early-attic pieces give a country charm, along with welcoming fresh flow-ers. Air conditioned. Guests' own fully equipped kitchen. Continental breakfast. Smokers, please step outside.

Hosts: Jovanna Kezar and John Paré
Rooms: 3 (1 PB; 2 SB) $55-95
Continental Breakfast
Credit Cards: A, B
Notes: 2, 7, 9, 10, 11, 12, 14

Old Fort Inn and Resort

Box M-30, 04046
(207) 967-5353; (800) 828-FORT
FAX (207) 967-4547

Discover the hospitality of a luxurious New England inn that combines all of yes-terday's charm with today's conve-niences—from the daily buffet breakfast to the comfort and privacy of antique-

Old Fort Inn and Resort

appointed rooms. Includes pool, tennis court, TV, telephones, air conditioning, and a charming antique shop, all in a secluded setting. AAA-rated four dia-monds. Closed mid-December through mid-April.

Hosts: David and Sheila Aldrich
Rooms: 16 (PB) $135-295
Full Breakfast
Credit Cards: A, B, C, D
Notes: 2, 7, 9, 10, 11, 12, 14

White Barn Inn

Beach Street, P.O. Box 560C, 04046
(207) 967-2321; FAX (207) 967-1100

This 1850s farmhouse and its signature white barn have been transformed into a sophisticated inn and award-winning restau-rant. Twenty-five elegant accommodations, all with private baths and lovely antiques, many with whirlpool baths and fireplaces. New heated outdoor pool. A five-minute walk to the beach or to downtown Kenneb-unkport. Member Relais et Chateaux. AAA five-diamond dining. Selected among the top 12 inns.

Hosts: Mr. Laurie Bongiorno (owner)
Rooms: 25 (PB) $160-395
Continental Breakfast
Credit Cards: A, B, C
Notes: 2, 4, 5, 7, 9, 10, 11, 12, 13, 14

NOTES: Credit cards accepted: A MasterCard; B Visa; C American Express; D Discover; E Diner's Club;
F Other; 2 Personal checks accepted; 3 Lunch available; 4 Dinner available; 5 Open all year; 6 Pets welcome;

KITTERY

Enchanted Nights Bed and Breakfast

29 Wentworth Street, Route 103, 03904
(207) 439-1489;
www.enchanted-nights-bandb.com

An 1890 Princess Anne Gothic Victorian between Boston and Portland. Three minutes to dining and dancing in Portsmouth, historic homes, scenic ocean drives, and the renowned Kittery outlet malls. Convenient day trips to neighboring resorts. For the romantic at heart who delight in the subtle elegance of yesteryear; for those who are soothed by the whimsical charm of a French country inn. Elegant breakfast. Enjoy the suites with whirlpool for two. Cable TV and air conditioning. Pets welcome with restrictions.

Hosts: Nancy Bogenberger and Peter Lamandia
Rooms: 7 (PB) $52-182
Full Breakfast
Credit Cards: A, B, C, D
Notes: 2, 5, 6, 7, 8, 9, 10, 11, 12, 14, 15

Gundalow Inn

6 Water Street, 03904
(207) 439-4040

Relax in elegant but comfortable surroundings, just a 10-minute stroll across the bridge from historic Portsmouth, New Hampshire, and a short drive to beaches and factory outlets. Brick Victorian with six romantic guest rooms furnished with antiques, each with private bath, most with harbor views. Enjoy widely acclaimed four-course breakfast by

Gundalow

the fireplace or on the screened patio. Recommended by the *New York Times*. A no-smoking inn; open year-round.

Hosts: Cevia and George Rosol
Rooms: 6 (PB) $80-125
Full Breakfast
Credit Cards: A, B, D
Notes: 2, 5, 7, 9, 10, 11, 12, 14

LUBEC

Breakers by the Bay

37 Washington, 04652
(207) 733-2487

One of the oldest houses in the 200-year-old town of Lubec, a small fishing village. Three blocks to Campobello Island, the home of Franklin D. Roosevelt. All rooms have refrigerators, TVs, hand-crocheted tablecloths, hand-quilted bedspreads, and private decks for viewing the bay.

Host: E. M. Elg
Rooms: 5 (PB) $53.50-74.90
Full Breakfast
Credit Cards: None
Notes: 2, 7, 10, 12, 14

Peacock House

27 Summer Street, 04652
(207) 733-2403
www.nemaine.com/peacock_house

Down East hospitality with a distinctly southern grace. Built in 1860, Peacock House overlooks the Bay of Fundy and boasts five guest rooms all with private baths. This old Federal Revival provides quiet ambiance, unrivaled comfort, and easy access to Roosevelt's cottage on Campobello. For the special guests, handicapped accessible first floor. Three-diamond rating from AAA. Peacock House is close to Quoddy Head State Park, golf, and whale watching from Lubec Marina.

Rooms: 5 (PB) $65-85
Full Breakfast
Credit Cards: A, B
Notes: 2, 3, 9, 12, 15

7 No smoking; 8 Children welcome; 9 Social drinking allowed; 10 Tennis nearby; 11 Swimming nearby; 12 Golf nearby; 13 Skiing nearby; 14 May be booked through a travel agent; 15 Handicapped accessible.

MOUNT DESERT

Reibers' Bed and Breakfast

585 Sound Drive, P.O. Box 163, Somesville, 04660
(207) 244-3047; e-mail: reibersbnb@acadia.net
www.acadia.net/reibers

This 150-year-old Colonial homestead, listed on the national register, enjoys meadows and a tidal creek. Full breakfast. Central location. Moderate prices. Open all year.

Hosts: Gail and David Reiber
Rooms: 2 (1 PB; 1 SB) $65-75
Full Breakfast
Credit Cards: A, B
Notes: 2, 5, 7, 9, 10, 11, 12, 13

NAPLES

The Augustus Bove House

The Augustus Bove House

Rural Route 1, Box 501, 04055
(207) 693-6365
www.maineguide.com/naples/augustus

Guests are always welcome at the historic 1850 hotel. Originally known as Hotel Naples, it is restored for comfort and a relaxed atmosphere at affordable prices. Guest rooms have elegant yet homey furnishings, some with views of Long Lake. An easy walk to the water, shops, and recreation in a four-season area. Open all year, with off-season and midweek discounts. Telephones in each room. Air conditioning, TV, VCR, and hot tub. Coffee or tea anytime. AAA-approved.

Hosts: David and Arlene Stetson
Rooms: 11 (7 PB; 2+2 SB) $49-125
Full Breakfast
Credit Cards: A, B, C, D
Notes: 2, 5, 6, 7, 8, 9, 10, 11, 12, 13, 14

Inn at Long Lake

P.O. Box 806, 04055
(207) 693-6226

Enjoy romantic elegance and turn-of-the-century charm at the Inn at Long Lake, nestled amid the pines and waterways of the beautiful Sebago Lakes region. The inn has 16 restored rooms with TVs, air conditioners, and private baths. One minute's walk from the Naples Causeway. Four-season activities and fine dining nearby. This three-diamond AAA facility is worth the trip. Midweek discounts available. Named as one of the top 10 bed and breakfasts in the United States in a video competition by Innovations, Inc., of Jersey City, New Jersey.

Hosts: Maynard and Irene Hincks
Rooms: 16 (PB) $65-150
Continental Breakfast
Credit Cards: A, B, D
Notes: 2, 5, 7, 8, 9, 11, 12, 13, 14

Lamb's Mill Inn

Lamb's Mill Road, Box 676, 04055
(207) 693-6253

A charming country inn in the foothills of Maine's western mountain and lake region. Romantic country atmosphere on 20 acres of fields and woods. Five rooms with private baths and a full country breakfast. Hot tub available. Near lakes, antique shops, skiing, and canoeing.

Hosts: Laurel Tinkham and Sandra Long
Rooms: 6 (PB) $85-105

Lamb's Mill Inn

NOTES: Credit cards accepted: A MasterCard; B Visa; C American Express; D Discover; E Diner's Club; F Other; 2 Personal checks accepted; 3 Lunch available; 4 Dinner available; 5 Open all year; 6 Pets welcome;

Full Breakfast
Credit Cards: A, B
Notes: 2, 5, 7, 8, 9, 10, 11, 12, 13, 14

NEWAGEN

Newagen Seaside Inn

P.O. Box 68, 04552
(207) 633-5242; (800) 654-5242
e-mail: seaside@wiscasset.net

The Newagen Seaside Inn is one of the few remaining coastal inns that still evoke the spirit of a bygone era. The inn's relaxing, unhurried atmosphere harkens back to its 19th-century roots and makes it an ideal venue for romantic escapes, weekend weddings, family reunions, and artists' workshops. Ideal for families. The inn is on a former nature preserve and is a nature lover's paradise. It sits on 85 acres of forest, lawns, and gardens. Its mile of rocky coastline, with crashing surf and tidal pools, was significant in the life of noted environmental writer Rachel Carson.

Hosts: Heidi and Peter Larsen
Rooms: 26 (PB) $75-200
Full Breakfast
Credit Cards: A, B
Notes: 2, 3, 4, 7, 8, 9, 10, 11, 12, 14, 15

NEWCASTLE

Flying Cloud Bed and Breakfast

River Road, P.O. Box 549, 04553
(207) 563-2484; FAX (207) 563-8640
e-mail: flyingcl@lincoln.midcoast.com
www.lincoln.midcoast.com/~flyingcl

A lovingly restored 1790 to 1840 sea captain's home which is now a romantic 1990s inn. Full country breakfasts, beautiful water views, great beds, fireplaces, and an extensive library containing books on history and Americana, especially the Civil War. Spacious lawn and decks, 1840s flower garden, open and screened porches. Short walk to Damariscotta Village shops, pubs, and restaurants. Ideal for visiting Boothbay Harbor and the historic

Flying Cloud

Pemaquid area. Day trips to Acadia National Park, Camden, and Freeport.

Hosts: Jeanne and Alan Davis
Rooms: 5 (PB) $75-95
Full Breakfast
Credit Cards: A, B, C, D
Notes: 2, 5, 7, 9, 10, 11, 12, 13

Glidden House

24 Glidden Street, 04553
(207) 563-1859

Charming Victorian on street of fine homes. Attractively decorated. Private baths. River views. Walk to town for shops, galleries, restaurants, and historical sites. Full breakfasts always bring compliments for quality and service. Inquire about accommodations for children. Golf and skiing is a short drive away.

Host: Doris E. Miller
Rooms: 4 (PB) $60-75
Full Breakfast
Credit Cards: A, B
Notes: 2, 5, 7, 11

NEW HARBOR

Gosnold Arms

146 State Route 32, 04554
(207) 677-3727

On the harbor, the Gosnold Arms Inn and cottages, all with private baths, most with water view. A glassed-in dining room overlooking the water is open for breakfast

7 No smoking; 8 Children welcome; 9 Social drinking allowed; 10 Tennis nearby; 11 Swimming nearby; 12 Golf nearby; 13 Skiing nearby; 14 May be booked through a travel agent; 15 Handicapped accessible.

and dinner. The Gosnold wharf and moorings accommodate cruising boats. Within a 10-mile radius are lakes, beaches, lobster pounds, historic sites, boat trips, golf, antiques, shops, and restaurants. Smoking in designated areas only. Limited handicapped accessibility.

Hosts: The Phinney Family
Rooms: 26 (PB) $79-124
Full Breakfast
Credit Cards: A, B
Notes: 2, 4, 8, 9, 10, 11, 12

NORTHEAST HARBOR

Harbourside Inn

Northeast Harbor, 04662
(207) 276-3272

Peace and quiet, flower gardens at the edge of the forest, and woodland trails into Acadia National Park add to the delights of this genuine 1888 country inn. Spacious rooms and suites, all with private baths, many with king- or queen-size beds. Beautiful antiques, working fireplaces in all first- and second-floor rooms. Guests can walk or drive into nearby Acadia National Park. Sailing, deep-sea fishing, and carriage rides in the park. Reservations accepted for two nights or more.

Hosts: The Sweet Family
Rooms: 11 (PB) $85-210

Harbourside Inn

Suites: 3 (PB)
Continental Breakfast
Credit Cards: None
Notes: 2, 7, 10, 11, 12

OGUNQUIT

Chestnut Tree Inn

93 Shore Road, P.O. Box 2201, 03907
(207) 646-4529; (800) 362-0757
www.chestnuttreeinn.com

Guests are encouraged to make themselves at home at this gracious 1870 Victorian inn, the oldest inn in Ogunquit. Relax on the large front porch or in the side yard with gardens and stone water fountain. Enjoy a Continental breakfast in the spacious fireplaced living/dining room. Easy walk to beach, restaurants, and shops—on trolley route. Nonsmoking environment.

Hosts: Cynthia, Diana and Ronald St. Laurent
Rooms: 22 (16 PB; 6 SB) $40-125
Continental Breakfast
Credit Cards: A, B, C
Notes: 2, 7, 8, 9, 10, 11, 12, 13, 14

Gorges Grant Hotel

239 Route 1, P.O. Box 2240, 03907
(207) 646-7003; (800) 646-5001
FAX (207) 646-0660
e-mail: gorgesgrant@ogunquit.com

A modern inn of 81 luxury units, the Gorges Grant is on acres of meticulously manicured grounds in the heart of Ogunquit. Heated indoor/outdoor pools, Jacuzzi, large patio/poolside area, fitness center. Casual, fine dining at Raspberri's, the hotel's own full-service restaurant. Bed and breakfast and dinner package plans are available. Oguniquit features miles of white-sand beaches, the famous Marginal Way footpath, and picturesque Perkins Cove. Nearby outlet shopping at Kittery and Freeport (L.L. Bean). AAA-rated three diamonds.

Hosts: Karen and Bob Hanson
Rooms: 81 (PB) $76-166
Full Breakfast
Credit Cards: A, B, C, D, E
Notes: 2, 4, 7, 8, 9, 10, 11, 12, 15

NOTES: Credit cards accepted: A MasterCard; B Visa; C American Express; D Discover; E Diner's Club; F Other; 2 Personal checks accepted; 3 Lunch available; 4 Dinner available; 5 Open all year; 6 Pets welcome;

Hartwell House

118 Shore Road, P.O. Box 393, 03907
(207) 646-7210; (800) 235-8883

In the tradition of fine European country inns, Hartwell House offers rooms and suites elegantly furnished with Early American and English antiques. A complimentary gourmet breakfast is served daily. Perkins Cove, fine restaurants, shops, the fabulous Ogunquit Beach, and the Marginal Way are all within walking distance. Seasonal package arrangements. Conference facility seats up to 65 people and an executive board room seats 18. Available year-round. Dinner packages available during the off-season.

Hosts: Jim and Trisha Hartwell;
   Christopher and Tracey Anderson
Rooms: 16 (PB) $85-185
Full Breakfast
Credit Cards: A, B, C, D
Notes: 2, 5, 7, 9, 10, 11, 12, 13, 14, 15

Holiday Guest House

P.O. Box 2247, 03907
(207) 646-5582

Fully restored historic 1814 Colonial close to beaches, restaurants, antique shops, outlets, and nature trails. Guest accommodations have private baths and refrigerators.

Hosts: Lou and Rose LePage
Rooms: 2 (PB) $55-85
Continental Breakfast
Credit Cards: A, B, C, D
Notes: 2, 5, 7, 8, 9, 10, 11, 12, 14

Terrace By The Sea

11 Wharf Lane, P.O. Box 831, 03907
(207) 646-3232

The Terrace By The Sea blends the best of both worlds, with the elegance of a Colonial inn and deluxe motel accommodations, both offering spectacular ocean views in a peaceful, secluded setting across from the beach. All rooms have private baths, air conditioning, telephones, color cable TV, heat, refrigerators; some efficiency kitchens. Easy

walking distance to Ogunquit's beautiful sandy beach, Marginal Way, village shops, restaurants, and link to the trolley. Dinner packages available.

Hosts: John and Daryl Bullard
Rooms: 36 (PB) $103-168
Continental Breakfast
Credit Cards: None
Notes: 2, 7, 10, 11, 12

The Trellis House

2 Beachmere Place, P.O. Box 2229, 03907
(207) 646-7909; www.trellishouse.com

A turn-of-the-century beach house, completely restored and appointed with an eclectic blend of antiques. All rooms have private baths. Breakfast consists of fresh fruits, muffins and breads, juices, coffee, tea, and special entrée. The Trellis House is just a short walk to all that is special in Ogunquit. Cross-country skiing nearby.

Hosts: Pat and Jerry Houlihan
Rooms: 4 (PB) $75-120
Full Breakfast
Credit Cards: A, B, D
Notes: 2, 5, 7, 9, 10, 11, 12, 13

West Highland Inn

14 Shore Road, 03907
(207) 646-2181

The West Highland Inn is an island of serenity in a New England village setting in the heart of Ogunquit, close to everything it has to offer. The Victorian house, built in 1890, is full of antiques. Hosts offer breakfast

West Highland Inn

7 No smoking; 8 Children welcome; 9 Social drinking allowed; 10 Tennis nearby; 11 Swimming nearby; 12 Golf nearby; 13 Skiing nearby; 14 May be booked through a travel agent; 15 Handicapped accessible.

each day, with home-baked goodies each afternoon. Ten rooms with private baths. Three efficiencies. Open from May to November with special holiday weekends from December through April. Pets welcome. Seasonal rates.

Hosts: Linda and Steve Williams
    Clementine and Ferguson, the West Highland
    terriers
Rooms: 10 (PB) $60-120
Full Breakfast
Credit Cards: A, B
Notes: 2, 6, 7, 9, 10, 11, 12

ORLAND

Alamosook Lodge

P.O. Box 16, 04472
(207) 469-6393; FAX (207) 469-2528

Welcome to the lodge and the marvelous views of the lake. Enjoy freshwater swimming, canoeing, and fishing. Listen to loons. Experience fall foliage transformed into a blaze of reflecting colors. The winters are magical, with skating, cross-country skiing, and cozy warmth. Start the day with a sumptuous breakfast, stroll along the water, browse through the gardens, bask in the sun, and soak up the view. The six cheerful rooms with private baths are nonsmoking. Convenient to Bar Harbor, Blue Hill, Castine, and Deer Isle. Three miles off Route 1.

Hosts: Jan and Doug Gibson
Rooms: 6 (PB) $65-93
Full Breakfast
Credit Cards: A, B, C
Notes: 2, 5, 7, 8, 9, 11, 12, 15

The Sign of the Amiable Pig

74 Castine Road, P.O. Box 232, 04472-0232
(207) 469-2561

The bed and breakfast is in Orland village, just off Route 1. The house, named for the delightful weathervane which tops the garage, was built in the 18th century. Furnished with interesting antiques and oriental rugs, it has six working fireplaces, including the large cooking fireplace in the

The Sign of the Amiable Pig

keeping room. Full breakfast is served in the dining room or the keeping room. The remodeled barn is now a guest house available on a weekly or monthly basis with breakfast available by reservation.

Hosts: Charlotte and Wes Pipher
Rooms: 3 (1 PB; 2 SB) $60-75
Guest House: $550; $1,900
Full Breakfast
Credit Cards: F
Notes: 2, 5, 7, 8, 9, 10, 11, 12, 13

PORTLAND

Andrews Lodging Bed and Breakfast

417 Auburn Street, 04103
(207) 797-9157; FAX (207) 797-9040
e-mail: andrewsbedandbreakfast@compuserve.com
www.travelguides.com/BB/andrews_lodging

On over an acre of beautifully landscaped grounds on the outskirts of the city of Port-

Andrews Lodging

land, this 250-year-old Colonial home has been completely renovated for year-round comfort. Hosts offer modern baths, one with whirlpool, a completely applianced guest kitchen, a library, and a solarium overlooking beautiful gardens or pristine snow in the winter. Close to ocean, lakes, golf, skiing, and the mountains.

Hosts: Elizabeth and Douglas Andrews
Rooms: 5 (2 PB; 3 SB) $78-165
Full Breakfast
Credit Cards: A, B, C
Notes: 2, 5, 6, 7, 9, 12

Bed and Breakfast Reservations North Shore, Greater Boston, Cape Cod

P.O. Box 600035, Greater Boston Branch,
  Newtonville, 02160-0001
(617) 964-1606; (800) 832-2632
FAX (617) 332-8572; e-mail: info@bbreserve.com
www.bbreserve.com

133. European-style inn in Portland's historic western promenade district of grand homes has six beautifully decorated guest rooms with private baths, telephones, cable TV, air conditioning, and some fireplaces. A large carriage house, adjacent to the inn, offers two additional accommodations, each with separate entrance. The handicapped accessible, downstairs room has private bath, TV, air conditioning, telephone, and private garden patio. The second-floor suite adds a sitting area. Full gourmet breakfast and complimentary afternoon wine. No smoking. Children over 15 welcome. $145-165.

Inn on Carleton

46 Carleton Street, 04102
(207) 775-1910; (800) 639-1779
www.innoncarleton.com

Guests are graciously welcomed to this restored 1869 Victorian home in Portland's historic western promenade neighborhood. Near the center of downtown Portland, the Inn on Carleton is on a quiet, tree-lined street in a quaint residential neighborhood of Vic-

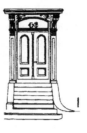

torian architecture. It's a short walk on the city's distinctive brick sidewalks to the Portland Museum of Art, Maine Medical Center, the arts district, the waterfront, and the busines district. And while in Portland, guests can enjoy the scenic Maine coastline, take the ferry to the Calendar Islands in Casco Bay, and stroll through the charming Old Port area with its cobbled streets, delightful shops, and fine restaurants. Children nine and older welcome.

Hosts: Philip and Sue Cox
Rooms: 7 (4 PB; 3 SB) $65-160
Full Breakfast
Credit Cards: A, B, D
Notes: 2, 5, 7, 9, 10, 11, 12, 13, 14

Inn at St. John

939 Congress Street, 04102
(207) 773-6481; (800) 636-9127
www.maineguide.com/portland/stjohn

A unique 100-year-old inn noted for its European charm and quiet gentility. Just a short walk to the Old Port, waterfront, and arts district. Tastefully decorated rooms with traditional and antique furnishings. Enjoy complimentary Continental breakfast, free parking, and value rates. All rooms offer free local calls and cable TV with HBO. An ideal inn for that off-season getaway. Air-conditioned and nonsmoking rooms available.

Host: Paul Hood
Rooms: 32 (20 PB; 12 SB)
Continental Breakfast
Credit Cards: A, B, C, D, E, F
Notes: 2, 5, 6, 8, 10, 11, 12, 13, 14

Pomegranate Inn

49 Neal Street, 04102
(207) 772-1006; (800) 356-0408
FAX (207) 773-4426

This 1884 Italianate inn in a historical neighborhood a few minutes' walk to

---

7 No smoking; 8 Children welcome; 9 Social drinking allowed; 10 Tennis nearby; 11 Swimming nearby; 12 Golf nearby; 13 Skiing nearby; 14 May be booked through a travel agent; 15 Handicapped accessible.

midtown Portland. Eight rooms, all with private bath, some with fireplace, air conditioned, hand-painted walls, antique furnishings, contemporary art. Beautiful garden. Tea offered in the afternoon. One room handicapped accessible.

Host: Isabel Smiles
Rooms: 8 (PB) $95-165
Full Breakfast
Credit Cards: A, B, C, D
Notes: 2, 5, 7, 9, 10, 11, 12, 13, 14

West End Inn

146 Pine Street, 04102
(207) 772-1377

A very special place where the elegance and charm of yesteryear have been preserved and blended with the amenities and convenience of today. All rooms are uniquely decorated and provide new four-poster canopied beds, private baths, cable TV, and telephone access. Breakfast is cooked to order and reflects the quality of this establishment. The staff create an atmosphere of relaxation and enjoyment throughout the guests' stay and are quick to assist with travel tips or dinner reservations.

Host: John Leonard
Rooms: 6 (PB) $89-189
Full Breakfast
Credit Cards: A, B, C, D, E
Notes: 2, 3, 4, 5, 7, 8, 9, 10, 11, 12, 13, 14

ROCKLAND _____

Captain Lindsey House Inn

5 Lindsey Street, 04841
(207) 596-7950; (800) 523-2145
FAX (207) 596-2758
e-mail: kebarnes@midcoast.com
www.midcoast.com/~kebarnes/

In the heart of Rockland's historic waterfront district, this in-town inn offers Old World charm with all the modern amenities in a comfortably elegant setting. Antiques and artifacts from around the world grace the spacious guest rooms, cozy lounge, and library. Cocktails are served fireside and a

sumptuous dinner awaits guests in the Waterworks restaurant. Nearby guests will enjoy antiquing, shopping, and windjamming, not to mention stunning coastal scenery and fine Down East hospitality. Seasonal rates. Children 9 and older welcome.

Hosts: Capts. Ken and Ellen Barnes
Rooms: 9 (PB) $65-160
Continental Breakfast
Credit Cards: A, B, C
Notes: 3, 4, 5, 7, 9, 10, 11, 12, 13, 14, 15

Lakeshore Inn

184 Lakeview Drive, 04841
(207) 594-4209; FAX (207) 596-6407
e-mail: lakshore@midcoast.com
www.midcoast.com/~lakeshore

The newly renovated Lakeshore Inn, originally built in 1767, is an elegant smoke-free bed and breakfast inn overlooking the all-season beauty of Lake Chickawaukie. Unwind in front of one of the fireplaces or relax on the deck. Hosts place their emphasis on personalized attention and delicious full gourmet breakfasts. Each of the four tastefully decorated guest rooms has a queen-size bed and its own private bath as well as air conditioning and telephone. The elegant headquarters for schooner cruising, antique hunting, art and artist viewing, summer concerts, or just relaxing in the enclosed outdoor hot tub/spa. Children over 12 welcome.

Hosts: Joseph P. McCluskey and Paula E. Nicols
Room: 4 (PB) $115-125
Full Breakfast
Credit Cards: A, B
Notes: 2, 5, 7, 9, 10, 11, 12, 14

ROUND POND _____

The Briar Rose

Route 32, P.O. Box 27, 04564
(207) 529-5478; e-mail: briarose@tidewater.net

Escape to an unspoiled fishing village close to the Pemaquid Lighthouse, beaches, Monhegan Island boat service, and other recreational facilities. The 150-year-old home

---

NOTES: Credit cards accepted: A MasterCard; B Visa; C American Express; D Discover; E Diner's Club;
F Other; 2 Personal checks accepted; 3 Lunch available; 4 Dinner available; 5 Open all year; 6 Pets welcome;

faces Round Pond Harbor and offers large, airy rooms filled with comfortable antique furnishings and collectibles. Relax in the gardens, enjoy walks in the village, visit local antique shops, country stores, studios, and galleries. Older children welcome; reservations recommended.

Hosts: Anita and Fred Palsgrove
Rooms: 3 (PB) $60-95
Full Breakfast
Credit Cards: None
Notes: 2, 5, 7, 9, 11, 12

RUMFORD CENTER

The Last Resort Bed and Breakfast
P.O. Box 112, 04278-0112
(207) 364-4986

A Colonial Cape in Rumford Corner, nestled in the foothills of western Maine. Country comfort, charm, and good home cooking are a specialty. Skiing within minutes; two state parks and golf courses in the area. Fishing, hunting, hiking, and boating by the back door. Children are welcome. Plenty of wide-open space for outside activities. Picnic lunch available at additional charge. Smoking permitted in designated areas only.

Host: Joan A. Tucker
Rooms: 3 (SB) $50
Full Breakfast
Credit Cards: None
Notes: 2, 5, 8, 9, 10, 11, 12, 13, 14

SACO

Crown 'n' Anchor Inn
121 North Street, P.O. Box 228, 04072-0228
(207) 282-3829; FAX (207) 282-7495

This Greek Revival two-story house was built during 1827-1828. The ornate Victorian furnishings, double parlors with twin mirrors, and bountiful country breakfast served on bone china by candlelight in the formal dining room afford many pleasant memories for guests. All rooms at the Crown 'n' Anchor Inn are furnished with period antiques, many collectibles, and provide private facilities. The Crown 'n' Anchor Inn provides yesterday's charm, today's comforts, for tomorrow's memories.

Rooms: 6 (PB) $60-110
Full Breakfast
Credit Cards: A, B, C
Notes: 2, 5, 6, 7, 8, 9, 10, 11, 12, 13, 14

SEARSPORT

Brass Lantern Inn
81 West Main Street, 04974
(207) 548-0150; (800) 691-0150
FAX (207) 548-0304 (call first)
e-mail: brasslan@agate.net

Sunlight streams through the windows of this beautiful sea captain's home, lifting the spirits. Guests will be greeted with warm hospitality, soft music, and scented candles. Spacious rooms, all with private baths, some with views of Penobscot Bay. Full breakfast served by candlelight in the elegant dining room. Relax in one of the parlors or explore the Penobscot Marine Museum, many antique shops, or oceanfront parks. Get away from it all and relax. "The lantern will be lit to welcome you!" Children over 12 welcome. Social drinking permitted in guests' own room.

Hosts: Maggie and Dick Zieg
Rooms: 5 (PB) $65-90

Brass Lantern Inn

7 No smoking; 8 Children welcome; 9 Social drinking allowed; 10 Tennis nearby; 11 Swimming nearby; 12 Golf nearby; 13 Skiing nearby; 14 May be booked through a travel agent; 15 Handicapped accessible.

Full Breakfast
Credit Cards: A, B, D
Notes: 2, 5, 7, 10, 11, 12, 13, 14

Homeport Inn

Box 647, East Main Street, Route 1, 04974
(207) 548-2259; (800) 742-5814
FAX (978) 443-6682; e-mail: hportinn@acadia.net
www.bnbcity.com/inns/20015

Homeport, listed in the National Register of Historic Places, is a fine example of a New England sea captain's mansion on beautiful landscaped grounds, with flower gardens extending to the ocean. This elegant home is furnished with family heirlooms and antiques. There are 10 guest rooms, seven with private baths. Victorian cottages are available. A visit offers a rare opportunity to vacation or be an overnight guest in a warm, homey, hospitable atmosphere without the customary travelers' commercialism. Children over three welcome.

Hosts: Edith and George Johnson
Rooms: 10 (7 PB; 3 SB) $55-90
Cottage: $600 per week
Full Breakfast
Credit Cards: A, B, C, D
Notes: 2, 5, 9, 10, 11, 12, 14

Thurston House Bed and Breakfast Inn

8 Elm Street, P.O. Box 686, 04974
(207) 548-2213; (800) 240-2213
e-mail: thurston@acadia.net

Beautiful circa 1830 Colonial home with well and carriage house. Built as a parson-

Thurston House

age for Stephen Thurston, uncle of Winslow Homer who visited often. Now guests can visit in a casual environment. Quiet village setting is steps away from Penobscot Marine Museum, beach park on Penobscot Bay, restaurants, tavern, galleries, and antiques. Relax in one of four beautiful guest rooms, and enjoy the "forget about lunch" breakfasts.

Hosts: Carl and Beverly Eppig
Rooms: 4 (2 PB; 2 SB) $50-65
Full Breakfast
Credit Cards: A, B, C
Notes: 2, 5, 7, 8, 9, 10, 11, 12, 13, 14

Watchtide... "B&B by the Sea"

190 West Main Street, (U.S. Route 1), 04974
(207) 548-6575; (800) 698-6575 (reservations)
e-mail: watchtyd@agate.net
www.agate.net/.~watchtyd/watchtide.html

Enjoy the wonders of beautiful Penobscot Bay while delighting in a sweet and savory breakfast elegantly served on the sun porch overlooking the bay and bird sanctuary. The charming Early American home, circa 1795, has been an inn since 1917—hosting many presidential wives. Serenely wander the acreage or browse the Angels to Antiques Shoppe where guests receive a discount.

Hosts: Nancy-Linn Nellis and Jack Elliott
Rooms: 4 (2-3 PB; 0-2 SB) $55-105
Full Breakfast
Credit Cards: A, B, D
Notes: 2, 5, 7, 9, 10, 11, 12, 13, 14

SOUTH BROOKSVILLE

Buck's Harbor Inn

Steamboat Wharf Road, P.O. Box 268, 04617
(207) 326-8660; FAX (207) 326-0730

Charming country inn on Buck's Harbor, Penobscot Bay, a famed yachting and boating center. Halfway between Acadia National Park/Bar Harbor and Camden. Historic Deer Isle, Castine, and Blue Hill are just a short drive away. Seasonal restaurant (the Landing) next door. Remote, beau-

NOTES: Credit cards accepted: A MasterCard; B Visa; C American Express; D Discover; E Diner's Club; F Other; 2 Personal checks accepted; 3 Lunch available; 4 Dinner available; 5 Open all year; 6 Pets welcome;

Buck's Harbor Inn

tiful, comfortable, Brooksville is just the way Maine should be experienced.

Hosts: Peter and Ann Ebeling
Rooms: 6 (SB) $65
Full Breakfast
Credit Cards: A, B
Notes: 2, 5, 7, 8, 9, 10, 11, 12

SOUTHWEST HARBOR

Harbour Woods

P.O. Box 1214, 04679
(207) 244-5388; www.acadia.net/harbourwoods/

Across from Hinckley Great Harbor Marina is this 1800s Maine farmhouse. Enjoy the retained charm and character of days gone by, such as family keepsakes, antiques, flowers, and soft glowing oil lamps. Breakfast is a dining experience of the finest kind. Anticipate evening tea and cookies, and the guest refrigerator is always stocked with complimentary soft drinks. Enjoy guest rooms with queen-size beds, fireplaces, candy, cable TVs, telephones with free local calling, and private baths with hair dryers, luxurious towels, and a selection of rich soaps. Privately reserve the indoor spa or take a leisurely swim in the heated pool, which awaits to refresh and relax after a full day of activities in Acadia National Park.

Hosts: Joe and Christine Titka
Rooms: 3 (PB) $69-115
Cottages: 11 (PB $59-125
Credit Cards: A, B, D
Notes: 5, 7, 9, 10, 11, 12, 13

The Heron House

1 Fernald Point Road, 04679
(207) 244-0221
e-mail: heronhouseme@acadia.net

This small bed and breakfast offers three rooms, all with private baths. There is a large country kitchen where breakfast is served. A large greenhouse is off the kitchen where guests may sit and relax. There are two dogs and a cat in residence. In the bed and breakfast, guests share space with the hosts and are free to make tea or coffee anytime. The hosts encourage guests to make themselves at home.

Hosts: Bob and Sue Bonkowski
Rooms: 3 (PB) $85-95
Full Breakfast
Credit Cards: None
Notes: 2, 4, 5, 7, 8, 9, 11, 12

The Island House

Box 1006, 04679
(207) 244-5180

Relax in a gracious, restful seacoast home on the quiet side of the island. Island House favorites, such as blueberry coffeecake and egg Florentine, are served for breakfast. Charming, private loft apartment available. Acadia National Park is just a five-minute drive away. The house is across the street from the harbor with swimming, sailing, biking, and hiking nearby. Children five and older welcome. Cross-country skiing nearby.

The Island House

7 No smoking; 8 Children welcome; 9 Social drinking allowed; 10 Tennis nearby; 11 Swimming nearby; 12 Golf nearby; 13 Skiing nearby; 14 May be booked through a travel agent; 15 Handicapped accessible.

Hosts: Charles and Ann Bradford
Rooms: 5 (1 PB; 4 SB) $50-165
Full Breakfast
Credit Cards: A, B
Notes: 2, 5, 7, 9, 10, 11, 12, 13, 14

Island Watch
Bed and Breakfast

Freeman Ridge Road, P.O. Box 1359, 04679
(207) 244-7229

Overlooking the harbors and mountains of
Mount Desert Island and the village of
Southwest Harbor, Island Watch sits atop
Freeman Ridge on the quiet side of the
island. The finest panoramic views, privacy, and comfort. Birds and wildlife
abound. Walk to Acadia National Park and
the fishing village of Southwest Harbor.
Private bath and a smoke-free environment. Full breakfasts served in dining room
or glass-enclosed garden room. Children
over 10 welcome.

Host: Maxine M. Clark
Rooms: 6 (PB) $75-85
Full Breakfast
Credit Cards: F
Notes: 2, 7, 9, 10, 11, 12, 15

The Kingsleigh Inn 1904

373 Main Street, Box 1426, 04679
(207) 244-5302

Surrounded by Acadia National Park, on the
quiet side of Mount Desert Island. Hosts
offer gracious hospitality in a warm, cozy
setting. All guest rooms are tastefully deco-

The Kingsleigh Inn 1904

rated, many having beautiful harbor views,
all with private baths. For that special occasion, try the secluded three-room turret suite
with panoramic views of the harbor. A full
gourmet breakfast is served. Afternoon
refreshments are available on the porch
overlooking the harbor or by a crackling
fire. AAA three-diamond-approved.

Hosts: Ken and Cyd Collins
Rooms: 8 (PB) $55-175
Full Breakfast
Credit Cards: A, B
Notes: 2, 5, 7, 9, 10, 11, 12, 13, 14

The Lambs Ear Inn

The Lambs Ear Inn

60 Clark Point Road, P.O. Box 30, 04679
(207) 244-9828; www.acadia.net/lambsear

The inn is a stately old Maine house, built
in 1857. Comfortable and serene, with a
sparkling harbor view. Have sweet dreams
on comfortable beds with crisp, fresh
linens. Start the day with a memorable
breakfast. Spend pleasant days filled with
salt air and sunshine. Please visit this special village in the heart of Mount Desert
Island surrounded by Acadia National
Park. Open May 1 through October 30.
Children over eight welcome.

Host: Elizabeth Hoke
Rooms: 6 (PB) $85-165
Full Breakfast
Credit Cards: A, B, C, D
Notes: 2, 7, 10, 11, 12, 14

NOTES: Credit cards accepted: A MasterCard; B Visa; C American Express; D Discover; E Diner's Club;
F Other; 2 Personal checks accepted; 3 Lunch available; 4 Dinner available; 5 Open all year; 6 Pets welcome;

Lindenwood Inn

118 Clark Point Road, P.O. Box 1328, 04679
(207)244-5335

Lindenwood Inn is next to Acadia National
Park, in the small fishing village of Southwest Harbor on Mount Desert Island. In this
turn-of-the-century sea captain's home, a
blend of the old and new, both in furnishings and art, creates an interesting and
relaxing atmosphere after one enjoys the
wide variety of outdoor activities available
nearby. The swimming pool, service bar,
restaurant, and lovely sitting rooms make
this a full-service inn. Open year-round.

Host: James King
Rooms: 17 (PB) $75-225
Full Breakfast
Credit Cards: A, B, D
Notes: 2, 5, 4, 7, 10, 11, 12

Penury Hall

374 Main Street, Box 68, 04679
(207) 244-7102; FAX (207) 244-5651
e-mail: tstrong@acadia.net
www.acadia.net/penury_n

On the quiet side of Mount Desert, 14 miles
from Bar Harbor, is Penury Hall, where
guests enjoy a breakfast of eggs Benedict,
blueberry pancakes, cinnamon waffles, or
popovers. Guests are welcome to use the
canoe. The sauna is relaxing after a hard day
of hiking or cross-country skiing. Inquire
about accommodations for children.

Hosts: Toby and Gretchen
Rooms: 3 (3 S2B) $70
Full Breakfast
Credit Cards: None
Notes: 2, 5, 7, 9, 10, 11, 12, 13, 14

STOCKTON SPRINGS

The Hichborn Inn

Church Street, P.O. Box 115, 04981
(800) 346-1522

This romantic Victorian inn is listed in the
National Register of Historic Places. Quiet
area just off Route 1. Period furnishings, beds

appointed with fine linens and down comforters, sumptuous full breakfasts, which may
feature crêpes made with the inn's own raspberries. Penobscot Marine Museum, numerous antique shops, and fine dining nearby.
Advance reservations recommended.

Hosts: Nancy and Bruce Suppes
Rooms: 4 (2 PB; 2 SB) $60-95
Full Breakfast
Credit Cards: None
Notes: 2, 5, 7, 11, 14

STONINGTON

Burnt Cove Bed and Breakfast

RFD 1, Box 2905, Whitman Road, 04681
(207) 367-2392

Waterfront, quiet on picturesque cove. Relax
on large deck or in interesting cedar-paneled
living room. Views of working lobster
wharves, sail boats, many birds. Small boat
launching available. Near nature conser-
vancy trails, Stonington Harbor, Isle au
Haute mailboat, shops, and restaurants.
Three guest rooms, all with water views.
Two upstairs rooms share bath; one has
queen-size bed, one a double and twin beds.
Downstairs room with king-size bed, TV,
and private bath. Children over 12 welcome.

Hosts: Diane Berlew and Bob Williams
Rooms: 3 (1 PB; 2 SB) $60-85
Full Breakfast
Credit Cards: A, B
Notes: 2, 7, 9, 10, 11, 12

STRATTON

The Widow's Walk

171 Main Street, P.O. Box 150, 04982
(207) 246-6901; (800) 943-6995

The Steamboat Gothic architecture of this
Victorian home led to a listing in the National
Register of Historic Places. Nearby Bigelow
Mountain, the Appalachian Trail, and
Flagstaff Lake present many opportunities
for boating, fishing, and hiking. In the
winter, Sugarloaf USA, Maine's largest ski

---

7 No smoking; 8 Children welcome; 9 Social drinking allowed; 10 Tennis nearby; 11 Swimming nearby;
12 Golf nearby; 13 Skiing nearby; 14 May be booked through a travel agent; 15 Handicapped accessible.

The Widow's Walk

resort, offers both alpine and cross-country skiing, as well as dogsled rides. Dogs and cats in residence. Inquire about accommodations for children.

Hosts: Mary and Jerry Hopson
Rooms: 6 (SB) $30-48
Full Breakfast
Credit Cards: A, B
Notes: 2, 5, 7, 9, 11, 12, 13

SULLIVAN HARBOR

Islandview Inn

Route 1, HCR 32, Box 24, 04664
(207) 422-3031

Turn-of-the-century summer cottage is just off Route 1, 15 minutes from Ellsworth and

Islandview Inn

35 minutes from Bar Harbor. Choose from six guest rooms with private baths. Each room features original furniture, detailed restoration work, and picturesque views of Frenchman's Bay and Mount Desert Island. Private beach, sailing, canoe, and dinghy available. Smoking restricted.

Host: Evelyn Joost
Rooms: 6 (PB) $70-105
Full Breakfast
Credit Cards: A, B, D
Notes: 2, 9, 10, 11, 12

TENANTS HARBOR

East Wind Inn

Mechanic Street, P.O. Box 149, 04860
(800) 241-VIEW (8439); FAX (207) 372-6366
e-mail: info@eastwindinn.com

Resting at water's edge in the lovely seaside town of Tenants Harbor, the East Wind Inn offers spectacular views of the harbor and the island-studded waters beyond. Lovingly restored, the East Wind features antique-filled rooms and suites tastefully decorated to mingle warmth and casual comfort. Fine dining is available in the inn's seaside dining room or enjoy a Maine lobster roll down at the inn's dock. For a unique Maine experience, cruise aboard the Friendship sloop *Surprise* that sails daily from the inn's private dock.

Hosts: Tim Watts and Joy Taylor
Rooms: 26 (19 PB; 7 SB) $90-275
Full Breakfast
Credit Cards: A, B, C, D
Notes: 2, 3, 4, 5, 6, 8, 9, 10, 11, 12, 14

THOMASTON

The Doorway Inn

145 Main Street, 04861
(207) 354-9551; (888) 300-4907
FAX (207) 357-6587; www.doorwayinn.com

This elegant Federal home that has been carefully restored awaits guests' visit to vacation land. The inn has four rooms, all with private baths. Three rooms have queen-

NOTES: Credit cards accepted: A MasterCard; B Visa; C American Express; D Discover; E Diner's Club; F Other; 2 Personal checks accepted; 3 Lunch available; 4 Dinner available; 5 Open all year; 6 Pets welcome;

size beds and the fourth has twin-size beds. Relax in the personal spa or sit by a cozy fire in the music room. On a hot summer day enjoy a glass of iced tea on the shady side porch. Thomaston is in mid-coast Maine, just a few minutes south of Rockland. Close to lighthouses, daysailing, hiking, antiquing, golf, fabulous dining, and museums. Free limo service provided within the area. Smoking not permitted on premises.

Hosts: Bruce and Carol Sue Greenleaf
Rooms: 4 (PB) $125-150
Full Breakfast
Credit Cards: A, B
Notes: 2, 5, 7, 8, 9, 10, 11, 12, 13

Serenity on the Oyster Bed and Breakfast

Rural Route 1, Box 5915, 04861
(207) 354-2063; (888) SERENE 1
www.midcoast.com/~serene1

Serenity sits on a bank overlooking the Oyster River. Five acres of wooded land with a quarter-acre pond in front. Four bedrooms, two large and two regular. A full-style breakfast served. Children over 12 welcome. Open year-round.

Hosts: Chuck and Terry Fleming
Rooms: 4 (1 PB; 3 SB) $65-85
Full Breakfast
Credit Cards: A, B
Notes: 2, 5, 7, 9, 11, 12, 13, 14

VINALHAVEN

Fox Island Inn

Carver Street, P.O. Box 451, 04863
(207) 863-2122; e-mail: gailrei@juno.com

Discover the unspoiled coastal Maine island of Vinalhaven. This comfortable, affordable bed and breakfast is in the quaint fishing village nestled around picturesque Carver's Harbor. Enjoy swimming in the abandoned granite quarries and exploring seaside nature preserves by foot or bicycle. State-operated car ferry from Rockland runs six times daily. Island activities include flea markets, church suppers, and wonderful local restaurants.

Host: Gail Reinertsen
Rooms: 6 (SB) $45-75
Continental Breakfast
Credit Cards: None
Notes: 2, 7, 9, 11

WALDOBORO

The Roaring Lion

995 East Main Street, 04572
(207) 832-4038

A 1905 Victorian home with tin ceilings; elegant woodwork throughout. The Roaring Lion accommodates special diets and serves miso soup, sourdough bread, homemade jams and jellies. Hosts are well traveled and lived for two years in West Africa. Their interests include books, gardening, art, and cooking. Gallery and gift shop on premises.

Hosts: Bill and Robin Branigan
Rooms: 4 (1 PB; 3 SB) $64.20-74.90
Full Breakfast
Credit Cards: None
Notes: 2, 5, 7, 8, 10, 11, 12, 13, 14

WATERFORD

The Parsonage House Bed and Breakfast

Rice Road, P.O. Box 116, 04088
(207) 583-4115

The Parsonage House, built in 1870 for the Waterford Church, overlooks Waterford

The Parsonage House

---

7 No smoking; 8 Children welcome; 9 Social drinking allowed; 10 Tennis nearby; 11 Swimming nearby; 12 Golf nearby; 13 Skiing nearby; 14 May be booked through a travel agent; 15 Handicapped accessible.

village, Keoka Lake, and Mount Tirem. In a four-season area that provides many opportunities for outdoor enthusiasts, the Parsonage is a haven of peace and quiet. Double guest rooms or private suite available. A full breakfast is served on the screened porch or in the large farm kitchen beside a glowing wood stove.

Hosts: Joseph and Gail St. Hilaire
Rooms: 3 (1 PB; 2 SB) $70-85
Full Breakfast
Credit Cards: None
Notes: 2, 3, 5, 7, 8, 11, 12, 13

The Waterford Inne

Chadbourne Road, Box 149, 04088
(207) 583-4037

Escape to country quiet in an inn offering the elegance of a fine country home. Nine uniquely decorated guest rooms and carefully furnished common rooms provide a fine setting for four-star dining in historic Waterford. Near mountains and coastline; water and woodland activities nearby. Closed April. Pets permitted with fee.

Host: Barbara Vanderzanden
Rooms: 9 (7 PB; 2 SB) $75-100
Full Breakfast
Credit Cards: C
Notes: 2, 4, 6, 8, 9, 10, 11, 12, 13

WELLS

The Victorian House Inn Bed and Breakfast

1616 Post Road, P.O. Box 1644, 04090
(207) 646-5355

Step back in time to enjoy the comfort and charm of this late-19th century southern Maine home. The inn offers three well-appointed rooms, each with a double bed and private bath. The parlor and first-floor guest room have a fireplace. Antiques, handmade crafts, memorablia of the past, and the large wraparound porch with white wicker furniture are all available for the

The Victorian House Inn

guests' enjoyment. Turndown service. Afternoon refreshments. Downhill skiing one and one-half hours away.

Hosts: Kathy and Jim Wright
Rooms: 3 (PB) $75-100
Full Breakfast
Credit Cards: A, B
Notes: 2, 5, 7, 10, 11, 12, 13

WINTER HARBOR

Main Stay Inn and Cottages

P.O. Box 459, 04693
(207) 963-5561

Restored Victorian home overlooks Henry's Cove. Housekeeping units with fireplaces. Walk to restaurants and post office. A quiet village within a mile of Acadia. Guests may enjoy hiking, biking, and local activities.

Hosts: Pearl and Roger Barto
Rooms: 3 plus 2 units (PB) $45
Credit Cards: A, B
Notes: 2, 5, 7, 8, 11, 12

WISCASSET

The Squire Tarbox Inn

1181 Main Road, Westport Island, 04578
(207) 882-7693; FAX (207) 882-7107
e-mail: squire@wiscasset.net
www.squiretarboxinn.com

Clean, casual, comfortable, and all country, this is a historic Colonial farmhouse on a

The Squire Tarbox Inn

back road near midcoast Maine harbors, beaches, antique shops, museums, and lobster shacks. Part of a working farm with a purebred goat dairy, the inn offers a balance of history, quiet country, good food, and relaxation. Delicious fresh goat cheese served by the fire before dinner. Known primarily for rural privacy and five-course dinners. Children over 14 welcome.

Hosts: Karen and Bill Mitman
Rooms: 11 (PB) $85-166
Full Breakfast
Credit Cards: A, B, C, D
Notes: 2, 4, 7, 9, 14

YORK

The Cape Neddick House

1300 Route 1, P.O. Box 70, Cape Neddick, 03902
(207) 363-2500

In the historic coastal community of York, this 1800s Victorian farmhouse is central to beaches, boutiques, antique shops, wildlife sanctuaries, boat cruises, factory outlets, and historical and cultural opportunities. Sleeping on antique high-back beds, snuggled under handmade quilts, guests are assured of pleasant dreams. No alarm clock needed, as the fragrant smells of cinnamon

popovers, apple almond tortes, or ham and apple biscuits drift by, gently waking guests. Reason enough to return time and again. All private baths. Two-room suite with fireplace available. Inquire about availability of dinner. Smoking restricted. Cross-country skiing nearby.

Hosts: John and Dianne Goodwin
Rooms: 5 (PB) $80-120
Full Breakfast
Credit Cards: None
Notes: 2, 5, 9, 10, 11, 12, 13

YORK BEACH

Homestead Inn Bed and Breakfast

5 Long Beach Avenue (Route 1A), 03910
(207) 363-8952; FAX (207) 363-8952

A converted 1905 summer boarding house, the inn is at Short Sands Beach. Individually decorated rooms have ocean views; each room has its own sink. Walk to beach, enjoy sunsets, or visit local Nubble Lighthouse. Historic landmarks; fine restaurants. Relax, be pampered, and let the seashore entertain. Continental plus breakfast served outside with an ocean view.

7 No smoking; 8 Children welcome; 9 Social drinking allowed; 10 Tennis nearby; 11 Swimming nearby; 12 Golf nearby; 13 Skiing nearby; 14 May be booked through a travel agent; 15 Handicapped accessible.

Hosts: Dan and Danielle Duffy
Rooms: 4 (S2B) $55-65
Continental Breakfast
Credit Cards: None
Notes: 2, 7, 9, 10, 11, 12

Hosts: Wes and Kathie Cook
Rooms: 5 (3 PB; 2 SB) $60-95
Full Breakfast
Credit Cards: None
Notes: 2, 5, 7, 8, 9, 11, 12

Red Shutters

7 Cross Street, P.O. Box 1281, 03910-1281
(207) 363-6292; (800) 890-9766
www.yorkme.org/inns/redshutters.html

Red Shutters, a cozy bed and breakfast for nonsmokers, is in a quiet residential neighborhood, a five-minute walk to ocean beach, shops, and restaurants. Three comfortably furnished guest rooms offer a refreshing night's rest. Homemade breakfast includes hot-from-the-oven muffins, fresh fruit, granola, assorted juices, and hot beverages. Special dietary needs are easily accommodated. Short drive to historic sites, shopping, antiques, scenic villages, and rocky coastline. Open mid-June through Labor Day.

Hosts: Gil and Evelyn Billings
Rooms: 3 (1 PB; 2 SB) $60-70
Continental Breakfast
Credit Cards: A, B
Notes: 2, 7, 9, 11

Bell Buoy Bed and Breakfast

570 York Street, 03911
(207) 363-7264

At the Bell Buoy, there are no strangers, only friends who have not met. Open year-round and minutes from US 95, Route 1, and the Kittery outlet malls. Only a short walk to sandy beaches, or guests may relax on the large porch or in the guests-only living room with fireplace. A full homemade breakfast will be served in the dining room or on the porch, as desired.

Dockside Guest Quarters

Harris Island Road, P.O. Box 205, York, 03909
(207) 363-2868; www.docksidegq.com

The Dockside Guest Quarters is a small resort on a private peninsula in York Harbor. Panorama of ocean and harbor activities. Spacious grounds with privacy and relaxing atmosphere. Beaches, outlet shopping, and numerous scenic walks nearby. Accommodations are in a seacoast inn and multiunit cottages. Full service marina, wedding facilities, and restaurant on-site. Packages and off-season rates are available. AAA-rated three diamonds.

Hosts: The Lusty Family
Rooms: 21 (19 PB; 2 SB) $60-145
Continental Breakfast
Credit Cards: A, B, D
Notes: 2, 3, 4, 5, 7, 8, 9, 10, 11, 12, 14, 15

Dockside Guest Quarters

Inn at Harmon Park

415 York Street, P.O. Box 495, 03911
(207) 363-2031; FAX (207) 351-2948
www.yorkme.org/inns/harmonpark.html

In the heart of York Harbor, within walking distance of the harbor beach and historic York village, the Inn greets its guests in an atmosphere of fresh flowers, wicker furniture, fireplaces, and helpful suggestions for dining, walking, and touring. The late-19th-century Victorian house, which has been the Antal family home for more than 20 years, offers four appealing rooms and one suite, all with private baths, and each intriguingly different in appointment.

Host: Sue Antal
Rooms: 5 (PB) $79-109
Full Breakfast
Credit Cards: None
Notes: 2, 5, 7, 9, 10, 11, 12, 14

York Harbor Inn

Route 1A, P.O.Box 573, 03911
(207) 363-5119; (800) 343-3869
www.yorkharborinn.com

Coastal country inn overlooks beautiful York Harbor in an exclusive residential neighborhood. There are 33 air-conditioned rooms with antiques, ocean views, and seven working fireplaces; some rooms have Jacuzzi spas and ocean-view decks. Fine dining year-round. An English pub on the premises with entertainment. The beach is within walking distance; boating, fishing, antique shops are all nearby. Banquet and meeting facilities available.

Hosts: Joe, Jean, Garry, and Nancy Dominguez
Rooms: 33 (PB) $89-199
Continental Breakfast
Credit Cards: A, B, C, E, F
Notes: 2, 3, 4, 5, 7, 8, 9, 11, 12, 14

7 No smoking; 8 Children welcome; 9 Social drinking allowed; 10 Tennis nearby; 11 Swimming nearby; 12 Golf nearby; 13 Skiing nearby; 14 May be booked through a travel agent; 15 Handicapped accessible.

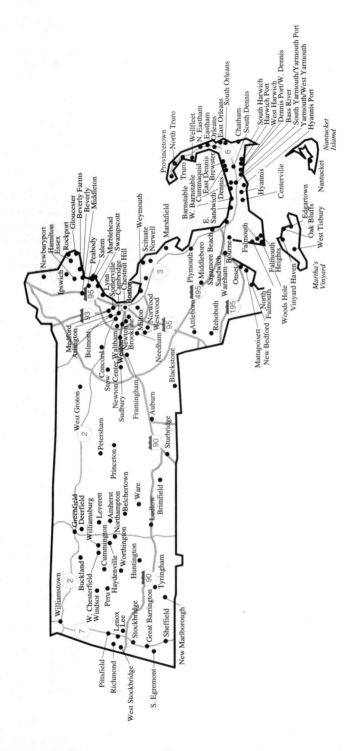

Massachusetts

Massachusetts

AMHERST

Allen House Victorian Bed and Breakfast Inn

599 Main Street, 01002
(413) 253-5000; www.allenhouse.com

Authentic 1886 Queen Anne-style Victorian, on three acres. Spacious bed chambers with telephones, central air conditioning. Antiques, art, and wall decor historically and accurate. Within walking distance of Emily Dickinson House. Amherst College, University of Massachusetts, galleries, museums, theaters, shops, and restaurants nearby. Free busing throughout five-college area. Formal full breakfast served. Afternoon and evening tea and refreshments. Winner of 1991 Historic Commission Award. Rated excellent by ABBA. AAA three-diamond-rated. *Boston* magazine's "Best Victorian in New England."

Hosts: Alan and Ann Zieminski
Rooms: 7 (PB) $55-135
Full Breakfast

Allen House

Credit Cards: A, B, C, D, E
Notes: 2, 5, 9, 10, 11, 12, 13

ARLINGTON

Bed and Breakfast Reservations North Shore, Greater Boston, Cape Cod

P.O. Box 600035, Greater Boston Branch,
  Newtonville, 02160-0001
(617) 964-1606; (800) 832-2632
FAX (617) 332-8572; e-mail: info@bbreserve.com
www.bbreserve.com

120. Arlington Victorian Manor. Elegance, luxury, romance, and comfort await guests in this glorious accommodation between Cambridge and Lexington. Seven miles from Boston, two from Harvard Square, with excellent public transportation nearby. Restored 1887 Queen Anne-style home retains much of its original architecture and superb detail: magnificent staircase, grand living room with hand-carved cherry mantel, solarium, dining room. Guest rooms have private baths, designer bed linens, ceiling fans. Continental plus breakfast featuring home-baked goods. Afternoon tea in solarium. Nonsmoking. Open year-round. $155-225.

ATTLEBORO

The Colonel Blackinton Inn

203 North Main Street, 02703
(508) 222-6022

The Colonel Blackinton Inn is a professionally operated country inn dedicated to

NOTES: Credit cards accepted: A MasterCard; B Visa; C American Express; D Discover; E Diner's Club; F Other; 2 Personal checks accepted; 3 Lunch available; 4 Dinner available; 5 Open all year; 6 Pets welcome; 7 No smoking; 8 Children welcome; 9 Social drinking allowed; 10 Tennis nearby; 11 Swimming nearby; 12 Golf nearby; 13 Skiing nearby; 14 May be booked through a travel agent; 15 Handicapped accessible.

serving guests in a friendly, relaxed atmosphere. Among the 12 sleeping rooms is the ideal accommodation for the business executive, the touring visitor, or those just visiting friends, relatives, or the area. The public areas include two small dining rooms, a tavern, a lovely sitting room, and a patio. The Carriage House across the patio is a beautiful function room.

Host: Joe Supinski
Rooms: 12 (PB) $75-125
Full Breakfast
Credit Cards: A, B, C, D, E
Notes: 2, 3, 4, 5, 7, 8, 9, 12, 14

AUBURN

Captain Samuel Eddy House

609 Oxford Street South, 01501
(508) 832-7282

The center-chimney Colonial home, circa 1765, has been restored and handsomely decorated in period style by the owners. In addition to the large keeping room where guests gather for breakfast, there are three common areas for guests to relax in. Each parlor has a fireplace, and the plant-filled sunroom allows guests to enjoy the country setting with views of Eddy Pond, the surrounding woods, and gardens. Children over five are welcome.

Hosts: Diedre and Michael Meddaugh
Rooms: 3 (PB) $70-90
Full Breakfast
Credit Cards: None
Notes: 2, 5, 7, 9, 12, 13, 14

BARNSTABLE (CAPE COD)

Ashley Manor

3660 Old Kings Highway, Box 856, 02630
(508) 888-2246; FAX (508) 362-9927
e-mail: ashleymn@capecod.net

Ashley Manor is a very special place, a gracious 1699 mansion on a two-acre estate in Cape Cod's historic district. Romantic rooms and suites feature private

Ashley Manor

baths and fireplaces. Elegant public rooms with antiques and oriental rugs. Delicious full breakfast in formal dining room or on terrace overlooking parklike grounds and new tennis court. Walk to the beach and village. Prices subject to change. Children over 12 welcome.

Host: Donald Bain
Rooms: 6 (PB) $120-180
Full Breakfast
Credit Cards: A, B, D, F
Notes: 2, 5, 7, 9, 10, 11, 12, 14

Bed and Breakfast Associates Bay Colony, Ltd.

P.O. Box 57166, Babson Park, Boston, 02157-0166
(781) 449-5302; (800) 347-5088
FAX (781) 449-5958; e-mail: info@bnbboston.com
www.bnbboston.com

CC221. A 200-year-old tavern on historic Old King's Highway on the enchanting north shore of Cape Cod. Here guests are treated to a true colonial atmosphere just one mile from a harbor beach and a 10-minute ride to the sandy beaches and ferry docks in Hyannis. Five guest rooms, all with queen-size or double beds, antique furnishings, and private baths. Lower rates off-season. $85-120.

CC222. This secluded classic 19th-century inn on the unspoiled north side of the mid-cape is nestled amid majestic trees and exquisite flower and herb gardens. Here every guest is treated to a generous home-made breakfast along with special ameni-

NOTES: Credit cards accepted: A MasterCard; B Visa; C American Express; D Discover; E Diner's Club; F Other; 2 Personal checks accepted; 3 Lunch available; 4 Dinner available; 5 Open all year; 6 Pets welcome;

ties, including daily turndown service. Six guest rooms, with private baths, queen-size, double, or twin beds. Lower rates off-season. $115-185.

Bed and Breakfast Cape Cod

P.O. Box 1312, Orleans, 02653
(508) 255-3824; (800) 541-6226
FAX (508) 240-0599
e-mail: bedandb@capecod.net
www.bandbcapecod.com

4. Built in 1754, it was operated as a tavern for many years. Wide-board floors and lovely antiques add to the charm of bedrooms with fireplaces, private baths, and air conditioning. Listed in the National Register of Historic Places. Walk to the shops in the village or the harbor from which the whale-watching ships depart. Four miles to Hyannis and ferry to Nantucket. Air conditioned. Continental breakfast. No smoking. Children over 14 welcome. $85-125.

Bed and Breakfast Reservations North Shore, Greater Boston, Cape Cod

P.O. Box 600035, Greater Boston Branch, Newtonville, 02160-0001
(617) 964-1606; (800) 832-2632
FAX (617) 332-8572; e-mail: info@bbreserve.com
www.bbreserve.com

62. Old Kings Highway Tavern. An original tavern built in 1754. This historic landmark invites guests to take a step back in history. Five guest rooms, canopied four-poster beds, all with private baths, some with working fireplaces. Relax in the parlor with a complimentary sherry next to a cozy fireplace. Enjoy lovely grounds and gardens. Walk to quaint Barnstable Village with its own picturesque harbor and beach. Whale watching, charter fishing, and great restaurants. Boats to Martha's Vineyard and Nantucket 10 minutes away. Elegantly served Continental breakfast. No smoking. Twenty dollars for third person in room. $85-125.

112. Barnstable Colonial Guest House. Federal Colonial house dates back to 1800. Walk through beautiful gardens and spacious grounds. Stroll along a rambling brook or take a morning walk to the ocean's edge. Relax on the porch and terrace. Two large sitting rooms with fireplaces. Short walk to village center with great restaurants and picturesque beach nearby. Guest kitchen for light use. Full gourmet breakfast. Three guest rooms, one with working fireplace, private baths. Thirty-five dollars for each additional person. No smoking. $105-125.

Beechwood

Beechwood

2839 Main Street, 02630
(508) 362-6618; (800) 609-6618
FAX (508) 362-0298
www.virtualcapecod.com/market/beechwood

Experience the romance of this romantic Victorian inn, with six large guest rooms, some with fireplaces or water views. All rooms are furnished with beautiful period antiques and have private baths. Gourmet breakfasts are served in the paneled dining room, and afternoon tea by the parlor fireplace in winter. In summer, iced tea and lemonade are served on the veranda that overlooks one and one-half acres of beautifully landscaped lawns and gardens. *Cape Cod Life* magazine rated Beechwood as "Best Mid-Cape Bed and Breakfast."

Hosts: Debbie and Ken Traugot
Rooms: 6 (PB) $90-160
Full Breakfast
Credit Cards: A, B, C, D
Notes: 2, 5, 7, 9, 10, 11, 12, 14

7 No smoking; 8 Children welcome; 9 Social drinking allowed; 10 Tennis nearby; 11 Swimming nearby; 12 Golf nearby; 13 Skiing nearby; 14 May be booked through a travel agent; 15 Handicapped accessible.

Crocker Tavern
Bed and Breakfast

3095 Main Street (Historic Route 6A), 02630
(508) 362-5115; (800) 773-5359
FAX (508) 362-5562
e-mail: crocktav@capecod.net
www.capecod.net/crockertavernbnb

The Crocker Tavern is a wonderfully restored 1750s Colonial with a lot of history, charm, and romance. The five beautifully decorated guest rooms have canopied beds, private baths, antiques, sitting areas, and air conditioning; and some have working fireplaces. Complimentary wine and sherry are served in the parlor, and breakfast is served by candlelight with soft music. The Tavern is a short walk to village restaurants and the water and is midcape, which is ideal for exploring all the cape and islands.

Hosts: Sue and Jeff Carlson
Rooms: 5 (PB) $85-130
Continental Breakfast
Credit Cards: A, B
Notes: 2, 5, 7, 9, 11, 12, 14

Crocker Tavern

BASS RIVER (CAPE COD) _____

The Anchorage

122 South Shore Drive, 02664
(508) 398-8265
e-mail: anchbb@masscot.com

The Anchorage is an ideal place to spend a holiday if people enjoy Cape Cod's broad sandy beaches and warm water. The ocean

The Anchorage

is just a few steps away. There are theaters, restaurants, hiking, fishing, boating, and all activities to complete your holiday. "Join us for a quiet, relaxing visit where the gentle sea breezes help you to leave all your cares behind."

Host: Ruth T. Masciarotte
Rooms: 3 (PB) $35-60
Continental Breakfast
Credit Cards: None
Notes: 2, 5, 9, 10, 11,12

BELCHERTOWN _____

Ingate Farms
Bed and Breakfast

60 Lamson Avenue @ South Amherst/Belchertown
  Line, 01007
(413) 253-0440 (phone/FAX)

Natural country environment amid 400 acres in Holyoke Mountain Range, yet within minutes to the culture and charms of the "Five Colleges Region" in the western Massachusetts Pioneer Valley. Ingate Farms—formerly a bobbin factory, tavern, and then a home—is decorated in Early American antiques and provides comfort, charm, and care via experienced hosts. Swim and ride on the property. Hike the horse trails, fish or bird watch, or boat on the famous Quabbin Reservoir nearby. Excellent restaurants abound. Extended stay, multiple room, and corporate discounts available. Continental plus breakfast served. Children 12 and older welcome.

Hosts: Virginia Kier and Bill McCormick
Rooms: 5 (3 PB; 2 SB) $55-85

NOTES: Credit cards accepted: A MasterCard; B Visa; C American Express; D Discover; E Diner's Club; F Other; 2 Personal checks accepted; 3 Lunch available; 4 Dinner available; 5 Open all year; 6 Pets welcome;

Continental Breakfast
Credit Cards: A, B, C
Notes: 2, 5, 7, 9, 10, 11, 12, 13, 14

BELMONT

Bed and Breakfast Associates Bay Colony, Ltd.

P.O. Box 57166, Babson Park, Boston, 02157-0166
(781) 449-5302; (800) 347-5088
FAX (781) 449-5958; e-mail: info@bnbboston.com
www.bnbboston.com

IN800. A large, attractive Georgian Colonial in a prestigious neighborhood in this fine suburban community. The hostess offers two guest rooms: one is in a private area with a twin bed and a bath en suite; the other has a double bed and is in the main house with private bath in the hall. Driveway parking. $70-85.

BEVERLY

Bed and Breakfast Reservations North Shore, Greater Boston, Cape Cod

P.O. Box 600035, Greater Boston Branch,
  Newtonville, 02160-0001
(617) 964-1606; (800) 832-2632
FAX (617) 332-8572; e-mail: info@bbreserve.com
www.bbreserve.com

13. A beautifully decorated, cozy Colonial-style home, offering three attractive guest rooms, a queen-size room with private hall bath on first floor, and two second-floor rooms and which can sleep up to four each, that share a bath. In hot weather, common areas have air conditioning. Guest rooms have fans. Guests enjoy use of kitchen facilities for fixing light snacks, color TV in living room, enclosed sun porch, telephone, and off-street parking. Continental breakfast provided each morning. Complimentary train pickup at Beverly Depot. Older children welcome. No smoking. Whole house may be rented to families/small group (up to nine). $75-100.

Bunny's Bed and Breakfast

17 Kernwood Heights, 01915
(978) 922-2392

This Dutch Colonial inn is on a scenic route leading along the state's northeastern coast. The Continental plus breakfast in the dining room feature made-from-scratch breads, muffins, and coffeecakes. Every effort is made to meet special dietary needs if notified in advance. Twenty miles north of Boston and one-half mile from Salem. Close to Gordon College, Endicott College, and Mintserrat College of Art.

Hosts: Bunny and Joe Stacey
Rooms: 3 (1 PB; 2 SB) $65-90
Continental Breakfast
Credit Cards: None
Notes: 2, 5, 7, 9, 11, 14

BEVERLY FARMS

Bed and Breakfast Reservations North Shore, Greater Boston, Cape Cod

P.O. Box 600035, Greater Boston Branch,
  Newtonville, 02160-0001
(617) 964-1606; (800) 832-2632
FAX (617) 332-8572; e-mail: info@bbreserve.com
www.bbreserve.com

71. The Jon Larcum House. Enjoy the warmth and charm of an authentic antique Colonial, dating back to 1839. Three guest rooms, tastefully decorated with handmade quilts and oriental rugs with private and shared bath. Downstairs dining room and common room with TV available for guest use. Continental plus breakfast. Weather permitting, guests are invited to use the outside deck or backyard. This accommodation is within walking distance to the town center, commuter train to Boston, and a lovely sandy oceanside beach. Children over 12 welcome. Resident pets. No smoking. $85-110.

---

7 No smoking; 8 Children welcome; 9 Social drinking allowed; 10 Tennis nearby; 11 Swimming nearby; 12 Golf nearby; 13 Skiing nearby; 14 May be booked through a travel agent; 15 Handicapped accessible.

BLACKSTONE

The Fieldstone Victorian

40 Edgewater Drive, 01504
(508) 883-4647

The 1905 Victorian waterfront home on a landscaped acre is minutes Providence, Rhode Island, and Boston and Worcester, Massachusetts. Antiques enhance the intricately carved woodwork in the common rooms and fireplaced dining room. The two guest rooms have private baths, queen-size beds, water views, cable TV, and homemade cookies. Candlelight gourmet breakfasts are served on antique family china, and include homemade breads, jams, and fruit syrups. Near many genealogical resources, museums, and Blackstone River canoe launches.

Hosts: Joe and Donna Emidy
Rooms: 2 (PB) $75
Full Breakfast
Credit Cards: A, B
Notes: 2, 5, 7, 8, 9, 11, 12

The Fieldstone Victorian

Morin's Victorian Hideaway Bed and Breakfast

48 Mendon Street, 01504
(508) 883-7045

A unique bed and breakfast, nestled on three and one-half acres, overlooking the scenic Blackstone River. The hosts provide a warm and cozy atmosphere for their guests with a fully stocked kitchen, where guests can help themselves to snacks or libations at any

Morin's Victorian Hideaway

time. Sleeping accommodations for the weary traveler include three spacious and charming rooms. Billiard room, exercise room, and in-ground pool and yard games are available. Walking distance to restaurants, shops, stores, and churches.

Hosts: Chip and Lynn Morin
Rooms: 3 (1 PB; 2 SB) $65-75
Continental Breakfast
Credit Cards: None
Notes: 2, 5, 7, 8, 9, 10, 11, 12, 14

BOSTON

Abercrombie's Farrington Inn

23 Farrington Avenue, 02134
(617) 787-1860; (800) 767-5337 (U.S. and
    Canada); 0-800-896-040 (U.K.)
FAX (617) 783-3869
e-mail: info@farringtoninn.com
www.farringtoninn.com

Small European-style inn catering to the budget-minded traveler. Features standard rooms, rooms with kitchenettes, and some lovely suites. Price includes unlimited local telephone service, parking, and breakfast. Near public transportation and points of interest, the Farrington is an economical choice in one of the most expensive cities in the world.

Hosts: Christine and Bob Terwilliger
Rooms: 36 (12 PB; 24 SB) $50-105
Continental Breakfast
Credit Cards: A, B, C
Notes: 8

NOTES: Credit cards accepted: A MasterCard; B Visa; C American Express; D Discover; E Diner's Club; F Other; 2 Personal checks accepted; 3 Lunch available; 4 Dinner available; 5 Open all year; 6 Pets welcome;

A Bed & Breakfast Agency of Boston and Boston Harbor Bed and Breakfast

47 Commercial Wharf, 02110
(617) 720-3540; (800) 248-9262
0 800 89 5128 (free phone from U.K.)
FAX (617) 523-5761; e-mail:bnbboston@erols.com
www.boston-bnbagency.com

Downtown Boston's largest selection of guest rooms in historic bed and breakfast homes including Federal and Victorian townhouses and beautifully restored 1840s waterfront lofts. Also a lovely selection of furnished private studio, or one- and two-bedroom condominiums that are great for families. Exclusive locations include waterfront, Faneuil Hall and Quincy Market, North End, Back Bay, Beacon Hill, Copley Square, Cambridge, Cape Cod, and the Islands. Yachts and houseboats are also available. Credit cards and personal checks accepted. Children welcome. No smoking. May be booked through a travel agent. $65-130.

Bed and Breakfast Associates Bay Colony, Ltd.

P.O. Box 57166, Babson Park, Boston, 02157-0166
(781) 449-5302; (800) 347-5088
FAX (781) 449-5958; e-mail: info@bnbboston.com
www.bnbboston.com

M104. Those seeking the charm of an old European hotel will enjoy staying in this prestigious private club with its elegant drawing room and small, gracious dining room. Convenient to Newbury Street shops, historic sites, and the Hynes Convention Center. Four guest rooms, two with private baths. Continental breakfast served. Elevator service. Children are welcome. $117-127.

M131. In Boston's prestigious Beacon Hill and adjacent to the historic Massachusetts State House, this inn is a loving restoration of two attached 1830s townhouses. The fine period furnishings include four-poster and canopied beds, decorative fireplaces, and reproduction desks. New private baths throughout, and guests are always welcome to use the kitchen, the dining room, and the parlors. $112-137.

M136. This handsome 46-room mansion at the foot of Beacon Hill is within walking distance of many Boston attractions. Modern amenities have been incorporated into this careful restoration, and rooms include telephone lines, private baths, color TVs, individual climate controls, and some kitchenettes. Elevator and handicapped access are available. The gracious double parlor with working fireplace and period furnishings serves as the lobby, and reproduction furnishings create a warm, elegant atmosphere. Continental breakfast. Laundry and valet. $90-155.

M137. Boston has only one Newbury Street, and it is the street for art galleries, designer clothing boutiques, and fine window shopping. This 32-room Newbury Street Inn puts all of this at the doorstep. Opened in 1991, this property is restored and offers warm, comfortable rooms with 19th-century reproductions. Breakfast is served on the front patio when the weather permits. Selectively priced rooms available on all four floors. Reserved parking available in the rear for $10 per day. Two blocks to Copley Square and Hynes Convention Center. $100-155.

M138. In Copley Square, this 64-room inn offers modern business amenities, a gracious lobby, and the best location in the city. All rooms have private bath, queen-size or twin beds, TV, telephone, and individual climate control. Discount on-site parking. $130-165.

M140. A floating bed and breakfast docked at Lewis Wharf on the Boston waterfront adjacent to Quincy Market and Faneuil

7 No smoking; 8 Children welcome; 9 Social drinking allowed; 10 Tennis nearby; 11 Swimming nearby; 12 Golf nearby; 13 Skiing nearby; 14 May be booked through a travel agent; 15 Handicapped accessible.

Bed and Breakfast Associates Bay Colony, Ltd. (continued)

Hall. Guests have the pleasure of complete privacy on this 40-foot Chris Craft with aft bedroom, small bath with shower, private deck, main salon with sofa bed and galley. Catered dinners available. Yacht stays in port. $140-160.

M142. Stay in a true Back Bay mansion! This opulent home defines luxury and in-town convenience. Just two blocks from the renowned shops and cafés of Newbury Street, this bed and breakfast features two lavish guest rooms and a breakfast buffet station. Queen-size canopied beds. In-hall baths are each shared with one tenant. $150-175.

M144. This 1940s New York-style apartment building offers one guest room with queen-size bed and private bath for double occupancy. Overlooks Boston's Public Garden. This immaculate, attractive apartment features both great location and grand views. $105-125.

M152. An 1864 Victorian brownstone in Boston's South End. The host and hostess are long-time residents of their neighborhood and are active in the preservation of the delightful enclosed private park behind their home. The guest room overlooks the park and affords a delightful garden view. Private attached bath with Victorian tub. $80-95.

M153. Across from the Boston Public Garden, near the *Cheers* bar and the Ritz Carlton Hotel, this private one-bedroom apartment provides an urban sanctuary in a quiet and highly desirable building. Stylish

decor, private brick terrace, full kitchen, double bed plus sofa bed in living room. $155-185.

M158. Just completed, this one bedroom apartment offers charm and style in a historic Beacon Hill townhouse. Entrance through a private courtyard garden. New queen-size bed, full kitchen, living room with beamed ceiling and queen-size sleeper sofa, pine floors, and fireplace. $150-200.

M159. Splendid accommodations in this wonderful Beacon Hill townhouse close to all the tourist attractions. Private guest accommodations on third and fourth floors. Each with queen-size beds and private baths. Third floor has separate parlor, while the fourth floor offers a massive fireplace and kitchenette. Romantic and wonderful. $150-200.

M160. The delightful hostess has an eye for detail and guests will marvel at her exquisite taste. Her immaculate guest room has a queen-size bed and private bath. Lots of stairs here—the condo occupies the third to fifth floors in a classic Victorian townhouse on Beacon Hill. Enjoy a great view of the city from the private roof deck. $135-160.

M224. This South End Victorian has been impeccably restored and offers two floors of guest space, including two guest rooms, two full baths, a sitting room, and kitchen, with private entrance and parking at additional $10. Can be rented to one party or two. Monthly rates available. Can rent entire apartment. $90-135.

M228. A fabulous private suite with queen-size bed, new kitchenette, private bath, designer built-ins, TV, telephone, working fireplace, and garden access. This deluxe accommodation is on the garden level of an

NOTES: Credit cards accepted: A MasterCard; B Visa; C American Express; D Discover; E Diner's Club; F Other; 2 Personal checks accepted; 3 Lunch available; 4 Dinner available; 5 Open all year; 6 Pets welcome;

elegant Back Bay mansion near the famed Newbury Street shops and cafés, and close to Copley Square. Sleeper sofa also available. Private parking for an additional $10. $120-155.

M300. Appleton is one of Boston's prettiest residential streets, and it is just two blocks from the Back Bay station in historic Copley Square. The hostess is delighted to offer two beautifully decorated and quiet guest rooms with queen-size beds, new private baths, TV, and telephone. $120-150.

M303. This bed and breakfast host couple offer a wealth of knowledge about Boston along with their kind attention to guest needs. Each of the two guest rooms reflects splendid taste and attention to detail. Near Copley Square, their brownstone townhouse is convenient to Boston's tourist and convention centers. $87-97.

M306. In a 19th-century townhouse three blocks from Copley Square, guests enjoy the privacy and convenience of this newly decorated studio apartment with a Murphy double bed, futon couch, cooking nook, and private bath. $92-102.

M309. Enjoy privacy in this newly renovated Victorian townhouse on a lovely South End street, three blocks from the Boston Common. This attractive third-floor room offers private bath en suite, color TV, and twin beds. Kitchenette with breakfast foods provided. $75-80.

M323. This well-kept and appealing 1869 brick townhouse, near the Hynes Convention Center, features two nicely decorated second-floor guest rooms; one includes a queen-size bed, "decorative" fireplace, delightful antiques, and a bay window breakfast spot. Shared bath. Parking is available on request at $10 per day. $89-99.

M356. For extended stays, ask about this one-bedroom apartment with a new eat-in kitchenette, queen-size bed, living room with sleeper-sofa, color TV, and private bath in an 1857 townhouse on a quiet street in the South End. Clean and well maintained. Inquire about monthly rates.

M362. This private-entry suite offers a comfortable home away from home in central Boston near Tremont Street's "restaurant row." The spacious two-room suite with 11-foot ceilings includes a kitchenette, a private bath, and a spacious living room with a large bay window. Monthly rates available. $125-135.

M365. This convenient and charming town house near Copley Square boasts two fully renovated and attractively furnished private entry apartments with cable TV, telephones, and air conditioning. The studio has a queen-size bed, a small full kitchen, and a private bath. The one bedroom apartment has a double bed plus a single sleeper-sofa in the living room. There is also a full kitchen and a private bath. Inquire about monthly rates. $112-137.

M366. A one-bedroom apartment on a quiet street in the South End near Copley Square. Guests will feel at home in this spotless unit with thoughtful amenities. Cable TV, telephone, full kitchen, and private bath. Please ask about this home's perfume and chemical-free policy. $125-150.

M370. The hostess, a former instructor with the Boston Ballet, enjoys telling her guests all about her South End neighborhood with its many great restaurants. Her immaculate condo in a Victorian townhouse features collectibles from her worldwide travels along with an appealing mix of antiques, from Early American through Victorian. Double bed, private bath,

7 No smoking; 8 Children welcome; 9 Social drinking allowed; 10 Tennis nearby; 11 Swimming nearby; 12 Golf nearby; 13 Skiing nearby; 14 May be booked through a travel agent; 15 Handicapped accessible.

delightful private parlor. Set in a serene park. $97.

M371. Two talented gentlemen have recently created this stylish new space on the garden level of their South End townhouse. This large studio apartment has its entry through a private neighborhood park and it features a sitting room, private bath with large soaking tub, kitchen area, and a queen-size bed in an alcove. Here designer contemporary decor mixes with antiques. $140-160.

M417. On Boston Harbor, this condo apartment offers stunning views of the waterfront and easy access to Faneuil Hall and Quincy Market. Two guest rooms, each with private bath, queen-size bed, and contemporary furnishings. $120-150.

M426. These Beacon Hill apartments are ideal for those visiting the waterfront, the financial district, or the Government Center area of Boston. Each one-bedroom apartment in this restored 19th-century building is fully furnished and includes full kitchen, cable TV, private telephone line with answering machine. Some have a working fireplace or a small deck with gas grill. Weekly and monthly rates available. $125-175.

M466. This ground-level apartment in Charlestown offers privacy and space in an 1870s Victorian townhouse near the base of the famed Bunker Hill Monument. The private entry suite features an antique double bed, a Pullman kitchen, a small living room with sleeper-sofa, TV, and private bath. Weekly rates offered. $90-105.

M482. In historic Charlestown, on Boston's famed Freedom Trail, guests enjoy a second-floor guest room with deck overlooking gardens and private entrance in this 1847 Greek Revival townhouse. The tradi-

tionally furnished guest room has queen-size bed and private bath. $87-97.

M483. On a hill overlooking Boston, in the Jamaica Plain neighborhood, this contemporary townhouse offers wonderful views from the guest suite and the outside deck and patio. Guests have the entire second floor, including a large bedroom, a private bath, and a sitting room with an impressive media center. Five blocks to "T" into central Boston. Free parking. $75-95.

Bed and Breakfast Reservations North Shore, Greater Boston, Cape Cod

P.O. Box 600035, Greater Boston Branch,
  Newtonville, 02160-0001
(617) 964-1606; (800) 832-2362
FAX (617) 332-8572; e-mail: info@bbreserve.com
www.bbreserve.com

46. Bed and Breakfast Afloat. For the adventurous bed and breakfast guest, a 40-foot Chris Craft docked in the heart of downtown Boston's waterfront on Lewis Wharf. Cozy and comfortable with separate bedroom, boat-shower private bath, living room with double futon, TV, VCR, air conditioning, telephone, table/chairs, and galley kitchen. Ample supply of self-serve breakfast foods. Host will cater for special occasions by advanced arrangement. Available May 1 through October 15. No smoking. $140-150.

68. Garden Bed Breakfast Suite. In Boston's South End neighborhood, designated as a landmark, preserved historic district. Victorian brick row house built in 1860 and owned by an artist has a separate private entrance leading to double Victorian parlor with beautiful painted ceilings, artwork, and antiques. Bedroom, TV, VCR, telephone, private bath, and fully equipped efficiency kitchen, self-serve breakfast, private bath. Twenty dollars for third person on

---

NOTES: Credit cards accepted: A MasterCard; B Visa; C American Express; D Discover; E Diner's Club; F Other; 2 Personal checks accepted; 3 Lunch available; 4 Dinner available; 5 Open all year; 6 Pets welcome;

rollaway. No smoking. Children over 12 welcome. $125-135.

93. Beacon Hill Townhouse. Historic brownstone townhouse in the heart of one of Boston's most requested neighborhoods, Beacon Hill. Three guest rooms include a king-size and two twin-size beds, sharing a bath, plus an oversized suite featuring king-size bed, sitting area with double sleeper sofa, TV, and private en suite bath. Rooms have air conditioning. Continental breakfast put out buffet style in fourth-floor sitting room. Walk to everything. Twenty dollars for each additional person in suite. No smoking. $85-120.

97. Harborside. In the heart of the Boston waterfront and adjacent to Faneuil Hall Market Place, this high-rise condo has two beautiful rooms each with private bath, queen-size bed, TV, climate control, and over-sized picture window with panoramic view of the harbor and Boston waterfront. Breakfast included, taken to guests' room, where they will enjoy the views of the harbor from their table. No smoking. $125-135.

113. The Townhouse. A stately Boston Victorian-era brownstone on a lovely tree-lined street. Beautifully appointed and aesthetically decorated by artist host. One lovely guest room with double bed and private bath on second floor. Daytime use of large parlor. Continental breakfast is contemporary kitchen with access to outside deck. Walk to Copley and many tourist sites. No smoking. $115.

128. Park Suite. In the heart of Boston's South End/Back Bay neighborhood. Garden level of restored brick row townhouse, private terrace overlooking private park, furnished with antiques and modern classics. Separate bedroom with queen-size bed, pri-

vate full bath, living room, and well-equipped kitchen. Cable TV, air conditioning, telephone. Self-serve breakfast. Under 10 minute's walk to Copley Place. Twenty dollars for third person on rollaway. Off-season and extended rates. No smoking. Children over 12 welcome. $135-165.

129. Melrose House. In Bay Village, a small historic enclave adjacent to Back Bay and Chinatown in the heart of downtown Boston. Convenient to everything. Second floor features a small private art gallery displaying well-known contemporary paintings/ sculptures. Two guest rooms, with private en suite baths, TV, air conditioning, and telephones on upper floors. One room has queen-size bed. The other is a larger suite with king-size bed, sitting area, table/chairs, and refrigerator. Continental breakfast. No smoking. $100-115.

Host Homes of Boston
P.O. Box 117, Waban Branch, 02468-0001
(617) 244-1308; FAX (617) 244-5156

Ailanthus House. Reminiscent of Victorian days, this brownstone in the historic district is named for its huge shade tree. Friendly host offers two large second-floor guest rooms, each with en suite bath. Two resident cats. Central location, three blocks to Prudential Center, subway, Hynes Convention Center, Copley Square, Back Bay Amtrak. Great neighborhood restaurants. No smoking. Private bath, telephone, and TV. $105-125.

Back Bay House. Host offers full first floor in 1868 French Academic-style townhouse on quiet street near the Public Garden and Copley Square. Spacious quarters include bedroom with queen-size bed, mirrored hall, comfortable parlor with fireplace, sofa bed, balcony, cable TV, VCR, and kitchen stocked for basic Continental breakfast. Great central location. Walk to Newbury

7 No smoking; 8 Children welcome; 9 Social drinking allowed; 10 Tennis nearby; 11 Swimming nearby; 12 Golf nearby; 13 Skiing nearby; 14 May be booked through a travel agent; 15 Handicapped accessible.

Street cafés and boutiques, Copley Square conference hotels, Hynes Convention Center. No more than two guests at one time and six-night limited stay. No smoking. Private bath, air conditioning, telephone. $150-160.

Braddock Close. This 1860 Victorian townhouse is on a quiet street. Two light-filled street-level apartments have separate entrances. The one-bedroom apartment has a large living room with sofa bed. The other is a spacious studio apartment. Each has a full bath, equipped kitchen stocked for breakfast, air conditioning, TV/VCR, and telephone. Three blocks to Hynes Convention Center, fine shops, subway. Four blocks to Copley Square, Back Bay Amtrak. Walk to Symphony Hall, restaurants. $115-130.

Coach House. Converted to a private home in 1890, the original structure housed 12 coaches and staff. Here, on a quiet gas-lit street, this host family offers two well-appointed guest rooms with private baths. Resident cat. Near Freedom Trail, hotels, restaurants, Massachusetts General Hospital, and MIT. No smoking. TV. Air conditioned. $125-150.

Copley Close. An 1870 brownstone in quiet area. Guest apartment has large, bright bedroom with garden view. Full bath. Comfortable living room with cable TV/VCR, air conditioning, telephone. Kitchen stocked for breakfast. Street-level entrance. Note: guests must maintain chemical-free environment—no smoking, strong perfumes, or sprays. Three blocks from Hynes Convention Center and Prudential Center, Copley Place, Back Bay, Amtrak, subway. $135.

1829 Federal. Brick townhouse with fan doorway. Recent renovation combines modern conveniences with early charm.

Spacious third-floor guest suite with bath, sofa bed, and view. Two fourth-floor rooms share bath and TV room. Near Boston Common, Faneuil Hall, antique shops, MIT, and subway. Air conditioned. TV. No smoking. $90-120.

Near Faneuil Hall. Boston's past and present meet in this colorful Faneuil Hall and Quincy Market area. Host's fifth- and sixth-floor walk-up has brick-and-beam decor and balcony. Spacious guest room with double bed, skylights, and private bath. Subway two blocks away. Walk to harbor hotels, Freedom Trail, financial center, and restaurants. TV. Air conditioned. No smoking. $87.

On the Avenue. Boston Common, Copley Place, convention hotels, and the subway are steps away from 19th-century ambiance in private professional club. Dining room; guest parlor. Three spacious doubles have telephone and private bath. Four small singles share two baths. Rollaway: $25. Air conditioning, TV, elevator. $75-115.

On the Park. This 1865 Victorian bowfront in a historic district features antiques and authentic decor. Two fourth-floor guest rooms share a bath. Resident dogs. Four blocks to Copley Square, Hynes Convention Center, Back Bay Orange Line, and Amtrak. No smoking. Air-conditioned. $87.

Popham House. This elegant 1940 New York-style brick townhouse overlooks the Public Garden. Host's second-floor home, replete with traditional antiques, has one guest room with private bath. TV in parlor. Steps from major hotels, theaters, restaurants, convention center, and subway. Air-conditioned. $108.

Proper Bostonian. Business people like this 1872 townhouse with authentic decor.

Spacious third-floor guest room has sitting area and small stocked kitchen where guests make their own breakfast. Another twin room often available for same party. Busy hosts offer privacy in best area. Four blocks to Copley Square and Hynes Convention Center. Near Boston Common. Air conditioning; private bath; TV. $95-105.

Two Fountains. Amid the Victorian brownstones (circa 1859) facing a central mall, this home retains the 19th-century decor of spacious rooms, molded ornamental ceilings, and wood detail. Three guest rooms; two at street-level share hall bath. The third room shares host's bath. Guests welcome in parlor and garden. Great restaurants around the corner. Back Bay, Copley Square, Amtrak, subway six blocks away. Air conditioned. TV. Telephone. No smoking. $85-90.

Victorian Bowfront. Brick townhouse, circa 1869, in historic neighborhood boasts the era's high ceilings, carved wood detail, and marble fireplaces. Two second-floor guest rooms share a bath. City Room has TV. Country Room has striking wall mural and basin. Breakfast is served in rooms. Resident dog and cat. Central location. Walk three blocks to convention center and subway. No smoking. Air conditioned. Telephone. $89.

Oasis Guest House

22 Edgerly Road, 02115
(617) 267-2262; FAX (617) 267-1920
e-mail: oasisgh@tiac.net
www.oasisgh.com

Two renovated Back Bay townhouses with color TV, telephones, central air, and private baths. Within walking distance of restaurants, museums, and points of interest. This is a great in-town location near the Hynes Convention Center. Enjoy the outside decks. Parking. Fine lodging accommodations, since 1982, in the heart of the city for a price much less than at major hotels. Most of the guests are repeats and referrals. Call, fax, or write for more information. Discounted winter rates.

Rooms: 16 (11 PB; 5 SB) $65-104
Continental Breakfast
Credit Cards: A, B, C
Notes: 5, 9, 14

BREWSTER (CAPE COD)

Bed and Breakfast Cape Cod

P.O. Box 1312, Orleans, 02653
(508) 255-3824; (800) 541-6226
FAX (508) 240-0599
e-mail: bedandb@capecod.net
www.bandbcapecod.com

78. In the village, 500 feet from Cape Cod Bay, is this spacious home. Two guest rooms with private baths are beautifully decorated and well maintained. Walk to the village shops, restaurants, and beach trails. The wing of the house has a living room for guests with a fireplace, TV and VCR, and comfortable seating. A Continental plus breakfast is served. No smoking. Children over 12 welcome. $85-95.

The Bramble Inn and Restaurant

2019 Main Street, 02631
(508) 896-7644

Two antique buildings in the heart of the historic district lovingly restored to reflect a bygone era. All eight rooms have private baths and air conditioning. Chef-owned nationally acclaimed restaurant with five intimate dining rooms, candlelight, antiques, and fresh flowers. Prix fixe four-course dinners by reservation. House specialties include rack of lamb and native seafoods presented with an innovative air. "Dining at its innovative best"—*New York Times*, 1997. Children eight and older welcome.

7 No smoking; 8 Children welcome; 9 Social drinking allowed; 10 Tennis nearby; 11 Swimming nearby; 12 Golf nearby; 13 Skiing nearby; 14 May be booked through a travel agent; 15 Handicapped accessible.

The Bramble Inn

Hosts: Cliff and Ruth Manchester
Rooms: 8 (PB) $105-135
Full Breakfast
Credit Cards: A, B, C, D
Notes: 2, 4, 7, 9, 10, 11, 12, 14

Candleberry Inn on Cape Cod

1882 Main Street, 02631
(508) 896-3300

Gracious 250-year-old sea captain's home on two acres of gardens and towering trees in the heart of Brewster's historic district. Walk to fine dining, antique shops, and beach. Nine romantic, spacious guest rooms, all with private baths, some with working fireplaces, amid antiques, art, and oriental carpets. Guests are pampered with every amenity, including terry-cloth robes in the rooms, and a full gourmet served breakfast.

Hosts: Gini and David Donnelly
Rooms: 9 (PB) $80-165
Full Breakfast
Credit Cards: A, B, C, D
Notes: 2, 5, 7, 9, 10, 11, 12

Isaiah Clark House

1187 Main Street (Route 6A), 02631
(508) 896-2223; (800) 822-4001 (reservations)
FAX (508) 896-2138; e-mail: rgriffin@capecod.net
www.isaiahclark.com

Seven handsomely appointed guest rooms in an authentic Colonial (circa 1780) sea captain's home. Private baths, air conditioning, cable TV, and fireplaces are featured. Gourmet full breakfast and afternoon tea are served hearthside or on the deck overlooking flower gardens, shade trees, and berry patches. A concert-quality grand piano graces the music room. This inn offers relaxed elegance, warm hospitality, and easy accessibility to beaches, bike trails, nature trails, whale watching, and other natural attractions. Children 10 and older welcome.

Host: Richard Griffin
Rooms: 7 (PB) $78-130
Full Breakfast
Credit Cards: A, B, C, D
Notes: 5, 7, 9, 10, 11, 12, 14

Isaiah Clark House

Old Sea Pines Inn

2553 Main Street, 02631
(508) 896-6114

Lovely turn-of-the-century mansion, once the Sea Pines School of Charm and Personality for Young Women, now a newly renovated and redecorated country inn. Furnished with antiques, some of the rooms have working fireplaces. On three and one-half acres of land, with a wraparound porch looking out over the lawn, trees, and flowers. Complimentary beverage on arrival. Dinner theater on Sunday evening, June, July, August, and September. Children over eight welcome.

NOTES: Credit cards accepted: A MasterCard; B Visa; C American Express; D Discover; E Diner's Club; F Other; 2 Personal checks accepted; 3 Lunch available; 4 Dinner available; 5 Open all year; 6 Pets welcome;

Old Sea Pines

Hosts: Stephen and Michele Rowan
Rooms: 16 (PB) $55-115
Full Breakfast
Credit Cards: A, B, C, D, E
Notes: 2, 5, 7, 9, 10, 11, 12, 14, 15

Orleans Bed and Breakfast Associates, Inc.

P.O. Box 1312, Orleans, 02653
(508) 255-3824; (800) 541-6226
FAX (508) 240-0599
e-mail: orleansbnb@capecod.net
www.capecod.net/bb

Pineapple Place. Nestled among the pines in the heart of Brewster, this Cape contemporary home offers a decor of vivid antique collections from around the world. There is a very private guest wing that faces the century-old forests of Cape Cod. The guest room has a canopied bed, spacious private bath, sitting area that opens onto guests' private patio. Enter this amazing home by guests' private entrance or use the main entrance that steps into a fabulous great room. Nearby a Cape Cod Bay beach, one mile to Route 6A, the Captain's Highway, a quarter of a mile to the Cape Cod bike trail. Very romantic. $85-110.

The Ruddy Turnstone

463 Main Street, 02631
(508) 385-9871; (800) 654-1995 (reservations)
FAX (508) 385-5696
www.sunsol.com/ruddyturnstone/

The Ruddy Turnstone bed and breakfast is on three private acres yet very close to all

the pleasures and activities of the area. The expansive back yard offers magnificent ocean views. Built in the early 1800s, this is truly an old Cape Cod property impeccably restored. All rooms, tastefully decorated, have queen-size beds, private baths, fresh flowers, and air conditioning. A most relaxing place where guests immediately feel at home. AAA three-diamond rating. Children over 10 welcome.

Hosts: Gordon and Sally Swanson
Rooms: 5 (PB) $85-150
Full Breakfast
Credit Cards: A, B
Notes: 2, 5, 7, 9, 10, 11, 12, 14

The Ruddy Turnstone

BRIMFIELD

Converse House Bed and Breakfast

7 Brookfield Road, 01010
(413) 245-7812; (413) 245-0455

This elegant 1823 Federal home is conveniently in central Massachusetts, five miles from historic Sturbridge Village and the Massachusetts Turnpike. Spacious bedrooms are tastefully decorated and furnished with poster and canopied beds. Guests may enjoy a parlor and dining room expressly for their use. Brimfield is host to this country's largest outdoor antique and collectibles market held three times a year. Boston, Cape Cod, and the Berkshires are a 90-minute drive. Antique shops and restaurants in nearby Sturbridge. Continental plus breakfast.

7 No smoking; 8 Children welcome; 9 Social drinking allowed; 10 Tennis nearby; 11 Swimming nearby; 12 Golf nearby; 13 Skiing nearby; 14 May be booked through a travel agent; 15 Handicapped accessible.

Hosts: Beth and Peter Baker
Rooms: 2 (PB) $79-129
Continental Breakfast
Credit Cards: None
Notes: 2, 5, 7

BROOKLINE

Bed and Breakfast Associates Bay Colony, Ltd.

P.O. Box 57166, Babson Park, Boston, 02157-0166
(781) 449-5302; (800) 347-5088
FAX (781) 449-5958; e-mail: info@bnbboston.com
www.bnbboston.com

M610. This quiet Brookline Hills neighborhood is convenient to the Longwood medical area as well as the "T" to central Boston. The guest suite is a large room featuring a fully stocked kitchenette, private bath, dining table, and sofa. Continental breakfast. Children welcome. No smoking allowed. Weekly and monthly rates available. $72-90.

M611. Near Washington Square and Beacon Street, this caterer, a former college professor, provides hilltop views from her tastefully decorated modern townhouse. Three guest rooms; one has private bath en suite. Free driveway parking. $65-87.

M617. A delightful Victorian home just three blocks from Commonwealth Avenue. Ideal for those wishing to have a quiet setting, driveway parking, and proximity to the subway system and Boston University. Three guest rooms with period furnishings. Double or queen-size beds, shared baths. $105-114.

M620. This beautifully restored and fully redecorated 1903 mansion offers 12 bed and breakfast guest rooms, eight with private baths, in the Beacon Street/Longwood medical area of Brookline. An easy walk to the hospitals and to the transit lines. Most baths are private. Limited free parking. Lower rates off-season. $109-179.

M641. Once part of the Underground Railroad, this 18th-century farm cottage in Brookline Village is steeped in history and is surrounded by imposing mansions on a quiet street near the Longwood medical area. Three guest rooms all feature antique furnishings. Guests have a choice of double, queen-size, or twin beds and private or shared bath. $70-87.

M646. Next to the Longwood medical area (Children's, Brigham and Women's, and Dana Farber Hospitals), this small suite with double bed is especially for stays of one week or longer. Guests will enjoy the convenience of a kitchenette and private bath on the first floor of this grand Victorian home. Weekly and monthly rates available. $94-104.

M661. On Beacon Street, between Boston University and Boston College, this historic townhouse dates back to 1894. Fully restored and tastefully furnished with antiques, the guest room has a bird's-eye maple four-poster queen-size bed and a twin bed, with a private bath in the hall. Free driveway parking. $85-95.

Bed and Breakfast Reservations North Shore, Greater Boston, Cape Cod

P.O. Box 600035, Greater Boston Branch,
    Newtonville, 02160-0001
(617) 964-1606; (800) 832-2632
FAX (617) 332-8572; e-mail: info@bbreserve.com
www.bbreserve.com

104. The Tree House. Brick townhouse on a lovely tree-lined street in Brookline, with short walk to public transportation. Easy access to Boston. Off-street parking included. Bright and sunny living room, dining area with access to outside deck. Great Continental plus breakfast. Three guest rooms with TV, air conditioning. One room with private bath and two rooms sharing a bath. Two resident Siamese cats. No smoking. $65-90.

NOTES: Credit cards accepted: A MasterCard; B Visa; C American Express; D Discover; E Diner's Club;
F Other; 2 Personal checks accepted; 3 Lunch available; 4 Dinner available; 5 Open all year; 6 Pets welcome;

Beech Tree Inn

83 Longwood Avenue, 02146
(617) 277-1620; (800) 544-9660
FAX (617) 277-0657

Neighborhood charm in the city, this Victorian-style bed and breakfast is just over the Boston line. Individually decorated guest rooms, all with telephones and air conditioning, some with shared baths, some with private baths. A fully equipped kitchen is available for guests as well as a sitting room with cable TV and movies for guests' pleasure. Enjoy downtown Boston via the nearby trolley, walk to local shops and restaurants, play in the park, or just sit under the apple tree...a pleasant interlude for a night, weekend, or week at affordable prices. Ask about winter discounts. Homemade breakfast.

Host: Bette Allen
Rooms: 11 (7 PB; 4 SB) $65-125
Continental Breakfast
Credit Cards: A, B
Notes: 2, 5, 6, 7, 8, 10, 12, 14

The Bertram Inn

92 Sewall Avenue, 02146
(617) 566-2234; (800) 295-3822
FAX (617) 277-1887; www.bertraminn.com

Come home to Victorian elegance at a 90-year-old house in a quiet neighborhood only 10 minutes by subway from central Boston. Freshly restored to its original splendor using period furniture and antiques, the inn boasts working fireplaces, a large front porch, rose garden, and a commons breakfast room with complimentary Continental plus breakfast and afternoon tea. Each of the 14 unique rooms includes cable TV, telephone, and air conditioning. A variety of shops and fine restaurants is only a stroll's distance away. Off-street parking included.

Host: Bryan Austin
Rooms: 14 (PB) $79-194
Continental Breakfast
Credit Cards: A, B, C
Notes: 5, 6, 7, 9, 14

Greater Boston Hospitality

P.O. Box 1142, 02146
(617) 277-5430; e-mail: bdfd@channel1.com
www.channel1.com/Bnb

Hundreds of accommodations in outstanding Georgian, Federal, Victorian, and Colonial homes, condos, and inns in the greater Boston area. All include breakfast, many include parking, and others are on excellent transport system. Many are minutes from colleges, medical area, museum, and Freedom Trail. Visit Boston as a  native while staying at Greater Boston Hospitality. Write or call today for free brochure. Some luxury accommodations available.

Manager: Kelly Simpson
Rooms: 125 (100 PB; 25 SB) $50-110
Full and Continental Breakfast
Credit Cards: A, B
Notes: 2, 3, 5, 7, 8, 10, 11, 12, 14

Host Homes of Boston

P.O. Box 117, Waban Branch, Boston, 02468-0001
(617) 244-1308; FAX (617) 244-5156

Beacon Street Victorian. An 1890 restored Victorian townhouse. Second-floor guest room (two-person limit) with private bath. Breakfast in spacious dining room with fireplace, comfortable sitting area. Green Line-C trolley outside door. Fifteen minute ride direct to Back Bay, Hynes Convention Center, Copley Square, Boston University, and Boston Common. Walk to restaurants. No smoking. TV. Air conditioning. Parking available. $85.

Bienvenue. This Tudor Provincial (circa 1939) home is in an elegant, quiet neighborhood. Two second-floor guest rooms with connecting bath. Small study. Also, first-floor bath available. Near Boston

7 No smoking; 8 Children welcome; 9 Social drinking allowed; 10 Tennis nearby; 11 Swimming nearby; 12 Golf nearby; 13 Skiing nearby; 14 May be booked through a travel agent; 15 Handicapped accessible.

Common, Pine Manor, Longwood Medical Center. Ten-minute walk to Green Line-D. Boston three miles away. Parking available. Telephone. TV. No smoking. Children over six welcome. $68-85.

Gardener's Cottage. Serenity, convenience, and comfort in this two story apartment. Enter through a spotless, fully equipped kitchen into the living room with broad windows facing the garden. Upstairs is bedroom with queen-size bed, study nook, and full private bath. Hosts provide food for Continental breakfast. Near Boston College, Longwood medical area, shops, restaurants. Green Line-D into the Back Bay four to five blocks away. No smoking. Air conditioning, TV, parking, and telephone. $135.

Studio Apartment. Colonial home (1620 Salem house replica) on quiet cul-de-sac offers above-ground basement room with sofa, galley kitchen, patio, private bath, and private entrance. Choice of breakfast on tray or self-serve. Five blocks to Green Line-C. Ten minutes to Copley Square. TV. Air conditioning. No smoking. $81.

BROOKLINE HILLS

Host Homes of Boston

P.O. Box 117, Waban Branch, Boston, 02468-0001
(617) 244-1308; FAX (617) 244-5156

The Tree House. Meg's modern townhouse with traditional decor has a sweeping view from the glass-walled living room and deck. Three second-floor guest rooms share a bath. Also a queen room with air conditioning and private bath. Two Siamese cats. Near Back Bay, Boston College, and Boston University. Ten minutes to Hynes Convention Center via Green Line-C and D (three blocks). Private bath. TV. No smoking. $75-85.

BUCKLAND

1797 House

Upper Street-Charlemont Road, 01338
(413) 625-2975

This 18th-century home is in a peaceful rural area, yet is convenient to many attractions and all points in New England. Large rooms, private baths, down quilts, and a lovely screened porch ensure comfort. Near historic Deerfield, five-college area, and Yankee Candle. Experience a modicum of civilization in an increasingly uncivilized world. One-bedroom apartment with kitchen available. Inquire about accommodations for children.

Host: Janet Turley
Rooms: 3 (PB) $60-80
Full Breakfast
Credit Cards: None
Notes: 5, 7, 10, 11, 12, 13

CAMBRIDGE

Bed and Breakfast Associates Bay Colony, Ltd.

P.O. Box 57166, Babson Park, Boston, 02157-0166
(781) 449-5302; (800) 347-5088
FAX (781) 449-5958; e-mail: info@bnbboston.com
www.bnbboston.com

M806. Walk to MIT or pick up the subway to Harvard from this immaculate home. The hostess, who lives nearby, maintains the two guest rooms, one with queen-size bed and the other with single bed. Kitchen, dining area, and spacious living room with fireplace for bed and breakfast guests. Additional futon available. The whole house can be rented for $150-175. Or the rooms can be rented individually for $70-90.

M807. In Central Square, between Harvard University and MIT, this Italianate duplex home, circa 1866, underwent a complete restoration in 1995. All period details were preserved and the decor features antique furnishings throughout. Three guest rooms are offered. Shared or private bath available. One block to Central Square subway and Massachusetts Avenue bus. Limited on-street parking. $105-114.

M816. In a stately brick apartment building, this bed and breakfast hostess offers her gracious home with traditional decor. One pleasant, quiet guest room with double bed shares bath with hostess. Spacious and charming. Three blocks from Massachusetts Avenue, just north of Harvard Square (a 10-minute walk or a 5-minute bus ride). $70-85.

M835. A pleasant apartment with one guest room just outside Harvard Square across from the Charles River shoreline. A wonderful setting! This traditional brick building is quiet and well kept. The delightful hostess will share her third-floor apartment with visitors to Harvard and other Cambridge locations. Excellent quality, firm queen-size sofa bed, shared bath. $99.

M875. A large informal home in a quiet neighborhood just west of Harvard Square (a 20-minute walk or a five-minute bus ride). Three simple guest rooms, with private baths, are offered in this plant-filled house with a fenced yard. Driveway parking. $55-70.

M900. This fine bed and breakfast inn is in a Harvard Square neighborhood. The recently completed historic restoration has produced 18 guest rooms with private baths and tasteful decor. Romantics enjoy the second-floor suite with fireplace. Limited reserved parking available. $99-229.

A Bed and Breakfast in Cambridge

A Bed and Breakfast in Cambridge

1657 Cambridge Street, 02138-4316
(617) 868-7082; (800) 795-7122
FAX (617) 876-8991
e-mail: DoanePerry@compuserve.com
www.cambridgebnb.com

Affordable elegance in 1897 house, great beds, fresh flowers, home-baked specialties, homemade jams, afternoon tea, off-street parking, cable TV, telephones in rooms, air conditioning. Hospitable hosts speak French and German. A full fancy Continental plus breakfast served.

Rooms: 3 (SB) $50-110
Continental Breakfast
Credit Cards: A, B, C
Notes: 2, 5, 7, 11, 14

Host Homes of Boston

P.O. Box 117, Waban Branch, Boston, 02468-0001
(617) 244-1308; FAX (617) 244-5156

Blue Hawthorne. This 100-year-old Victorian home off Brattle Street is a quiet oasis near bustling Harvard Square. The host offers two first-floor guest rooms with private baths, telephones, and TVs. Shady side garden. Three blocks to the square, Red Line, Charles Hotel, restaurants, and shops. Air conditioning. TV. No smoking. $75-87.

---

7 No smoking; 8 Children welcome; 9 Social drinking allowed; 10 Tennis nearby; 11 Swimming nearby; 12 Golf nearby; 13 Skiing nearby; 14 May be booked through a travel agent; 15 Handicapped accessible.

Cambridge Suite. This large home, circa 1855, is on a quiet road only three blocks from bustling Harvard Square. The first-floor guest suite has a sitting room with sofa and desk and private bath. Breakfast served in the dining room. Near William James Hall and law school. Red Line three blocks. TV. Telephone with answering machine. Parking available. Air conditioning. No smoking. $105.

Near Harvard Square. Just a seven-minute walk to the square, Harvard Yard, Brattle Street, and Red Line. Quiet, shady location. European decor. Coffee ground fresh for breakfast. Private first-floor guest room with shared bath. Air conditioning. TV. $85.

True Victorian. Host's Victorian jewel sits on a quiet hill near Massachusetts Avenue between Harvard and Porter Squares. Three second-floor guest rooms. Guest rooms are air conditioned. Only four guests at a time, except families. Hearty breakfast in sunny kitchen, often self-serve on weekdays. Red Line and train at Porter Square two blocks. TV. No smoking. $85.

Wit and Wisdom. Tucked between Harvard and Porter Square near the Radcliffe Quad, this bright bed and breakfast is ideal for visiting academics. Guest room has large desk overlooking the courtyard and one twin-size bed. Guest shares host's bathroom. Five-minute walk to subway, observatory, law school. Near restaurants and shops. No smoking. Air conditioning. Permit parking. $68-75.

Isaac Harding House

288 Harvard Street, 02139
(617) 876-2088; FAX (617) 497-0953
e-mail: reserve@irvinghouse.com

Guests will like the style and grace of this 1860s Victorian. Spacious guest rooms include a queen-size bed and private bath,

TV, telephone, and air conditioning. Enjoy breakfast in the sunny dining room. Harding House is large enough to let guests be and small enough to make guests feel at home. In mid-Cambridge, guests will find Harvard Square, MIT, or Boston easy to get to by foot or by T. Limited parking available.

Host: Jane Jones
Rooms: 14 (PB) $125-220
Continental Breakfast
Credit Cards: A, B, C, D, E
Notes: 2, 5, 7, 8, 15

Prospect Place

112 Prospect Street, 02139
(617) 864-7500; (800) 769-5303
FAX (617) 576-1159

An elegant Italianate bed and breakfast built in 1866 and in the center of Cambridge near Harvard and MIT, just across the river from Boston. Owned by the same family for over 100 years until 1994. Period details abound, from classic archways to marble fireplaces and cut-glass windows. Eclectically furnished in wonderful antiques; two grand pianos grace the spacious parlor. Complete breakfast served in the Victorian dining room. Early American history, a variety of museums, world-class universities, and musical concerts are all within a few minutes of the front door.

Hosts: Eric and Judy Huenneke
Rooms: 3 (1 PB; 2 SB) $80-125
Full Breakfast
Credit Cards: A, B
Notes: 5, 7, 8, 14

CENTERVILLE

Adam's Terrace Gardens Inn

539 Main Street, 02632
(508) 775-4707 (phone/FAX)

Beautiful historic captain's home, circa 1835. Entirely renovated, the eight bedrooms are very nice and airy, all equipped with cable TV. Breakfasts are served outside on the screened porch or in the dining

Adam's Terrace Gardens Inn

room. Specialties are quiches and crêpes served with fresh fruits. Fresh flowers. One-half mile to the beach on Cape Cod.

Rooms: 8 (5 PB; 3 SB) $80-105
Full Breakfast
Credit Cards: A, B, D
Notes: 2, 5, 8, 9, 11, 12, 14

Bed and Breakfast Cape Cod

P.O. Box 1312, Orleans, 02653
(508) 255-3824; (800) 541-6226
FAX (508) 240-0599
e-mail: bedandb@capecod.net
www.bandbcapecod.com

67. This is a comfortable bed and breakfast host home overlooking beautiful Lake Wequaquet. Beautifully landscaped grounds and lake water views are part of the natural appeal of this accommodation. Room one, on the first floor, has a private bath. Room two is a small room with a shared bath. Enjoy freshwater swimming in the nearby lake and visit Hyannis. A Continental plus breakfast is served from 8 to 10 A.M. in the dining area. $70.

82. Lake Wequaquet is the largest freshwater lake on Cape Cod. Nestled along the shore of the lake is this home featuring two guest rooms that share a bath. Air conditioned. Great swimming, fishing, or simply sitting on the lakeshore are but some of the

pleasures here. The great restaurants, shops, and the ferry to either Martha's Vineyard or Nantucket are four miles away. Continental breakfast is served. A great spot for a family of up to four persons. No smoking. $70.

On the Pond Bed and Breakfast

160 Huckins Neck Road, 02632
(508) 775-0417; (401) 454-0246 (off season)

"Come to our lakefront mid-Cape Cod inn for an unforgettable vacation." Boat, swim, fish, enjoy the deck or sauna or "veg out" watching the latest movies on cable TV/VCR. Suite with living room, refrigerator, and one or two bedrooms (queen- or twin-size beds). All-you-can-eat gourmet breakfast served on sun deck or in glass-walled dining room with great views of lake. Close to beaches, tennis, golf, shopping, movies, and ferries to Nantucket and Martha's Vineyard.

Hosts: Dotty and Don Horowitz
Rooms: 2 (PB) $60-125
Full Breakfast
Credit Cards: A, B
Notes: 2, 5, 7, 8, 9, 10, 11, 12, 14

On The Pond

7 No smoking; 8 Children welcome; 9 Social drinking allowed; 10 Tennis nearby; 11 Swimming nearby; 12 Golf nearby; 13 Skiing nearby; 14 May be booked through a travel agent; 15 Handicapped accessible.

CHATHAM (CAPE COD)

The Azubah Atwood Inn

177 Cross Street, P.O. Box 668, 02633-0668
(508) 945-7075; (888) 265-6220

Historically significant, a lovely old sea captain's home (complete with cupola), circa 1789. Three charming rooms for adults, with queen-size beds, private baths, color cable TV, air conditioning, and telephone. Spacious grounds with magnificent old trees and a large screened veranda. Parlor and dining room with original fireplaces. Some antique furnishings throughout. Hearty Continental breakfast included. Restricted smoking areas. Several friendly resident cats also extend their welcome. Short walk to village and beach. Open seasonally and some winter holidays.

Hosts: William P. and Audrey E. Gray
Rooms: 3 (PB) $149
Continental Breakfast
Credit Cards: A, B
Notes: 2, 9, 10, 11, 12

Bed and Breakfast Cape Cod

P.O. Box 1312, Orleans, 02653
(508) 255-3824; (800) 541-6226
FAX (508) 240-0599
e-mail: bedandb@capecod.net
www.bandbcapecod.com

12. This reproduction of an Early American Cape Cod home offers a first-floor room with a private bath, double bed; the second floor offers two rooms with double beds. (These rooms are never rented separately, so they share a "private" bath.) A short walk to the village, fish pier, and the beach. Air conditioned. Continental breakfast. $80.

65. This Cape Cod-style home built more than 40 years ago was expanded in 1987 and now is a spacious, convenient, and beautifully maintained home. It is only a few hundred yards from Oyster Pond, an ocean inlet, and only one mile from popular Hardings Beach on the Atlantic Ocean. The guest rooms on the second floor each have a private bath. Air conditioned and with glimpses of the ocean, it is a quiet and relaxing environment. No smoking. No children. $70-89.

Bed and Breakfast Reservations North Shore, Greater Boston, Cape Cod

P.O. Box 600035, Greater Boston Branch,
    Newtonville, 02160-0001
(617) 964-1606; (800) 832-2632
FAX (617) 332-8572; e-mail: info@bbreserve.com
www.bbreserve.com

130. Chatham Gardens. Chatham's most historic inn, meticulously restored and elegantly decorated to blend the charm of the past with modern day luxuries. The inn is a short stroll to the center of Chatham Village with its quaint shops and fine restaurants, or a more leisurely walk to beautiful Lighthouse Beach. Most of the 18 guest rooms feature four-poster beds, original pine flooring, private baths, telephones, beamed ceilings, and wet bars. Relax by the fireplace, enjoy a drink in the English-style pub, or stroll through the gardens. Sumptuous breakfast buffet. Open year-round. No smoking. $85-235.

Carriage House Inn

407 Old Harbor Road, 02633
(508) 945-4688 phone/FAX; (800) 355-8868
www.capecodtravel.com/carriagehouse

Charming traditional cape home tastefully decorated and furnished with antiques and family pieces. Six bright and airy guest rooms feature private baths and air conditioning. Carriage house rooms offer fireplaces, private entrances, and outside sitting areas. Fireplaced living room with piano, spacious grounds, lovely flowers. Home-baked breakfast served. Guest pantry stocked with beverages and homemade cookies. Easy walk to village attractions. Bicycles and beach towels available.

NOTES: Credit cards accepted: A MasterCard; B Visa; C American Express; D Discover; E Diner's Club; F Other; 2 Personal checks accepted; 3 Lunch available; 4 Dinner available; 5 Open all year; 6 Pets welcome;

Carriage House Inn

Hosts: Patty and Dennis O'Neill
Rooms: 6 (PB) $95-185
Full Breakfast
Credit Cards: A, B, C, D
Notes: 2, 5, 7, 9, 10, 11,12, 14

The Cyrus Kent House Inn

63 Cross Street, 02633
(800) 338-5368

Comfortably elegant, the inn is an award-winning restoration of a 19th-century sea captain's mansion. Rooms are large, bright, and airy, furnished with antiques. Private baths, telephone, and TV. On a quiet lane in the quaint seaside village of Chatham, a historic district. Excellent restaurants and beaches are within steps. Children over 10 are welcome.

Host: Sharon Mitchell Swan
Rooms: 10 (PB) $80-175
Continental Breakfast
Credit Cards: A, B
Notes: 2, 5, 7, 9, 10, 11, 12, 14

The Cyrus Kent House Inn

Moses Nickerson House Inn

364 Old Harbor Road, 02633
(508) 945-5859; (800) 628-6972
FAX (508) 945-7087; e-mail: tmnhi@capecod.net
www.virtualcapecod.com/market/
  mnickerson/

Quiet, elegant, romantic. Built in 1839 by whaling captain Moses Nickerson, this small inn has seven individually decorated guest rooms featuring canopied beds, fireplaces, oriental rugs, private baths, and air conditioning. TV optional. Glass-enclosed breakfast room. Walk to the quaint village of Chatham with its fine shops, galleries, and restaurants, or turn right at the end of the driveway and walk to the beach or fishing pier. AAA-rated. Children over 12 welcome.

Hosts: George and Linda Watts
Rooms: 7 (PB) $95-179
Full Breakfast
Credit Cards: A, B, C, D
Notes: 2, 5, 7, 9, 10, 11, 12, 14

Moses Nickerson House Inn

The Old Harbor Inn

22 Old Harbor Road, 02633
(508) 945-4434; (800) 942-4434
FAX (508) 945-7665; e-mail: brazohi@capecod.net

Casual elegance invites guests to stay. Eight guest rooms decorated in English country style with designer fabric and linen are a perfect setting to relax. Each room has twins, queen- or king-size bed with full private bath in each room. Some rooms have fireplaces, TVs, and more. A short walk to historic seaside village of Chatham.

7 No smoking; 8 Children welcome; 9 Social drinking allowed; 10 Tennis nearby; 11 Swimming nearby; 12 Golf nearby; 13 Skiing nearby; 14 May be booked through a travel agent; 15 Handicapped accessible.

Old Harbor Inn

Explore...Discover...be Pampered! Children 14 and older welcome. Inquire about social drinking.

Hosts: Judy and Ray Braz
Rooms: 8 (PB) $109-229
Continental Breakfast
Credit Cards: A, B, C, D, E, F
Notes: 2, 5, 7, 10, 11, 12, 14

Orleans Bed and Breakfast Associates, Inc.

P.O. Box 1312, 02653-1312
(508) 255-3824; (800) 541-6226
FAX (508) 240-0599
e-mail: orleansbnb@capecod.net
www.capecod.net/bb

The Breakaway. This meticulously maintained old house is entered through an attractive front door just a short walk from the famous Chatham Lighthouse. A charming guest parlor has a TV. Upstairs there are three guest rooms and two full baths off the hall. Breakfast in a lovely dining room or enjoy a cup of coffee on the large screened side porch. Less than a mile to town with its many boutiques and fine restaurants. Walk to the sea. Continental plus breakfast served. $95.

Woods Hill. On a quiet wooded cul-de-sac, the private entrance opens to a cathedral ceiling sitting room with French doors opening to a large sun deck. The stairway from the sitting room leads to an oversized bedroom with sitting area, a Palladian window at the head of the queen-size bed. Private bath with twin sinks, separate shower stall, and oversized tub. Complete with guest refrigerator, color TV/VCR.

Continental breakfast provided, all just a short drive to the center of Chatham village and many area beaches. $95.

Port Fortune Inn

201 Main Street, 02633
(800) 750-0792; FAX (508) 945-0792
e-mail: porfor@capecod.net
www.capecod.net/portfortune

Two beautifully restored historic buildings 100 yards from ocean in Old Village near lighthouse. Fourteen elegantly decorated rooms, some with ocean views, all with queen-size beds, private baths, air conditioning, telephones. Many antiques, four-poster beds. Delicious breakfast in ocean-view dining room. Two graciously appointed common rooms, breezy patio surrounded by colorful gardens. Open all year. Children eight and older welcome.

Rooms: 14 (PB) $85-170
Continental Breakfast
Credit Cards: A, B, C
Notes: 5, 7, 9, 10, 11, 12, 14

Port Fortune Inn

CHESTNUT HILL

Bed and Breakfast Reservations North Shore, Greater Boston, Cape Cod

P.O. Box 600035, Greater Boston Branch,
  Newtonville, 02160-0001
(617) 964-1606; (800) 832-2632
FAX (617) 332-8572; e-mail: info@bbreserve.com
www.bbreserve.com

NOTES: Credit cards accepted: A MasterCard; B Visa; C American Express; D Discover; E Diner's Club; F Other; 2 Personal checks accepted; 3 Lunch available; 4 Dinner available; 5 Open all year; 6 Pets welcome;

7. The Suite at Chestnut Hill. Within Boston's city limits, about eight miles outside the downtown area. This is a private separate suite nestled in a neighborhood of elegant homes. Just a seven-minute walk to public transportation for easy access to Boston. Suite is very tastefully decorated, with many extras, including skylights, dining area, efficiency kitchen, TV, air conditioning, telephone, sitting area, daily maid service. Host provides self-serve breakfast. Queen-size bed with couches converting to two singles to comfortably sleep four. Parking included. Twenty dollars for each additional person in room. No smoking. $100-115.

CONCORD

Bed and Breakfast Associates Bay Colony, Ltd.

P.O. Box 57166, Babson Park, Boston, 02157-0166
(781) 449-5302; (800) 347-5088
FAX (781) 449-5958; e-mail: info@bnbboston.com
www.bnbboston.com

CW230. Built in 1775, this five-bedroom inn retains the original moldings and beams while the thoughtful restoration provides all the modern guest room amenities. Private bath, desk, and TV in each room. Light breakfast buffet. Family rates available. Two-bedroom apartment for $165 is available. $100-110.

Bed and Breakfast Reservations North Shore, Greater Boston, Cape Cod

P.O. Box 600035, Greater Boston Branch,
Newtonville, 02160-0001
(617) 964-1606; (800) 832-2632
FAX (617) 332-8572; e-mail: info@bbreserve.com
www.bbreserve.com

20. The 1775 Colonial Inn. In historic Concord, just 20 miles west of Boston, with easy access from main highways. This is a meticulously restored colonial inn with five guest rooms, all with private baths, color TV, air conditioning, and telephones. Continental buffet breakfast is included. Afternoon tea or sherry is served by the fireplace, in the 200-year-old sitting room. There is also a two-bedroom apartment with queen-size/single bedrooms, small kitchen, and living room/dining area. Business support services are available nearby for business travelers. Children over 12 welcome. No smoking. Reduced rates for weekly and monthly stays. $95-165.

Colonel Roger Brown House

1694 Main Street, 01742
(978) 369-9119; (800) 292-1369

This 1775 Colonial home is on the historic register and close to the Concord and Lexington historic districts, 18 miles west of Boston and Cambridge. Five rooms with air conditioning, private baths, color TV, and telephones. Complimentary beverages at all times. Complimentary use of Concord Fitness Club adjacent to the inn in the restored Damon Mill. Comfortable and cozy atmosphere. Inquire about accommodations for children. Hearty Continental plus buffet breakfast.

Host: Lauri Berlied
Rooms: 5 (PB) $75-100
Continental Breakfast
Credit Cards: A, B, C
Notes: 2, 5, 7, 9, 10, 11, 12, 13, 14

Hawthorne Inn

462 Lexington Road, 01742
(978) 369-5610; FAX (978) 287-4949
www.concord.mass.com

Built circa 1870 on land once owned by Emerson, Hawthorne, and the Alcotts. Alongside the "battle road" of 1775 and within walking distance of authors' homes, battle sites, and Walden Pond. Furnished with antiques, handmade quilts, original artwork, Japanese prints, and sculpture.

Hosts: G. Burch and M. Mudry
Rooms: 7 (PB) $110-215

7 No smoking; 8 Children welcome; 9 Social drinking allowed; 10 Tennis nearby; 11 Swimming nearby; 12 Golf nearby; 13 Skiing nearby; 14 May be booked through a travel agent; 15 Handicapped accessible.

Hawthorne Inn

Continental Breakfast
Credit Cards: A, B, C, D
Notes: 2, 5, 7, 8, 9, 10, 11, 12, 13, 14

CUMMAQUID (CAPE COD)

The Acworth Inn

4352 Old Kings Highway, P.O. Box 256, 02637
(508) 362-3330; (800) 362-6363

The Acworth Inn sits among the trees along the Old Kings Highway that winds through the historic, unspoiled north side of Cape Cod. The inn offers an opportunity to experience the gracious lifestyle of a bygone era. Built in 1860, it is a classic Cape house, completely renovated and out-

The Acworth Inn

fitted with charming hand-painted pieces and colorful fabrics. From its central location near Barnstable Harbor one can easily reach all points on the cape, Martha's Vineyard, and Nantucket.

Hosts: Jack and Cheryl Ferrell
Rooms: 5 (PB) $85-185
Full Breakfast
Credit Cards: A, B, C, D
Notes: 2, 5, 7, 9, 10, 11, 12, 14

Bed and Breakfast Cape Cod

P.O. Box 1312, Orleans, 02653
(508) 255-3824; (800) 541-6226
FAX (508) 240-0599
e-mail: bedandb@capecod.net
www.bandbcapecod.com

51. Built in 1790, this Cape Cod-style house was expanded through the years and fully restored into a comfortable historic house offering expansive views of Hallett's Pond, an ocean inlet from Cape Cod Bay. Two bedrooms with private bath are in the house. A separate cottage with privacy, two bedrooms, private bath, living room, and deck makes a great spot for up to four persons or a honeymoon hideaway. Continental plus breakfast served. No smoking. Children 12 and older welcome. $95-145.

CUMMINGTON

Cumworth Farm

472 West Cummington Road, 01026
(413) 634-5529

A 200-year-old house with a sugar house and blueberry and raspberry fields on the premises. Pick berries in season. The farm raises sheep and is close to Tanglewood, Smith College, the William Cullen Bryant Homestead, cross-country skiing, and hiking trails. Hot tub. Closed from November 1 to May 1. Lower rate midweek.

Host: Ed McColgan
Rooms: 6 (SB) $75
Full Breakfast
Credit Cards: None
Notes: 2, 7, 8, 9, 10, 11, 12

NOTES: Credit cards accepted: A MasterCard; B Visa; C American Express; D Discover; E Diner's Club; F Other; 2 Personal checks accepted; 3 Lunch available; 4 Dinner available; 5 Open all year; 6 Pets welcome;

DEERFIELD

Deerfield's Yellow Gabled House

111 North Main Street, South Deerfield, 01373
(413) 665-4922

Built in the 1800s, this inn presents a mixture of Colonial with Gothic Revival and boasts gabled roofs, two-story wood clapboards, Gothic arched windows, and old wide-pine boards for flooring. Guest rooms feature custom window treatments, sofas, canopied beds, and antiques. One room is a suite with a private bath. Gathering room with library and telephone. Walk to restaurants, Yankee Candle Company, and museum. Drive to historic Deerfield, Sugarloaf Mountain, area colleges, and farmlands. Two hours from Boston and three and one-half hours from New York City. AAA three-diamond rating.

Rooms: 3 (1 PB; 2 SB) $75-120
Full Breakfast
Credit Cards: None
Notes: 2, 5, 7, 9, 10, 11, 12, 13, 14

Deerfield's Yellow Gabled House

DENNIS

Captain Nickerson Inn

333 Main Street, 02660
(508) 398-5966; (800) 282-1619

Delightful Victorian sea captain's home on a bike path in historic section of Dennis. Comfortable front porch is lined with white wicker rockers. Five guest rooms are decorated in period four-poster or white iron queen-size beds and oriental or hand-woven rugs. Cozy terry robes and air conditioning available in all rooms. Breakfast is served in fireplaced dining room. Walk to Indian Lands Trail and the Bass River. Only one-half mile from Cape Cod Bike Trail (22+ miles). Close to shops and good restaurants. No smoking. Children are welcome.

Hosts: Pat and Dave York
Rooms: 5 (3 PB; 2 SB) $65-95
Full Breakfast
Credit Cards: A, B, D
Notes: 2, 7, 8, 9, 10, 11, 12, 14

The Four Chimneys Inn

946 Main Street, 02638
(508) 385-6317

Newly restored, spacious 1881 Victorian home with lovely gardens on historic Route 6A. Across from Scargo Lake, it's a short walk to Cape Cod Bay beaches, the Cape Playhouse, art museum, restaurants, auctions, concerts, and shops. Golf, tennis, and bike trails within two miles. Central to all of Cape Cod. Closed for the month of January. No smoking. Children over eight are welcome.

Host: Kathy Clough
Rooms: 8 (PB) $75-115
Full Breakfast
Credit Cards: A, B, C, D
Notes: 2, 7, 9, 10, 11, 12, 14

The Four Chimneys Inn

7 No smoking; 8 Children welcome; 9 Social drinking allowed; 10 Tennis nearby; 11 Swimming nearby; 12 Golf nearby; 13 Skiing nearby; 14 May be booked through a travel agent; 15 Handicapped accessible.

Isaiah Hall

Isaiah Hall
Bed and Breakfast Inn
P.O. Box 1007, 152 Whig Street, 02638
(508) 385-9928; (800) 736-0160
www.virtualcapecod.com/isaiahhall

Enjoy country ambiance and hospitality in the heart of Cape Cod. This lovely 1857 farmhouse is tucked away on a quiet historic side street. Within walking distance of the beach and village shops, restaurants, museums, cinema, and playhouse. Nearby bike trails, tennis, and golf. Comfortably appointed with antiques and orientals. Guest rooms have air conditioning and cable TV. Excellent central location for day trips. Continental plus breakfast is served. Closed mid-October through mid-April. Children over seven welcome.

Host: Marie Brophy
Rooms: 10 (PB) $91-128
Suite: 1–$156
Continental Breakfast
Credit Cards: A, B, C
Notes: 2, 7, 9, 10, 11, 12, 14

Scargo Manor
Bed and Breakfast
909 Main Street, Route 6A, 02638
(508) 385-5534; (800) 595-0034

Elegance on historic Scargo Lake. Beautifully updated 1895 sea captain's home on two and one-half meticulously landscaped acres. Large rooms and suites with king- or queen-size canopied beds and private baths. Large common area with fireplace, TV, and telephone. Continental plus breakfast served in dining room with fireplace or on sun-filled enclosed porch. Nearby beaches, golf, tennis, bike trails, historic sites, restaurants, and the famous Cape Playhouse. Access to all points on Cape Cod. Open April 1 to December 31.

Hosts: Jane and Chuck MacMillin
Rooms: 6 (PB) $80-140
Continental Breakfast
Credit Cards: A, B, C, D, E
Notes: 2, 7, 11, 12

DENNIS PORT

Bed and Breakfast Cape Cod
P.O. Box 1312, Orleans, 02653
(508) 255-3824; (800) 541-6226
FAX (508) 240-0599
e-mail: bedandb@capecod.net
www.bandbcapecod.com

60. Built in 1721, this lovely restored Colonial house is across the street from one of the most popular beaches on the cape. The house has four guest rooms with private baths, and extra rooms for a third or fourth person in the party. Within walking distance of several restaurants, tennis, and lots of shopping. A unique spot on the beach in a historic home. All rooms are air conditioned. A full Continental breakfast served. No smoking. Children over 10 welcome. $85-140.

The Rose Petal
Bed and Breakfast
152 Sea Street, Box 974, 02639
(508) 398-8470
www.virtualcapecod.com/market/rosepetal/

Picket-fenced gardens surround traditional 1872 New England home in a delightful seaside resort neighborhood. Stroll past century-old houses to a sandy Nantucket Sound beach. Home-baked pastries highlight a full breakfast. A comfortable parlor

The Rose Petal

offers TV, piano, reading. Enjoy queen-size brass beds; antiques; hand-stitched quilts; spacious and bright baths; air conditioning. Between Hyannis and Chatham, it is convenient to all Cape Cod attractions. AAA three-diamond rating.

Hosts: Dan and Gayle Kelly
Rooms: 3 (2 PB; 1 SB) $55-96
Full Breakfast
Credit Cards: A, B, C
Notes: 2, 5, 7, 8, 9, 10, 11, 12, 14

EAST DENNIS

Bed and Breakfast Cape Cod

P.O. Box 1312, Orleans, 02653
(508) 255-3824; (800) 541-6226
FAX (508) 240-0599
e-mail: bedandb@capecod.net
www.bandbcapecod.com

56. This Cape Cod-style house, built in 1994, is a short walk to two beaches on Cape Cod Bay, each of which is easily accessible for a swim or fishing. The house has two bedrooms, each with private bath, cable TV, and air conditioning. Ten-minute walk to Cape Playhouse, several fine restaurants, and shopping. There is an apartment (three-night or weekly) available with a king-size bed, kitchen facilities, and a pull-out sofa for one or two additional persons. No smoking. Children 10 and older welcome. $70-85.

EASTHAM

Bed and Breakfast Cape Cod

P.O. Box 1312, Orleans, 02653
(508) 255-3824; (800) 541-6226
FAX (508) 240-0599
e-mail: bedandb@capecod.net
www.bandbcapecod.com

76. The village of Eastham is the center of some of the most scenic sections of Cape Cod. This lovely Cape Cod-style house is built on the harbor with views of the water from all rooms. The in-ground pool offers a freshwater swim for guests while the ocean beach is nearby. The queen-size, private-bath, air-conditioned bedrooms are decorated with antiques. Walk to everything in the village of Orleans for great restaurants, shops, and bike or boat rentals. Full breakfast. No smoking. Children 12 and older welcome. $115.

Orleans Bed and Breakfast Associates, Inc.

P.O. Box 1312; Orleans, 02653
(508) 255-3824; (800) 541-6226
FAX (508) 240-0599
e-mail: orleansbnb@capecod.net
www.capecod.net/bb

The Aerie. This light-filled attractive guest wing has a high outlook over the marsh with unimpeded view of Cape Cod Bay. Guest accommodation has a private entrance, private bath, refrigerator, and sitting area with TV and air conditioning. In addition, guests have a deck on which to sit and observe spectacular sunsets. Breakfast is served in the greenhouse or on the deck overlooking the bay. Three-night minimum stay. $115.

Back Acres. Cozy grade-level studio apartment in secluded area. It has a kitchenette with microwave and fully stocked refrigerator for self-serve breakfasts. Spacious sitting room with queen-size sofa bed, VCR, and cable TV. Large private patio faces lovely

7 No smoking; 8 Children welcome; 9 Social drinking allowed; 10 Tennis nearby; 11 Swimming nearby; 12 Golf nearby; 13 Skiing nearby; 14 May be booked through a travel agent; 15 Handicapped accessible.

small freshwater pond with dock. Short distance to bicycle trail, National Seashore visitor center, and ocean beaches. $70.

Bayside Path. An attractive and comfortable home in a wonderful location. Walk five minutes to beautiful private beach and scenic views of Cape Cod Bay. Home is nestled in secluded setting. Quiet bedrooms on the first floor share modern bath. Comfortable, furnished adjacent guest living room offers cable TV and VCR. Popular walking and biking area. Breakfast served. $75-85.

Ocean Walk. A wooded path winds past the Three Sisters lighthouses and leads from this comfortable house to the Nauset Light Beach nearby. There is a large separate living room with fireplace for guests. Big windows and deep couches invite relaxed reading or watching TV. The bedroom has a private bath with extra-large tub and shower. There are a guest microwave and refrigerator. $90.

On Target. Watch the spectacular sunsets from the screened-in porch from this most beautiful bay-view location in Eastham. There is one spacious bedroom facing the bay. The second bedroom can be used for family or friends traveling together. Only steps away from a small bay beach or take a morning stroll out onto the bay flats at low tide. Perfect location and perfect home. $80-90.

The Over Look Inn. Those interested in Victoriana will particularly enjoy this romantic inn. Scottish hosts add special charm to afternoon tea in the parlor, browsing in the Churchill Library, or a game of billiards in the Hemingway Room. There are 10 comfortable bedrooms, each with private bath. Brass beds and other period furniture reflect the authentic atmosphere of the inn. Relax on large, graceful veranda after bicycle trips

in the nearby Cape Cod National Seashore. Family suites available. $75-135.

Quail Cover. For those seeking the restfulness of the lower cape this is the perfect place. Close to Cape Cod Bay, the famous Audubon Bird Sanctuary, and the bike trail, this lovely home has one guest room with private bath, TV/VCR, and private entrance. Enjoy the sights and sounds of nature from the sunroom. Delightful hosts will let guests know about the cape's best-kept secrets. $75.

Windmill View. An adult-sized doll house just perfect for two or with one small child ($20 additional). Host will serve breakfast in guests' "house" or on guests' private patio. Bedroom with TV plus single sofa bed. Fully equipped eat-in kitchen and full bath (also warm-water outside shower). This little house sits in a uniquely landscaped garden with grassy lawn and a path leading to Long Pond for freshwater bathing. Short walk to convenience stores and library. Close to National Seashore visitor center. $85.

The Whalewalk Inn

220 Bridge Road, 02642
(508) 255-0617

The welcoming hosts promise an unspoiled environment on outer Cape Cod—one of the country's most beautiful areas. Only minutes by car or bike to beaches, bike trails, or Orleans village. This 1830s home has been restored and creatively decorated with handsome antiques. The 11 guest rooms and five large suites with wet bars are furnished with country antiques, fine linens, and local art. All are air conditioned, have private baths; some have fireplaces. Breakfast and afternoon hors d'oeuvres.

Hosts: Carolyn and Richard Smith
Rooms: 16 (PB) $140-240
Full Breakfast
Credit Cards: A, B
Notes: 2, 7, 9, 11, 12, 14

NOTES: Credit cards accepted: A MasterCard; B Visa; C American Express; D Discover; E Diner's Club; F Other; 2 Personal checks accepted; 3 Lunch available; 4 Dinner available; 5 Open all year; 6 Pets welcome;

EAST ORLEANS

The Farmhouse at Nauset Beach

163 Beach Road, Orleans, 02653
(508) 255-6654

This bed and breakfast is an 1870 Greek Revival historic farmhouse which was once part of a duck farm in East Orleans one-half mile to beautiful sand dunes and surf of the Atlantic Ocean. Quiet, residential area, 1.6 acres, 90 feet from road. Ocean-view rooms. Gift certificates available. The Standish children, Clark and Florence, are 11th generation descendants of Myles Standish. "Be our guests."

Hosts: The Standishes
Rooms: 8 (PB) $42-95
Continental Breakfast
Credit Cards: A, B
Notes: 2, 5, 8, 9, 10, 11, 12, 14

The Farmhouse at Nauset Beach

Nauset House Inn

143 Beach Road, Box 774, 02643
(508) 255-2195; e-mail: jvessel@capecod.net
www.nausethouseinn.com

The Nauset House Inn is a place where the gentle amenities of life are still observed, a place where sea and shore, orchard and field all combine to create a perfect setting for tranquil relaxation. The Nauset House Inn is ideally near one of the world's great ocean beaches, yet is close to antique and craft shops, restaurants, art galleries, scenic

Nauset House Inn

paths, and remote places for sunning, swimming, and picnicking. Closed November 1 through March 31.

Hosts: Diane and Al Johnson, Cindy and
    John Vessella
Rooms: 14 (8 PB; 6 SB) $75-135
Full Breakfast
Credit Cards: A, B, D
Notes: 2, 7, 9, 10, 11, 12

Orleans Bed and Breakfast Associates, Inc.

P.O. Box 1312; Orleans, 02653
(508) 255-3824; (800) 541-6226
FAX (508) 240-0599
e-mail: orleansbnb@capecod.net
www.capecod.net/bb

The Captain Nelson Homestead. A spacious Federal antique home with newly renovated guest rooms. Enjoy the sun on the open deck overlooking the gardens and secluded forest. Steps away to the East Orleans shops and restaurants. Nauset Beach is just one mile down the road. One room with two twin beds with private bath and a second room with a single twin bed with private or shared bath. $60-120.

The China Clipper. This spacious country home is on the way to Nauset Beach in East Orleans. The name represents the extensive antique collection the hosts have from the China trade. Two comfortable bedrooms share a large bath. Each room has a TV and

7 No smoking; 8 Children welcome; 9 Social drinking allowed; 10 Tennis nearby; 11 Swimming nearby; 12 Golf nearby; 13 Skiing nearby; 14 May be booked through a travel agent; 15 Handicapped accessible.

is air conditioned. Linger leisurely on the expansive deck or in the comfortable living room. The garden apartment has a bedroom, private bath, spacious living room with sofa bed, complete kitchen, and air conditioning. $65-115.

The Family House. Spacious and child friendly, this lovely home is within walking distance to East Orleans and only a mile and a half to Nauset Beach. There is a large guest suite that has a sitting area, full kitchen, TV, private full bath, and attached bedroom. A second room with private bath and a step-down sitting and TV area. There is also a smaller room for those people traveling with other family members. Have breakfast on the brick patio facing a large manicured back yard or in guests' own room. Twenty dollars for additional persons. Off-season rates available. $70-95.

High Nauset. Experience spectacular views of the Atlantic Ocean and Nauset Beach. Four new, bright, and airy guest rooms on the second floor of this home which sits high on a knoll overlooking Nauset Beach. The rooms offer private attached baths with tub/shower combination, large picture windows, and cable TV. Separate guest entrance. Awaken to a panoramic view from the window, the surf pounding along the shore or perhaps a passing fishing boat. A Continental breakfast is offered in the guest living room. $90-140.

The Lyttle House. Excellent location for biking to Nauset Beach. A sunny apartment with separate entrance. Living room with sofa bed, cable TV, telephone. Nice dining area and full kitchen stocked for breakfast. A separate bedroom and modern bath with shower. Private deck. Children welcome. Twenty dollars additional per child; crib available. $80-100.

Orissa House. This rambling Greek Revival gets its name from an 1857 ship-wreck on Nauset Beach. Parklike setting with apple orchard and flower gardens. Nauset Beach is one-half mile away and 400 yards to saltwater landing, dock, and small beach on Meeting House Pond. Large, sunny bedroom with private bath. Two additional bedrooms with shared bath or have a private bath at an additional charge. Relax in upstairs sitting area, enjoy breakfast in the sunroom or outdoors on brick patio. $80-95.

Ship's Knees Inn

Ship's Knees Inn

186 Beach Road, P.O. Box 756, 02643
(508) 255-1312; FAX (508) 240-1351

A 170-year-old restored sea captain's home; rooms individually appointed with their own Colonial color schemes and authentic antiques. Only a three-minute walk to popular sand-duned Nauset Beach. Swimming pool and tennis on premises. Also available three miles away, overlooking Orleans Cove, are an efficiency and two heated cottages where children of all ages are welcome and smoking is permitted. Children over 12 are welcome at the inn.

Rooms: 22 (11 PB; 11 SB) $45-120
Continental Breakfast
Credit Cards: A, B
Notes: 2, 5, 7, 9, 10, 11, 12, 14

EAST SANDWICH

Wingscorton Farm Inn

Route 6A, Olde Kings Highway, 02537
(508) 888-0534; (508) 888-0545

Historic 1756 estate on 13 acres, with private beach, working farm, full farm breakfast.

NOTES: Credit cards accepted: A MasterCard; B Visa; C American Express; D Discover; E Diner's Club; F Other; 2 Personal checks accepted; 3 Lunch available; 4 Dinner available; 5 Open all year; 6 Pets welcome;

Children welcome; well-behaved pets welcome also. Carriage house with full kitchen, living room, bedroom, and sunning deck. Breakfast is included in all rates. Also available is a two-bedroom cottage with full kitchen and fireplace in living room. Suites with private bath and working fireplace.

Hosts: Sheila Weyers and Richard Loring
Rooms: 4 (PB) $115-150
Full Breakfast
Credit Cards: A, B, C
Notes: 2, 3, 4, 5, 6, 8, 9, 10, 11, 12, 14

EDGARTOWN (CAPE COD)

Bed and Breakfast Associates Bay Colony, Ltd.

P.O. Box 57166, Babson Park, Boston, 02157-0166
(781) 449-5302; (800) 347-5088
FAX (781) 449-5958; e-mail: info@bnbboston.com
www.bnbboston.com

MV100. This delightful old whaling captain's home now offers 15 unique guest rooms, each with private bath; some with fireplaces, decks, or private entrances. Two blocks to town for shops, restaurants, and harbor. Enjoy cookies and lemonade in the gazebo or croquet on the lawn. $110-325.

Hob Knob Inn

128 Main Street, P.O. Box 239, 02539
(508) 627-9510; (800) 696-2723
FAX (508) 627-4560
e-mail: hobknob@vineyard.net
www.hobknob.com

Sixteen luxurious rooms in the heart of Edgartown village. Large, airy bedrooms with king-size beds, cotton bed linens, and down comforters. Delicious breakfast prepared to order served in two dining rooms. Charter fishing boat may take guests to an undiscovered beach complete with personalized picnic basket. Classic bicycles available for island touring. Fresh flowers and newspapers delivered to door. Welcoming and courteous staff. Inquire about accommodations for children.

Host: Margaret H. White
Rooms: 19 (18 PB; 1 SB) $100-375
Full Breakfast
Credit Cards: A, B, C
Notes: 2, 5, 7, 10, 12, 14, 15

EDGARTOWN (MARTHA'S VINEYARD)

The Arbor

222 Upper Main Street, P.O. Box 1228, 02539
(508) 627-8137

This turn-of-the-century home was originally built on the adjoining island of Chappaquiddick and was moved by barge to its present location. A short stroll to village shops, fine restaurants, and the bustling activity of Edgartown Harbor, the Arbor is filled with the fragrance of fresh flowers. Peggy will gladly direct visitors to the walking trails, unspoiled beaches, fishing, and all the delights of Martha's Vineyard. Smoking in designated areas only. Children over 12 welcome.

Host: Peggy Hall
Rooms: 10 (8 PB; 2 SB) $80-150
Continental Breakfast
Credit Cards: A, B
Notes: 2, 9, 10, 11, 12

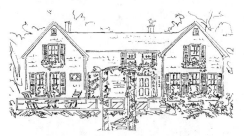

The Arbor

Bed and Breakfast Nantucket/Martha's Vineyard

P.O. Box 341, West Hyannisport, 02672-0341
(800) 686-5252; FAX (508) 775-2884
e-mail: bedandb@capecod.net
www.bandbcapecod.net

204. This 1840s sea captain's house offers 11 rooms with private baths, some with fireplaces and air conditioning. The decor is Victorian. Transportation to the beach is right outside the door, and a short walk takes guests to the village shops and restaurants. Continental breakfast. Children over 11 welcome. $95-195.

210. Built in 1840 by a whaling captain and restored in 1996 by the present owner, this charming, luxuriously appointed four-guest-room bed and breakfast is nothing short of spectacular. From the wonderful heated in-ground pool to the very private carriage house with fireplace and Jacuzzi, there are amenities for every desire. Full breakfast, air-conditioned rooms, and convenience to all Edgartown's shops, restaurants, and points of interest are a few blocks away. No smoking. $110-350.

Captain Dexter House of Edgartown

35 Pease's Point Way, P.O. Box 2798, 02539
(508) 627-7289; FAX (508) 627-3328

This historic inn offers both charm and hospitality. Enjoy beautiful gardens. Savor a home-baked Continental plus breakfast and evening apéritif. Relax in a four-poster, lace-canopied bed in a room with a working fireplace. Stroll to the harbor, town, and restaurants. Bicycle or walk to the beach. Let the innkeepers make a vacation special!

Captain Dexter House of Edgartown

Host: Birdie
Rooms: 11 (PB) $65-190
Continental Breakfast
Credit Cards: A, B, C
Notes: 2, 7, 8, 9, 10, 11, 12, 14

The Charlotte Inn

The Charlotte Inn

27 South Summer Street, Edgartown, 02539
(508) 627-4751

Fine English antiques and fireplaces in a romantic garden setting with private courtyards and porches. Has 25 impeccably maintained and individually decorated guest rooms. Attention to detail is the Charlotte Inn's trademark. Walking distance to shops, beaches, tennis, and sailing. Excellent French restaurant called l'Étoile in the inn serves dinner. Member of Relais et Chateaux. Voted one of two Country House Hotels of the year—*Andrew Harper's Hideaway Report.*

Hosts: Gery and Paula Conover
Rooms: 25 (PB) $175-750
Full or Continental Breakfast
Credit Cards: A, B, C
Notes: 2, 4, 5, 9, 10, 11, 12

Colonial Inn of Martha's Vineyard

38 North Water Street, P.O. Box 68,
   Edgartown, 02539
(508) 627-4711; (800) 627-4701

In the heart of historic Edgartown overlooking the harbor sits the Colonial Inn. It

NOTES: Credit cards accepted: A MasterCard; B Visa; C American Express; D Discover; E Diner's Club; F Other; 2 Personal checks accepted; 3 Lunch available; 4 Dinner available; 5 Open all year; 6 Pets welcome;

offers 43 newly renovated and lovingly refurbished rooms, all with heat, air conditioning, color TVs, telephones, and private baths. Continental breakfast is served daily in the solarium and garden courtyard. Affordable luxury. Closed December through March.

COLONIAL INN

Host: Linda Malcouronne
Rooms: 43 (PB) $90-225
Continental Breakfast
Credit Cards: A, B, C
Notes: 3, 4, 8, 9, 10, 11, 12, 14, 15

The Edgartown Inn

56 North Water Street, 02539
(508) 627-4794

Historic inn built in 1798 as the home for a whaling captain. Early guests included Daniel Webster, Nathaniel Hawthorne, and Charles Summer. Later, John Kennedy stayed here as a young senator. Completely restored over the last 150 years, today it is filled with antiques. Convenient to beaches, harbor, and restaurants. Famous for breakfast, including homemade breads and

cakes. Member of the National Trust for Historic Preservation.

Hosts: Liliane and Earle Radford
Rooms: 20 (16 PB; 4 SB) $95-190
Full and Continental Breakfast
Credit Cards: None
Notes: 2, 9, 10, 11, 12

Point Way Inn

Box 5255, 02539
(508) 627-8633; (888) 711-6633

Now under new ownership. This delightful country inn provides a warm, relaxed retreat with working fireplaces in 9 out of 14 guest rooms. Tea and scones are provided in the winter; in the summer, lemonade and cookies are served in the beautiful newly landscaped gardens. Complimentary courtesy car available. Air conditioned. Two-night minimum stay on weekends. Seasonal rates available.

Hosts: John Glendon and Claudia Miller
Rooms: 14 (PB) $175-325
Continental Breakfast
Credit Cards: A, B, C, D
Notes: 2, 5, 6, 7, 8, 10, 11, 12, 14

Shiretown Inn

44 North Water Street, P.O. Box 921, 02539
(508) 627-3353; (800) 541-0090
FAX (508) 627-8478

In downtown Edgartown is the Shiretown Inn, circa 1817, consisting of two whaling captain's houses and carriage house rooms. Listed in the National Register of Historic Places. All rooms in the captain's houses have private entrances off of the garden walkways or shared deck areas. These clean, comfortable, country-style rooms feature private baths, cable color TVs, telephones, and air conditioning. Carriage house rooms, although more basic and modest, have private baths.

Host: Sonya A. Lima
Rooms: 33 (PB) $59-259
Continental Breakfast
Credit Cards: A, B, D
Notes: 4, 8, 9, 10, 11, 12, 14

7 No smoking; 8 Children welcome; 9 Social drinking allowed; 10 Tennis nearby; 11 Swimming nearby; 12 Golf nearby; 13 Skiing nearby; 14 May be booked through a travel agent; 15 Handicapped accessible.

ESSEX

Bed and Breakfast Reservations North Shore, Greater Boston, Cape Cod

P.O. Box 600035, Greater Boston Branch,
   Newtonville, 02160-0001
(617) 964-1606; (800) 832-2632
FAX (617) 332-8572; e-mail: info@bbreserve.com
www.bbreserve.com

56. Essex River Inn. Historic 1830 Federal-style inn retaining many of its original features; folding Indian shutters, working fireplaces, and wood carvings. Several porches and balconies overlook salt marsh and Essex River. Seven charming guest rooms, all with private bath, air conditioning, color cable TV, telephone. Spacious penthouse suite features fireplace, efficiency kitchen area, private deck. Walk to restaurants, antique shops, and Woodman's famous "lobster-in-the-rough." Full gourmet breakfast. No smoking. Children 16 and older welcome. Resident cat in common areas. $99-150.

George Fuller House

148 Main Street, 01929
(978) 768-7766; (800) 477-0148
FAX (978) 768-6178

Essex shipwrights built this home with the same pride and craftsmanship used to build the famous "Essex-built" fishing schooners. This 1830 Federal-style house retains many of its fine architectural features. The seven guest rooms are furnished with antiques and period reproductions. Each has a unique atmosphere with features such as brass and canopied beds, braided rugs, and hand-caned Boston rockers. All rooms have private baths, individual heat/air conditioning, color TV, and telephones. Four guest rooms have working fireplaces that add unique charm to these rooms.

Hosts: Cindy and Bob Cameron
Rooms: 7 (PB) $100-150

Full Breakfast
Credit Cards: A, B, C, D
Notes: 2, 5, 7, 8, 9, 10, 11, 12, 14

FALMOUTH (CAPE COD)

Bed and Breakfast Associates Bay Colony, Ltd.

P.O. Box 57166, Babson Park, Boston, 02157-0166
(781) 449-5302; (800) 347-5088
FAX (781) 449-5958; e-mail: info@bnbboston.com
www.bnbboston.com

CC129. Antique house, circa 1820, with lovely period furnishings and three guest rooms with private baths. On the village green, just two blocks from the shuttle bus to the ferry to Martha's Vineyard. $85-95.

CC127. Waquoit Village. This perfect sanctuary is a 1996 restoration of a circa 1800 sea captain's mansion. Along with six exquisite guest rooms, visitors are treated to an indoor heated swimming pool, hot tub, sauna, grand parlor, and classic card room with double French doors overlooking the expansive grounds. Ideal for corporate groups or families, this secluded inn is only 20 minutes from the ferry to Martha's Vineyard and one-fourth mile to Waquoit Bay. $65-135.

Bed and Breakfast Cape Cod

P.O. Box 1312, Orleans, 02653
(508) 255-3824; (800) 541-6226
FAX (508) 240-0599
e-mail: bedandb@capecod.net
www.bandbcapecod.com

42. This gracious Federal Colonial home, built in 1822, is on the beautiful village green in Falmouth. Through the years this prominent home has been photographed many times as a reflection of picturesque New England. Restored some years ago by the hostess, the home now offers two bedrooms with private baths, air conditioning, and canopied four-poster beds. Walk to the bus to Martha's Vineyard ferry or stroll across the green to shops and fine restaurants. Full breakfast. $85-95.

Bed and Breakfast Reservations North Shore, Greater Boston, Cape Cod

P.O. Box 600035, Greater Boston Branch,
  Newtonville, 02160-0001
(617) 964-1606; (800) 832-2632
FAX (617) 332-8572; e-mail: info@bbreserve.com
www.bbreserve.com

84. Falmouth Heights Bed and Breakfast. A short walk to the Martha's Vineyard ferry, pristine beaches, and seaside restaurants. This contemporary bed and breakfast has a large deck and in-ground pool. Each of seven guest rooms, all with private baths, is a colorful work of art, with hand-crafted New England-made furnishings. Comfortable sitting room with fireplace. A delicious breakfast buffet is served in café-style kitchen overlooking deck and pool. $129-149.

Capt. Tom Lawrence House

75 Locust Street, 02540
(508) 540-1445; (800) 266-8139
FAX (508) 457-1790
www.sunsol.com/captaintom/

Beautiful 1861 Victorian, former whaling captain's residence in the historic village of

Capt. Tom Lawrence House

Falmouth. Central air conditioning throughout the whole facility. Comfortable, spacious, corner guest rooms with TVs. Firm beds—some with canopies. Steinway piano and working fireplace. One completely furnished apartment sleeps four. Gourmet breakfast consists of fresh fruit, breads, pancakes made from freshly ground organic grain, and a variety of other delicious specialties. German spoken. Two-night minimum stay.

Rooms: 6 (PB) $80-165
Full Breakfast
Credit Cards: A, B
Notes: 2, 9. 10, 11, 12, 14

The Elms

495 Route 28A West Falmouth Highway, 02574
(508) 540-7232; FAX (508) 540-7295

Charming Victorian, built in the early 1800s, features nine beautifully appointed bedrooms, seven private baths, and antique decor throughout. A full Continental breakfast is served. Tour the manicured grounds to survey the flower and herb gardens or relax in the gazebo. In the historic district; also walk to restaurants, antique shops, and one-half mile to ocean. Children over 14 welcome.

Hosts: Betty and Joe Mazzucchelli
Rooms: 9 (7 PB; 2 SB) $75-100
Continental Breakfast
Credit Cards: A, B, C
Notes: 2, 5, 7, 9, 10, 11, 12, 15

Gladstone Inn

219 Grand Avenue South, 02540
(508) 548-9851
www.sunsol.com/gladstoneinn

A 1996 editor's pick, *Yankee* magazine. An oceanfront Victorian inn overlooking Martha's Vineyard. Established in 1910. Light, airy guest rooms have period furniture and their own wash stations. Buffet breakfast is served on the glassed-in porch that also provides a cozy place to read, watch cable TV, or relax. Five guest rooms

7 No smoking; 8 Children welcome; 9 Social drinking allowed; 10 Tennis nearby; 11 Swimming nearby; 12 Golf nearby; 13 Skiing nearby; 14 May be booked through a travel agent; 15 Handicapped accessible.

Gladstone Inn

have private baths and TVs. Refrigerators, bikes, and gas grill are provided for guests to use. Closed October 15 through May 15.

Hosts: Jim and Gayle Carroll
Rooms: 15 (5 PB; 10 SB) $70-145
Full Breakfast
Credit Cards: A, B
Notes: 2, 9, 10, 11, 12

Grafton Inn

261 Grand Avenue South, 02540
(508) 540-8688; (800) 642-4069
FAX (508) 540-1861

Cape Cod oceanfront Queen Anne Victorian. Thirty steps to sandy beach. Breathtaking views of Martha's Vineyard. Full gourmet breakfast served at private tables

Grafton Inn

overlooking Nantucket Sound. Complimentary evening wine and cheese. Immaculate accommodations. Thoughtful amenities. Homemade chocolates, fresh flowers, sand chairs, beach towels. Individual air conditioning and heat. Cable color TV. On bike path. Year-round golf, tennis, deep-sea fishing minutes away. Walk to restaurants, shops, and island ferry. AAA and Mobil three-star rated.

Hosts: Liz and Rudy Cvitan
Rooms: 11 (PB) $85-169
Full Breakfast
Credit Cards: A, B, C
Notes: 7, 9, 10, 11, 12, 14

Hewins House Bed and Breakfast

20 Hewins Street, 02540
(508) 457-4363; (800) 555-4366

At the Hewins House Bed and Breakfast it is the hostess's pleasure to share one of Falmouth's historic homes with guests. Through the years this home has been lovingly preserved. Step back in time and enjoy comfortable elegance and delicious homemade breakfasts. Walk to restaurants, shopping, island ferries, beaches, and bus station from the convenient location. Once guests have stayed at the Hewins House, they will want to return again and again.

Host: Virginia Price
Rooms: 3 (PB) $85-105
Full Breakfast
Credit Cards: A, B, C, D
Notes: 2, 7, 8, 9, 10, 11, 12, 14

The Inn at One Main Street

One Main Street, 02540
(508) 540-7469

This elegant 1892 Victorian is in Falmouth's historic district, where the road to Woods Hole begins. The inn is within walking distance to beaches, bike path, restaurants, shops, and ferry shuttle. Enjoy a romantic getaway in one of six freshly decorated rooms, each with private bath.

NOTES: Credit cards accepted: A MasterCard; B Visa; C American Express; D Discover; E Diner's Club; F Other; 2 Personal checks accepted; 3 Lunch available; 4 Dinner available; 5 Open all year; 6 Pets welcome;

The Inn at One Main Street

Whatever wishes guests may have, the hosts will do their very best to ensure an enjoyable stay and send guests home feeling fully refreshed.

Hosts: Ilona Cleveland and Jeanne Dahl
Rooms: 6 (PB) $95-125
Full Breakfast
Credit Cards: A, B, C, D
Notes: 5, 7, 10, 11, 12

Mostly Hall
Bed and Breakfast Inn

27 Main Street, 02540
(508) 548-3786; (800) 682-0565
FAX (508) 457-1572
www.sunsol.com/mostlyhall/

Romantic 1849 southern plantation-style Cape Cod home with wraparound veranda

Mostly Hall

and widow's walk. Set back from the road on an acre of beautiful gardens with a gazebo. Close to restaurants, shops, beaches, and island ferries. Spacious corner rooms with queen-size canopied beds, central air conditioning, gourmet breakfast, bicycles, and private baths. Minimum stay Memorial Day through Columbus Day is two nights. Closed January through mid-February.

Hosts: Caroline and Jim Lloyd
Rooms: 6 (PB) $95-140
Full Breakfast
Credit Cards: A, B, C, D
Notes: 2, 7, 9, 10, 11, 12

The Palmer House Inn

The Palmer House Inn

81 Palmer Avenue, 02540-2857
(508) 548-1230; (800) 472-2632
FAX (508) 540-1878

Turn-of-the-century Victorian bed and breakfast in the historic district. Antique furnishings return guests to the romance of a bygone era. Full gourmet breakfast featuring Belgian waffles, creamed eggs with fresh chives, and chocolate-stuffed French toast. Close to island ferries, beaches, and shops. Bicycles available. Personal checks accepted for deposits only. Children over 10 welcome.

Hosts: Ken and Joanne Baker
Rooms: 13 (PB) $78-185
Full Breakfast
Credit Cards: A, B, C, D, E
Notes: 5, 7, 9, 10, 11, 12, 14, 15

7 No smoking; 8 Children welcome; 9 Social drinking allowed; 10 Tennis nearby; 11 Swimming nearby; 12 Golf nearby; 13 Skiing nearby; 14 May be booked through a travel agent; 15 Handicapped accessible.

Village Green Inn

40 Main Street, 02540
(508) 548-5621; (800) 237-1119
FAX (508) 457-5057; e-mail: vgi40@aol.com
www.villagegreeninn.com

Gracious old Victorian, ideally on historic village green. Walk to fine shops and restaurants, bike to beaches, tennis, and the picturesque bike path to Woods Hole. Enjoy 19th-century charm and warm hospitality in elegant surroundings. Four lovely guest rooms and one romantic suite all have private baths. Also bicycles, seasonal beverages, and working fireplaces. Personal checks accepted as deposit only. Children 12 and older welcome. Open year-round.

Hosts: Diane and Don Crosby
Rooms: 5 (PB) $85-160
Full Breakfast
Credit Cards: A, B, C
Notes: 2, 5, 7, 9, 10, 11, 12, 14

Village Green Inn

The Wildflower Inn

167 Palmer Avenue, 02540
(508) 548-9524; (800) 294-5459
FAX (508) 548-9524; e-mail: wldflr167@aol.com
www.wildflower-inn.com

Built before the turn of the century, this award-winning inn is in the heart of Falmouth's historic district and a five-minute

The Wildflower Inn

walk to Falmouth village. Each upstairs guest rooms has its own personality; all have private bath, some with whirlpool. A cottage, with private entrance, kitchen, living room, and spiral staircase leading to a romantic loft bedroom is available weekly. A gourmet breakfast, as seen on PBS *Country Inn Cooking*, is served in the gathering room or on the wraparound porch. Complimentary refreshments available 24 hours. Air conditioning throughout.

Hosts: Donna and Phil Stone
Rooms: 6 (PB) $90-160
Full Breakfast
Credit Cards: A, B, C
Notes: 5, 7, 8, 9, 10, 11, 12, 14

Woods Hole Passage Bed and Breakfast Inn

186 Woods Hole Road, 02540
(508) 548-9575; (800) 790-8976
FAX (508) 540-4771
e-mail: woods.hole.inn@usa.net
www.woodsholepassage.com

This 100-year-old carriage house sits on spacious grounds adorned by shade trees and berry bushes. The inn is close to the bike path, Martha's Vineyard, Nobska Lighthouse, the Woods Hole Oceanographic Institution, and the many beaches of the cape. Rooms have private baths and are graciously appointed in a comfortable, clean, airy atmosphere. A full gourmet breakfast is served by a huge multi-paned window on the patio overlooking the grounds or in the secret garden.

Host: Deb Pruitt
Rooms: 5 (PB) $75-115
Full Breakfast
Credit Cards: A, B, C, D, E
Notes: 2, 5, 7, 8, 9, 10, 11, 12, 14

FALMOUTH HEIGHTS

Inn on the Sound

313 Grand Avenue, 02540
(800) 564-9668

The oceanfront Inn on the Sound boasts a million-dollar view of Martha's Vineyard, Vineyard Sound, and miles of shoreline. The inn is across the street from the beach and a short walk to the Martha's Vineyard ferry, bicycle rental, the harbor, restaurants, and shops. Spacious, upscale, casual, beach-house-style guest rooms provide queen-size beds, private baths, lounge seating, and a panoramic view. Included is a sumptuous gourmet breakfast.

Hosts: Renée Ross and David Ross
Rooms: 10 (PB) $95-160
Full Breakfast
Credit Cards: A, B, C, D
Notes: 2, 5, 7, 9, 10, 11, 12, 14

The Moorings Lodge

207 Grand Avenue South, 02540
(508) 540-2370

Enjoy homemade breads for buffet breakfast served on a large glassed-in porch with lovely ocean view. This charming old sea captain's home with spacious, airy rooms overlooks Vineyard Sound and Martha's Vineyard. Just opposite a safe and clean family beach and within a short walking distance of good restaurants and the island ferry. Delicious breakfast served. Fifteen dollars for extra adult in room.

Hosts: Ernie and Shirley Benard
Rooms: 8 (PB) $85-139
Full Breakfast
Credit Cards: A, B, C
Notes: 2, 7, 8, 9, 10, 11, 12, 14

FRAMINGHAM

Bed and Breakfast Associates Bay Colony, Ltd.

P.O. Box 57166, Babson Park, Boston, 02157-0166
(781) 449-5302; (800) 347-5088
FAX (781) 449-5958; e-mail: info@bnbboston.com
www.bnbboston.com

CW625. This is an idyllic country setting at the end of a private road, yet a short walk to Framingham Centre shops and public transportation. The home was once a barn. The contemporary restoration was completed just over 20 years ago but the weathered siding has the rich hues of age. Exit the first-floor suite via French doors to acres of open land. The guest room has a cathedral ceiling and an attached sitting area. Full breakfast. Children welcome. Monthly rates available. $72-92.

CW605. Very pleasant ranch-style home overlooking Japanese gardens and acres of woodland. Three appealing guest rooms for one party only. Living room with fireplaces and cathedral ceiling. $68-85.

GLOUCESTER

Bed and Breakfast Associates Bay Colony, Ltd.

P.O. Box 57166, Babson Park, Boston, 02157-0166
(781) 449-5302; (800) 347-5088
FAX (781) 449-5958; e-mail: info@bnbboston.com
www.bnbboston.com

NS505. Originally an 1898 Victorian "cottage," this splendid seaside retreat has been completely updated and redecorated. It is on the banks of the Annisquam River, and guests may enjoy watching passing boats from each of the guest rooms, the inviting decks, or the gardens below. There is also a private swimming beach. These three beautifully decorated rooms share two full baths. Continental breakfast. Children over 12 welcome. Family rates available. $80-95.

7 No smoking; 8 Children welcome; 9 Social drinking allowed; 10 Tennis nearby; 11 Swimming nearby; 12 Golf nearby; 13 Skiing nearby; 14 May be booked through a travel agent; 15 Handicapped accessible.

Bed and Breakfast Reservations North Shore, Greater Boston, Cape Cod

P.O. Box 600035, Greater Boston Branch,
   Newtonville, 02160-0001
(617) 964-1606; (800) 832-2632
FAX (617) 332-8572; e-mail: info@bbreserve.com
www.bbreserve.com

1. Riverview Bed and Breakfast. Turn-of-the-century waterfront home high above the Annisquam River. Enjoy fabulous panoramic views of river and small-boating activity from 100-foot wraparound porch or from own private waterfront deck. Gorgeous terraced gardens and landscaped grounds lead to private dock at water's edge. Guest rooms are beautifully decorated and share two full baths. Private decks. Third person in room is an additional $15-20. Children welcome when whole house is rented by same family. No smoking. $70-90.

79. Oceanside Cottage. Small one-bedroom cottage, with breathtaking setting on grounds that slope right to the rugged coastline and ocean's edge. Enjoy spectacular sunsets right at the front door. Cottage has double bed, small living room with TV, shower bath, and galley kitchen stocked with self-serve breakfast foods. Sleeps two. Weekly rates available. Smoking permitted outside only. Open Memorial weekend through September. Three-night minimum stay. $90.

105. The Inn at Gloucester Harbor. Charming three-story Colonial directly across from America's oldest harbor, and just a short walk to beaches, restaurants, and waterfront park. All six designer-decorated guest rooms have private baths. Some have direct ocean views and fireplaces. Relax on the front terrace or back yard garden deck enjoying the ocean breezes and harbor activity. Children seven and older welcome. No smoking. Open year-round. $89-149.

Gray Manor Bed and Breakfast

14 Atlantic Road, 01930
(978) 283-5409; (407) 784-8766 (winter)
http: //www.capeann.com/graymanor

Gray Manor Bed and Breakfast is 30 miles north of Boston on picturesque Cape Ann, which has 25 miles of coastline including America's oldest and most historic fishing port. Gray Manor is only a three-minute walk to a beautiful white sandy beach. Private baths, air conditioning, cable TV, refrigerators, decks, kitchenettes, outdoor gas-fired barbecue grills, patio and porches for relaxation. TV in lounge plays movies at night. Open May 1 through October 25. Seasonal rates.

Host: Madeline Gray
Rooms: 9 (PB) $45-65
Continental Breakfast
Credit Cards: A, B
Notes: 9, 10, 11

GREAT BARRINGTON

American Country Collection

1353 Union Street, Schenectady, NY 12308
(518) 370-4948; (800) 810-4948
FAX (518) 393-1634 (call first)
e-mail: Carolbnbres@msn.com

138. This 1700s Victorian rural farm is on 500 acres of rolling hills, woods, and fields. It is furnished with antiques and oriental rugs. There are four guest rooms, two with private baths. Tanglewood, Norman Rockwell Museum, Berkshire Festival, and skiing are all within 15 minutes. There is an in-ground pool available for guest use. Full breakfast. Smoking outdoors. Resident dog. Children over 10 welcome. $75-100.

Coffing-Bostwick House

98 Division Street, 01230
(413) 528-4511

Unique, historic Greek Revival home (1825). Spacious, well-appointed guest rooms. Cozy parlor with TV; commodious library-living room; elegant mahogany-paneled dining

---

NOTES: Credit cards accepted: A MasterCard; B Visa; C American Express; D Discover; E Diner's Club; F Other; 2 Personal checks accepted; 3 Lunch available; 4 Dinner available; 5 Open all year; 6 Pets welcome;

room; all with fireplaces. Lavish homemade full breakfasts with fresh produce and fruits. Relaxed, informal atmosphere. Four acres with lovely river to stroll. Convenient to Tanglewood, Jacob's Pillow, theaters, ski areas, museums, art galleries, antique shops, and fine dining. Midweek discounts; special weekly packages. No smoking is preferred.

Hosts: Diana and William Harwood
Rooms: 6 (2 PB; 4 SB) $60-95
Full Breakfast
Credit Cards: None
Notes: 2, 5, 7, 8, 9, 10, 11, 12, 13

Elaine's Bed and Breakfast Selections

4987 Kingston Road, Elbridge, NY 13060
(315) 689-2082 (after 10 A.M.)

1. Very nice newer nonsmoking Colonial offers two guest rooms. The spacious master bedroom has a color remote-controlled TV and large private bath with deep whirlpool tub. The second guest room shares a bath with the hostess. Continental breakfast. Entire house can be rented for larger groups. $65-100.

2. Contemporary ranch set far back from the street, overlooks the Housatonic River. Hot tub on deck. Living room-size suite has a sitting area, wood stove, and color remote-controlled TV. There is a separate entrance that leads outdoors. The bath is shared with the owner. Resident cat. No smoking. No guest pets. Continental breakfast.

The Turning Point Inn

3 Lake Buel Road, 01230
(413) 528-4777

An 18th-century former stagecoach inn. Full, delicious breakfast. Featured in the *New York Times*, *Boston Globe*, and *Los Angeles Times*. Adjacent to Butternut Ski Basin; near Tanglewood and all Berkshire attractions. Hiking and cross-country ski trails. Sitting rooms with fireplaces, piano,

The Turning Point Inn

cable TV. Groups and families welcome. Two-bedroom cottage with kitchen and living room available for $200 per night.

Hosts: The Yosts
Rooms: 8 (6 PB; 2 SB) $80-100
Full Breakfast
Credit Cards: A, B, C
Notes: 2, 5, 7, 8, 9, 10, 11, 12, 13, 14

Windflower Inn

684 South Egremont Road, 01230
(413) 528-2720; (800) 992-1993
www.windflowerinn.com

The Windflower is a gracious, antique-filled country inn on 10 acres in the heart of the Berkshire Hills of southwestern Massachusetts. There are two large living rooms, screened porch, and beautiful gardens and grounds for guests' relaxation. All of the rooms are air conditioned, have color TV, and many have working fireplaces. Afternoon tea and cookies are served. Smoking permitted in designated areas only.

Rooms: 13 (PB) $100-180
Full Breakfast
Credit Cards: C
Notes: 2, 5, 8, 9, 10, 11, 12, 13

GREENFIELD

The Brandt House Country Inn

29 Highland Avenue, 01301-3605
(413) 774-3329; (800) 235-3329
FAX (413) 772-2908
e-mail: brandt@brandt_house.com
www.brandt_house.com

High on a hill just five minutes from historic Deerfield, and a five-minute walk to

7 No smoking; 8 Children welcome; 9 Social drinking allowed; 10 Tennis nearby; 11 Swimming nearby; 12 Golf nearby; 13 Skiing nearby; 14 May be booked through a travel agent; 15 Handicapped accessible.

town, this 16-room estate offers privacy, elegance, and comfort. Private baths, wraparound porches, a clay tennis court, fireplaces, pool table, feather beds, antiques, glowing hardwood floors, fresh flowers, and cozy bathrobes await guests. A sumptuous home-cooked breakfast is included. Inquire about accommodations for pets.

Owner/Innkeeper: Phoebe Compton
Rooms: 7 (PB) $105-175
Credit Cards: A, B, C, D, E
Notes: 2, 5, 7, 8, 9, 10, 11, 12, 13, 14

HAMILTON

Bed and Breakfast Reservations North Shore, Greater Boston, Cape Cod

P.O. Box 600035, Greater Boston Branch,
   Newtonville, 02160-0001
(617) 964-1606; (800) 832-2632
FAX (617) 332-8572; e-mail: info@bbreserve.com
www.bbreserve.com

30. The Elms Bed and Breakfast. Surrounded by tall elms, this very cozy and immaculate bed and breakfast invites guests to relax and enjoy its secluded patio and gardens. Location is central to many tourist attractions. Short walk to village center and Boston commuter rail. Two rooms share a bath. Breakfast with homemade goodies. No smoking. $65-75.

HARWICH PORT (CAPE COD)

Augustus Snow House

528 Main Street, 02646
(508) 430-0528; (800) 320-0528
www.augustussnow.com

Romantic Victorian mansion built in 1901, the Augustus Snow House remains one of Cape Cod's most breathtaking examples of Queen Anne Victorian architecture. Today, this turn-of-the-century home with its gabled dormers and wraparound veranda is one of the cape's most elegant and exclu-

sive inns, catering to a small number of discerning guests. Five exquisite bedrooms with queen- or king-size beds, private baths (some with Jacuzzis), fireplaces, color TVs, air conditioning, gourmet breakfast, and afternoon refreshments. The private beach is just a three-minute stroll away.

Hosts: Joyce and Steve Roth
Rooms: 5 (PB) $105-160
Full Breakfast
Credit Cards: A, B, C, D
Notes: 2, 5, 7, 9, 10, 11, 12, 14

Bed and Breakfast Associates Bay Colony, Ltd.

P.O. Box 57166, Babson Park, Boston, 02157-0166
(781) 449-5302; (800) 347-5088
FAX (781) 449-5958; e-mail: bnbboston@aol.com
www.bnbboston.com

CC365. This eight-bedroom inn sits just footsteps from the famed sandy beaches of the cape's south shore. Guests are delighted by the facilities, which include elegant guest rooms with private baths, welcoming common rooms, and romantic decor. Full breakfast provided. Lower rates off-season. $155-220.

CC359. This luxurious Victorian mansion provides an unforgettable setting for a romantic getaway. There are five richly appointed guest rooms with fine period furnishings, elegant baths, and modern amenities. Savor the full gourmet breakfasts and afternoon beverage service in the gracious parlor. Stroll over to the quaint shopping area and to the nearby beach on Nantucket Sound. All rooms have private baths. No children, please. Off-season rates available. $145-160.

Bed and Breakfast Cape Cod

P.O. Box 1312, Orleans, 02653
(508) 255-3824; (800) 541-6226
FAX (508) 240-0599
e-mail: bedandb@capecod.net
www.bandbcapecod.com

30. This Cape Cod-style home built in 1730 and restored in 1977 is 500 feet from the warm waters of Nantucket Sound. The charming accommodation is decorated with both Colonial and Shaker designs. From the private deck from each room one can see the beach and the ocean. Walk to all the village points of interest, including shops, restaurants, and tennis or golf. Full gourmet breakfast served. $100-150.

Bed and Breakfast Reservations North Shore, Greater Boston, Cape Cod

P.O. Box 600035, Greater Boston Branch,
 Newtonville, 02160-0001
(617) 964-1606; (800) 832-2632
FAX (617) 332-8572; e-mail: info@bbreserve.com
www.bbreserve.com

25. Inn by the Sea. Less than 500 feet from a private mile-long beach on Nantucket Sound. Guests will enjoy the casual elegance of this inn in quiet setting, with great midcape location. Nine decorator-designed guest rooms, en suite baths, some with private entrances, fireplaces, and Jacuzzis. Full country breakfast in formal dining room. Living room with fireplace and spacious sun porch overlooking grounds. Cottage with canopied bed, fireplace, kitchen, sleeps three to four. $205 per night for cottage plus $35 of each additional person. No smoking. $165-185.

102. Queen Anne Victorian. Grand turn-of-the century inn, with gabled dormers and wraparound veranda on lovely grounds. Short walk to a beautiful sandy beach on Nantucket Sound. Five elegant and beautifully decorated guest rooms feature private baths (some with Jacuzzis), TV, and working fireplaces, each encased in hand-carved mantels and wood surrounds to match the existing decor. Memorable, multi-course gourmet breakfast, private individual tables in formal dining room. Location close to Harwich Port ferries to Nantucket. No smoking. $105-160.

Captain's Quarters

Captain's Quarters

85 Bank Street, 02642
(800) 992-6550
www.virtualcapecod.com/market/
 captainsquarters

A romantic 1850s Victorian with a classic wraparound porch, nostalgic gingerbread trim, and a graceful curving front stairway. Guest rooms have private baths, queen-size brass beds with eyelet-lace-trimmed sheets, lace curtains, color cable TVs, and comfortable reading chairs. Just a three-minute walk into town and to a lovely ocean beach. Experience Cape Cod in a relaxed and friendly atmosphere.

Hosts: Ed and Susan Kenney
Rooms: 5 (PB) $89-109
Continental Breakfast
Credit Cards: A, B, C, D
Notes: 2, 7, 9, 10, 11, 12, 14

Country Inn

86 Sisson Road, 02646
(508) 432-2769; (800) 231-1722

A Colonial farmhouse (circa 1780) on six and one-half acres features six guest rooms, all with private baths and cable TVs. On Cape Cod in close proximity to bike trails, fishing, beaches, and sightseeing. A full-service inn. Guests enjoy the 134-seat restaurant featuring contemporary New England cuisine as well as the inn's Old English-style tavern. Open year-round. The country charm abounds with nine blazing

7 No smoking; 8 Children welcome; 9 Social drinking allowed; 10 Tennis nearby; 11 Swimming nearby; 12 Golf nearby; 13 Skiing nearby; 14 May be booked through a travel agent; 15 Handicapped accessible.

fireplaces in the winter and the comfort of air conditioning, an in-ground swimming pool, and use of private beach with parking nearby in the summer.

Hosts: James and Wendi Dings
Rooms: 6 (PB) $55-110
Continental Breakfast
Credit Cards: A, B, C
Notes: 2, 4, 5, 7, 9, 10, 11, 12, 14, 15

Harbor Breeze of Cape Cod

326 Lower County Road, 02646
(508) 432-0337; (800) 272-4343
FAX (508) 432-1276
e-mail: dvangeld@capecod.net
www.harborbreezeinn.com

Walk to the beach, shopping, and dining. Relaxed bed and breakfast with nine country guest rooms gathered around the garden courtyard—private entrances, refrigerators, TVs, some air conditioning, and fireplaces. Family suites and private honeymoon rooms with sitting decks. Hearty Continental buffet breakfast with homemade baked goods served in the comfortable common room overlooking the pool. Picnic area with charcoal grills. The best central location for touring Cape Cod, Martha's Vineyard, and Nantucket!

Hosts: Kathleen and David VanGelder
Rooms: 9 (PB) $75-129
Continental Breakfast
Credit Cards: A, B, C, D
Notes: 2, 5, 8, 9, 10, 11, 12, 14

HAYDENVILLE

Shingle Hill Bed and Breakfast

7 Mountain Street, P.O. Box 212, 01039
(413) 268-8320

Goat herd and guard donkey roam past spectacular mountain view on this 40-acre hillside retreat just 10 minutes from downtown Northampton in the Berkshire foothills. Guests have the use of a living room, dining area, and kitchen that are completely separate from hosts' quarters. Enjoy a leisurely country breakfast—Continental breakfast

weekdays; full breakfast weekends—on the enclosed deck overlooking the front pasture. Convenient to I-91, Massachusetts Turnpike, and the Five College (Northampton/Amherst) area.

Host: Sara Sullivan
Rooms: 5 (2 PB; 3 SB) $60-85
Full and Continental Breakfast
Credit Cards: None
Notes: 2, 5, 7, 8, 9, 10, 11, 12, 13

HUNTINGTON

Carmelwood

8 Montgomery Road, 01050
(413) 667-5786

Beautiful Victorian home on bluff above Westfield River. Three double rooms share two baths off upstairs foyer. Grand piano in gracious parlor. Fireplace. Sunny dining room. Full country breakfasts feature home-grown organic fruits and berries. Extensive gardens, two par-three golf holes. Children over 12 welcome.

Host: Katheryn Corrigan
Rooms: 3 (S2B) $65-80
Full Breakfast
Credit Cards: C
Notes: 2, 5, 7, 9, 11, 12, 13

HYANNIS

The Inn on Sea Street

358 Sea Street, 02601
(508) 775-8030; FAX (508) 771-0878
e-mail: innonsea@capecod.net

This elegant Victorian inn, with nine romantic guest rooms plus a white wicker cottage is just steps from the beach. Antiques, Persian carpets, canopied beds, TVs, and air conditioning are features of this friendly, unpretentious inn. Refrigerators, telephones, beach chairs and towels are available for guests' use. A full hot gourmet breakfast of homemade delights is served at individual tables set with sterling silver, china, crystal, and fresh flowers. One-night stays welcome.

NOTES: Credit cards accepted: A MasterCard; B Visa; C American Express; D Discover; E Diner's Club; F Other; 2 Personal checks accepted; 3 Lunch available; 4 Dinner available; 5 Open all year; 6 Pets welcome;

The Inn on Sea Street

Host: Lois Nelson and J.B. Whitehead
Rooms: 10 (8 PB; 2 SB) $78-125
Full Breakfast
Credit Cards: A, B, C, D
Notes: 2, 7, 9, 10, 11, 12, 14

Mansfield House

70 Gosnold Street, 02601
(508) 771-9455

This charming New England Bed and Breakfast is set in a quiet residential neighborhood, yet within walking distance of three public beaches and the boats to Nantucket and Martha's Vineyard. This 100-year-old English-style farm house has been totally renovated without losing its 19th-century ambiance. Guest rooms include private bath, king-size or twin beds, cable TV, VCRs. Enjoy a full gourmet breakfast in the charming dining

Mansfield House

room or on the adjacent porch. Open May through October.

Host: Donald Patrell
Rooms: 4 (PB) $75-90
Full Breakfast
Credit Cards: None
Notes: 2, 7, 8, 9, 10, 11, 12, 14

Sea Beach Inn

388 Sea Street, P.O. Box 2428, 02601
(508) 775-4612

A charming restored 1860 sea captain's house and carriage barn in the heart of Cape Cod. Sea Beach Inn is noted for its warm hospitality and comfortable, air conditioned rooms with private baths. Family units are available in the rustic carriage barn. Just 200 yards from Sea Street Beach. An easy walk to Hyannis Main Street with its unique shops and ferries to Nantucket and Martha's Vineyard. From Hyannis it is an easy trip to Provincetown, Falmouth, and other cape towns. Bus, plane, and train pick-up available.

Hosts: Neil and Elizabeth Carr
Rooms: 9 (7 PB; 2 SB) $55-75
Continental Breakfast
Credit Cards: A, B, C
Notes: 2, 8, 10, 11, 12

Sea Breeze Inn

397 Sea Street, 02601
(508) 771-7213; FAX (508) 862-0663
e-mail: seabreeze@capecod.net
www.capecod.net/seabreeze/

A Victorian bed and breakfast—closest to the beach, five-minute drive to the boats for the islands, restaurants, shopping, and the Kennedy compound. All of the rooms have private baths and air conditioning. A Continental plus breakfast of cereals, homemade muffins, and scones is served each morning in the dining room. Personal checks accepted on advanced reservations only.

Host: Patricia Gibney
Rooms: 14 (PB) $55-130
Continental Breakfast
Credit Cards: A, B, C, D
Notes: 5, 8, 9, 10, 11, 12, 14, 15

7 No smoking; 8 Children welcome; 9 Social drinking allowed; 10 Tennis nearby; 11 Swimming nearby; 12 Golf nearby; 13 Skiing nearby; 14 May be booked through a travel agent; 15 Handicapped accessible.

HYANNIS PORT _____

The Simmons Homestead Inn

288 Scudder Avenue, 02647
(508) 778-4999; (800) 637-1649
FAX (508) 790-1342
e-mail: SimmonsInn@aol.com
www.capecod.com/simmonsinn

This sea captain's estate was built in 1820
and was made into a great bed and breakfast inn in 1988. Beautiful and fun-filled
rooms, private baths, fireplaces, full breakfasts, wine hours, and much more make this
one of the very best inns on Cape Cod.
Within a mile of town, beaches, and the
harbor, the inn is in quiet Hyannis Port.

Host: Bill Putman and Betsy Reney
Rooms: 10 (PB) $110-200
Full Breakfast
Credit Cards: A, B, C, D
Notes: 2, 5, 8, 9, 10, 11, 12, 14

IPSWICH _____

Bed and Breakfast Reservations North Shore, Greater Boston, Cape Cod

P.O. Box 600035, Greater Boston Branch,
 Newtonville, 02160-0001
(617) 964-1606; (800) 832-2632
FAX (617) 332-8572; e-mail: info@bbreserve.com
www.bbreserve.com

106. Hillside Cottage. Perfect summer getaway. Wonderful two-bedroom cottage with
beautiful views of ocean, private landscaped grounds. Fully equipped, modern
kitchen. Dining area with ocean view, sitting area with cable TV, and large screened
porch. Picnic table, lawn furniture, and barbecue for guest use. Walk to beach. Families welcome. Sleeps four. No smoking.
Seasonal from $975.

116. The Inn at Ipswich Center. This 1850
Colonial inn in historic district, overlooking Ipswich Center. Central to all towns of

the North Shore and just minutes from the
world-famous Crane Beach. Walk to wonderful shops, restaurants, and the commuter rail. Eleven guest rooms, most with
private baths. Air conditioning. Sun room
with TV. Breakfast included. Restricted
smoking. Children 16 and older welcome.
$85-125.

Town Hill Bed and Breakfast

16 North Main Street, 01938
(978) 356-8000; (800) 457-7799

A 1945 Greek Revival. Eleven comfortable rooms individually decorated. Walking distance to restaurants, shops, train to
Boston. Historic homes and beautiful
Crane Beach.

Hosts: Chere and Bob
Rooms: 11 (9 PB; 2 SB) $75-150
Full Breakfast
Credit Cards: A, B, C
Notes: 12, 14

LEE _____

American Country Collection

1353 Union Street, Schenectady, NY 12308
(518) 370-4948; (800) 810-4948
FAX (518) 393-1634 (call first)
e-mail: Carolbnbres@msn.com

202. This 250-year-old farmhouse stands
on a hillside overlooking the first Shaker
settlement in the Berkshires. Tanglewood,
Stockbridge, and the Norman Rockwell
Museum are within nine miles. One of two
common rooms has couches, chairs, a TV,
and a fireplace. Air conditioned. Shared
baths. An apartment on the second floor
has a double bed, an air-conditioned
kitchen, a living area, and bath. Intimate
dinners are available for an additional
charge Thursdays through Saturday in late
spring, summer, and early fall. Full breakfast. Inquire about accommodations for
children and pets. Smoking outside only.
$75-110.

Applegate

Applegate

279 West Park Street, 01238
(413) 243-4451; (800) 691-9012
www.applegateinn.com

A circular driveway leads to this pillared Georgian Colonial home set on six peaceful acres. Applegate is special in every way, with canopied beds, antiques, fireplaces, pool, and manicured gardens. Its mood is warm, hospitable, and relaxed. Enjoy complimentary wine and cheese in the living room, complete with a baby grand piano. Candlelight breakfast is served. New TV room with VCR and a small video library. Near Norman Rockwell Museum and Tanglewood in the heart of the Berkshires. Children over 12 are welcome.

Hosts: Nancy Begbie-Cannata and Richard Cannata
Rooms: 6 (PB) $95-230
Continental Breakfast
Credit Cards: A, B
Notes: 2, 5, 7, 9, 10, 11, 12, 13

Ashley Inn Bed and Breakfast

182 West Park Street, 01238
(413) 243-2746; FAX (413) 243-2489
e-mail: innkeeper@ashleyinn.com

New England hospitality in a classic Revival home. Guest rooms with antiques, private baths. Enjoy hosts' antique clock collection in the parlor, TV room, and dining room. Sit down to a delicious home-made breakfast. Afternoon tea served in the parlor or on the marble veranda. Minutes to Tanglewood and all Berkshire attractions. Walk to a public golf course or tennis court. Fine dining nearby.

Hosts: Dawn and Paul Borst
Rooms: 4 (PB) $55-120
Full Breakfast
Credit Cards: A, B, C, D
Notes: 2, 5, 7, 10, 12, 13

Chambéry Inn

199 Main Street, 01238
(413) 243-2221; (800) 537-4321
FAX (413) 243-3600

Restful, romantic, and rejuvenating; this school house teaches guests the three Rs of travel. Come visit the Berkshires' 1885 *petite chateau*. All 400- to 500-square-foot schoolhouse suites are individually decorated. Standard features include 13-foot ceilings, 8-foot windows, sitting areas with fireplaces, private baths with whirlpools, air conditioning, telephones, and color TV. Choose a king-size canopied or two queen-size beds, or a guest room with a Jacuzzi for two. Room-delivered Continental plus breakfast included. Hospitality and facilities—par excellence!

Hosts: Joseph and Lynn Toole
Rooms: 9 (PB) $75-265
Continental Breakfast
Credit Cards: A, B, C, D
Notes: 2, 3, 4, 5, 7, 9, 10, 11, 12, 13, 14, 15

Devonfield

85 Stockbridge Road, 01238
(413) 243-3298; (800) 664-0880
FAX (413) 243-1360

Historic country estate offering the charm of yesterday and the amenities of today. Set on 40 acres of lawn and fields yet near all Berkshire attractions (Tanglewood, etc.). King- or queen-size beds, some suites, fireplaces in four bedrooms, heated pool, tennis court, bicycles, and golf course nearby. Smoking permitted in designated

7 No smoking; 8 Children welcome; 9 Social drinking allowed; 10 Tennis nearby; 11 Swimming nearby; 12 Golf nearby; 13 Skiing nearby; 14 May be booked through a travel agent; 15 Handicapped accessible.

Devonfield

areas only. Children welcome except in July and August.

Hosts: Sally and Ben Schenck
Rooms: 10 (PB) $70-260
Full Breakfast
Credit Cards: A, B, C, D
Notes: 2, 5, 9, 10, 11, 12, 13, 14

The Parsonage on the Green

20 Park Place, 01238
(413) 243-4364
www.bbhost.com/parsonageonthegreen

Historic 1851 village gem nestled in the pines. High ceilings, wide floorboards, family antiques. Quiet, cozy, homey. Library with TV, parlor with piano and fireplace. Hearty breakfast on elegant table setting. Afternoon tea and sweets. Walk to shops and restaurants. Minutes to Tanglewood, museums, outlets, golf, tennis. Skiing, hiking, swimming nearby.

Hosts: Donald and Barbara Mahony
Rooms: 4 (2 PB; 2 SB) $65-125
Continental Breakfast
Credit Cards: A, B
Notes: 2, 5, 7, 10, 11, 12, 13

LENOX

Amadeus House

15 Cliffwood Street, 01240
(800) 205-4770; FAX (413) 637-4770
e-mail: info@amadeushouse.com

Amadeus House is a restored Victorian set on a quiet residential street of grand homes in the center of historic Lenox village. Fine restaurants, shops, and art galleries are a short walk away. Each of the eight comfortable guest rooms is named after a favorite composer. Most rooms have queen-size beds and private baths. Enjoy the classic wraparound porch or, during chillier weather, savor afternoon tea by the fireplace in the living room.

Hosts: Martha Gottron and John Felton
Rooms: 8 (6 PB; 2 SB) $65-185
Full Breakfast
Credit Cards: A, B, C, D
Notes: 2, 5, 7, 9, 10, 11, 12, 13

Amadeus House

American Country Collection

1353 Union Street, Schenectady, NY 12308
(518) 370-4948; (800) 810-4948
FAX (518) 393-1634 (call first)
e-mail: Carolbnbres@msn.com

154. A Berkshire tradition since 1780, this gracious country home with Dutch-gabled roofs has 18 guest rooms: seven with jet tubs and private porches, eight with fireplaces, five with air conditioning, and all with private baths. Rooms are cozy and comfortable. The 72-foot swimming pool is available for guest use. A full breakfast is served daily. Children over 12 welcome; smoking permitted. $100-253.

Birchwood Inn

7 Hubbard Street, 01240
(413) 637-2600; (800) 524-1646

Drive through the village of Lenox, and at the top of the hill stands the historic Birchwood Inn. The first town meeting was held here in 1767. Elegant and beautifully restored, the inn is known throughout the region for its hospitality. Enjoy antiques, fireplaces, library, and wonderful porch. Cultural activities include the Boston Symphony at Tanglewood and performing arts. There is marvelous fall foliage, hiking, and biking. Full breakfast with international specialities daily.

Hosts: Joan, Dick, and Dan Toner
Rooms: 12 (10 PB; 2 SB) $60-210
Full Breakfast
Credit Cards: A, B, C, D, E, F
Notes: 2, 5, 7, 9, 10, 11, 12, 13, 14

Blantyre

16 Blantyre Road, P.O. Box 995, 01240
(413) 637-3556

A gracious country house/hotel surrounded by 85 acres of grounds. The hotel has a European atmosphere and exceptional cuisine. Offers tennis, croquet, and swimming as its leisure activities. Open May through November.

Host: Roderick Anderson
Rooms: 23 (PB) $265-675
Full or Continental Breakfast
Credit Cards: A, B, C
Notes: 2, 3, 4, 10, 11, 12, 14

Brook Farm Inn

Brook Farm Inn

15 Hawthorne Street, 01240
(413) 637-3013

There is poetry here. A lovely century-old Victorian home, nestled in a wooded glen amid gardens and a pool. There is a large library with fireplace, and several guest rooms feature fireplaces and canopied or brass beds. Poetry readings with tea and scones are offered each Saturday. Near Tanglewood, theater, ballet, and museums. Enjoy hiking, biking, and wonderful fall foliage. In winter, cross-country and downhill skiing are nearby. Relax and enjoy. Afternoon tea

Blantyre

7 No smoking; 8 Children welcome; 9 Social drinking allowed; 10 Tennis nearby; 11 Swimming nearby; 12 Golf nearby; 13 Skiing nearby; 14 May be booked through a travel agent; 15 Handicapped accessible.

served. Children over 15 welcome. Smoking permitted in designated areas only.

Hosts: Joe and Anne Miller
Rooms: 12 (PB) $80-200
Full Breakfast
Credit Cards: A, B, D
Notes: 2, 5, 9, 10, 11, 12, 13

The Gables Inn

The Gables Inn

81 Walker Street, 01240
(413) 637-3416; (800) 382-9401

Former home of novelist Edith Wharton. Queen Anne-style with period furnishings, pool, tennis, fireplaces, and theme rooms.

Host: Frank Newton
Rooms: 18 (PB) $80-210
Full Breakfast
Credit Cards: A, B, D
Notes: 2, 5, 9, 10, 11, 12, 13

Garden Gables Inn

141 Main Street, P.O. Box 52, 01240
(413) 637-0193; FAX (413) 637-4554

A charming 18-room, 200-year-old gabled inn in the historic center of Lenox on five wooded acres dotted with gardens, maples, and fruit trees. A 72-foot outdoor swimming pool, fireplaces, and Jacuzzi. Fully air conditioned. Minutes from Tanglewood and other attractions. Good skiing in winter. In-room telephones. Breakfast included. All rooms are air conditioned.

Hosts: Mario and Lynn Mekinda
Rooms: 18 (PB) $95-225

Full Breakfast
Credit Cards: A, B, C, D
Notes: 2, 5, 7, 9, 10, 12, 13

The Kemble Inn

2 Kemble Street, 01240
(800) 353-4113; www.kembleinn.com

Nestled in the beautiful Berkshire Hills and perched on the edge of historic Lenox village stands the Kemble Inn. With its distant panoramic mountain views to the west and its spacious Georgian elegance, the Kemble Inn has 15 rooms and central air. Each room has a color TV and a telephone, and some rooms have a fireplace and Jacuzzi. Nearby is Jacob's Pillow Dance Festival, the Berkshire Theatre Festival, Tanglewood, and the Chesterwood and Norman Rockwell Museums. Cross-country and downhill skiing nearby. Children over 12 welcome.

Hosts: Richard and Linda Reardon
Rooms: 15 (PB) $85-275
Continental Breakfast
Credit Cards: A, B, D, E
Notes: 2, 5, 7, 9, 10, 11, 12, 13, 14, 15

The Kemble Inn

Summer Hill Farm

950 East Street, 01240
(413) 442-2057; (800) 442-2059
e-mail: innkeeper@summerhillfarm.com
www.summerhillfarm.com

Comfortable 200-year-old farmhouse and converted-barn guest cottage on 20-acre horse farm are tastefully furnished with genuine English antiques and oriental rugs. The satisfying country breakfast is served in the dining room or on the sun porch looking out over the gardens and view. The atmosphere is peaceful, relaxed, friendly, and unpretentious. Close to Tanglewood, Jacob's Pillow Dance Festival, museums, galleries, theaters, Hancock Shaker Village, good restaurants, and shops. There is also a three-bedroom, two-bath farmhouse available to rent by the week or month. Inquire about accommodations for children. Cottage is handicapped accessible.

Hosts: Michael and Sonya Chassell Wessel
Rooms: 7 (PB) $55-160
Full or Continental Breakfast
Credit Cards: A, B, C
Notes: 2, 5, 7, 9, 10, 11, 12, 13, 14

Summer Hill Farm

Whistler's Inn

5 Greenwood Street, 01240
(413) 637-0975; FAX (413) 637-2190
e-mail: rmears3246@aol.com

Old World elegance and modern comfort in an antique-filled Tudor mansion on seven acres of gardens and woodlands. Eleven rooms with private baths, air conditioning; eight rooms with fireplaces;

Whistler's Inn

library; French music room. Sun porch overlooking gardens.

Rooms: 14 (PB) $100-225
Full Breakfast
Credit Cards: A, B, C, D
Notes: 2, 5, 7, 8, 9, 10, 11, 12, 13, 14

LEVERETT

Hannah Dudley House Inn

114 Dudleyville Road, 01054
(413) 367-2323

This elegant country inn is on 110 tranquil, rural acres and is the ideal getaway. The 200-year-old house has been romantically restored with spacious guest rooms, private baths, fireplaces throughout, and attention to detail. Each room is meticulously and individually decorated with its own theme and comfortably furnished in Colonial style. Three common rooms, two patios, and an array of benches and hammocks offer a variety of relaxation options both inside and out. The inn's intimate setting

Hannah Dudley House Inn

7 No smoking; 8 Children welcome; 9 Social drinking allowed; 10 Tennis nearby; 11 Swimming nearby; 12 Golf nearby; 13 Skiing nearby; 14 May be booked through a travel agent; 15 Handicapped accessible.

also includes a swimming pool, hiking trails, scenic picnic spots, ponds, and special places just waiting to be discovered.

Hosts: Erni and Daryl Johnson
Rooms: 4 (PB) $125-185
Full Breakfast
Credit Cards: A, B
Notes: 2, 5, 7, 9, 10, 12, 13

LUDLOW

Misty Meadows, Ltd.

467 Fuller Street, 01056
(413) 583-8103

One of Ludlow's oldest, this 200-year-old house has 85 acres on which to wander. A country scenic atmosphere on a working farm that raises Scottish Highlanders. A scenic patio overlooks the Minechoag Mountain Range. Screened cabana with in-ground pool. Brook fishing nearby. An area with a lot of history and many historical sites less than one-half hour away.

Host: Donnabelle Haluch
Rooms: 2 (SB) $30-50
Continental Breakfast
Credit Cards: None
Notes: 2, 5, 6, 8, 9, 10, 11, 12, 13

LYNN

Bed and Breakfast Reservations North Shore, Greater Boston, Cape Cod

P.O. Box 600035, Greater Boston Branch,
Newtonville, 02160-0001
(617) 964-1606; (800) 832-2632
FAX (617) 332-8572; e-mail: info@bbreserve.com
www.bbreserve.com

96. Oceanside Victorian. Beautiful Queen Anne Victorian, very accessible to Boston and directly across from the ocean. Filled with oriental rugs, antiques, and many interesting works of art from host's travels. Two large and very comfortable common sitting rooms feature ocean views and baby grand pianos. Elegant formal dining room with ocean view. Steps from a wonderful ocean walkway to shops and restaurants. Two lovely guest rooms share a bath. No smoking. Resident pet. Available weekends only from Memorial Day through October 31. $85.

111. Maplewood Bed and Breakfast. This stately turn-of-the-century Victorian home is just 10 miles north of Boston, one mile from the ocean, and within easy access to historic North Shore towns. Enjoy back-yard patio and gardens or relax on outside decks. Four beautifully furnished guest rooms include two oversized suites, sleeping four to five. Family suite has crib. In-room amenities include TV, air conditioning, telephones, refrigerator, and coffee maker. Parlor and large living room with fireplace. Private and shared baths. Sumptuous full breakfast. No smoking. Open year-round. Resident pets. $75-155.

Diamond District Breakfast Inn

142 Ocean Street, 01902-2007
(781) 599-4470; (800) 666-3076
FAX (781) 599-4470

Architect-designed Georgian mansion in historic "Diamond District" built in 1911 for a Lynn shoe manufacturer. Features include gracious foyer and grand staircase, spacious fireplace, living and dining room with ocean view, French doors leading to veranda overlooking the gardens, ocean. Guest rooms contain antiques, individual

Diamond District Breakfast Inn

NOTES: Credit cards accepted: A MasterCard; B Visa; C American Express; D Discover; E Diner's Club; F Other; 2 Personal checks accepted; 3 Lunch available; 4 Dinner available; 5 Open all year; 6 Pets welcome;

decor, air conditioning, TVs, telephones, down comforters, some fireplaces, whirlpool, deck, ocean views, and private baths. King suites with TV, VCR, CD player. Only 300 feet off three-mile sandy beach for swimming, walking, and jogging. Walk to restaurants. Home-cooked breakfast; vegetarian, low-fat available.

Hosts: Sandra and Jerry Caron
Rooms: 11 (7 PB; 4 SB) $80-235
Full Breakfast
Credit Cards: A, B, C, D, E
Notes: 2, 5, 7, 8, 10, 11, 12, 14

MARBLEHEAD

Bed and Breakfast Associates Bay Colony, Ltd.

P.O. Box 57166, Babson Park, Boston, 02157-0166
(781) 449-5302; (800) 347-5088
FAX (781) 449-5958; e-mail: info@bnbboston.com
www.bnbboston.com

NS264. Magnificently in Marblehead's historic Old Town and overlooking the harbor, this Victorian-era home has been fully restored to offer the very best bed and breakfast accommodations: water views, private baths, TV, telephones, king-size beds. Common areas include: parlor with fireplace, kitchen, and roof deck with ocean view. Lower winter rates. $165.

NS268. The feeling of another era, expressed through the chimes of the mantel clock, chandeliers, brasswork, hand carvings, paintings and etching, is evidence of the fortunes brought home from centuries of seafarers. This exquisite 18th-century inn with 10 guest rooms, all with private baths en suite, is in Old Marblehead within walking distance to the harbor. $95-245.

NS269. On the ocean, with private terrace, this spectacular old English Tudor mansion has endless views from most of its seven elegant guest rooms and from the guest

dining/living room. The designer decor features wicker, antiques, and a welcoming upscale style. One-minute walk to Preston Beach, five-minute drive into town. Lower rates off-season. $190-200.

Bed and Breakfast Reservations North Shore, Greater Boston, Cape Cod

P.O. Box 600035, Greater Boston Branch,
    Newtonville, 02160-0001
(617) 964-1606; (800) 832-2632
FAX (617) 3332-8572; e-mail: info@bbreserve.com
www.bbreserve.com

73. Oceanside Tudor. Grand oceanside Tudor with spectacular panoramic views. Luxury, romance, privacy, personal attention. Seven rooms with en suite baths, several with working fireplaces. Ground-level guest room features private oceanfront patio. Large common area with kitchen facilities and fireplace. Continental breakfast at own private table by oceanside picture windows. Private courtyard and gardens. $175-225.

Compass Rose

36 Gregory Street, 01945
(781) 631-7599

Studio-by-the-Sea. Garden entrance studio overlooking Marblehead Harbor. Queen-size bed, kitchenette stocked with Continental breakfast, private bath—all in a nautical theme.

Cottage on the Avenue. Charming, newly renovated one-bedroom cottage, furnished with new and antique treasures. Queen-size bed, kitchen stocked with Continental breakfast, private patio, garden. Walk to beaches, historical sights, etc.

Hosts: Carol and Bob Swift
Rooms: 2 (PB) $95-125
Continental Breakfast
Credit Cards: A, B
Notes: 2, 5, 7, 8, 9, 10, 11

7 No smoking; 8 Children welcome; 9 Social drinking allowed; 10 Tennis nearby; 11 Swimming nearby; 12 Golf nearby; 13 Skiing nearby; 14 May be booked through a travel agent; 15 Handicapped accessible.

The Harbor Light Inn

58 Washington Street, 01945
(781) 631-2186

Premier inn one block from the harbor with rooms featuring air conditioning, TV, private baths, and working fireplaces. Two rooms have double Jacuzzis and sun decks. Beautiful 18th-century-period mahogany furniture. Recent acquisition of an adjacent Federalist manor provides more room and amenities, including a conference room and swimming pool. Continental plus breakfast served.

Hosts: Peter and Suzanne Conway
Rooms: 20 (PB) $95-155
Suites: (PB) $165-245
Continental Breakfast
Credit Cards: A, B, C
Notes: 2, 5, 7, 9, 10, 11, 12, 14

Harborside House

Host: Susan Livingston
Rooms: 2 (SB) $70-85
Continental Breakfast
Credit Cards: None
Notes: 2, 5, 7, 10, 11, 14

The Harbor Light Inn

Harborside House

23 Gregory Street, 01945-3241
(781) 631-1032; e-mail: swliving@shore.net

This handsome 1850 home in the historic district overlooks Marblehead Harbor. Enjoy water views from a fireplaced parlor, period dining room, third-story sun deck, and summer breakfast porch where guests may sample home-baked breads and muffins. Walk to historic sights, excellent restaurants, and unique shops. Hostess is a professional dressmaker and nationally ranked competitive swimmer. Enjoy quiet comfort and convenience. Children over 10 welcome.

The Nesting Place

16 Village Street, 01945
(781) 631-6655; (800) 877-5656
e-mail: louisehir@aol.com

This charming 19th-century home is in historic Marblehead and within walking distance of the renowned harbor, beaches, historic homes, galleries, eateries, shops, and parks. A relaxing, refreshing home away from home. Two comfortably furnished guest rooms feature a homemade Continental plus breakfast, outdoor hot tub, and a smoke-free environment. One-half hour from Boston, or one hour from New Hampshire. Bike trails and public transportation to Boston. Massage and facials available by appointment. Seasonal rates.

Host: Louise Hirshberg
Rooms: 2 (SB) $65-75
Continental Breakfast
Credit Cards: A, B
Notes: 2, 5, 7, 8, 9, 10, 11, 12

Seagull Inn

106 Harbor Avenue, 01945
(781) 631-1893; FAX (781) 631-3535

Sun-drenched and comfort-filled suites with flexible occupancy offer TVs, VCR, telephones, and private baths. Glorious gardens in the summer and spectacular views from the decks throughout the year make every season special at the Seagull. Take a short walk to a beach or lighthouse. Watch sailboat races or fishing fleets. Enjoy sunrises or sunsets from the porch or decks. Business travelers are welcomed; meeting space is available.

Hosts: Skip and Ruth Sigler
Rooms: 3 (PB) $100-200
Continental Breakfast
Credit Cards: A, B
Notes: 2, 5, 6, 7, 8, 9, 10, 11, 14

MARSHFIELD

Bed and Breakfast Associates Bay Colony, Ltd.

P.O. Box 57166, Babson Park, Boston, 02157-0166
(781) 449-5302; (800) 347-5088
FAX (781) 449-5958; e-mail: info@bnbboston.com
www.bnbboston.com

SS350. What enthusiasm and hospitality this retired couple bring to hosting! Their New England farm-style home is one block from Marshfield Beach. Built in 1875, it is furnished with warmth and charm; guests will find this bed and breakfast a welcoming retreat. Three guest rooms with private baths. Full breakfast served. Children are welcome. No smoking allowed. Family rates available. $60-80.

Bed and Breakfast Reservations North Shore, Greater Boston, Cape Cod

P.O. Box 600035, Greater Boston Branch,
   Newtonville, 02160-0001
(617) 964-1606; (800) 832-2632
FAX (617) 332-8572; e-mail: info@bbreserve.com
www.bbreserve.com

127. Rexhame Shores. This is as good as it gets! Private oceanfront setting, on five acres of beach and dunes in historic seaside village of Rexhame. Forty minutes to Boston and Falmouth/Cape Cod. This

seven-room home has three bedrooms, three full baths (two with Jacuzzis), huge decks for viewing spectacular sunsets. Great living room with fireplace. Sleeps up to six. Families with children 12 and older welcome. Subject to availability, may be rented with three-night minimum stay. Continental breakfast provided. Inquire about self-catered weekly rental. $250.

MATTAPOISETT

Bed and Breakfast Associates Bay Colony, Ltd.

P.O. Box 57166, Babson Park, Boston, 02157-0166
(781) 449-5302; (800) 347-5088
FAX (781) 449-5958; e-mail: info@bnbboston.com
www.bnbboston.com

SS900. Built circa 1835, this lovely home has a delightful old-fashioned porch for viewing the beautiful flower beds on warm summer evenings. The large, comfortable living room welcomes guests for reading and conversation. There are two guest rooms. One has a sitting room. Both have a fireplace, TV, and a private bath en suite. Continental breakfast served on English china in the formal dining room. $85-105.

MEDFORD

Bed and Breakfast Associates Bay Colony, Ltd.

P.O. Box 57166, Babson Park, Boston, 02157-0166
(781) 449-5302; (800) 347-5088
FAX (781) 449-5958; e-mail: info@bnbboston.com
www.bnbboston.com

IN205. This host couple offers two beautiful properties in Medford's finest neighborhood of stately homes near Tufts University. Fully restored and attractively furnished, the guest rooms offer all bed sizes and most share baths with one other room. A three-room family suite has a private bath and balcony with view of Boston. $95-110.

7 No smoking; 8 Children welcome; 9 Social drinking allowed; 10 Tennis nearby; 11 Swimming nearby; 12 Golf nearby; 13 Skiing nearby; 14 May be booked through a travel agent; 15 Handicapped accessible.

Bed and Breakfast Reservations North Shore, Greater Boston, Cape Cod

P.O. Box 600035, Greater Boston Branch,
Newtonville, 02160-0001
(617) 964-1606; (800) 832-2632
FAX (617) 332-8572; e-mail: info@bbreserve.com
www.bbreserve.com

85. Medford Manor. Elegant Greek Revival-style home meticulously restored and beautifully decorated in Victorian decor. Atmosphere is cozy and comfortable without sacrificing the elegance of the original architectural details. Location is close to Tufts plus great access into Boston. Large porch with stately pillars fronts house. Inside there are several comfortable sitting areas and a formal dining room, where a Continental breakfast is set out buffet-style each morning. Guest rooms are beautifully appointed with fine coordinated linens and period furnishings and are air conditioned for guest's comfort. Children over 12 welcome. Favorable rates for longer stays. No smoking. $95-125.

MIDDLEBORO _____

On Cranberry Pond Bed and Breakfast

43 Fuller Street, 02346
(508) 946-0768

Snuggled away among the hills and bogs of northeastern Middleboro is a haven from the daily routine that offers a restful, cozy, country escape with all the modern amenities and more. Three working fireplaces, two common rooms, flower room, corporate meeting room, and dining room. Bass fishing, canoeing, mountain biking, and lots of walking trails are nearby. Thirty minutes from Plymouth, 45 minutes from Boston, Fall River, and New Bedford, and 40 minutes to Cape Cod. Children over seven welcome.

Hosts: Jeannine and Tim LaBossiere
Rooms: 6 (3 PB; 3 SB) $85-140
Full Breakfast

Credit Cards: A, B, C, D, E, F
Notes: 2, 5, 7, 9, 10, 11, 12, 13, 14

MIDDLETON _____

Bed and Breakfast Associates Bay Colony, Ltd.

P.O. Box 57166, Babson Park, Boston, 02157-0166
(781) 449-5302; (800) 347-5088
FAX (781) 449-5958; e-mail: info@bnbboston.com
www.bnbboston.com

CN501. A special retreat for those seeking a romantic getaway. This 1692 saltbox is set on landscaped grounds just eight miles from Salem. Two private guest rooms are available. The Victorian Room, with a working fireplace, furnished in the period; and the Roaring Twenties Room, authentic in every detail, with private entry, cathedral ceiling, and Jacuzzi tub for two. Both have double bed and private bath. Just the place for a true escape or a fun base for touring. Free driveway parking. $100-125.

Bed and Breakfast Reservations North Shore, Greater Boston, Cape Cod

P.O. Box 600035, Greater Boston Branch,
Newtonville, 02160-0001
(617) 964-1606; (800) 832-2632
FAX (617) 332-8572; e-mail: info@bbreserve.com
www.bbreserve.com

3. Blue Door Bed and Breakfast. The original parts of this now 10-room historic home date back to 1698. Location neighbors Salem/Marblehead area and is just 35 minutes from Boston. Two spacious and luxurious guest rooms have private baths. Large enclosed sunroom overlooks two acres of private grounds with goldfish pond, gazebo, and perennial gardens. In-room amenities include working fireplace in the Victorian Room, and whirlpool tub in Twenties Room. Twenties Room has adjoining room for third person. Host is gourmet cook who will arrange romantic dinners by advanced arrangement at additional charge. No smok-

NOTES: Credit cards accepted: A MasterCard; B Visa; C American Express; D Discover; E Diner's Club; F Other; 2 Personal checks accepted; 3 Lunch available; 4 Dinner available; 5 Open all year; 6 Pets welcome;

ing. Special occasion small gatherings can be catered by host. Thirty-five dollars for third person. $125-140.

NANTUCKET

The Carriage House

5 Ray's Court, 02554
(508) 228-0326

Lovingly cared for by hosts Jeanne McHugh and son, Haziel, this picturesque converted carriage house is perfectly, and romantically, positioned just behind the magnificent whaling mansions of Main Street, down a meandering flowered lane—"paved with crushed scallop shells—where it's beautifully quiet, yet right in town."—*Yankee*, 1989. The charming 1865 Victorian has seven distinctive guest rooms, private baths, heirloom antiques, guest library, parlor, and cheerful terrace. It is quality-rated by AAA and Mobil and has been written up in *National Geographic*, the *New York Times*, and many more.

Hosts: Jeanne McHugh and son, Haziel
Rooms: 7 (PB) $65-150
Continental Breakfast
Credit Cards: None
Notes: 2, 5, 7, 8, 10, 11, 12, 14

Danforth House Bed and Breakfast

121 Main Street, 02554
(508) 228-0136; (800) 484-7247 ext. 0136

People seem to feel comfortable here. The house was purchased by the hosts' grandmother in 1940 and has been a family house ever since. All the furnishings are antique and the house reflects the many generations of Nantucketers who have lived here. The walk down the exceptionally gracious Main Street into town takes 10 minutes. The hosts enjoy well-mannered pets and children and know of many enjoyable places for dogs and children to run and play with their parents.

Hosts: Lyn Danforth, Peter Arsenault, and Anne Haskell
Rooms: 4 (2 PB; 2 SB) $75-120
Continental Breakfast
Credit Cards: None
Notes: 2, 5, 6, 7, 8, 9, 10, 11, 12

Hawthorn House

2 Chestnut Street, 02554
(508) 228-1468 (phone/FAX)
e-mail: hhguests@nantucket.net

The Hawthorn House is a lovely Nantucket home built in 1849. The bed and breakfast is in the heart of Nantucket's historic district, three blocks from Steamboat Wharf. Entertainment, dining, shopping, and historic sites are within walking distance and beaches and fishing are a short bicycle ride away. Each of the 10 guest rooms is lovingly decorated with antique furnishings and original art and crafts by local artists. A full breakfast is provided year-round.

Hosts: Mitchell and Diane Carl
Rooms: 10 (8 PB; 2 SB)
Full Breakfast
Credit Cards: A, B
Notes: 2, 5, 7, 8, 9, 10, 11, 12, 14

House of Seven Gables

32 Cliff Road, 02554
(508) 228-4706

A quiet Victorian with bright sunny rooms in the historic district of Nantucket. A

House of Seven Gables

7 No smoking; 8 Children welcome; 9 Social drinking allowed; 10 Tennis nearby; 11 Swimming nearby; 12 Golf nearby; 13 Skiing nearby; 14 May be booked through a travel agent; 15 Handicapped accessible.

Continental breakfast is served in the room. Walk to museums, beaches, restaurants, and shops.

Host: Suzanne Walton
Rooms: 10 (8 PB; 2 SB) $65-175
Continental Breakfast
Credit Cards: A, B, C
Notes: 2, 7, 9, 10, 11, 12

Inn at Captains Corners

89 Easton Street, P.O. Box 628, 02554
(508) 228-1692; (800) 319-9990
FAX (978) 740-0036
e-mail: captainscorners@nii.net

This gracious captain's home offers 10 rooms with mostly private baths. Central residential area near beaches, shops, and restaurants. Nantucket Island welcomes guests with 88 miles of beaches, manicured yards, and gracefully maintained history in its homes.

Host: Barbara Bowman
Rooms: 15 (11 PB; 4 SB) $99-160
Continental Breakfast
Credit Cards: A, B, C
Notes: 2, 7, 8, 9, 10, 11, 12, 14

The Martin House Inn

61 Centre Street, P.O. Box 743, 02554
(508) 228-0678; e-mail: martinn@nantucket.net

In a stately 1803 mariner's home in the Nantucket historic district, a romantic sojourn awaits guests. A glowing fire in

The Martin House Inn

the spacious living room-dining room is the perfect place to read and relax. Large, airy guest rooms with authentic period pieces and four-poster beds and a lovely yard and veranda for peaceful summer afternoons make sure guests have a memorable stay. Continental plus breakfast featuring homemade breads and muffins, fresh fruits, and granola is served in the dining room. Working fireplaces in four rooms. Seasonal rates available.

Host: Debbie Wasil
Rooms: 13 (9 PB; 4 SB) $85-160
Continental Breakfast
Credit Cards: A, B, C
Notes: 2, 5, 7, 8, 9, 10, 11, 12

The White House

48 Centre Street, 02554
(508) 228-4677; FAX (508) 228-1934

Ideally in the old historic district. Adjacent to the lovely Jared Coffin Garden and within easy walking distance of ferry terminals as well as fine dining museums, entertainment, shops, and galleries. Afternoon wine and cheese in season. Also available is an apartment accommodating two to four persons and rents by the week.

Rooms: 3 (PB) $75-135
Continental Breakfast
Credit Cards: A, B, C
Notes: 2, 5, 7, 8, 10, 11, 12

The Woodbox Inn

29 Fair Street, 02554
(508) 228-0587

Nantucket's oldest inn, built in 1709, is one and a half blocks from the center of town. The Woodbox offers three queen-size rooms and six suites with working fireplaces, all with private baths. A full breakfast is available along with candlelight gourmet dinners. Voted Wine Spectator Award of Excellence, Nantucket's Most Romantic Dining Room, and rated Nantucket's Finest Dining. Closed January 2 through June 1.

The Woodbox Inn

Host: Dexter Tutein
Rooms: 9 (PB) $140-250
Full Breakfast
Credit Cards: None
Notes: 2, 4, 7, 8, 9, 10, 11, 12

NANTUCKET ISLAND

Bed and Breakfast Associates Bay Colony, Ltd.

P.O. Box 57166, Babson Park, Boston, 02157-0166
(781) 449-5302; (800) 347-5088
FAX (781) 449-5958; e-mail: info@bnbboston.com
www.bnbboston.com

NT18. This circa 1835 sea captain's home has been restored and enlarged as a fine bed and breakfast inn just outside of Nantucket town. Decorated with antiques and reproduction pieces, including four-poster and canopied beds, many with working fireplaces and color TVs. Family suites available. Full breakfast. Seasonal rates. $75-195.

NT830. On historic Cliff Road overlooking Nantucket Harbor, this 10-room guest house offers a lovely Victorian decor and an ambiance designed to create romantic memories. Nearby Jetties Beach awaits and guests can easily stroll into Nantucket town. No car is needed here as the ferry dock is just a 10-minute walk from the door. Lower rates off-season. $110-175.

NT831. This in-town "family of inns" offers everything guests would imagine. With sev-
eral buildings and cottages, guests may select the location best suited to their tastes. Guest room amenities include: fireplaces, four-poster canopied beds, private baths, air conditioning, telephones, TVs. Two-room cottages. Seasonal rates. $50-400.

NT835. In this delightful six-room bed and breakfast inn, guests are treated to a romantic gem. Enchanting collectibles and lovely antiques abound. Each guest room has private bath, small refrigerator, TV, and telephone. The suite has a large private living room with a sleeper-sofa, marble Jacuzzi bathroom, and a canopied bed in the cozy guest bedroom. A studio apartment is also available. Two blocks from town center. A perfect romantic escape. $185-325.

NT836. This 220-year-old inn just outside of town is authentic in its details with antique furnishings, original wide-plank floors, raised wood panel walls, and six period fireplaces. Guests may choose from 12 rooms ranging from simple to deluxe. Ten rooms with private baths. Full breakfast. Seasonal rates. $90-240.

NT837. Across from Jetties Beach, this sunny inn is just a short stroll from town. The 90 cheerful guest rooms with white wicker furnishings and French doors have air conditioning and access to the central swimming pool. Seasonal rates. $105-235.

NEEDHAM

Bed and Breakfast Associates Bay Colony, Ltd.

P.O. Box 57166, Babson Park, Boston, 02157-0166
(781) 449-5302; (800) 347-5088
FAX (781) 449-5958; e-mail: info@bnbboston.com
www.bnbboston.com

IW630. This sweet little Cape-style home epitomizes New England suburban serenity. Convenient to commuter railway, or Boston

7 No smoking; 8 Children welcome; 9 Social drinking allowed; 10 Tennis nearby; 11 Swimming nearby; 12 Golf nearby; 13 Skiing nearby; 14 May be booked through a travel agent; 15 Handicapped accessible.

is only 20 minutes by car. Two guest rooms (large room with double bed or smaller room with twin beds) share a bath on the second floor. Host quarters are on the first floor. Driveway parking. $58-75.

IW635. Immaculate Cape-style home near Needham center. Available hosted or unhosted. Two guest rooms, each with queen-size bed and full bath. Very pleasant, traditional decor. Weekly and monthly rates available. $130-150 for entire unhosted house. $85-95 per room.

IW638. A delightful multilevel Colonial home with a tasteful and appealing decor. Three guest rooms on the third floor with shared or private designer baths. This is a delightful neighborhood, 25 minutes west of downtown Boston. Family rates available. $65-110.

Bed and Breakfast Reservations North Shore, Greater Boston, Cape Cod

P.O. Box 600035, Greater Boston Branch,
   Newtonville, 02160-0001
(617) 964-1606; (800) 832-2632
FAX (617) 332-8572; e-mail: info@bbreserve.com
www.bbreserve.com

55. South Court. This multilevel contemporary Colonial, beautifully designed and decorated by the hosts, is in a lovely suburb, west of Boston, just minutes from Route 128. Its peaceful surroundings, including a nearby river and wooded area, give guests the feel of being miles from it all. Within walking distance to the town center, close to many area colleges, and less than one-half mile to the commuter rail into Boston. Three guest rooms share a bath, but rooms can be taken at private bath rates subject to availability. Several lovely sitting rooms and outside deck for guests' use. Continental breakfast. Light kitchen privileges for longer stays. Children welcome. No smoking. $75-100.

Host Homes of Boston

P.O. Box 117, Waban Branch, Boston, 02468-0001
(617) 244-1308; FAX (617) 244-5156

Hilltop House. Quiet, sylvan setting with Boston skyline view in winter. Host offers a large second-floor guest room and en suite bath in Colonial home. Relax on screened porch or shady lawn. Ten minutes to Boston. Near Boston Common, Pine Manor, Wellesley, and Route 128 businesses. Half-mile to commuter train. TV. Air conditioned. Parking. No smoking. $85.

NEW BEDFORD

1875 House

367 Seventh Street, 02740
(508) 997-6433; FAX (508) 984-1696

The 1875 House is a wooden house built in the early Victorian era. The home has undergone thoughtful restoration which is reflected in the tasteful decor throughout. Close to the newly designated Whaling National Historic Park, two blocks from the Rotch-Jones-Duff Museum, in the historic area of New Bedford, and in a neighborhood which figured prominently in the Underground Railroad. Also convenient to Cape Cod, Newport, Providence, and Boston—all within an hour's drive. Pets welcome with prior arrangements.

1875 House

Rooms: 3 (PB) $55-70
Continental Breakfast
Credit Cards: None
Notes: 2, 5, 8, 9, 11, 12

NEWBURYPORT

The Windsor House in Newburyport

38 Federal Street, 01950
(978) 462-3778; (888) TRELAWNY
FAX (978) 465-3443; e-mail: tintagel@greennet.net

Built as a wedding present, this 18th-century Federal mansion offers a rare blend of Yankee hospitality and the English tradition of bed and breakfast. Designed as a residence/ship's chandlery, the inn recalls the spirit of an English country house. In a historic seaport near a wildlife refuge. Whale watching, museums, theater, and antiques. Rates include afternoon tea, English cooked breakfast, tax, and service.

Hosts: Judith and John Harris
Rooms: 4 (PB) $135
Full Breakfast
Credit Cards: A, B, C, D
Notes: 2, 5, 6, 7, 8, 10, 11, 12, 13, 14

NEWBURYPORT (SALISBURY)

Bed and Breakfast Reservations North Shore, Greater Boston, Cape Cod

P.O. Box 600035, Greater Boston Branch,
    Newtonville, 02160-0001
(617) 964-1606; (800) 832-2632
FAX (617) 332-8572; e-mail: info@bbreserve.com
www.bbreserve.com

125. The Old Salts Bed and Breakfast. Minutes from Newburyport, Plum Island, and gorgeous beaches of the Massachusetts and New Hampshire shores, this Greek Revival farmhouse has been lovingly restored. A glass-enclosed sunroom overlooks three acres of secluded gardens. A sumptuous full country breakfast is served. Three beautiful rooms with private baths. Resident dog. $90-115.

NEW MARLBOROUGH

Old Inn on the Green and Gedney Farm

Route 57, 01230
(413) 229-3131; (800) 286-3139
FAX (413) 229-8236

A 1760 inn with period guest rooms and private baths. Three-star (*Boston Globe*) restaurant with candlelight, fireplaces, and alfresco dining. Gedney Farm is a turn-of-the-century renovated barn with deluxe guest rooms and suites with granite fireplaces and whirlpool. Banquet facilities available. Superb wedding site. Lunch is available seasonally.

Hosts: Brad Wagstaff and Leslie Miller
Rooms: 21 (PB) $120-285
Continental Breakfast
Credit Cards: A, B, C
Notes: 2, 4, 5, 8, 9, 10, 11, 13, 14

NEWTON

Bed and Breakfast Associates Bay Colony, Ltd.

P.O. Box 57166, Babson Park, Boston, 02157-0166
(781) 449-5302; (800) 347-5088
FAX (781) 449-5958; e-mail: info@bnbboston.com
www.bnbboston.com

IW255. This stately Victorian in a neighborhood of grand 19th-century homes has a private two-room guest suite with light cooking facilities, a charming sitting room, and a dazzling new private bath. Walk to the express bus for a 10-minute trip to central Boston. Amenities include cable TV, VCR, telephone, a small refrigerator, microwave, built-in sandwich bar, and a Victorian desk and sofa. Ten to 20 minutes west of Boston. $95-105.

Host Homes of Boston

P.O. Box 117, Waban Branch, Boston, 02468-0001
(617) 244-1308; FAX (617) 244-5156

Alderwood. Guests migrate to the gourmet kitchen in this 1930 Colonial. Second-floor

7 No smoking; 8 Children welcome; 9 Social drinking allowed; 10 Tennis nearby; 11 Swimming nearby; 12 Golf nearby; 13 Skiing nearby; 14 May be booked through a travel agent; 15 Handicapped accessible.

guest room has twin beds. Pumpkin the cat lives here. Children welcome. Quiet road near Boston College law campus. One mile to Green Line-D. Ten-minute drive to Boston. Private bath. TV. Air conditioned. $85.

Briarwood. Historic Chestnut Hill landmark home (1875) combines Early American antiques with modern amenities. Exceptional guest wing with private entrance and bath, featuring queen-size bed, two twin beds that double as sofas, skylights, air conditioning, TV, an alcove with dining table, picture window, and light-cooking facilities. Guests prepare own breakfast, food provided. Near restaurants and elegant mall, four blocks to public transit (Green Line-D), one block to Boston College. Boston, three miles. No smoking. $100.

Rockledge. Stately 1882 Victorian in prime location where guests return again and again. Cordial hosts offer bright, spacious rooms, antiques, and gardens. Three second-floor guest rooms, parlor with TV. Queen-size and twin rooms share hall bath. Double room with bath en suite. Ceiling fans. Chloe the cat in residence. Two blocks to lake, village restaurants, shops, and Green Line-D. Fifteen minutes to Back Bay, Copley Square. No smoking. $75-87.

NEWTON CENTER

Bed and Breakfast Associates Bay Colony, Ltd.

P.O. Box 57166, Babson Park, Boston, 02157-0166
(781) 449-5302; (800) 347-5088
FAX (781) 449-5958; e-mail: info@bnbboston.com
www.bnbboston.com

IW245. This large Victorian home has two pleasant third-floor guest rooms with shared bath and a master suite with private bath. Fully restored and beautifully furnished, this family home is on a quiet street close to shops and public transit. $73-105.

Bed and Breakfast Reservations North Shore, Greater Boston, Cape Cod

P.O. Box 600035, Greater Boston Branch,
    Newtonville, 02160-0001
(617) 964-1606; (800) 832-2632
FAX (617) 332-8572; e-mail: info@bbreserve.com
www.bbreserve.com

2. Crescent Bed and Breakfast. In a beautiful suburb about seven miles west of Boston. Five-minute walk to public transportation. A large and gracious Greek Revival, truly a house beautiful. Lovely gardens and in-ground pool. Two guest rooms each have double beds, private baths, TVs, air conditioning. Continental plus breakfast in elegant dining room or on screen porch. Pets in residences. No smoking. Extra $20 for third person in room. $95-115.

Host Homes of Boston

P.O. Box 117, Waban Branch, Boston, 02468-0001
(617) 244-1308; FAX (617) 244-5156

Park Lane. This large Baronial-style stucco (1911) on quiet street has a Victorian motif. Friendly host offers two third-floor guest rooms, one with double bed and the other with trundle bed; second floor has queen-size bed, private bath Jacuzzi, air conditioning, cable TV. First-floor guest parlor with fireplace. Village, public transit (Green Line-D), restaurants all within 10-minute walk. Five miles from Boston. No smoking. Children welcome. $68-85.

NORTH EASTHAM (CAPE COD)

Bed and Breakfast Reservations North Shore, Greater Boston, Cape Cod

P.O. Box 600035, Greater Boston Branch,
    Newtonville, 02160-0001
(617) 964-1606; (800) 832-2632
FAX (617) 332-8572; e-mail: info@bbreserve.com
www.bbreserve.com

NOTES: Credit cards accepted: A MasterCard; B Visa; C American Express; D Discover; E Diner's Club; F Other; 2 Personal checks accepted; 3 Lunch available; 4 Dinner available; 5 Open all year; 6 Pets welcome;

92. The Old Farmhouse Bed and Breakfast. A 1720 farmhouse in rustic setting with lovely perennial gardens. Short walk along a winding footpath to a great sandy beach. Perfect for young couples on a budget and families with children, who enjoy outdoor activities. Barbecue and light kitchen privileges. Three cozy guest rooms, one and one-half baths, Jacuzzi. Enjoy views of gardens and grounds from outside deck. Resident pets. No smoking. $65-80.

NORTHAMPTON (FLORENCE) _____

American Country Collection

1353 Union Street, Schenectady, NY 12308
(518) 370-4948; (800) 810-4948
FAX (518) 393-1634 (call first)
e-mail: Carolbnbres@msn.com

239. Step out onto a huge deck and see Mount Tom in the view. Enjoy watching the sheep and goats fenced in the 40 acres of pastures just minutes from downtown Northampton. This trilevel homestay bed and breakfast offers guests a unique open floor plan. The second-floor suite and third-floor rooms share a dining area and living room. Near colleges and historic Deerfield. Great park nearby for golf, swimming, tennis, hiking, and cross-country skiing. $75-110.

The Knoll

230 North Main Street, 01062-1221
(413) 584-8164

The Knoll can be found on 17 acres overlooking farmland and forest. It is in town and yet in a rural setting, with an acre of lawn and a large circular driveway. This is the five-college area of western Massachusetts: Smith, Amherst, Mount Holyoke, and Hampshire Colleges, and the University of Massachusetts.

Host: Mrs. Lee Lesko
Rooms: 3 (SB) $45-55
Full Breakfast
Credit Cards: None
Notes: 2, 5, 7, 10, 12, 13

Lupine House

185 North Main Street, P.O. Box 60483, Florence, 01060-0483
(413) 586-9766; (800) 890-9766
www.westmass.com/lupinehouse

Lupine House Bed and Breakfast, a recently remodeled circa 1870 home, is three miles from downtown Northampton in the village of Florence. Three tastefully decorated guest rooms have private baths. Bike trail abuts hosts' property. Homemade breakfast includes fresh breads, fruit, granola, juices, and hot beverages. Special dietary needs are easily accommodated. A short drive to Smith, Amherst, Hampshire, and Mount Holyoke Colleges, University of Massachusetts, Deerfield Academy, and the Williston Northampton School. Open mid-September through early June.

Hosts: Gil and Evelyn Billings
Rooms: 3 (PB) $70
Continental Breakfast
Credit Cards: A, B
Notes: 2, 7, 9, 12, 13

NORTH TROY (CAPE COD)_____

Bed and Breakfast Reservations North Shore, Greater Boston, Cape Cod

P.O. Box 600035, Greater Boston Branch, Newtonville, 02160-0001
(617) 964-1606; (800) 832-2632
FAX (617) 332-8572; e-mail: info@bbreserve.com
www.bbreserve.com

115. Truro Winery Bed and Breakfast. Beautiful 1836 Federal style on five acres of rolling hills and vineyards. A working winery, the first of its kind on Cape Cod. A romantic and peaceful retreat. Five beautifully appointed rooms, with private baths, one with double Jacuzzi. Breakfast room overlooks patio and vineyards. Full breakfast. Location close to Provincetown and many area beaches. No smoking. $89-129.

7 No smoking; 8 Children welcome; 9 Social drinking allowed; 10 Tennis nearby; 11 Swimming nearby; 12 Golf nearby; 13 Skiing nearby; 14 May be booked through a travel agent; 15 Handicapped accessible.

NORWELL

1810 House Bed and Breakfast

147 Old Oaken Bucket Road, 02061
(781) 659-1810; e-mail: tuttle1810@aol.com

The 1810 House has been lovingly restored and added to by the owners. The antique half-Cape with its original beamed ceilings, three working fireplaces, wide-pine floors, and hand-stenciled walls is furnished with antiques, oriental carpets, and interesting accessories. Three bright cheery rooms share two full baths. An ideal spot for day trips to Cape Cod, Concord, Lexington, Salem, Rockport, and Newport, Rhode Island. Public transportation to Boston by subway or commuter boat is nearby. Enjoy a ride in the host's restored 1915 Model T depot hack. Ten-dollar surcharge for single-night bookings.

Hosts: Susanne and Harold Tuttle
Rooms: 3 (2 PB; 1 SB) $65-85
Full Breakfast
Credit Cards: None
Notes: 2, 5, 7, 10, 11, 12, 14

NORWOOD

Bed and Breakfast Associates Bay Colony, Ltd.

P.O. Box 57166, Babson Park, Boston, 02157-0166
(781) 449-5302; (800) 347-5088
FAX (781) 449-5958; e-mail: info@bnbboston.com
www.bnbboston.com

IW560. Just 15 minutes from Boston, this four-bedroom inn was built in 1850 and is authentically furnished with antiques and reproduction pieces. Each room has a private bath, TV, and telephone. $80-85.

OAK BLUFFS (MARTHA'S VINEYARD)

The Beach House Bed and Breakfast

Corner of Seaview and Pennacook Avenue, 02557
(508) 693-3955

A newly renovated 1890s house directly across from large, sandy swimming beach. Friendly, helpful, and relaxed atmosphere. Rooms have brass queen-size beds, ceiling fans, and TVs. Close to town, shops, restaurants, ferries, shuttle bus, and tours; moped, car, bike, and boat rentals. Oak Bluffs is a magnificent town for strollers and photographers, with its many-hued gingerbread cottages. It is also home to the Flying Horses, the nation's oldest carousel.

Hosts: Pamela, Calvin, and Justin Zaiko
Rooms: 9 (PB) $75-140
Continental Breakfast
Credit Cards: A, B, C, D, E
Notes: 5, 10, 11, 12

Bed and Breakfast Associates Bay Colony, Ltd.

P.O. Box 57166, Babson Park, Boston, 02157-0166
(781) 449-5302; (800) 347-5088
FAX (781) 449-5958; e-mail: info@bnbboston.com
www.bnbboston.com

MV101. This lovely Victorian mansion overlooks the sandy beaches of Nantucket Sound in historic Oak Bluffs. Walk to restaurants, shops, the world-famous gingerbread houses, and the historic Flying Horses carousel just down the road. Ten guest rooms. Summer rates, including breakfast and afternoon tea, start at $150.

MV102. A new candy-colored Victorian-styled inn on lively Oak Bluffs harbor with all modern amenities. Several rooms with harbor view and some kitchen suites. $125-275.

Bed and Breakfast Nantucket/Martha's Vineyard

P.O. Box 341, West Hyannisport, 02672-0341
(800) 686-5252; FAX (508) 775-2884
e-mail: bedandb@capecod.net
www.bandbcapecod.net

201. This 1872 Victorian cottage has seven bedrooms for bed and breakfast and is one

NOTES: Credit cards accepted: A MasterCard; B Visa; C American Express; D Discover; E Diner's Club; F Other; 2 Personal checks accepted; 3 Lunch available; 4 Dinner available; 5 Open all year; 6 Pets welcome;

city block from the beaches. Bedrooms have private baths. Public tennis and public transportation to other parts of the island are two blocks away. Continental breakfast is served from 8:00 to 10:00 A.M. $80-140.

206. The Victorian cottage was built 95 years ago, 500 feet from the ocean on Nantucket Sound. It is a unique house that has been in the owner's family for generations. The four bedrooms share two baths. Enjoy the beach a few steps away from the house. Shops, restaurants, tennis, golf, and biking are within three-fourths mile of the house. Relax in the parlor, savoring great music in front of a fireplace. A great getaway any time of the year. No children. No smoking. $55-98.

209. Oak Bluffs is a Victorian village at the heart of the island. The ferry, buses, and the beach are steps away. The inn was built in 1989 and reflects the quaint style of the houses in the community. All rooms are air conditioned, with private full baths, TVs, and telephones. Lovely grounds offer outdoor breakfasts and spots for lounging. Harbor views from some rooms. Several suites for three to four persons are available. A great island accommodation. Bike, jeep, or car rentals available nearby. Continental breakfast. $75-175.

ONSET

Bed and Breakfast Reservations North Shore, Greater Boston, Cape Cod

P.O. Box 600035, Greater Boston Branch,
   Newtonville, 02160-0001
(617) 964-1606; (800) 832-2632
FAX (617) 332-8572; e-mail: info@bbreserve.com
www.bbreserve.com

77. Inn on the Beach. Directly on the beach in small seaside village midway between Plymouth and Hyannis. This award-winning Spanish-style bed and breakfast mansion

has seven romantic rooms, panoramic ocean views and private baths. Guest house and original carriage house with large suites, some with kitchens, TV, refrigerator, one- to two- bedrooms, patios, and decks meeting sandy beach. Great for families and longer stays. Inquire about weekly rates for guest house and carriage house. Continental breakfast included for guests staying in main inn. $90-160.

The Henderson-Berford Inn

2 Fairway Drive, 02532
(508) 759-8860

Master bedroom with walk-in closet/dressing room, private bath, king-size bed, and guest dining room. The home is at the gateway to Cape Cod near clean and beautiful beaches, the Cape Cod Coral, deep-sea fishing, whale watching, golf, museums, Hyannis, shopping malls, outlets. Fifteen minutes to Falmouth ferry to Martha's Vineyard. Plymouth is 22 miles north, offering a view of historic Plymouth Rock and Cranberry World Visitors Center. One-hour drive to Boston, 45 minutes to Rhode Island. Open May through October.

Hosts: Mr. and Mrs. Henderson
Rooms: 1 (PB) $65-75
Continental Breakfast
Credit Cards: None
Notes: 7, 9, 12

The Reynolds House on the Harbor

11 South Boulevard, 02558
(508) 291-4036

On a windswept knoll overlooking Onset Harbor and facing Onset Beach is the Reynolds House. Its three guest rooms are light and airy and comfortably decorated in turn-of-the-century decor. They feature spectacular views and beds with superior mattresses. There are two private baths, with footed tubs and showers and one shared bath. Guests are drawn to the porches which overlook Wickets Island and

7 No smoking; 8 Children welcome; 9 Social drinking allowed; 10 Tennis nearby; 11 Swimming nearby; 12 Golf nearby; 13 Skiing nearby; 14 May be booked through a travel agent; 15 Handicapped accessible.

The Reynolds House on the Harbor

the multicolored vistas which are inspiration to any artist. There is nearby fishing, boating, golfing. A generous home-cooked breakfast is served in the dining room or on the porch facing the rising sun. Boston and the lower cape are minutes away.

Rates: $85-100
Full Breakfast
Credit Cards: None
Notes: 2, 5, 7, 8, 9, 10, 11, 12, 14

ORLEANS

Academy Place Bed and Breakfast

8 Academy Place, P.O. Box 1407, 02653
(508) 255-3181; FAX (508) 247-9812

This 1790s sea captain's home, on the village green, is at the edge of Orleans's shopping district. Many fine shops and restaurants are a short walk away. Accom-

Academy Place

panied by candlelight, Sandy serves a Continental plus breakfast of homemade muffins and breads with chilled juices and fresh fruit, freshly brewed coffee, teas, or hot chocolate. The entire house is air conditioned. Beaches and fishing, two and one-half miles; Cape Cod National Seashore visitor center, four miles; bike trail, one-third mile. Children six and older welcome.

Hosts: Sandy and Charles Terrell
Rooms: 5 (3 PB; 2 SB) $75-95
Continental Breakfast
Credit Cards: A, B
Notes: 2, 7, 9, 10, 11, 14

Bed and Breakfast Cape Cod

P.O. Box 1312, Orleans, 02653
(508) 255-3824; (800) 541-6226
FAX (508) 240-0599
e-mail: bedandb@capecod.net
www.bandbcapecod.com

8. This dramatic contemporary home is built on high ground and overlooks five acres of wooded land. The large deck is next to an in-ground pool. Interior features include a soaring cathedral ceiling, oriental carpets, wood-burning fireplaces, and a spiral staircase. Bedrooms have air conditioning and private baths. Nauset Beach is two miles away. A cottage is also available. Full breakfast. No smoking. Children over 11 welcome. $115.

Orleans Bed and Breakfast Associates, Inc.

P.O. Box 1312; Orleans, 02653
(508) 255-3824; (800) 541-6226
FAX (508) 240-0599
e-mail: orleansbnb@capecod.net
www.capecod.net/bb

Bay Cottage Bed and Breakfast. On one and one-half acres by Cape Cod Bay, this English-style bed and breakfast cottage is the perfect haven for a seaside vacation. Two bedrooms, each with canopied bed, attached private bath. Living room with fireplace, TV, air conditioning, porches, and decks all invite comfort and relaxation. A

NOTES: Credit cards accepted: A MasterCard; B Visa; C American Express; D Discover; E Diner's Club; F Other; 2 Personal checks accepted; 3 Lunch available; 4 Dinner available; 5 Open all year; 6 Pets welcome;

short distance from Skaket Beach and the bike trail. Also available is a lovely studio apartment rented weekly. No breakfast with apartment. $95-98.

The 1840 House. This Greek Revival house, built in 1840, is within walking distance to Orleans's lovely town center and is on the way to Nauset Beach. *Stately* and *elegant* best describe this fine old home inside and out. One double bedroom and one twin bedroom. Bath is private. Be surrounded with antiques while relaxing or watching TV in the sitting room. $60-75.

Gray Gables. An enormous old elm shades a secluded yard with furniture set out for guests' pleasure. A private entrance leads to guest wing of fine old house with plenty of charm and wonderfully warm hosts. Comfortable, spacious, air-conditioned guest room has queen-size bed plus single bed, refrigerator, and TV. Adjacent bath has huge tiled shower. Continental breakfast set out for guests to enjoy at their leisure in privacy of own room or under the elm. $80.

Honeysuckle House. Steps away from Skaket Beach and a one-minute bike ride to the bike trail, this contemporary saltbox has good location. Nature beckons from the shaded deck overlooking gardens, marshes, and woods filled with sights and sounds of nature. Bedrooms with private baths downstairs and upstairs. A second bedroom upstairs is available with a double bed for another member of guests' party, in which case the bedrooms upstairs share a bath. Guest refrigerator. $65-75.

Just around the Bend. A charming guest wing with two private entrances and a porch overlooking a rolling backyard and woods. In a residential neighborhood within walking distance of town center and a short bicycle ride to beaches and bike trails. Decorated in a comfortable yet contemporary style, the spacious wing offers a bedroom with queen-size bed, private bath with shower, air-conditioned living room with sleeper-sofa, telephone, TV, and a fully equipped eat-in kitchen. Stocked refrigerator for breakfast; guest wing suite is self-catered. $100.

Morgan's Way. This dramatic Cape contemporary home built on high ground overlooks five acres of lovely gardens, lawns, and woods. A massive deck is next to heated swimming pool. Interior features include soaring cathedral ceilings, oriental carpets, original art, and a wood-burning fireplace. Two miles to Nauset Beach and one mile to the village center. Air conditioned bedrooms have private baths. Also available is a pool house rented by the week. Full breakfast is included with rooms in the house. No breakfast is included with pool house. $115.

Rive Gauche. Imagine waking up with a private view of a lovely ocean pond. This artist's house and gardens were recently featured in the book *Cape Cod Gardens and Houses*. The spacious studio features a king-size bed, adjoining private bath, kitchenette, sitting area, and balcony. Use the private dock to swim from or take the canoe out to Pleasant Bay. This studio offers the quintessential Cape Cod experience. Very romantic and private. Three-night minimum. $120.

Room with a View. On the waterfront with beautiful views of Town Cove, a swimming pool surrounded by rose hedges, antiques, plenty of charm, close to beaches and the Cape Cod National Seashore. This is what Cape Cod is all about. Watch the sailboats and the fishermen while enjoying breakfast. Two lovely bedrooms with private baths. Romantic. $100-115.

7 No smoking; 8 Children welcome; 9 Social drinking allowed; 10 Tennis nearby; 11 Swimming nearby; 12 Golf nearby; 13 Skiing nearby; 14 May be booked through a travel agent; 15 Handicapped accessible.

Squire Doane. Set on a hill overlooking Pilgrim Lake, this elegant 1820 sea captain's home is furnished with authentic antiques and classic good taste. Upstairs, a spacious bedroom has a private bath and view of the lake. A second bright bedroom has a private bath. The carriage house, a lovely studio apartment, has a private entrance, efficiency kitchen, bath with shower, double bed, queen-sized futon sofa. Five-night minimum for the carriage house. $80-115.

Sweet Retreat. A delightful in-town studio. Outside stairs lead to deck with view of attractive garden and to private entrance into fully equipped breakfast area. A step down into bedroom suite with canopied queen-size bed, private bath, desk, TV, VCR, and telephone. Host owns beautiful little patisserie and imaginative catering business. Count on good things provided for breakfast. Bike to beaches, walk to village. $80-90.

Waterside Gardens. Extraordinary waterfront on Pochet Inlet with blue herons, bountiful gardens, and warm hospitality. All rooms have air conditioning and private baths in this spacious, luxurious contemporary Cape. Easy access to fishing, swimming, biking, tennis, golf, and antiquing. Bring your camera. Separate apartment with water view, full kitchen, living room area with fireplace, sleep sofa, TV/VCR, separate bedroom, private bathroom. Three people maximum. Thirty dollars for each additional person. $145-135.

Winterwell. Restored 19th-century Cape Cod farmhouse, just a three-tenths of a mile stroll to Skaket Beach yet close to town and bike path, offers two comfortable accommodations. In the main house, a first floor air-conditioned guest room with separate entrance has full private bath, double bed and twin bed. Main living room for occasional reading and TV. Guest refrigerator available. A spacious guest wing with separate entrance offers an air-conditioned bedroom, private bath, sitting room, and kitchen/dining area. $80-95.

Woodhead House. Set on a quiet street, this house is a homey place named after the host's ancestral cottage in Ireland. A private suite on the second floor has antique-furnished air-conditioned bedroom with nice bath and small eat-in kitchen. There is also a sitting area with cable TV. A second room can be made available to a family that might need extra accommodations for one or two members traveling together. An easy bike ride or five minutes' drive to Nauset Beach and the center of town. Twenty dollars for extra persons. $70.

PEABODY

Joan's Bed and Breakfast

210 R Lynn Street, 01960
(978) 532-0191

Twenty-five minutes from Boston and 10 minutes from historic Salem. Just five minutes from Routes 95 and 128 and US Route 1. There is an in-ground pool that guests use in the summer. A very nice walking area around a local pond. Wonderful restaurants and theaters. Great shopping. All pastries and breads are homemade. The hostess serves a Continental plus breakfast. There can be arrangements made for private baths. "We make sure our home is your home when you are traveling."

Host: Joan Hetherington
Rooms: 3 (3 SB) $55-80
Continental Breakfast
Credit Cards: None
Notes: 2, 5, 7, 8, 9, 11, 14

PERU

American Country Collection

1353 Union Street, Schenectady, NY 12308
(518) 370-4948; (800) 810-4948
FAX (518) 393-1634 (call first)
e-mail: Carolbnbres@msn.com

NOTES: Credit cards accepted: A MasterCard; B Visa; C American Express; D Discover; E Diner's Club; F Other; 2 Personal checks accepted; 3 Lunch available; 4 Dinner available; 5 Open all year; 6 Pets welcome;

069. Built in 1830 as the town parsonage, this private homestay features the original wide-plank floors and floor-to-ceiling windows that look out onto old stone walls and 13 acres of woods. Guests dine in a sunroom with bay windows and French doors that lead onto a patio. The decor is French country, and the home is furnished with antiques and colorful Waverly and Laura Ashley chintz fabrics. Three excellent cross-country centers and one downhill ski area are within an eight-mile radius. Two bedrooms with private baths and double beds. No smoking. $65.

PETERSHAM

Winterwood at Petersham

19 North Main Street, 01366
(508) 724-8885

An elegant 16-room Greek Revival mansion built in 1842, just off the common of a classic New England town. The inn boasts numerous fireplaces and several porches for relaxing. Cocktails available. In the National Register of Historic Places.

Hosts: Jean and Robert Day
Rooms: 6 (PB) $63.42-84.56
Continental Breakfast
Credit Cards: A, B, C, D
Notes: 2, 5, 7, 8, 9, 12, 13, 14

Winterwood at Petersham

PITTSFIELD

The Olde White Horse Inn

378 South Street, 01201
(413) 442-2512

The Olde White Horse Inn is a charming, spacious Colonial home built around the turn of the century. Found in the Berkshires near Tanglewood. Eight cozy guest rooms, each with a private bath, air conditioning, TV, and telephone. Guest rooms are tastefully decorated with country charm, fresh flowers, and fluffy comforters on double beds. The White Horse Inn is guests' home away from home. Open year-round.

Hosts: Joe and Linda Kalisz
Rooms: 8 (PB) $90-175
Full Breakfast
Credit Cards: A, B, C, D, E, F
Notes: 2, 5, 7, 8, 9, 10, 11, 12, 13, 14

PLYMOUTH

Bed and Breakfast Associates Bay Colony, Ltd.

P.O. Box 57166, Babson Park, Boston, 02157-0166
(781) 449-5302; (800) 347-5088
FAX (781) 449-5958; e-mail: info@bnbboston.com
www.bnbboston.com

SS766. This classic Colonial bed and breakfast was built to be the perfect romantic retreat. Three guest rooms, two with ocean views, all with private baths. Walk to beach and Plimoth Plantation. Twenty-minute drive to Cape Cod. Sumptuous full breakfast. $75-125.

SS767. This magnificent home provides glorious ocean views from each of its three guest rooms, all decorated to perfection. The Delft Room, named for the tiles that surround the fireplace, has an antique cherry bed. The Master Suite has a four-poster bed. And the Garden Room boasts an iron bed, garden motif, and private sitting room. Full breakfast served in oceanfront dining room. $98-125.

7 No smoking; 8 Children welcome; 9 Social drinking allowed; 10 Tennis nearby; 11 Swimming nearby; 12 Golf nearby; 13 Skiing nearby; 14 May be booked through a travel agent; 15 Handicapped accessible.

Bed and Breakfast Cape Cod

P.O. Box 1312, Orleans, 02653
(508) 255-3824; (800) 541-6226
FAX (508) 240-0599
e-mail: bedandb@capecod.net
www.bandbcapecod.com

50. This recently built spacious home has left no stone unturned to assure a comfortable and relaxing environment. Four large rooms with queen-size or twin beds have ocean views from private-bath bedrooms. A fourth room is a honeymoon suite with a Jacuzzi and beautiful ocean view. The *Mayflower*, the rock, and great restaurants nearby. Full breakfast. No smoking. Children over 12 welcome. $90-113.

Bed and Breakfast Reservations North Shore, Greater Boston, Cape Cod

P.O. Box 600035, Greater Boston Branch,
   Newtonville, 02160-0001
(617) 964-1606; (800) 832-2632
FAX (617) 332-8572; e-mail: info@bbreserve.com
www.bbreserve.com

119. The 1820 English Cottage. A beautifully restored Cape-style bed and breakfast on 40 acres of pastures and wonderful grounds with breathtaking views. Large outside deck where breakfast is served in warmer weather. Three elegantly decorated guest rooms, en suite private baths, working fireplaces, and air conditioning. Large common room with fireplace, TV/VCR. Close to all historic sites. Great location for easy day trips to Boston, Cape Cod, Newport, Rhode Island. Full breakfast. $95-115.

Foxglove Cottage

101 Sandwich Road, 02360
(508) 747-6576; (800) 479-4746
FAX (508) 747-7622
e-mail: tranquility@foxglove-cottage.com
www.foxglove-cottage.com

Nestled in the heart of historic Plymouth, Foxglove Cottage (circa 1820) is a fully restored, authentic Cape farmhouse furnished with American and Victorian antiques. Its rooms all have en suite private baths, air conditioning/heat, working fireplaces, and reading and sitting areas. Enjoy the common room with its large comfortable sitting area and cable TV/VCR. Minutes from Plimoth Plantation and other historic sites and activities. Open year-round so that guests may enjoy not only the seasons, but the ambiance and warm New England hospitality. Children over 12 welcome.

Hosts: Mr. and Mrs. Charles K. Cowan
Rooms: 3 (PB) $80-95
Full Breakfast
Credit Cards: D
Notes: 2, 5, 7, 9, 10, 11, 12, 14

Remembrance

265 Sandwich Street, 02360
(508) 746-5160

Remembrance is an old cedar-shingled Cape-style home in a lovely residential neighborhood one mile from historic Plymouth, Plimoth Plantation, and the expressway; two blocks from the ocean. It is delightfully decorated with antiques, wicker, original art, plants, and flowers. Delicious full breakfasts served at guests' convenience in the greenhouse overlooking the garden and bird feeders. Tea time. No smoking. Gentle resident pets.

Host: Beverly Bainbridge
Rooms: 2 (SB) $65
Full Breakfast
Credit Cards: None
Notes: 2, 5, 7, 9, 10, 11, 12, 14

The Thornton Adams House

73C Warren Avenue, 02360
(888) 747-9700 (toll-free)

Enjoy the lovely ocean view from the classic Colonial home. Walk to the beach or plantation (home of the Pilgrims). Historic Plymouth center offers antiquing, whale watching, the rock, and *Mayflower II*, to

The Thornton Adams House

name a few. All the rooms have private baths, cable TV, and are air conditioned. The stunning "suite" has an oversized Jacuzzi. An elegant full breakfast served. Off-season rates available.

Hosts: Aldine and Bob Thornton
Rooms: 3 (PB) $75-95
Full Breakfast
Credit Cards: None
Notes: 2, 5, 7, 8, 9, 10, 11, 12

PRINCETON

Fernside Bed and Breakfast

162 Mountain Road, P.O. Box 303, 01541
(978) 464-2741; (800) 545-2741
FAX (978) 464-2065

An elegant Federal mansion with a breathtaking view of Boston on the eastern slope of Mount Wachusett in central Massachusetts. This gracious home has been carefully restored and exquisitely furnished in antiques and period reproductions. The

Fernside

eight fireplaces, numerous porches, and sitting rooms offer guests the opportunity to renew themselves, enjoy a romantic retreat, or just escape and relax. The Wachusett region provides opportunities for hiking, bird watching, snow shoeing, cross-country and downhill skiing.

Hosts: Jocelyn and Richard Morrison
Rooms: 6 (PB) $105-155
Full Breakfast
Credit Cards: A, B, C, D, E, F
Notes: 2, 5, 7, 9, 10, 11, 12, 13, 15

PROVINCETOWN

Bradford Gardens Inn

178 Bradford Street, 02657
(508) 487-1616; (800) 432-2334
e-mail: bradgard@capecod.net

An 1820 Colonial country inn with rooms offering fireplaces, ceiling fans, and antiques. Fireplaced cottages set in the beautiful gardens. All units have private baths. One block from the ocean and a five-minute stroll to town center for shopping, fine dining, art galleries, and whale watching. Nonsmoking rooms available. Children and pets welcome in some rooms.

Host: Susan Culligan
Rooms: 8 (PB)$65-250
Cottages/townhomes: 10
Full Breakfast
Credit Cards: A, B, C
Notes: 5, 9, 10, 14

The Captain's House

350A Commercial Street, 02657
(508) 487-9353; (800) 457-8885

Open year-round, the house in the center of town is within walking distance to shopping, restaurants, and night life. Reasonable rates and immaculate accommodations. Continental breakfast with home-baked pastries. Private and shared baths with cable TV and a pleasant common room with VCR and music for guests' pleasure. A private patio for sunbathing is also provided. Major

7 No smoking; 8 Children welcome; 9 Social drinking allowed; 10 Tennis nearby; 11 Swimming nearby; 12 Golf nearby; 13 Skiing nearby; 14 May be booked through a travel agent; 15 Handicapped accessible.

credit cards accepted. Off-season rates available. Smoking permitted in designated areas only.

Hosts: Bob Carvalho and David Brennan
Rooms: 11 (3 PB; 8 SB) $55-95
Continental Breakfast
Credit Cards: A, B, C, D
Notes: 2, 5, 9, 10, 11, 12

Gabriel's Apartments and Guest Rooms

104 Bradford Street, 02657
(508) 487-3232; (800) 969-2643
FAX (508) 487-1605
e-mail: gabriels@provincetown.com
www.provincetown.com/gabriels

Since 1979 Gabriel's has welcomed friends to two beautiful homes graced by antique furnishings, patios, and gardens. Each guest room and suite, decorated differently, is distinguished by its own personality. Amenities include Continental plus breakfast in the large skylit common room, fireplaces, exercise equipment, hot tubs, a steam room, cable TV, VCRs, in-room telephones, air conditioning, fully equipped kitchens, a sauna, business services; a book and video library, bikes, and private parking. Personal checks are accepted for deposits only. Inquire about accommodations for pets.

Host: Gabriel Brooke
Rooms: 20 (PB) $65-200
Continental Breakfast
Credit Cards: A, B, C, D, E, F
Notes: 5, 7, 8, 9, 10, 11, 12, 14

Land's End Inn

22 Commercial Street, 02657
(508) 487-0706; (800) 276-7088

At the very tip of Cape Cod, perched high atop Gull Hill, Land's End Inn commands a panoramic view of Provincetown and all of Cape Cod Bay. Large, airy, comfortably furnished living rooms, a large front porch, and lovely antique-filled bedrooms provide relaxation and visual pleasure to guests. Seasonal rates available.

Host: Anthony Arakelian
Rooms: 16 (PB) $87-285
Continental Breakfast
Credit Cards: A, B
Notes: 2, 5, 7, 9, 11

Watership Inn

Watership Inn

7 Winthrop Street, 02657
(508) 487-0094

Rustic 1820 sea captain's home, with Colonial rooms, private baths, and spacious lobby. Open year-round, serving Continental breakfast daily. Parking is available, and a five-minute walk gets visitors to the beach or to the center of town.

Host: Jim Foss
Rooms: 15 (PB) $32-110
Continental Breakfast
Credit Cards: A, B, C, D
Notes: 5, 9, 10, 11, 12, 14

White Wind Inn

174 Commercial Street, 02657
(508) 487-1526
www.provincetown.com/whitewindinn

A white Victorian, circa 1845, featuring some of the finest accommodations available in New England. The decor is tastefully accented with period antiques, all adding to the warm and cozy atmosphere of the inn.

Innkeepers: Michael Valenti and Robert Tosner
Rooms: 11 (PB) $85-190
Continental Breakfast
Credit Cards: A, B, C, D
Notes: 5, 9, 10, 11, 12

NOTES: Credit cards accepted: A MasterCard; B Visa; C American Express; D Discover; E Diner's Club; F Other; 2 Personal checks accepted; 3 Lunch available; 4 Dinner available; 5 Open all year; 6 Pets welcome;

REHOBOTH

Five Bridge Farm Inn Bed and Breakfast

154 Pine Street, P.O. Box 462, 02769
(508) 252-3190

Five Bridge Farm is a unique property near Providence, Newport, Cape Cod, and Boston. Enjoy hiking, cross-country skiing, tennis, swimming, or quiet time in the library, gazebo, on 60 acres. Guests are treated to old-fashioned hospitality and delicious home-cooked breakfasts. Horseback riding, golf, fine restaurants, beaches, and antiquing are all nearby. Inquire about accommodations for children.

Hosts: Harold and Ann Messenger
Rooms: 5 (3 PB; 2 SB) $75-105
Full Breakfast
Credit Cards: A, B, D
Notes: 2, 3, 5, 6, 7, 9, 10, 11, 12

Gilbert's Tree Farm Bed and Breakfast

30 Spring Street, 02769
(508) 252-6416

A 150-year-old New England Cape home with authentic hardware, wood floors, and windows is on a 15-acre tree farm only 12 miles east of Providence. Guests may enjoy in-ground pool, hiking, and pony cart rides. Delicious full country breakfasts. Within one hour of Boston, Plymouth, Newport, and Mystic. An additional $15 to stable horses.

Host: Jeanne Gilbert
Rooms: 3 (SB) $60
Suite: 1 (PB) $80
Full Breakfast
Credit Cards: None
Notes: 2, 5, 6, 7, 8, 9, 10, 11, 12, 14

Perryville Inn

157 Perryville Road, 02769
(508) 252-9239

This 19th-century restored Victorian in the National Register of Historic Places is on four

Perryville Inn

and one-half wooded acres with a quiet brook, mill pond, stone walls, and shaded paths and is overlooking an 18-hole public golf course. Bicycles available for guests, including a tandem. Nearby are antique stores, museums, Great Woods Performing Arts Center, fine seafood restaurants, and an old-fashioned New England clambake. Arrange for a horse-drawn hayride or a hot-air balloon ride. Within 15 minutes of Providence; one hour of Boston, Plymouth, Newport, and Mystic. Central air conditioning.

Hosts: Tom and Betsy Charnecki
Rooms: 4 (PB) $65-95
Continental Breakfast
Credit Cards: A, B, C, D
Notes: 2, 5, 7, 8, 9, 12, 14

RICHMOND

A Bed and Breakfast in the Berkshires

1666 Dublin Road, 01254
(413) 698-2817; (800) 795-7122
FAX (413) 698-3158
e-mail: doaneperry@compuserve.com

Stroll through serene gardens in the Berkshire Hills, relax in hammock in apple orchard on a country lane. Three and one-half miles to Tanglewood Music Festival and Hancock Shaker Village. Three rooms with private baths, great king- and queen-size beds, cable TV, air conditioning. No smoking. Berkshire apple pancakes, blueberry crêpes, and banana bread are among

7 No smoking; 8 Children welcome; 9 Social drinking allowed; 10 Tennis nearby; 11 Swimming nearby; 12 Golf nearby; 13 Skiing nearby; 14 May be booked through a travel agent; 15 Handicapped accessible.

A Bed and Breakfast in the Berkshires

the home-baked specialties served for breakfast, along with fresh fruit. Enjoy afternoon tea and scones on the screened porch. Children and pets welcome.

Hosts: Doane Perry and Family
Rooms: 3 (PB) $75-145
Continental Breakfast
Credit Cards: A, B, C
Notes: 2, 5, 6, 7, 8, 10, 11, 12, 13, 14

ROCKPORT

Addison Choate Inn

49 Broadway, 01966
(508) 546-7543; (800) 245-7543
www.cape-ann.com/addison-choate

An 1851 Greek Revival residence with six bright and cheerful rooms and a stable house with two one-bedroom apartments. All have original wide-pine floors, quilts, rag rugs, white wicker chairs, antique and reproduction furniture, private baths. Living room with fireplace; TV room; suites. Pri-

Addison Choate Inn

vate-blend coffee, home-baked cakes, breads. Air conditioning. Perennial gardens, pool, parking, porches, two friendly cats. Walk to galleries, shops, restaurants, beaches, Boston trains.

Hosts: Knox and Shirley Johnson
Rooms: 8 (PB) $85-130
Continental Breakfast
Credit Cards: A, B, F
Notes: 2, 5, 7, 11, 14

Bed and Breakfast Associates Bay Colony, Ltd.

P.O. Box 57166, Babson Park, Boston, 02157-0166
(781) 449-5302; (800) 347-5088
FAX (781) 449-5958; e-mail: info@bnbboston.com
www.bnbboston.com

NS558. Guests at this delightful inn can lounge at the beach or stroll to the many galleries, shops, and eateries and famous tourist sites on Rockport Harbor. Relaxing is the first order of business on the large front porch, or the spacious lawn, or at the gazebo on Observatory Point, where the land meets the rocky shoreline. Beautiful grounds, 33 attractive guest rooms (many with ocean views), and freshly baked Continental breakfast await guests. $85-130.

NS559. On a picturesque street near the beach and harborside shops, this Victorian home has 14 charming guest rooms with private baths, formal dining room, and sun porch. There is a carriage house which is also available. Seasonal rates. $75-97.

Bed and Breakfast Reservations North Shore, Greater Boston, Cape Cod

P.O. Box 600035, Greater Boston Branch,
  Newtonville, 02160-0001
(617) 964-1606; (800) 832-2632
FAX (617) 332-8572; e-mail: info@bbreserve.com
www.bbreserve.com

98. The Inn at Mill Pond. A stately 1840 Victorian inn with 14 tastefully decorated guest rooms with private baths. Some larger suites and efficiencies available. Relax on grounds with beautiful flowering gardens and picnic tables. Short walk to sandy beach and town center with quaint shops, many restaurants, and scenic harbor. Commuter rail station nearby for day trip into Boston. Families with children welcome in the annex rooms and carriage house. No smoking. Delicious home-baked Continental breakfast. Twenty dollars for third person in room. $99-125.

The Inn on Cove Hill

37 Mount Pleasant Street, 01966
(508) 546-2701; (888) 546-2701

Offering a friendly atmosphere with the option of privacy, this painstakingly restored 200-year-old Federal home is just two blocks from the harbor and shops. Meticulously appointed cozy bedrooms are furnished with antiques, and some have canopied beds. Wake up to the delicious aroma of hot muffins, and enjoy a Continental breakfast at the umbrella tables in the Pump Garden. The fresh sea air is preserved in the nonsmoking facility.

Hosts: John and Marjorie Pratt
Rooms: 11 (9 PB; 2 SB) $48-115
Continental Breakfast
Credit Cards: A, B
Notes: 2, 7, 9, 11, 12

Peg Leg Inn and Restaurant

2 King Street, 01966
(978) 546-2352; (800) 346-2352
www.cape-ann.com/pegleg

The original charm of five Colonial New England homes on the edge of the sea overlooking beautiful Front Beach and Rockport's picturesque shoreline. Panoramic ocean views from the guest rooms. Each welcomes with a warm and pleasant atmosphere, including private bath and TV. Lawns, gardens, and decks for guests' pleasure and relaxation. A short stroll to the quaint village that abounds with lovely shops and art galleries. The inn's own ocean-view restaurant

is famous for fresh local seafood and Yankee specialities, and an original working greenhouse serves as an added dining room.

Rooms: 33 (PB) $85-140
Continental Breakfast
Credit Cards: A, B, C
Notes: 2, 4, 7, 8, 10, 11, 12, 14

Ralph Waldo Emerson Inn

1 Cathedral Avenue, 01966
(978) 546-6321; FAX (978) 546-7043
e-mail: emerson@cove.com

In the 1850s Ralph Waldo Emerson sat on the Cathedral Rocks and made his "acquaintance with the sea." Today guests enjoy leisurely strolls along quiet tree-shaded streets, shopping in the art galleries, or relaxing in the inn's heated pool or whirlpool and sauna. Some enjoy fishing trips or whale watching out of nearby Gloucester, while others enjoy the ocean view from the inn's wide old-fashioned veranda. Rates without breakfast available.

Hosts: Gary and Diane Wemyss
Rooms: 36 (PB) $99-150
Continental Breakfast
Credit Cards: A, B, D
Notes: 2, 4, 8, 9, 10, 11, 12, 14, 15

Ralph Waldo Emerson Inn

Rocky Shores Inn and Cottages

65 Eden Road, 01966
(978) 546-2823; (800) 348-4003
www.rockportusa.com/rockyshores

Rocky Shores Inn sits on the easternmost point of Cape Ann, between the picturesque harbors of Rockport and Gloucester. The inn is a 1905 seaside mansion that overlooks the historic twin lights of Thacher Island and the open sea. Guests enjoy the beautiful beaches, whale watching, sailing, fishing, shopping on famous Bearskin Neck, and tasting lobsters in harbor-front restaurants. Continental plus breakfast.

Rooms: 21 (PB) $78-130
Continental Breakfast
Credit Cards: A, B, C
Notes: 2, 7, 8, 10, 11, 12, 14

Sally Webster Inn

34 Mount Pleasant Street, 01966
(978) 546-9251

Gracious Colonial Inn (circa 1832) steeped in local history sits just two blocks from the galleries, shops, and restaurants of Rockport village and is surrounded by ocean beaches. Whether guests come to Rockport to whale watch, sail, golf, shop, or antique, coming home to the inn will be the best part of the day. Rockport is a wonderful place to settle in and explore New England—Boston, Salem, Newburyport, Essex, Gloucester, Marblehead, all within 35 miles.

Hosts: Rick and Carolyn Steere
Rooms: 8 (PB) $68-94
Continental Breakfast
Credit Cards: A, B
Notes: 2, 7, 9, 10, 11, 12

Seacrest Manor

Seacrest Manor

99 Marmion Way, 01966
(978) 546-2211

Decidedly small, intentionally quiet. Gracious hospitality in luxurious surroundings with magnificent views overlooking woods and sea. Spacious grounds, lovely gardens, and ample parking. Famous full breakfast and afternoon tea included. No pets. Not recommended for children. Fresh flowers, cable TV, free daily paper, mints, and turndown. Mobil-rated three stars. Across from the nine-acre John Kieran Nature Preserve. An hour north of Boston by car or train. Nonsmoking. Closed December through March.

Hosts: Leighton Saville and Dwight MacCormack
Rooms: 8 (6 PB; 2 SB) $98-146
Full Breakfast
Credit Cards: None
Notes: 2, 7, 9, 11, 12

The Tuck Inn Bed and Breakfast

17 High Street, 01966
(978) 546-7260; (800) 789-7260
www.rockportusa.com/tuckinn/

A cozy 1790 Colonial home on a quiet secondary street, one block from the village center. The inn features the charm of yesterday with antiques, quilts, wide-pine floors, and living room with fireplace, coupled with modern conveniences such as private baths,

Sally Webster Inn

NOTES: Credit cards accepted: A MasterCard; B Visa; C American Express; D Discover; E Diner's Club; F Other; 2 Personal checks accepted; 3 Lunch available; 4 Dinner available; 5 Open all year; 6 Pets welcome;

cable TVs, air conditioning, and a pool. Guests have remarked on the lavish home-baked buffet breakfast and are treated to good old-fashioned New England hospitality. Golfing is three blocks away. Smoke-free.

Hosts: Liz and Scott Wood
Rooms: 11 (PB) $55-95
Continental Breakfast
Credit Cards: A, B
Notes: 2, 5, 7, 8, 9, 10, 11, 12, 13, 14

SAGAMORE BEACH

Widow's Walk

152 Clark Road, P.O. Box 605, 02562
(508) 888-0762

Just 200 feet from beautiful Sagamore Beach on Cape Cod Bay, this Cape-style country home gives guests that "homecoming feeling." It has two beautifully decorated bedrooms on the second floor and also has an authentic widow's walk. Hosts offer a lovely, fully equipped apartment with private entrance on the ground floor.

Rooms: 2 (SB) $80-85
Continental Breakfast
Credit Cards: F
Notes: 2, 5, 7, 9, 10, 11, 12

SALEM

Amelia Payson House

16 Winter Street, 01970
(978) 744-8304; e-mail: bbamelia@aol.com
www.salemweb.com/biz/ameliapayson/

A five-minute stroll from the elegantly restored 1845 Greek Revival finds the Peabody & Essex Museum, the Salem Witch Museum, Salem Maritime National Historic Site, the House of Seven Gables, shops, waterfront dining, and the Amtrak train to Boston. The seaside towns of Rockport and Gloucester are a short drive up the coast. Comfort amenities include private baths, TV, and air conditioning. Color brochure available. Children over 12 welcome. Nonsmoking host home.

Hosts: Ada and Donald Roberts
Rooms: 4 (PB) $75-125
Continental Breakfast
Credit Cards: A, B, C
Notes: 7, 9, 10, 11, 12

Bed and Breakfast Associates Bay Colony, Ltd.

P.O. Box 57166, Babson Park, Boston, 02157-0166
(781) 449-5302; (800) 347-5088
FAX (781) 449-5958; e-mail: info@bnbboston.com
www.bnbboston.com

CN178. These two glorious 19th-century sea captains' homes have been restored and decorated with the warmth and charm of yesterday and all the amenities and conveniences that everyone expects and enjoys today. The two inns offer a total of 30 guest rooms, suites, and family apartments, all with private baths, individual climate controls, cable color TVs, and telephones. Several rooms have Jacuzzis and fireplaces. The inn's restaurant offers two intimate dining rooms, a patio, and garden. Honeymoon suite available. Seasonal rates. $119-185.

Bed and Breakfast Reservations North Shore, Greater Boston, Cape Cod

P.O. Box 600035, Greater Boston Branch,
    Newtonville, 02160-0001
(617) 964-1606; (800) 832-2632
FAX (617) 332-8572; e-mail: info@bbreserve.com
www.bbreserve.com

5. Inn on the Green. In the heart of Salem, this historic Greek Revival-style inn was built in 1846. It has been elegantly restored. Each of seven guest rooms has period furnishings, queen-size bed, private bath, cable TV, and air conditioning. Sunny breakfast room where complimentary Continental breakfast is served. Relax in the beautiful formal living room with marble decorative fireplace. Walk to historic sites, shopping, great restaurants, and commuter rail train to Boston. Cat in residence. No smoking. $95-110.

7 No smoking; 8 Children welcome; 9 Social drinking allowed; 10 Tennis nearby; 11 Swimming nearby; 12 Golf nearby; 13 Skiing nearby; 14 May be booked through a travel agent; 15 Handicapped accessible.

107. Salem House. In Salem, two-bedroom apartment in first floor of historic Ephraim Wood House. Tastefully decorated, fully equipped, modern eat-in kitchen, dining room, living room, air conditioning, TV, off-street parking. Weekly in season from $975.

Coach House Inn

284 Lafayette Street, 01970
(978) 744-4092; (800) 688-8689
FAX (978) 745-8031; e-mail: coachhse@star.net
www.salemweb.com/biz/coachhouse

Victorian mansion, built by a sea captain in 1879, retains the charm and elegance of an earlier era. Colorful, bright rooms are decorated with antique furnishings. In historic district two blocks from the ocean.

Host: Patricia Kessler
Rooms: 11 (9 PB; 2 SB) $78-135
Continental Breakfast
Credit Cards: A, B, C, D
Notes: 5, 7, 8, 9, 10, 11, 12

The Inn at Seven Winter Street

7 Winter Street, 01970
(508) 745-9520; (800) 932-5547

Come, be a guest at the Inn at Seven Winter Street! This magnificently restored French Victorian inn is an award winner. Each room finely appointed with period antiques and furnishings. All rooms have

The Inn at Seven Winter Street

something beautifully unique: marble fireplace, canopied bed, Jacuzzi, or sun deck. In a historic area, within a one-minute walk of the waterfront, historic sites, dining, and museums. Off-street parking available. No smoking.

Hosts: Sally Flint, Jill and D. L. Coté
Rooms: 10 (PB) $85-185
Continental Breakfast
Credit Cards: A, B, C
Notes: 2, 5, 7, 9

The Salem Inn

7 Summer Street, 01970
(508) 741-0680; (800) 446-2995

Three elegantly restored 1834, 1854, and 1874 Federal, Italianate, and Colonial townhouses, in the heart of Salem's historic district, have 39 luxuriously appointed rooms with private baths and some working fireplaces. Direct-dial telephones, cable TVs, and air conditioning. Hearty Continental breakfast and lovely rose garden. Jacuzzi and canopied suites available. Smoking in designated areas only. Within walking distances of the museums and other attractions. Limited handicapped accessibility.

Hosts: Richard and Diane Pabich
Rooms: 39 (PB) $99-200
Continental Breakfast
Credit Cards: A, B, C, D, E, F
Notes: 2, 5, 6, 8, 9, 10, 11, 12, 14

Stephen Daniels House

1 Daniels Street, 01970
(508) 744-5709

Built by a sea captain in 1667 and enlarged in 1756, the house is beautifully restored and furnished with antiques. Wood-burning fireplaces in the bedrooms with charming canopied beds. Continental breakfast is served before two huge fireplaces. Walk to 11 points of interest in Salem.

Host: Catherine Gill
Rooms: 5 (3 PB; 2 SB) $50-115

NOTES: Credit cards accepted: A MasterCard; B Visa; C American Express; D Discover; E Diner's Club; F Other; 2 Personal checks accepted; 3 Lunch available; 4 Dinner available; 5 Open all year; 6 Pets welcome;

Continental Breakfast
Credit Cards: C
Notes: 2, 5, 6, 8, 9, 10, 11, 12, 14

Suzannah Flint House

98 Essex Street, 01970
(508) 744-5281; (800) 893-9973
www.salemweb.com/biz/suzannahflint

Built in 1808, the Suzannah Flint House is
a fine example of Federal period architecture. Each spacious room features antique
furnishings, oriental rugs over original
hardwood floors, decorative fireplaces, private baths, cable color TV/VCR, and air
conditioning. The inn is in Salem's historic
district, adjacent to Salem Common, and
one block to the waterfront wharves, museums, historic sites, shops, and fine dining.
Also walk to train station.

Host: Scott Eklind
Rooms: 3 (PB) $55-110
Continental Breakfast
Credit Cards: A, B, C, D
Notes: 2, 5, 7, 9, 10, 11, 12

SANDWICH (CAPE COD)

Bay Beach Bed and Breakfast

1-3 Bay Beach Lane, Box 151, 02563
(508) 888-8813; (800) 475-6398

Luxury beachfront bed and breakfast with
super amenities in a romantic setting overlooking Cape Cod Bay. Six spacious guest
rooms with decks and ocean views, plus
three honeymoon suites with king-size bed
and Jacuzzi are available for guests to
choose. A full breakfast is served each morning. All rooms have air conditioning, telephones, cable TV, refrigerators, and compact
disk players; some with fireplaces. Exercise
room. AAA four-diamond inn. Four-crown
ABBA. Adults only. Nonsmoking.

Hosts: Emily and Reale Lemieux
Rooms: 6 (PB) $160-225
Continental Breakfast
Credit Cards: A, B
Notes: 2, 7, 9, 10, 11, 12

Bed and Breakfast Associates Bay Colony, Ltd.

P.O. Box 57166, Babson Park, Boston, 02157-0166
(781) 449-5302; (800) 347-5088
FAX (781) 449-5958; e-mail: info@bnbboston.com
www.bnbboston.com

CC256. A lovingly restored 250-year-old
Colonial home overlooking Shawme Pond
in historic Sandwich Village. Four guest
rooms with private baths, gift and book
shop, and delightful tea room and garden.
$85-100.

Bed and Breakfast Cape Cod

P.O. Box 1312, Orleans, 02653
(508) 255-3824; (800) 541-6226
FAX (508) 240-0599
e-mail: bedandb@capecod.net
www.bandbcapecod.com

27. Built in 1741 in the heart of what is
now the center of the village, this lovely
restored Colonial-style home is in the
National Register of Historic Places. Walk
to all village sites, including the pond off
the village square. Start the day with a full
breakfast, or walk the village streets enjoying the picture of a community not much
changed from 200 years ago. The English
hosts will treat guests as special visitors,
offering a meal with every reservation in
their authentic English tearoom. A special
place that will give guests memories to
cherish. No smoking. $85-95.

Belfry Inne and Bistro

8 Jarves Street, P.O. Box 2211, 02563
(508) 888-8550; (800) 844-4542
FAX (508) 888-3922; e-mail: info@belfryinn.com
www.belfryinn.com

Belfry Inne exemplifies an era renowned for
gentility and grace. Authentic "painted
lady" in the heart of Sandwich, Cape Cod
historic district. All rooms with private bath,
some with whirlpools, fireplaces, soaking
tubs, and private balconies. Pamperings

7 No smoking; 8 Children welcome; 9 Social drinking allowed; 10 Tennis nearby; 11 Swimming nearby;
12 Golf nearby; 13 Skiing nearby; 14 May be booked through a travel agent; 15 Handicapped accessible.

include down comforters and individual selected antiques—room service, telephones, some TVs. Hospitality at its finest. Bistro offers beverages, desserts as well as dinner—neo-French cuisine. Relax on the porch with a glass of wine or iced tea.

Host: Christopher Wilson
Rooms: 9 (PB) $85-165
Full Breakfast
Credit Cards: A, B, C
Notes: 2, 3, 4, 5, 7, 8, 10, 11, 12, 14

Capt. Ezra Nye House

152 Main Street, 02563
(508) 888-6142; (800) 388-2278

Comfort and warmth amid antique-filled rooms, some with fireplaces and canopies, make any stay a treat in this 1829 Federal home. Museums, lake, and restaurants within a block. Featured in *Glamour* and *Innsider* magazines and chosen Best Bed and Breakfast, Upper Cape, by *Cape Cod Life* magazine in 1993, 1994, and 1996. "Thank you for opening your hearts and your home to us....You have made our first trip to Cape Cod a memorable one!" Children over 10 welcome.

Hosts: Elaine and Harry Dickson
Rooms: 5 (PB) $75-110
Suite: 1 (PB)
Full Breakfast
Credit Cards: A, B, C, D, F
Notes: 2, 5, 7, 9, 10, 11, 12, 14

Capt. Ezra Nye House

The Cranberry House

50 Main Street, 02563
(508) 888-1281

The Cranberry House is a friendly place to stay on Cape Cod. A full breakfast is served in the dining room or on the deck. Relax in the den overlooking the beautifully landscaped yard. Hosts offer cable TV and complimentary soft drinks. Sandwich, the cape's oldest town, has many shops, restaurants, museums, gardens, and beaches. The Cape Cod canal has walking and biking trails. No smoking in house. Children over 10 welcome.

Hosts: John and Sara Connolly
Rooms: 4 (PB) $65-85
Full Breakfast
Credit Cards: F
Notes: 5, 7, 9, 10, 11, 12

Dillingham House

71 Main Street, 02563
(508) 833-0065

Built circa 1650, the Dillingham House is one of the oldest in the country. It offers its guests an interesting historical experience while providing a quiet and comfortable natural environment off the beaten path. Sandwich has many historical attractions, as well as quiet beaches for relaxation and a scenic waterfront nearby.

Host: Kathy Kenney
Rooms: 4 (2 PB; 2 SB) $70-80
Continental Breakfast
Credit Cards: None
Notes: 2, 9, 10, 11, 12

The Dunbar House

1 Water Street, 02563
(508) 833-2485; FAX (508) 833-4713
e-mail: dunbar@capecod.net

An old Colonial home, circa 1740, in the heart of historic Sandwich village offers three en suite guest rooms, a full breakfast, and an English tearoom in the adjacent carriage house. The Dunbar House overlooks Shawme Pond and is within walking distance of five museums and the beach.

NOTES: Credit cards accepted: A MasterCard; B Visa; C American Express; D Discover; E Diner's Club; F Other; 2 Personal checks accepted; 3 Lunch available; 4 Dinner available; 5 Open all year; 6 Pets welcome;

The Dunbar House

Hosts: Nancy Iribarren and David Bell
Rooms: 3 (PB) $65-95
Full Breakfast
Credit Cards: A, B, D
Notes: 3, 4, 5, 7, 8, 9, 10, 11, 12, 14

Inn at Sandwich Center

118 Tupper Road, 02563
(508) 888-6958; (800) 249-6949
FAX (508) 833-0574; e-mail: innsan@aol.com
www.bfbooks.com/innsan.html

Elegant 1829 inn listed in the National Register of Historic Places in historic Sandwich village. Antique and art lovingly create warm ambiance. Five bedrooms, fireplaces, four-poster beds, private bathrooms. Breakfast served in keeping room with circa 1750 fireplace. Homemade Continental plus breakfast. Special amenities. Nonsmoking. French, Italian, and some Spanish spoken. Children over 12 welcome.

Hosts: Eliane and Alan Thomas
Rooms: 5 (PB) $75-120
Continental Breakfast
Credit Cards: A, B, C, D
Notes: 2, 5, 7, 9, 10, 11, 12, 14

Isaiah Jones Homestead

165 Main Street, 02563
(508) 888-9115; (800) 526-1625

Elegant 1849 Victorian Italianate bed and breakfast fully restored with Victorian antique furniture, oriental rugs, accessories, and tapestries throughout. Five guest rooms, four with queen-size beds, one with a double and twin bed. All private baths, two with oversize whirlpool tubs. Three rooms with fireplaces. Full breakfast and afternoon tea. On Main Street of historic Sandwich village, the oldest town on Cape Cod, and a 15-minute walk to the beach.

Hosts: Jan and Doug Klapper
Rooms: 5 (PB) $75-155
Full Breakfast
Credit Cards: A, B, C, D
Notes: 2, 5, 7, 9, 10, 11, 12, 14

The Summer House

158 Main Street, 02563
(508) 888-4991; (800) 241-3609

Elegant circa 1835 Greek Revival bed and breakfast featured in *Country Living* magazine, in the heart of historic Sandwich village, Cape Cod's oldest town (settled 1637). Antiques, hand-stitched quilts, working fireplaces, flowers, large sunny rooms, and English-style gardens. Close to dining, museums, shops, pond, and gristmill; boardwalk to beach. Bountiful breakfast, elegantly served. Afternoon tea in the garden included. Working fireplaces in all guest rooms, plus one in the parlor, and one in the breakfast room. Children over six welcome. Seasonal rates.

Hosts: Erik Suby and Phyllis Burg
Rooms: 5 (PB) $65-105
Full Breakfast
Credit Cards: A, B, C, D
Notes: 2, 5, 7, 10, 11, 12

The Summer House

7 No smoking; 8 Children welcome; 9 Social drinking allowed; 10 Tennis nearby; 11 Swimming nearby; 12 Golf nearby; 13 Skiing nearby; 14 May be booked through a travel agent; 15 Handicapped accessible.

The Village Inn at Sandwich

4 Jarves Street, 02563
(508) 833-0363; (800) 922-9989
FAX (508) 833-2063; e-mail: capecodinn@aol.com
www.capecodinn.com

The Allen House

This beautifully restored 1830s Federal-style inn is in the heart of historic Sandwich village, the oldest town on Cape Cod. It's a short stroll to museums, antique shops, galleries, and restaurants or over the boardwalk to the beach on Cape Cod Bay for swimming, boating, or fishing. Relax on the wraparound porch surrounded by gardens, or in comfortable parlors filled with antiques. Eight beautifully decorated guest rooms, some with fireplaces, each unique. Queen-size beds, private baths. Full gourmet breakfast. Art workshops are offered in the sunny new studio tucked behind the inn.

Host: Susan Fehlinger
Rooms: 8 (6 PB; 2 SB) $75-105
Full Breakfast
Credit Cards: A, B, C, D
Notes: 2, 5, 7, 8, 9, 10, 11, 12, 14

The Village Inn at Sandwich

SCITUATE

The Allen House

18 Allen Place, 02066
(781) 545-8221

Sleep comfortably and quietly in a gracious, gabled Victorian merchant's home overlooking an unspoiled New England fishing town and harbor, only an hour's drive south of Boston. Then wake to classical music and gourmet cuisine. The hosts are English, professional caterers, and cat lovers. On every sunny, warm day expect a full breakfast—and sometimes afternoon tea—on the porch overlooking the harbor.

Hosts: Christine and Iain Gilmour
Rooms: 6 (PB) $69-169
Full Breakfast
Credit Cards: A, B, C, D
Notes: 2, 5, 7, 9, 11, 12, 14, 15

Bed and Breakfast Associates Bay Colony, Ltd.

P.O. Box 57166, Babson Park, Boston, 02157-0166
(781) 449-5302; (800) 347-5088
FAX (781) 449-5958; e-mail: inf@bnbboston.com
www.bnbboston.com

SS260. This circa 1905 home is a two-minute walk from Scituate Harbor. It has been remodeled and is filled with period furniture and English-style hospitality. Guests make themselves comfortable in the cheerful parlor, indulge in the fabulous gourmet full breakfast (or ask for a low-cal or "happy heart" diet), relax before the Edwardian fireplace, or gaze out at the yachts in the harbor. A short stroll brings visitors to local shops and seafood restaurants. Six guest rooms, four with private baths. Children over 16 are welcome. Smoking is not permitted. Lower rates for stays of three or more days and off-season. $99-159.

Bed and Breakfast Reservations North Shore, Greater Boston, Cape Cod

P.O. Box 600035, Greater Boston Branch,
   Newtonville, 02160-0001
(617) 964-1606; (800) 832-2632
FAX (617) 332-8572; e-mail: info@bbreserve.com
www.bbreserve.com

108. Seashell Bed and Breakfast. Halfway between Cape Cod and Boston, this bed and breakfast offers panoramic ocean views from guests' suite and private patio. On "third cliff," just one mile from scenic Scituate Harbor, where guests will enjoy quaint shops and a variety of interesting restaurants. Guest quarters include own private suite, private bath, dining/living room, full kitchen, TV, air conditioning, telephone. Full breakfast is served in the upstairs dining room for shorter stays. For longer stays, the host will stock guests' cupboards and refrigerator with breakfast foods. Extra bedroom upstairs with private bath available only in conjunction with suite. Smoking is not permitted. Infants and children over 12 are welcome. $75-125.

Host Homes of Boston

P.O. Box 117, Waban Branch, Boston, 02468-0001
(617) 244-1308; FAX (617) 244-5156

Seashells. Watch a spectacular sunrise over the ocean, sunbathe, walk along the beach, or visit quaint Scituate Harbor. Great escape between Boston and Cape Cod. Quiet area. The guest suite includes a spacious living/dining room, awood stove, and glass doors overlooking water. Modern kitchen, bath, bedroom with king-size or twin beds. The second-floor room has a double bed and hall bath, if in the same party. Telephone. TV. Air conditioned. Parking. No smoking. $130.

SHEFFIELD _____

American Country Collection

1353 Union Street, Schenectady, NY 12308
(518) 370-4948; (800) 810-4948
FAX (518) 393-1634 (call first)
e-mail: Carolbnbres@msn.com

173. An authentic 1840s Colonial barn conversion of hand-hewn beams, plank floors, and stenciled walls nestled on three wooded acres below Mount Everett in the Berkshire's Taconic Range. Hike from the inn on a connecting trail that runs along a racing stream to the Appalachian Trail via Mount Race Falls. Thirteen guest rooms in the main house, and three guest rooms in each of two cottages. Several rooms are interconnecting, offering suite arrangements for families. A kitchen and laundry are available for guest use. Continental breakfast. No resident pets; guest pets welcomed with prior arrangements. $90-135.

Covered Bridge

69 Maple Avenue, Norfolk, CT 06058
(860) 542-5944; FAX (860) 542-5690

1SHMA. This charming log home, commanding a sweeping view of the Berkshires, is the perfect spot for an idyllic, pastoral retreat. A horse grazes nearby, and it's a short walk across the fields to the swimming pond. A full breakfast is served in the kitchen or on the porch. The host, an actress, has traveled extensively and is also well informed about area activities. There are two double guest rooms that share a bath. $85-95.

Ivanhoe Country House

254 South Undermountain Road (Route 41), 01257
(413) 229-2143

In the Berkshire Hills on 20 wooded acres. Swimming pool, hiking trails including the Appalachian. All rooms with private baths, some with fireplace and kitchen. Near Tanglewood, antique shops, shopping outlets, ski areas, golf, and tennis. Excellent restaurants

---

7 No smoking; 8 Children welcome; 9 Social drinking allowed; 10 Tennis nearby; 11 Swimming nearby; 12 Golf nearby; 13 Skiing nearby; 14 May be booked through a travel agent; 15 Handicapped accessible.

Ivanhoe Country House

nearby. Continental breakfast served outside each bedroom. Brochure available.

Hosts: Carole and Dick Maghery
Rooms: 9 (PB) $65-110
Continental Breakfast
Credit Cards: None
Notes: 2, 5, 6, 8, 9, 10, 12, 13

Ramblewood Inn

Box 729, 01257
(413) 229-3363

This stylish country house, furnished for comfort and romance, is in a beautiful natural setting of mountains, pine forest, and serene private lake for swimming and canoeing. Private baths, fireplaces, central air, lovely gardens, and gourmet breakfasts. Convenient to all Berkshire attractions: Tanglewood, drama/dance festivals, antiques, Lime Rock racing, skiing, and hiking. Minimum stay requirements for weekends and holidays. Suite available.

Ramblewood Inn

Hosts: June and Martin Ederer
Rooms: 6 (PB) $80-125
Full Breakfast
Credit Cards: A, B
Notes: 2, 5, 7, 8, 9, 10, 11, 12, 13, 14

SOMERVILLE

Bed and Breakfast Reservations North Shore, Greater Boston, Cape Cod

P.O. Box 600035, Greater Boston Branch,
   Newtonville, 02160-0001
(617) 964-1606; (800) 832-2632
FAX (617) 332-8572; e-mail: info@bbreserve.com
www.bbreserve.com

82. Morrison House. Large 1910 Victorian mansard-style home, offering two cozy guest rooms. First-floor room has private half-bath and shares bath with second-floor guest room. Both rooms have TV and air conditioning. Off-street parking. Continental breakfast in kitchen or on private back yard deck, weather permitting. One block from Red Line "T" in Davis Square, making Harvard and MIT only a short train ride away. Walking distance to Tufts University. Cat in residence. No smoking. Longer stays preferred at discounted rates. $75-80.

Cobble Hill Bed and Breakfast

74 Mount Vernon Street, 02145-4319
(617) 666-1975

Cobble Hill Bed and Breakfast is a charming Second Empire Victorian Mansard home, minutes from downtown Boston. There are three guest rooms and a shared parlor. Decorated with period furnishings, Cobble Hill maintains a Victorian ambiance and is registered as one of greater Boston's historic properties. Hosts Sharon and Paul Turcotte serve a full breakfast. Free off-street parking. There is a minimum of two nights.

Hosts: Sharon and Paul Turcotte
Rooms: 3 (3 SB) $70
Full Breakfast
Credit Cards: None
Notes: 2, 5, 7, 8, 9, 11

NOTES: Credit cards accepted: A MasterCard; B Visa; C American Express; D Discover; E Diner's Club; F Other; 2 Personal checks accepted; 3 Lunch available; 4 Dinner available; 5 Open all year; 6 Pets welcome;

SOUTH DENNIS

Country Pineapple Inn

370 Main Street, P.O. Box 719, 02660
(508) 394-7474; e-mail: irret8848@aol.com

Enjoy the elegant simplicity of a restored 1839 sea captain's home in the historic village of South Dennis, Cape Cod. Hosts strive to make their guests feel as family. Hosts serve a full country breakfast, along with house specialties that are available throughout the day. The inn is in the "Sea Captains' Village," close to the beautiful Bass River, three golf courses, boating, and swimming, and the famous Cape Cod Bike Rail Trail. Enjoy one acre of grounds and solitude. Children over 10 welcome.

Rooms: 4 (3 PB; 1 SB) $65-95
Full Breakfast
Credit Cards: None
Notes: 2, 5, 7, 9, 10, 11, 12, 15

Country Pineapple Inn

SOUTH EGREMONT

The Egremont Inn

Old Sheffield Road, P.O. Box 418, 01258
(413) 528-2111; FAX (413) 528-3284

In the National Register of Historic Places, this 1780 stagecoach stop has 20 rooms, suites, and connecting rooms, all with private baths, air conditioning. Three fireplaced first-floor sitting rooms, lovely wraparound porch, tavern, and dining room with outstanding cuisine. Pool and tennis courts on premises. The inn is a short drive to downhill and cross-country skiing, hiking, cycling, water attractions, a wealth of live theater, concerts, and dance festivals, and world-renowned antique shops.

Hosts: Karen and Steven Waller
Rooms: 20 (PB) $90-165
Full and Continental Breakfast
Credit Cards: A, B, C, D
Notes: 2, 4, 5, 8, 10, 11, 12, 13, 14

SOUTH HARWICH

The House on the Hill

968 Main Street, Route 28, 02661-0051
(508) 432-4321

A lovely Cape Cod farmhouse built in 1832 and furnished with antiques and family pieces. Enjoy a sunny deck, or the warm-water beach one mile away, or the Nantucket ferry one-half mile away. A Continental breakfast of freshly baked muffins, breads, and fresh fruit is served in a country dining room. The living room with original paneling and fireplace offers guests a relaxed atmosphere to read, watch TV, or converse with other guests. Children welcome; a crib and cot are available.

Hosts: Allen and Carolyn Seanson
Rooms: 3 (PB) $55-65
Continental Breakfast
Credit Cards: None
Notes: 2, 5, 7, 8, 11, 12

SOUTH ORLEANS

Hillbourne House

Route 28, #654, 02662
(508) 255-0780

This charming bed and breakfast was built in 1798 and during the Civil War was part of the Underground Railroad. A circular hiding place is still in evidence beneath the trap door in the common room. Enjoy a magnificent view of Pleasant Bay and the great dunes of Outer Beach on the

Atlantic. Convenient to all cape activities. Private beach and dock. Continental plus breakfast served.

Hosts: Jack and Barbara Hayes
Rooms: 8 (PB) $50-95
Continental Breakfast
Credit Cards: None
Notes: 2, 5, 7, 9, 10, 11, 12

Orleans Bed and Breakfast Associates, Inc.

P.O. Box 1312; Orleans, 02653
(508) 255-3824; (800) 541-6226
FAX (508) 240-0599
e-mail: orleansbnb@capecod.net
www.capecod.net/bb

Mayflower House. Handsome reproduction bow roof house on a picturesque rural road leading to Paw Wah Pond on Pleasant Bay. Two guest rooms, each with private bath, color TV, and air conditioning. Relax or read in first-floor parlor or on secluded deck. There is also a lovely guest wing with kitchenette, air conditioning, ceiling fan, large bathroom with Jacuzzi tub, canopied bed, and private entrance. Twenty dollars extra for additional persons. $80-115.

White Pines. Nestled among pines with colorful gardens, this lovely home invites quiet and privacy. Large bedroom with private Jacuzzi bath, cathedral ceiling, ceiling fan, TV/VCR, working space, and guest refrigerator. There is a large deck to watch birds. Minutes to Pleasant Bay. Cot available. Twenty dollars extra for additional persons. $75.

SOUTH YARMOUTH (CAPE COD)

Bed and Breakfast Associates Bay Colony, Ltd.

P.O. Box 57166, Babson Park, Boston, 02157-0166
(781) 449-5302; (800) 347-5088
FAX (781) 449-5958; e-mail: info@bnbboston.com
www.bnbboston.com

CC380. Contemporary elegance in an antique setting. Ten wonderful guest rooms in this 1845 sea captain's mansion. Every amenity thoughtfully provided in this magnificent restoration. Lower rates off-season. $95-185.

Bed and Breakfast Cape Cod

P.O. Box 1312, Orleans, 02653
(508) 255-3824; (800) 541-6226
FAX (508) 240-0599
e-mail: bedandb@capecod.net
www.bandbcapecod.com

68. This 1880 sea captain's house has a belvedere, reflecting the character of architecture in the whaling ship days. Charming restorations with Victorian decor and wide-board, highly burnished floors characterize this house. Bedrooms with private baths, queen-size beds, and a Jacuzzi are some of the features. Hyannis and the ferry to either Nantucket or Martha's Vineyard are only 15 minutes away by car. This home has been featured in Fodor's travel guide. Breakfast is a special full-service treat. No smoking. Children over 12 welcome. $75-120.

STOCKBRIDGE

Arbor Rose Bed and Breakfast

8 Yale Hill, 01262-0114
(413) 298-4744

Charming 1810 mill and farmhouse with flowing pond, gardens, antiques, tranquility, home baking, and smiles. Close to Stockbridge center, museums, restaurants, and Berkshire Theater. Private baths, four-poster beds, fireplaces, gallery shop, ski packages. No smoking. Families welcome.

Hosts: Christina Alsop and Family
Rooms: 6 (PB) $60-155
Full Breakfast
Credit Cards: A, B, C
Notes: 2, 5, 7, 8, 9, 10, 11, 12, 13, 14

NOTES: Credit cards accepted: A MasterCard; B Visa; C American Express; D Discover; E Diner's Club; F Other; 2 Personal checks accepted; 3 Lunch available; 4 Dinner available; 5 Open all year; 6 Pets welcome;

Four Seasons on Main Bed and Breakfast

47 Main Street, P.O. Box 634, 01262
(413) 298-5419

Lovingly restored and refurbished 1860 Greek Revival home in the heart of the village of Stockbridge, "Norman Rockwell's Main Street," with beautiful gardens and large front porch. The bed and breakfast has four guest rooms, private baths, paddle fans, air conditioning, and fine heirloom antique furnishings. Fireplace and TV in front parlors. An easy walk to shops, fine restaurants, Berkshire theater, and recreation in a four-season area. Dog in residence. Afternoon refreshments and seasonal package arrangements. Inquire about cancellation policy. Minimum two-to-three-night stay Tanglewood weekends and holidays. Not suitable for children.

Hosts: Greg and Pat O'Neill
Rooms: 4 (PB) $100-165
Full Breakfast
Credit Cards: A, B, C
Notes: 2, 5, 7, 9, 10, 11, 12, 13, 14

Historic Merrell Inn

1565 Pleasant Street, South Lee, 01260
(413) 243-1794; (800) 243-1794
FAX (413) 243-2669; e-mail: merey@bcn.net
www.merrell-inn.com

This 200-year-old brick stagecoach inn in a small New England village along the banks

Historic Merrell Inn

of the Housatonic River is listed in the National Register of Historic Places. Rooms with fireplaces, canopied beds, and antique furnishings. Full breakfast is served in the original tavern room. One mile to Norman Rockwell's beloved Stockbridge.

Hosts: Charles and Faith Reynolds
Rooms: 9 (PB) $75-165
Full Breakfast
Credit Cards: A, B
Notes: 2, 5, 7, 8, 9, 11, 13, 14

The Inn at Stockbridge

The Inn at Stockbridge

Route 7 North, P.O. Box 618, 01262
(413) 298-3337; FAX (413) 298-3406

Consummate hospitality and outstanding breakfasts distinguish a visit at this turn-of-the-century Georgian Colonial estate on 12 secluded acres in the heart of the Berkshires. Close to the Norman Rockwell Museum, Tanglewood, Hancock Shaker Village, summer theaters, and four-season recreation. The inn has a gracious, English country feeling, with two well-appointed living rooms, a formal dining room, and a baby grand piano.

Hosts: Alice and Len Schiller
Rooms: 12 (PB) $95-260
Full Breakfast
Credit Cards: A, B, C, D
Notes: 2, 5, 7, 9, 10, 11, 12, 13, 14, 15

7 No smoking; 8 Children welcome; 9 Social drinking allowed; 10 Tennis nearby; 11 Swimming nearby; 12 Golf nearby; 13 Skiing nearby; 14 May be booked through a travel agent; 15 Handicapped accessible.

The Roeder House

The Roeder House Bed and Breakfast

Route 183, Box 525, 01262
(413) 298-4015; www.roederhouse.com

On four acres in Stockbridge near the Rockwell and Chesterwood museums. Full breakfast served on porch in summer with views of pool and grounds. Queen-size four-poster beds, private baths, air conditioning, period antiques, and Audubon print collection. Cancellation and no smoking policies. Winter ski package.

Hosts: Diane and Vernon Reuss
Rooms: 7 (PB) $95-245
Full Breakfast
Credit Cards: A, B, C, D
Notes: 2, 5, 7, 9, 10, 12, 13, 14

STOW

Bed and Breakfast Associates Bay Colony, Ltd.

P.O. Box 57166, Babson Park, Boston, 02157-0166
(781) 449-5302; (800) 347-5088
FAX (781) 449-5958; e-mail: info@bnbboston.com
www.bnbboston.com

CW325. Authentic Colonial farmhouse, circa 1734, features three romantic guest rooms. Honeymoon suite has a sitting room, Jacuzzi in the bath, and queen-size canopied bed. All guest rooms have handmade quilts, decorative fireplaces, and antique furnishings. $95-115.

STURBRIDGE

Bed and Breakfast Reservations North Shore, Greater Boston, Cape Cod

P.O. Box 600035, Greater Boston Branch,
Newtonville, 02160-0001
(617) 964-1606; (800) 832-2632
FAX (617) 332-8572; e-mail: info@bbreserve.com
www.bbreserve.com

24. The Village Bed and Breakfast. Less than one hour from Boston and the Berkshires, tour Old Sturbridge Village, where life in an 1830s rural New England town is re-created. This accommodation is very convenient to the town of Brimfield, where one of the largest and most famous flea markets in Massachusetts is held. At day's end enjoy the comforts of this cozy gambrel-roofed Colonial-style bed and breakfast with three beautiful guest rooms (shared/private baths). There is also a separate entrance suite, perfect for extended stays, with half-bath, refrigerator, microwave, desk. Guests may use the cozy sitting room with TV or relax on outside screened porch/deck. Full breakfast and afternoon tea included. Children over 12 welcome. No smoking. $85-100.

Colonel Ebenezer Crafts Inn

Fiske Hill Road, P.O. Box 187, 01566-0187
(508) 347-3313; (800)-PUBLICK

The Colonel Ebenezer Crafts Inn was built in 1786 by David Fiske, Esquire, on one of the highest points of land in Sturbridge, which offered him a commanding view of his cattle and farmland. The house has since been restored by the management of the Publick House. Accommodations at Crafts Inn are charming. There are two canopied beds, as well as some four-poster beds. Guests may relax by the pool or in the sunroom, take afternoon tea, or enjoy sweeping views of the countryside. Those seeking a more hearty breakfast, lunch, or dinner can stroll down to the Publick House just over a mile away. Cross-country skiing nearby.

NOTES: Credit cards accepted: A MasterCard; B Visa; C American Express; D Discover; E Diner's Club; F Other; 2 Personal checks accepted; 3 Lunch available; 4 Dinner available; 5 Open all year; 6 Pets welcome;

Host: Albert Cournoyer
Rooms: 8 (PB) $69-150
Continental Breakfast
Credit Cards: A, B, C, E
Notes: 2, 5, 7, 8, 9, 10, 11, 12, 13, 14, 15

Sturbridge Country Inn

530 Main Street, P.O. Box 60, 01566
(508) 347-5503; FAX (508) 347-5319

Historic 1840s inn, near Old Sturbridge Village. Each room features a fireplace and whirlpool tub. Complimentary breakfast and wine. Walk to antique shops, boutiques, crafts, and more. Live theater in the Loft. Off-season discounts and packages available. Smoking in designated areas only. Children over four welcome.

Host: Patricia Affenito
Rooms: 9 (PB) $59-159
Continental Breakfast
Credit Cards: A, B, C, D
Notes: 2, 4, 5, 9, 10, 11, 12, 13, 14

SUDBURY

Bed and Breakfast Associates Bay Colony, Ltd.

P.O. Box 57166, Babson Park, Boston, 02157-0166
(781) 449-5302; (800) 347-5088
FAX (781) 449-5958; e-mail: info@bnbboston.com
www.bnbboston.com

CW644. Delightful 19th-century Arabian horse farm on nine acres. Luxurious master suite with four-poster canopied bed, fireplace, and elegant bath with whirlpool tub. Three pleasant smaller rooms. Central air conditioning. Fabulous for outdoor weddings. $85-160.

Sudbury Bed and Breakfast

3 Drum Lane, 01776
(978) 443-2860

A large Garrison Colonial home with traditional furnishings on a quiet tree-studded acre. A Continental breakfast is served with homemade muffins and rolls. Close to Boston, Lexington, and Concord. An abundance of outdoor recreation and historical sights nearby. Friendly hospitality for the New England visitor.

Hosts: Don and Nancy Somers
Rooms: 2 (S1.5B) $55-65
Continental Breakfast
Credit Cards: None
Notes: 2, 5, 7, 8, 10, 11, 12, 13

SWAMPSCOTT

Bed and Breakfast Associates Bay Colony, Ltd.

P.O. Box 57166, Babson Park, Boston, 02157-0166
(781) 449-5302; (800) 347-5088
FAX (781) 449-5958; e-mail: info@bnbboston.com
www.bnbboston.com

NS210. On the beach, this bed and breakfast inn offers moderately priced rooms with traditional decor, private baths, color TVs, refrigerators; plus oceanside pool, patio, and hot tub. $95-155.

Bed and Breakfast Reservations North Shore, Greater Boston, Cape Cod

P.O. Box 600035, Greater Boston Branch,
Newtonville, 02160-0001
(617) 964-1606; (800) 832-2632
FAX (617) 332-8572; e-mail: info@bbreserve.com
www.bbreserve.com

6. Oceanview Victorian. Easy access to Boston and North Shore. Wonderful ocean views. American country decor. Scenic ocean walkway to harbor with shops and restaurants. Deck/porch with ocean views. Three beautifully furnished rooms with two and one-half baths. Cable TV, air conditioning. Continental breakfast. No smoking. Children 10 and older welcome. Twenty dollars for third person in room. $75-90.

122. Monument Hill Manor. Magnificent 1880 Queen Anne mansion tucked away on one acre of terraced gardens, close to ocean. Guests can feel the ocean breezes! Antique

---

7 No smoking; 8 Children welcome; 9 Social drinking allowed; 10 Tennis nearby; 11 Swimming nearby; 12 Golf nearby; 13 Skiing nearby; 14 May be booked through a travel agent; 15 Handicapped accessible.

furnishings, exquisite carved fireplace mantels and grand stairwell. Four beautiful guest rooms have shared and private baths. All rooms are equipped with telephone, TV, compact refrigerator, coffee service. Some rooms have working fireplaces. Full gourmet breakfast is served. Friendly cats in residence, not allowed in eating or guest rooms. No smoking. $95-175.

TRURO

Bed and Breakfast Cape Cod

P.O. Box 1312, Orleans, 02653
(508) 255-3824; (800) 541-6226
FAX (508) 240-0599
e-mail: bedandb@capecod.net
www.bandbcapecod.com

9. From 1836 this Colonial-style home has been the site of a working farm and now a vineyard. Restoration was completed in 1994. Featured are wide-board floors, open-beam ceilings, and tasteful decor of the Victorian era. Bedrooms have queen-size beds and private baths, one with a Jacuzzi. Beaches, a lighthouse, restaurants, golf, tennis, and Provincetown are a few miles away. Continental breakfast. Children over 12 welcome. No smoking. $79-129.

Orleans Bed and Breakfast Associates, Inc.

P.O. Box 1312; Orleans, 02653
(508) 255-3824; (800) 541-6226
FAX (508) 240-0599
e-mail: orleansbnb@capecod.net
www.capecod.net/bb

The Moorland's Inn. A gracious old Victorian inn restored with Old World charm and elegance. There are five spacious guest rooms. Three with king-size beds have private baths; one has a kitchenette, and two with double beds share a bath. Relax in the Jacuzzi or spend a lazy afternoon on the grand front porch. Near the National Seashore beaches and minutes from

Provincetown. There are also three cottages that belong to this grand dame. The cottages are pet friendly. Special weekly rates available. $59-139.

South Hollow Vineyards Inn. On five picturesque acres, the historic Hughes-Rich Farmstead, circa 1836, remains one of the last working farms on Cape Cod. In 1993, a French vinifera winegrape vineyard was planted, the first of its kind on the cape. The Federal-style farmhouse has been restored and furnished and offers romantic, spacious rooms with four-poster beds and ensuite tiled baths. Sheltered and quiet; only one mile to Highland Golf Course, Cape Cod Light and beaches; a short drive to Provincetown. $89-129.

Parker House

Parker House

P.O. Box 1111, 02666
(508) 349-3358

The Parker House is an 1820 classic full-Cape nestled into the side of Truro Center between the Cobb Memorial Library and the Blacksmith Shop restaurant. Clean ocean and bay beaches two miles to east or west. Many art galleries and restaurants in Provincetown and Wellfleet are 10 minutes away by car. Golf, tennis, sailing, and whale watches nearby. The Cape Cod National Seashore and Audubon Sanctuary offer many trails and guided walks. The Parker House offers haven to a limited

---

NOTES: Credit cards accepted: A MasterCard; B Visa; C American Express; D Discover; E Diner's Club; F Other; 2 Personal checks accepted; 3 Lunch available; 4 Dinner available; 5 Open all year; 6 Pets welcome;

number of guests who can rest and read or enjoy the many activities nearby.

Host: Stephen Williams
Rooms: 2 (SB) $55
Continental Breakfast
Credit Cards: None
Notes: 2, 5, 9, 10, 11, 12

TYRINGHAM

The Golden Goose

123 Main Road, Box 336, 01264
(413) 243-3008

Small, friendly, 1800 country house nestled in Tyringham Valley in the Berkshires. Victorian antiques. Within one-half hour are Tanglewood, Stockbridge, Jacob's Pillow, Hancock Shaker Village, the Norman Rockwell Museum, Berkshire Theatre Festival, skiing, golf, and tennis. One mile off the Appalachian Trail. Near Butternut, Otis, Jiminy Peak, and Catamount ski slopes. Air-conditioned guest rooms. Children welcome. Coffee, tea, and cereals provided in rooms. Seven-night minimum stays summer and fall. Shorter stay accepted two weeks before desired reservation date, if available.

Hosts: Lilja and Joe Rizzo
Studio Apartment: $90-125
Barn Loft: $130-180
Credit Cards: A, B, C, D
Notes: 2, 5, 7, 8, 9, 10, 11, 12, 13, 14

The Golden Goose

VINEYARD HAVEN (MARTHA'S VINEYARD) _

Bed and Breakfast Associates Bay Colony, Ltd.

P.O. Box 57166, Babson Park, Boston, 02157-0166
(781) 449-5302; (800) 347-5088
FAX (781) 449-5958; e-mail: info@bnbboston.com
www.bnbboston.com

MV105. This exquisite mansion has 13 very special guest rooms with private baths, working wood-burning fireplaces, cable color TVs, and telephones. One- or two-person Jacuzzis, private hot tubs, and canopied four-poster beds available. Includes full breakfast. Seasonal rates. $160-450.

Bed and Breakfast Nantucket/Martha's Vineyard

P.O. Box 341, West Hyannisport, 02672-0341
(800) 686-5252; FAX (508) 775-2884
e-mail: bedandb@capecod.net
www.bandbcapecod.net

205. This home was built nearly 100 years ago as a private home. Later it was used for 40 years as a guest house. It was restored several years ago, and the present owner uses eight rooms for bed and breakfast. Each room has a private bath, air conditioning, and all are clean and bright with tasteful decor. Walk to all Vineyard Haven shops, stores, and restaurants. Bike rental available on the premises. Continental breakfast. $75-160.

208. Vineyard Haven, a popular community on the island, is the setting for this 15-room inn that features all private baths, TVs, and air-conditioned bedrooms. Decks from the rooms offer sunning areas and private entrances, making this a very private yet convenient location within walking distance of the shops, restaurants, and the ferry in the village. Many rooms have a pull-out available for a third or fourth person in the room. Continental breakfast. No smoking. $85-150.

7 No smoking; 8 Children welcome; 9 Social drinking allowed; 10 Tennis nearby; 11 Swimming nearby; 12 Golf nearby; 13 Skiing nearby; 14 May be booked through a travel agent; 15 Handicapped accessible.

Captain Dexter House of Vineyard Haven

92 Main Street, Box 2457, 02568
(508) 693-6564; FAX (508) 693-8448

A perfect country inn! Built in 1840, the house has been meticulously restored and exquisitely furnished to reflect the charm of that period. Be surrounded by flowers from the garden and pampered by innkeepers who believe in old-fashioned hospitality. The inn's eight romantic guest rooms are distinctively decorated. Several rooms have working fireplaces (as does the parlor) and four-poster canopied beds. Stroll to town and harbor. Continental plus breakfast.

Host: Birdie
Rooms: 8 (PB) $55-160
Continental Breakfast
Credit Cards: A, B, C, E
Notes: 2, 5, 7, 8, 9, 10, 11, 12, 14

The Hanover House

28 Edgartown Road; P.O. Box 2107, 02568
(508) 693-1066; (800) 339-1066
FAX (508) 696-6009

Within walking distance of the Vineyard Haven harbor and the ferries from the mainland, the Hanover House offers the charm of a cozy country house with the convenience of a village inn. The impeccably maintained guest rooms and suites all feature private baths, color TV, queen-size or two double beds, and air conditioning. A homemade Continental plus breakfast is served on the sun porch. The Hanover House is a AAA three-diamond, Mobil three-star, nonsmoking property.

Hosts: Kay and Ron Nelson
Rooms: 15 (PB) $95-250
Continental Breakfast
Credit Cards: A, B, C, D
Notes: 7, 8, 9, 10, 11, 12, 14

High Haven House

85 Summer Street, P.O. Box 289, 02568
(508) 693-9204; (800) 232-9204
FAX (508) 693-7807

A charming bed and breakfast on Martha's Vineyard. A perfect vacation spot with something for everyone. The beautiful beaches bring visitors from all over the world. High Haven House offers a variety of meticulously maintained accommodations that will suit everyone's budget and needs. Pool. Hot tub. Homemade Vineyard breakfast. In-room telephones. Call for details and off-season rates. "Best ambiance in Vineyard Haven."—*Boston's Best Guide.*

Hosts: Joe and Kathleen Schreck
Rooms: 12 (7 PB; 5 SB) $79-199
Continental Breakfast
Credit Cards: A, B, D
Notes: 2, 5, 8, 9, 10, 11, 12, 14

Lambert's Cove Country Inn

Rural Route 1, Box 422, 02568
(508) 693-2298

Once a lovely country estate, Lambert's Cove Country Inn in West Tisbury offers guest rooms in three charming buildings: the original 1790 residence, a converted 18th-century barn, and a carriage house. The setting is seven and one-half acres of lawn, meadows, gardens, and woodlands, with towering trees, an orchard, and vine-covered stone walls. Each room has its own charm. The dining room, which is open to the public, features some of the finest meals on the island.

The Hanover House

NOTES: Credit cards accepted: A MasterCard; B Visa; C American Express; D Discover; E Diner's Club; F Other; 2 Personal checks accepted; 3 Lunch available; 4 Dinner available; 5 Open all year; 6 Pets welcome;

Lambert's Cove Country Inn

Hosts: Katherine and Louis Costabel
Rooms: 15 (PB) $85-185
Full Breakfast
Credit Cards: A, B, C
Notes: 2, 4, 5, 7, 8, 10, 11, 12

Lothrop Merry House

Owen Park, Box 1939, 02568
(508) 693-1646

The Lothrop Merry House, built in the 1790s, overlooks Vineyard Haven Harbor and has a flower-bordered terrace, a private beach, and an expansive lawn. Most rooms have ocean views and a fireplace. All are furnished with antiques and fresh flowers. Complimentary canoe and Sunfish for guests' use. Close to ferry and shops. Personal checks accepted for deposit only.

Hosts: John and Mary Clarke
Rooms: 7 (4 PB; 3 SB) $68-215
Continental Breakfast
Credit Cards: A, B
Notes: 2, 5, 8, 9, 10, 11

Lothrop Merry House

The 1720 House

130 Main Street, 02568
(508) 693-6407

In the historic district of Vineyard Haven, a few minutes' walk to ferry, town, and beach, this authentic and totally renovated landmark structure was the home of prominent island families. Now owned by a TV producer from New York, the guests include a mix of celebrities and other interesting guests. The hosts can arrange for fishing, sailing charters, historic tours, horseback riding, and admission to a health club. Free bikes and maps of trails.

Rooms: 8 (4 PB; 4 SB) $75-175
Continental Breakfast
Credit Cards: A, B
Notes: 2, 5, 9, 10, 11, 12, 14, 15

The 1720 House

WALTHAM

Bed and Breakfast Associates Bay Colony, Ltd.

P.O. Box 57166, Babson Park, Boston, 02157-0166
(781) 449-5302; (800) 347-5088
FAX (781) 449-5958; e-mail: info@bnbboston.com
www.bnbboston.com

IW300. The friendly hostess will welcome guests to this charming little house with a white picket fence and a screened porch. It

7 No smoking; 8 Children welcome; 9 Social drinking allowed; 10 Tennis nearby; 11 Swimming nearby; 12 Golf nearby; 13 Skiing nearby; 14 May be booked through a travel agent; 15 Handicapped accessible.

is in a neighborhood of manicured lawns just one and one-half miles from I-95, which circles Greater Boston. Two guest rooms on the second floor share a bath. Full breakfast upon request. Children welcome. Family rates available. $55-65.

IW305. The hostess welcomes guests to her immaculate Cape-style home on a quiet street just one and one-half miles from Brandeis University and two miles from Route 195/128. Two guest rooms, each with double bed, share a bath on the second floor. $62-65.

WARE (STURBRIDGE)

Antique 1880 Inn Bed and Breakfast

14 Pleasant Street, 01082
(413) 967-7847

Relax in yesterday's charm. This 12-room Colonial is complete with six fireplaces, rustic beams, and hardwood floors. Breakfast may be served on the porch or in the dining room. Enjoy afternoon tea before the cozy fireplace. Midpoint between Boston and the Berkshires. Enjoy a country drive to Sturbridge Village and historic Deerfield. A short drive to five area colleges: Amherst, Mass-Hampshire, Mount Holyoke, and Smith.

Host: Margaret Skutnik
Rooms: 3 (1 PB; 2 SB) $55-75
Full Breakfast
Credit Cards: None
Notes: 2, 5, 7, 8, 9, 10, 11, 12, 14

WAREHAM

Mulberry Bed and Breakfast

257 High Street, 02571-1407
(508) 295-0684; FAX (508) 291-2909

Mulberry Bed and Breakfast sits on a half-acre lot shaded by the majestic mulberry

tree in the historic section of Wareham. This Cape Cod-style bed and breakfast home, built in 1847 by a blacksmith, offers three cozy guest rooms with shared baths. Furnishings and decor are in keeping with the home's vintage. Enjoy a hearty New England breakfast. Within an hour's drive are historic Plymouth, Boston, and Newport, the whaling-fishing city of New Bedford, and scenic Cape Cod. Wareham boasts 54 miles of coastline. Thus saltwater activities of every description are available. Two cats in residence. Cross-country skiing nearby. Inquire about handicapped accessibility. Two-night minimum stay on weekends July and August. Ask about a clambake to go.

Host: Frances A. Murphy
Rooms: 3 (3 S2B) $50-75
Full Breakfast
Credit Cards: A, B, C, D
Notes: 2, 5, 7, 8, 9, 10 ,11, 12, 13, 14

WELLFLEET

Aunt Sukie's Bayside Bed and Breakfast

525 Chequessett Neck Road, 02667
(508) 349-2804; (800) 420-9999
www.thold.com/auntsukies/

Historic home with contemporary addition. Bedrooms with private baths, refrigerator, telephone, and balcony overlooking private beach and National Seashore. Separate entrances, fireplaces, home-baked breakfast served at water-view table.

Hosts: Sue and Dan Hamar
Rooms: 3 (PB) $110-170
Full Breakfast
Credit Cards: A, B
Notes: 5, 7, 10, 11, 12, 14

The Inn at Duck Creeke

P.O. Box 364, 02667
(508) 349-9333; FAX (508) 349-0234

On a rustic five acres with views of pond and tidal marsh, this cozy country inn has

The Inn at Duck Creeke

25 attractive guest rooms within three lodging buildings, an exceptional restaurant, and the town's oldest tavern. Within the historic district, just a short walk to galleries and shops, it is also close to the harbor, ponds, and beaches. The friendly and energetic staff work to make guests' stay a pleasant and memorable one. "We welcome your visit."

Hosts: Bob Morrill and Judy Pihl
Rooms: 25 (17 PB; 8 SB) $65-95
Continental Breakfast
Credit Cards: A, B, C
Notes: 2, 4, 8, 9, 10, 11, 12

Orleans Bed and Breakfast Associates, Inc.

P.O. Box 1312; Orleans, 02653
(508) 255-3824; (800) 541-6226
FAX (508) 240-0599
e-mail: orleansbnb@capecod.net
www.capecod.net/bb

Pine Moorings. Only 150 yards from a beach on the other side of the Wellfleet Harbor. Walk to Wellfleet Center from Uncle Tim's bridge. This is a perfect upside down three-fourths Cape house. The first floor is completely private, with a queen-size bedroom and large full bath. There is a trundle bedroom available for families or people traveling together. Breakfast is served on a spacious deck with peeks of water. Forty dollars for extra person. $90.

WEST BARNSTABLE

Bed and Breakfast Reservations North Shore, Greater Boston, Cape Cod

P.O. Box 600035, Greater Boston Branch, Newtonville, 02160-0001
(617) 964-1606; (800) 832-2632
FAX (617) 332-8572; e-mail: info@bbreserve.com
www.bbreserve.com

117. Summersea Bed and Breakfast. Luxury and romance await guests in this sparkling contemporary nestled in a most beautiful and secluded setting with a view of Cape Cod Bay/Sand Neck Beach. Three luxurious guest rooms feature French country decor, private baths, balconies, skylights, fireplace, and wonderful views. Full gourmet breakfast. Common rooms are elegantly furnished. No smoking. Two-room suites available at $250. $130-165.

Honeysuckle Hill Bed and Breakfast

591 Old Kings Highway, Route 6A, 02668
(508) 362-8418; (800) 441-8418

On the edge of the small village of West Barnstable, the Honeysuckle Hill Bed and Breakfast has been welcoming guests for generations. Listed in the National Register of Historic Places, circa 1810, this enchanting seaside cottage offers comfortably elegant rooms and graciously served breakfasts. Built in the Queen Anne style, the inn is surrounded by lush, green lawns and colorful gardens. The five sparkling

Honeysuckle Hill

7 No smoking; 8 Children welcome; 9 Social drinking allowed; 10 Tennis nearby; 11 Swimming nearby; 12 Golf nearby; 13 Skiing nearby; 14 May be booked through a travel agent; 15 Handicapped accessible.

rooms are furnished in antiques and white wicker, along with featherbeds and Battenburg lace. The baths are outfitted in marble and brass and feature big fluffy towels and English toiletries. A full breakfast is included in the rates and is served in the sunny dining room.

Hosts: Bill and Mary Kilburn
Rooms: 5 (PB) $115-175
Full Breakfast
Credit Cards: A, B, C, D
Notes: 2, 5, 7, 9, 10, 11, 12

WEST CHESTERFIELD

Cliffside Bed and Breakfast

592 Main Road, P.O. Box 5, 01084
(413) 296-4022

The Cliffside Bed and Breakfast is in the hilltop community of Chesterfield. The bed and breakfast is surrounded by 150 acres of woodland. Guests are welcome to wander around the property and enjoy nature at its best, or just sit in the gazebo by the pond and enjoy the quiet trickle of the water, or conclude the day by observing a spectacular sunset.

Rooms: 2 (2 SB)
Full Breakfast
Credit Cards: None
Notes: 2, 7, 8, 10, 11, 12, 13

WEST GROTON

Bed and Breakfast Associates Bay Colony, Ltd.

P.O. Box 57166, Babson Park, Boston, 02157-0166
(781) 449-5302; (800) 347-5088
FAX (781) 449-5958; e-mail: info@bnbboston.com
www.bnbboston.com

CW550. Get away to this "gentleman's farm" in the country. This gracious home was recently built as a reproduction of the owner's circa 1800 farmhouse that was destroyed by fire at this site. The new home is grand in every detail and provides the finest accommodations in a country retreat:

elegant furnishings, thoughtful amenities, in-ground pool gloriously set on the meadow, and nearby canoeing, cross-country skiing, biking, and renowned antiquing. Three guest rooms. Master suite has bath en suite and working fireplace. $92-100.

WEST HARWICH (CAPE COD)

Bed and Breakfast Reservations North Shore, Greater Boston, Cape Cod

P.O. Box 600035, Greater Boston Branch, Newtonville, 02160-0001
(617) 964-1606; (800) 832-2632
FAX (617) 332-8572; e-mail: info@bbreserve.com
www.bbreserve.com

109. The Inn at West Harwich. This fully restored 200-year-old inn is five minutes from the Nantucket ferry. Six sparkling guest rooms, all with private bath, TV, air conditioning, and refrigerator. Two of the rooms are large deluxe suites with Jacuzzis and fireplaces. One suite is handicapped accessible. Cozy sitting room with fireplace. A wonderful Continental plus breakfast is delivered to room. Great central location for all Cape Cod attractions. Families with children welcome. No smoking. $85-130.

WESTON

Webb-Bigelow House

863 Boston Post Road, 02193
(617) 899-2444

Built in 1827, this elegantly furnished Federal house on three acres is 20 minutes from Boston, ideal for visiting colleges, corporations, historic areas, or family. Whether visiting, attending business meetings, or sightseeing, the restful atmosphere in an exclusive suburb is a place to relax with amenities of a pool and deck. Three bedrooms and adjoining baths include terry-cloth robes, hair dryers, and air conditioning. No children under 10. Excellent restaurants nearby. Open since 1983. Closed January through March.

Hosts: Jane and Bob Webb
Rooms: 3 (2 PB; 1 SB) $95-100
Full Breakfast
Credit Cards: None
Notes: 2, 7, 9, 10, 11, 14

WEST STOCKBRIDGE

Elaine's Bed and Breakfast Selections

4987 Kingston Road, Elbridge, 13060
(315) 689-2082 (after 10 A.M.)

Traditional country inn with first-floor public restaurant, tavern, and patio dining. This 200-year-old inn was originally a stagecoach stop. Guest rooms on the second floor have antique brass and iron beds. Quick drive to Stockbridge, Lenox, and Lee. Seasonal rates.

Shaker Mill Inn

#2 Oak Street, Box 521, 01266
(413) 232-8596; (800) 322-8565
FAX (413) 232-4644; e-mail: shakerInn@aol.com
www.shakermillinn.com

Ten luxury suites. All units have kitchenettes, balconies or decks, king- or queen-size beds, color cable TVs, fireplaces, and private whirlpool baths. Great for extended stays. On-premises laundry. Two-day minimum on summer weekends. Complimentary Continental breakfast. VCRs and large video library. Bike rentals. Tennis, swimming, and hiking nearby.

Host: Jonathan Rick
Suites: 10 (PB) $75-195
Continental Breakfast
Credit Cards: A, B, C
Notes: 2, 5, 6, 8, 9, 10, 11, 12, 13, 14, 15

The Williamsville Inn

Route 41, 01266
(413) 274-6118; FAX (413) 274-3539

The Williamsville Inn offers gracious lodging and candlelight dining in a historic 1797

Berkshire farmhouse, a peaceful country setting at the foot of Tom Ball Mountain. The restaurant, which serves elegant country cuisine nightly, except Tuesdays, is recommended by the *New York Times* and *Bon Appétit*. Old World charm and modern amenities, cordial atmosphere, and the opportunity to enjoy the gentle pleasures of quiet country life bring guests from all over the world. Antiquing, shopping, and hiking are nearby. Minutes from Tanglewood and the Norman Rockwell Museum.

Hosts: Gail and Kathleen Ryan
Rooms: 16 (PB) $120-185
Full Breakfast
Credit Cards: A, B, C
Notes: 2, 4, 5, 8, 9, 10, 11, 12, 13, 14

WEST TISBURY

The House at New Lane

44 New Lane, P.O. Box 156, 02578
(508) 696-7331; e-mail: housenl@vineyard.net

A simple and elegant West Tisbury bed and breakfast comfortably on seven acres of woods and gardens. Access to all-season country walks, beaches, nature trails, bike paths. Fireplaces in breakfast and sitting rooms.

Rooms: 4 (4 S2B) $65-85
Full Breakfast
Credit Cards: None
Notes: 2, 5, 7, 8, 9, 10, 11, 12

WEST TISBURY (MARTHA'S VINEYARD)

Bed and Breakfast Nantucket/Martha's Vineyard

P.O. Box 341, West Hyannisport, 02672-0341
(800) 686-5252; FAX (508) 775-2884
e-mail: bedandb@capecod.net
www.bandbcapecod.net

207. Built in 1790 as a rural farmhouse and converted into an inn, this charming building is in a very quiet, remote section of the island and boasts a fine gourmet restaurant for evening meals only. Eighteen rooms in

7 No smoking; 8 Children welcome; 9 Social drinking allowed; 10 Tennis nearby; 11 Swimming nearby; 12 Golf nearby; 13 Skiing nearby; 14 May be booked through a travel agent; 15 Handicapped accessible.

four buildings offer private baths and queen-size beds. Many rooms have air conditioning but it is seldom needed. A library with fireplace and a wonderful outside deck for guest use provide a variety of spots for relaxation. This is a great place for weddings as well as for a romantic honeymoon getaway. Children over six welcome. $75-175.

WESTWOOD

Bed and Breakfast Associates Bay Colony, Ltd.

P.O. Box 57166, Babson Park, Boston, 02157-0166
(781) 449-5302; (800) 347-5088
FAX (781) 449-5958; e-mail: info@bnbboston.com
www.bnbboston.com

IW725. This country house and barn are graced by an inviting brick patio with a large in-ground pool. The first floor has been redesigned to provide a view of the grounds through walls of glass. Antiques throughout. King-, queen-size, or twin beds. A Boston tour guide, this hostess claims there is a "friendly ghost" in the house. Children welcome. Family rates available. $60-75.

IW726. This private hideaway is a converted schoolhouse. A party of five can enjoy the two-story apartment with two bedrooms, two full baths, a kitchen, dining area, living room, and deck. Sleeping space includes an antique double bed, two twins that can be made up as a king, and one single. Children welcome; no smoking. Rates are based on four adults or family of four. $150-175.

WEST YARMOUTH

The Manor House Bed and Breakfast

57 Maine Avenue, 02673
(508) 771-3433; (800) 9MANOR9

The Manor House is a lovely 1920s six-bedroom Dutch Colonial bed and breakfast

The Manor House

overlooking Lewis Bay. Each room has a private bath and all are decorated differently and named after special little touches of Cape Cod, such as Cranberry Bog and Whale Watch. Easy access to virtually everything the cape has to offer. Enjoy a bountiful breakfast, afternoon tea, and friendly hospitality at the Manor House.

Hosts: Rick and Liz Latshaw
Rooms: 6 (PB) $78-128
Full Breakfast
Credit Cards: A, B, C
Notes: 2, 5, 7, 9, 10, 11, 12

WEST YARMOUTH (CAPE COD)

Bed and Breakfast Reservations North Shore, Greater Boston, Cape Cod

P.O. Box 600035, Greater Boston Branch,
    Newtonville, 02160-0001
(617) 964-1606; (800) 832-2632
FAX (617) 332-8572; e-mail: info@bbreserve.com
www.bbreserve.com

124. West Yarmouth Bed and Breakfast. This stately Greek Revival originally was a schoolhouse built in 1854. Central location, close to Hyannis and ferries to Martha's Vineyard/Nantucket. Spacious entrance, many original painting, lovingly rescued and restored by owners. Large sitting area

NOTES: Credit cards accepted: A MasterCard; B Visa; C American Express; D Discover; E Diner's Club; F Other; 2 Personal checks accepted; 3 Lunch available; 4 Dinner available; 5 Open all year; 6 Pets welcome;

with Victorian bar, piano, and outside deck. Four attractive guest rooms, with private baths and Jacuzzis. Full breakfast served in sunroom, where guests will find afternoon goodies and complimentary beverages. Children welcome when whole house is taken by family group. $90-135.

WEYMOUTH

Host Homes of Boston

P.O. Box 117, Waban Branch, Boston, 02468-0001
(617) 244-1308; FAX (617) 244-5156

Willowreeds. Bright and spacious 1990 Williamsburg Colonial with 18th-century furnishings, country atmosphere. Large deck overlooking huge swimming pool and adjacent wooded conservation land. Second-floor guest room with double canopied bed. Pine room with queen-size bed. Two hall baths. Resident toy poodle. First-floor guest parlor. Breakfast in sunny gourmet kitchen or on deck. Three miles to Red Line. Near fine restaurants. No smoking. Air conditioning. TV and swimming pool. $68-85.

WILLIAMSTOWN

American Country Collection

1353 Union Street, Schenectady, NY 12308
(518) 370-4948; (800) 810-4948
FAX (518) 393-1634 (call first)
e-mail: Carolbnbres@msn.com

029. This 600-acre dairy farm is nestled in a valley, but energetic guests can hike up the rolling hills to the pond to swim, fish, or just feast on the beautiful three-state view. Barn cats and calves delight visiting children. Join the host family in the living room for conversation, TV, or perhaps playing the piano. The two cozy, paneled guest rooms have comfortable beds and are cool, clean, and quiet. Shared bath. Breakfast is served on antique china and may be enjoyed on the porch on nice summer days. $50.

167. This newly renovated facility on 350 acres in the Berkshires offers cozy rooms with private bath; one-, two-, and three-bedroom suites with living room and fireplace, kitchen, and bedroom with queen-size bed; and secluded cottages with one, two, or three bedrooms, each with a fireplace. Heated pool. Air conditioned, with telephone and TV. Children under 16 are welcome and stay free. Pets permitted in cottages. Continental breakfast. Smoking permitted. $88-238.

Field Farm Guest House

554 Sloan Road, 01267
(413) 458-3135

At the foot of the Taconic Range, Field Farm offers charming accommodations in a country setting. Four miles of trails wind through 296 acres of forest, fields, and wetlands, home to a variety of wildlife. The 1948 American modern-style house has large dining and living rooms with fireplace, games, and books. Verandas overlook the swimming pool and tennis court. Picture windows frame formal gardens, sculptures, and stunning views of Mount Greylock—Massachusetts's highest mountain.

Hosts: Jean and Sean Cowhig (innkeepers);
Owners: The Trustees of Reservations
Rooms: 5 (PB) $125
Full Breakfast
Credit Cards: A, B, D
Notes: 2, 5, 7, 9, 10, 11, 12, 13

Steep Acres Farm Bed and Breakfast

520 White Oaks Road, 01267
(413) 458-3774

Two miles from Williams College and the Williamstown Theatre Festival. A country home on a high knoll with spectacular views of the Berkshire Hills and Vermont's Green Mountains. Trout and swimming pond are tempting on this farm's 52 acres adjacent to the Appalachian and Long Trails. Short distance to Tanglewood and Jacob's Pillow.

7 No smoking; 8 Children welcome; 9 Social drinking allowed; 10 Tennis nearby; 11 Swimming nearby; 12 Golf nearby; 13 Skiing nearby; 14 May be booked through a travel agent; 15 Handicapped accessible.

Hosts: Mary and Marvin Gangemi
Rooms: 4 (SB) $50-85
Full Breakfast
Credit Cards: None
Notes: 2, 5, 7, 9, 10, 11, 12, 13, 14

WINDSOR

Windfields Farm

154 Windsor Bush Road, Cummington, 01026
(413) 684-3786

Secluded 100-acre homestead on a dirt road surrounded by gardens, birds, fields, and forests, with swimming pond and hiking and ski trails. Guests have private  entrance, book-lined living room, fireplace, piano, and dining room. Family antiques, paintings, and flowers. Organic produce, eggs, maple syrup, raspberries, and wild blueberries enrich the hearty breakfasts. Near Tanglewood, Williams and Smith Colleges, and the new Norman Rockwell Museum. Closed March and April. Children over 12 are welcome.

Hosts: Carolyn and Arnold Westwood
Rooms: 2 (SB) $63-70
Full Breakfast
Credit Cards: None
Notes: 2, 7, 9, 10, 11, 13

WOODS HOLE

The Marlborough

320 Woods Hole Road, P.O. Box 238, 02543
(508) 548-6218; (800) 320-2322 (reservations)
FAX (508) 457-7519

Romantic Cape Cod cottage complete with picket fence, trellis, and garden, sits up on a hill among the trees. Rooms are air conditioned, have private baths, and are individually decorated with quilts, coordinated

The Marlborough

scented linens, collectibles, and thoughtful amenities. A wonderful full breakfast is served by pool or fireplace depending on season. Guests say the coffee is exceptional. Woods Hole Oceanographic Institute is within walking distance; minutes to Martha's Vineyard ferry, beaches, shopping, and bike paths. Great vacation home for Cape Cod sightseeing. Gift certificates available. Children over two welcome.

Host: Al Hammond
Rooms: 6 (PB) $75-135
Full Breakfast
Credit Cards: A, B, C
Notes: 2, 5, 7, 9, 10, 11, 12, 14

WORTHINGTON

The Hill Gallery

137 East Windsor Road, 01098
(413) 238-5914

On a mountaintop in the Hampshire Hills on 25 acres. Enjoy relaxed country living in an owner-built contemporary country home with art gallery, fireplaces, and swimming pool. Filled with antiques and collections. More than the usual bed and breakfast. Plenty of peace and quiet. Two-night minimum stay on holidays. Children over 10 welcome.

Host: Walter Korzec
Rooms: 3 (2 PB; 1 SB) $60-80
Full Breakfast
Credit Cards: None
Notes: 2, 5, 7, 9, 10, 11, 12, 13

NOTES: Credit cards accepted: A MasterCard; B Visa; C American Express; D Discover; E Diner's Club; F Other; 2 Personal checks accepted; 3 Lunch available; 4 Dinner available; 5 Open all year; 6 Pets welcome;

YARMOUTH PORT (CAPE COD)

Agapé Bed and Breakfast
168 Main Street, 02675
(508) 362-2800; (800) 379-3393 (in U.S.)

A newly restored sea captain's home built in 1843. Agapé Bed and Breakfast is a beautiful example of Greek Revival architecture with wide-board floors throughout the home, wainscoting, molding, and romantic fireplaces. True to the period, antiques and fresh flowers add to Agapé's charm. Private baths, one with Jacuzzi tub, add to comfort. Central to beaches, antique shops, nature trails. Cape Cod hospitality, family ambiance.

Hosts: John and Melissa O'Rourke
Rooms: 3 (PB) $90-125
Continental Breakfast
Credit Cards: A, B, C
Notes: 5, 7, 8, 9, 10, 11, 12, 14

Bed and Breakfast Cape Cod
P.O. Box 1312, Orleans, 02653
(508) 255-3824; (800) 541-6226
FAX (508) 240-0599
e-mail: bedandb@capecod.net
www.bandbcapecod.com

71. This Cape Cod-style house, built in 1800, has three air-conditioned bedrooms with private baths, one with a queen-size bed, one with a double, and one with twin beds. A parlor with a TV is available for guests. Enjoy a nice Continental breakfast. Walk to the freshwater pond or to the beach nearby, or simply relax on the pleasant grounds. $65-85.

Crook' Jaw Inn and Antiques
186 Main Street (Route 6A), 02675
(508) 362-6111; (888) 38 WHALE (9-9253)

This 1700s weathered Cape is on two and one-half acres on Captains Row. The rooms have king-size, twin, or double beds, all with private baths and one with a Jacuzzi. The large living room, library, and dining room, all with fireplaces, offer lots of atmosphere for the guests. A Continental plus buffet breakfast can be enjoyed in those rooms as well as on the secluded terrace. The convenient mid-cape location is close to all amenities and there is a gift and antique shop attached. Inquire about accommodations for children. Air conditioned.

Hosts: Paul and Donna Snow
Rooms: 5 (PB) $70-120
Continental Breakfast
Credit Cards: A, B, C
Notes: 2, 5, 9, 10, 11, 12, 14

Liberty Hill Inn on Cape Cod
77 Main Street, 02675
(508) 362-3976; (800) 821-3977
e-mail: libertyh@capecod.net
www.capecod.net/libertyhillinn

Casual elegance in a historic seaside village on the old Kings Highway. Romantic fireplaces, canopied beds, whirlpool, gourmet breakfast. Stroll to village shops and first-class restaurants. Meander country lanes to Cape Cod Bay. Take a run on the beach. A perfect central location provides easy access to all of Cape Cod's attractions. Mobil-rated three stars. Special honeymoon package. Handicapped accessible. Cable TV, air conditioning. "An elegant country inn...in an attractive setting of trees and flower-edged lawns. Romantic"–Fodor's.

Hosts: Jack and Beth Flanagan
Rooms: 9 (PB) $90-190
Full Breakfast
Credit Cards: A, B, C
Notes: 2, 5, 8, 9, 10, 11, 12, 14, 15

Olde Captain's Inn
101 Main Street, 02675-1709
(508) 362-4496

Charming restored captain's home in the historic district. Fine lodgings and superb Continental breakfast. Cable TV. The inn has a truly friendly, elegant atmosphere. Walk to shops and restaurants. No smoking in the inn. Continental plus breakfast is served. Stay two nights and the third night

7 No smoking; 8 Children welcome; 9 Social drinking allowed; 10 Tennis nearby; 11 Swimming nearby; 12 Golf nearby; 13 Skiing nearby; 14 May be booked through a travel agent; 15 Handicapped accessible.

is free. Suites are available starting at $300 per week.

Hosts: Betsy O'Connor and Sven Tilly
Rooms: 5 (3 PB; 2 SB) $50-100
Continental Breakfast
Credit Cards: None
Notes: 2, 5, 7, 8, 9, 10, 11, 12, 14

One Centre Street Inn

Route 6A and Old Kings Highway, 02675
(508) 362-8910; (888) 407-1653

Step back in time in this 1824 parsonage on the historic north side of Cape Cod. Its understated elegance affords guests both comfort and style in six individually decorated guest rooms. Most rooms are hand-stenciled and most have private baths. Fresh coffee awakens guests, along with homemade muffins and scones, seasonal fruits, and a special entrée—perhaps French toast with strawberry Grand Marnier sauce or cranberry-toasted pecan pancakes. Beaches, antiques, galleries, restaurants one mile away. Children over eight welcome.

Host: Karen Iannello
Rooms: 6 (4 PB; 2 SB) $75-120
Full Breakfast
Credit Cards: A, B, D
Notes: 2, 5, 7, 9, 10, 11, 12, 14

Wedgewood Inn

83 Main Street, 02675
(508) 362-5157

In the historic area of Cape Cod, the inn is in the National Register of Historic Places and has been featured in *Country Inns of America*. Near beaches, art galleries, antique shops, golf, boating, and fine restaurants. Fireplaces and private screened porches. Smoking in designated areas only. Children over 10 welcome.

Hosts: Milt and Gerrie Graham
Rooms: 9 (PB) $125-185
Full Breakfast
Credit Cards: A, B, C, E
Notes: 2, 5, 12, 14

Wedgewood Inn

The Village Inn

92 Main Street, Route 6A, P.O. Box 1, 02675
(508) 362-3182

This charming sea captain's home built in 1795 has been an inn since 1946. Noted for cordial hospitality and comfortable rooms with private baths. Public rooms, screened porch, and shaded lawn. The inn is within easy walking distance of Cape Cod Bay, excellent restaurants, and antique shops. No smoking.

Hosts: Mac and Esther Hickey
Rooms: 10 (8 PB; 2 SB) $40-85
Full Breakfast
Credit Cards: A, B
Notes: 2, 5, 6, 7, 8, 9, 10, 11, 12, 14

The Village Inn

NOTES: Credit cards accepted: A MasterCard; B Visa; C American Express; D Discover; E Diner's Club; F Other; 2 Personal checks accepted; 3 Lunch available; 4 Dinner available; 5 Open all year; 6 Pets welcome;

New Hampshire

ALEXANDRIA

Stone Rest Bed and Breakfast

1755 Fowler River Road, 03222
(603) 744-6066

Contemporary home in a rural setting on 10 acres with 200 feet on
a mountain stream
with swimming
hole. Close to
Newfound Lake,
Mount Cardigan,
Ragged Moun-
tain, shopping, and
other major tourist attractions. Adjacent one-bedroom apartments
also available. Hearty country breakfasts.
Barbecue grills, picnic tables, horseshoes,
and volleyball on grounds. Videos, library,
spa, ski packages available. Individual heat.

Stone Rest Bed and Breakfast
Alexandria, New Hampshire

Hosts: Dick and Peg Clarke
Rooms: 7 (5 PB; 2 SB) $45-65
Full Breakfast
Credit Cards: None
Notes: 2, 5, 7, 8, 9, 10, 11, 12, 13

ASHLAND

Country Options

27-29 North Main Street, P.O. Box 730, 03217
(603) 968-7958

The hosts' goal is to provide guests with tasteful, comfortable, clean accommodations and bountiful, delicious breakfasts at a reasonable rate. Guests are invited to experience the relaxed, friendly atmosphere which is both smoke and pet free. An appealing mix of country antiques, a wood fire in winter, the sun porch for warm weather are a few of the special features at Country Options. An abundance of scenic, recreational, and historical attractions, as well as shops, outlet malls, and restaurants combine to provide great variety. "When seeking distinctive but unpretentious accommodations, we suggest you give us a call."

Hosts: Sandra Ray and Nancy Puglisi
Rooms: 5 (5 SB) $45-55
Full Breakfast
Credit Cards: None
Notes: 2, 5, 7, 8, 10, 11, 12, 13

Elaine's Bed and Breakfast Selections

4987 Kingston Road, Elbridge, NY 13060
(315) 689-2082 (after 10 A.M.)

Perfect romantic getaway in Victorian style. Extremely popular—booked months in advance. Imagine rich dark woodwork, carved lace-canopied beds, in-room fireplaces, and Jacuzzis. If guests love the grandeur of old, then they will love this Victorian bed and breakfast. In the heart of the White Mountains, just minutes away from Squaw Lake, as well as world-class alpine skiing and cross-country trails, swimming, fishing, hiking, biking, tennis, golf, and antiquing.

Glynn House Victorian Inn

43 Highland Street, P.O. Box 719, 03217
(603) 968-3775; (800) 637-9599
FAX (603) 968-3129; e-mail: glynnhse@lr.net
www.bbonline/nh/glynnhouse

Step back in time to Victorian yesteryear. A romantic escape in the heart of the White Mountains and *On Golden Pond* lakes region of New Hampshire. Come enjoy the local

---

7 No smoking; 8 Children welcome; 9 Social drinking allowed; 10 Tennis nearby; 11 Swimming nearby; 12 Golf nearby; 13 Skiing nearby; 14 May be booked through a travel agent; 15 Handicapped accessible.

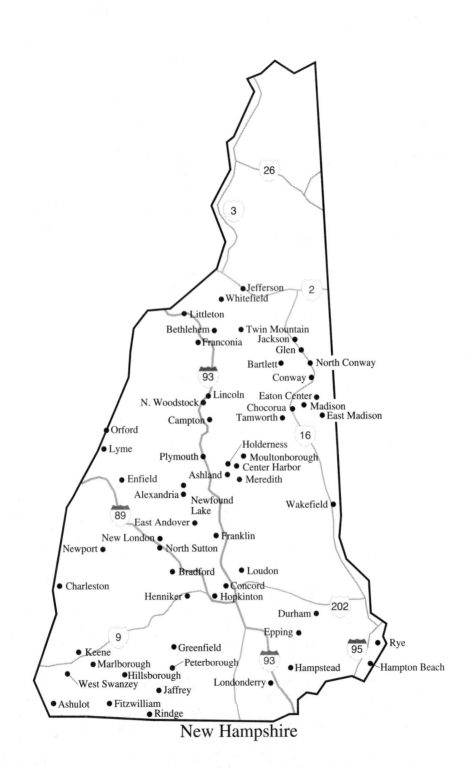

New Hampshire

Glynn House Victorian Inn

colors of each season. Nine gracious bedrooms with private baths. Whirlpool tub and fireplace amenities. Gourmet breakfast is served. Waterville Valley and Tenney Mountain nearby. Just two hours from Boston; I-94, exit 24. No smoking in bedrooms.

Hosts: Karol and Betsy Paterman
Rooms: 9 (PB) $85-145
Full Breakfast
Credit Cards: A, B, C, D, E
Notes: 2, 5, 8, 9, 10, 11, 12, 13, 14

ASHUELOT

Elaine's Bed and Breakfast Selections

4987 Kingston Road, Elbridge, NY 13060
(315) 689-2082 (after 10 A.M.)

Owner-designed and built, this dream pavilion guest house is on top of a mountain with a view of three states. Marble floors throughout except in the master bedroom where there is wall-to-wall carpet. Complete kitchen, spacious marble bath with large whirlpool tub and separate shower. Thick terry-cloth robes for guests' comfort. A full gourmet breakfast is delivered from the owner's house in the morning. Nice location for parties, conferences, and weddings with a chapel on premises. Rated A plus by the ABBA. Two-

night minimum on weekends and three-night minimum for holiday weekends. $250.

BARTLETT

The Notchland Inn

Hart's Location, 03812
(603) 374-6131; (800) 866-6131
FAX (603) 374-6168; e-mail: notchland@aol.com
www.notchland.com

A traditional country inn where hospitality has not been forgotten. There are 12 guest rooms, all with working fireplaces and private baths; several with Jacuzzi tubs. Delicious gourmet dining, spectacular mountain views, hiking, cross-country skiing, and swimming are some of the many recreations offered at this secluded mountain estate.

Hosts: Les Schoof and Ed Butler
Rooms: 12 (PB) $145-270
Full Breakfast
Credit Cards: A, B, C, D
Notes: 2, 4, 5, 7, 9, 10, 11, 12, 13, 14

BETHLEHEM

The Notchland Inn

Adair Country Inn

80 Guider Lane, 03574
(603) 444-2600; (888) 444-2600
FAX (603) 444-4823; e-mail: adair@connriver.net
www.adairinn.com

Adair Country Inn is of classic Georgian Colonial Revival design and offers

NOTES: Credit cards accepted: A MasterCard; B Visa; C American Express; D Discover; E Diner's Club; F Other; 2 Personal checks accepted; 3 Lunch available; 4 Dinner available; 5 Open all year; 6 Pets welcome; 7 No smoking; 8 Children welcome; 9 Social drinking allowed; 10 Tennis nearby; 11 Swimming nearby; 12 Golf nearby; 13 Skiing nearby; 14 May be booked through a travel agent; 15 Handicapped accessible.

extensive gardens and landscaping originally designed by the Olmsted Brothers of
Boston's Emerald Neckland and New
York's Central Park fame. There are dramatic views of the Presidential and Dalton
mountain ranges in addition to terrific
breakfasts, an all-weather tennis court, and
strolling paths. Golf, skiing, hiking, and
fine shops are nearby. Evening dining is
available in season. Adair is a recipient of
the prestigious AAA four-diamond award.

Hosts: Judy and Bill Whitman
Rooms: 10 (PB) $140-285
Full Breakfast
Credit Cards: A, B, C
Notes: 2, 4, 5, 7, 10, 11, 12, 13, 14

The Mulburn Inn at Bethlehem

2370 Main Street, 03574
(603) 869-3389; www.mulburninn.com

Step back in time and visit this picturesque
English Tudor-style mansion which served
as the Woolworth family summer estate.
Built by the famous architect Sylvanius D.
Morgan, the intricate details of this home
are breathtaking. Relax in the cozy yet
romantic atmosphere where legends such
as Cary Grant and Barbara Hutton spent
their honeymoon. Spacious rooms include
private baths. The inn boasts three fireplaces and two wraparound porches. Nestled in the White Mountains; golf, skiing,
hiking, and a variety of other activities are
just minutes away.

The Mulburn Inn

Hosts: Alecia Loveless and Christina Ferraro
Rooms: 7 (PB) $70.20-97.20
Full Breakfast
Credit Cards: A, B, C, D
Notes: 2, 5, 7, 8, 9, 10, 12, 13, 14

Wayside Inn

Wayside Inn

Route 302 at Pierce Bridge, P.O. Box 480, 03574
(603) 869-3364; (800) 448-9557
FAX (603) 869-5765

A traditional New England country inn in
the White Mountains. Quiet location by the
Ammonoosuc River. Spacious, newly renovated rooms with a European flair. Rooms
in the River House are suitable for families
with children and offer cable TV, small
refrigerators, and balconies overlooking the
river. Sandy beach by the river. Tennis and
fishing on premises. Excellent meals in the
dining room. Swiss specialties. B&B, MAP,
Golf packages. AAA- and Mobil-rated.

Hosts: Victor and Kathe Hofmann
Rooms: 26 (PB) $75-135
Full Breakfast
Credit Cards: A, B, C, D
Notes: 4, 8, 9, 10, 11, 12, 13, 14, 15

BRADFORD _____

Rosewood Country Inn

67 Pleasant View Road, 03221
(603) 938-5253 (phone/FAX–call first)
(800) 938-5273; e-mail: rosewood@conknet.com

Elegant and romantic country inn on a quiet
country road, but just minutes away from
the lakes and mountains. Cross-country
skiing from the front door. Twelve tastefully

NOTES: Credit cards accepted: A MasterCard; B Visa; C American Express; D Discover; E Diner's Club;
F Other; 2 Personal checks accepted; 3 Lunch available; 4 Dinner available; 5 Open all year; 6 Pets welcome;

Rosewood Country Inn

decorated suites, all with private baths. Drift off to sleep in a canopied or four-poster bed. Mozart and Vivaldi set the mood for the three-course candlelight and crystal breakfast served before a crackling fire in the dining room, or on one of the lovely sunlit porches. The perfect romantic getaway.

Hosts: Lesley and Dick Marquis
Rooms: 12 (PB) $85-150
Full Breakfast
Credit Cards: A, B, C
Notes: 2, 5, 7, 9, 11, 12, 13, 14

Thistle and Shamrock Inn and Restaurant

11 West Main Street, 03221
(603) 938-5553; (888) 938-5553
FAX (603) 938-5554
e-mail: thstle&shmrk@conknet.com

Turn-of-the-century country hotel, furnished with pieces that reflect the era. Guest rooms with private baths. Guests will enjoy a homemade breakfast in the dining room downstairs. A grand parlor with fire-

Thistle and Shamrock Inn

place is always ready for guests to enjoy. The restaurant offers casual gourmet dining in an elegant setting.

Hosts: Jim and Lynn Horigan
Rooms: 11 (PB) $75-91
Full Breakfast
Credit Cards: A, B, C, D
Notes: 2, 4, 5, 7, 8, 9, 10, 11, 12, 13, 14, 15

CAMPTON

Mountain-Fare Inn

Mad River Road, P.O. Box 553, 03223
(603) 726-4283

Lovely 1840s village home full of the antiques, fabrics, and feel of country cottage living. Flowers and gardens in summer and foliage in fall; a true skier's lodge in the winter. Accessible, peaceful, warm, friendly, and affordable. Featuring White Peaks Room for honeymoons or special occasions. Hearty breakfasts, great local dining. Sauna now available. Unspoiled beauty from Franconia Notch to Squam Lake. Wonderful four-season sports, music, theater, and wandering in the Whites.

Hosts: Susan and Nick Preston
Rooms: 10 (8 PB; 2 SB) $50-90
Full Breakfast
Credit Cards: None
Notes: 2, 5, 7, 8, 9, 10, 11, 12, 13, 14

CENTER HARBOR

Red Hill Inn

Rural Free Delivery 1, Box 99M, 03226
(603) 279-7001; (800) 5-RED HILL
FAX (603) 279-7003

Restored country estate on 60 acres overlooking Squam Lake and White Mountains. Twenty-six rooms, each with private bath, many with fireplace and Jacuzzi. Outdoor hot tub and swimming pool. Air conditioned. Country gourmet restaurant serving all meals; entertainment in the Runabout Lounge. Cross-country skiing and rentals on property. Two hours north of Boston.

7 No smoking; 8 Children welcome; 9 Social drinking allowed; 10 Tennis nearby; 11 Swimming nearby; 12 Golf nearby; 13 Skiing nearby; 14 May be booked through a travel agent; 15 Handicapped accessible.

Hosts: Rick Miller and Don Leavitt
Rooms: 26 (PB) $105-175
Full Breakfast
Credit Cards: A, B, C, D, E
Notes: 3, 4, 5, 7, 9, 10, 11, 12, 13, 14

CHARLESTOWN

MapleHedge
Bed and Breakfast Inn

355 Main Street, P.O. Box 638, 03603
(800) 9-MAPLE-9; FAX (603) 826-5237
e-mail: debrine@fmis.net

An elegant home in the national historic
register equipped with all modern amenities, MapleHedge is in historic rural New
Hampshire on a site with 200-year-old
maples and beautiful gardens. MapleHedge
is remembered for its three-course breakfast
and friendly, caring hosts. All rooms and
their private baths are individually decorated with antiques. Hosts pamper guests
with exquisitely ironed sheets, fluffy towels,
and a turndown service. Inn is on the Connecticut River, the western boundary
between New Hampshire and Vermont, and
is highly rated by both Mobil and ABBA.
Children over 12 welcome.

Hosts: Joan and Dick DeBrine
Rooms: 5 (PB) $85-100
Full Breakfast
Credit Cards: A, B
Notes: 2, 7, 9, 10, 11, 12, 13, 14

MapleHedge Inn

CHOCORUA

Riverbend Country Inn

273 Chocorua Mountain Highway, P.O. Box 288,
    03817
(603) 323-7440; (800) 628-6944
FAX (603) 323-7554
www.nettx.com/riverbend.html

North of Chocorua village guests will see a
sign for Riverbend Country Inn on the west
side of Route 16. The inn is 800-feet deep
in the woods and overlooks a bend in the
Chocorua River. Breakfast is served in the
breezeway and in warm weather on a deck
over the riverbank. The inn has bright, airy
guest rooms and two pleasantly furnished
sitting rooms with fireplaces, a library,
three decks, and a patio beside the river.
Rates may vary seasonally.

Hosts: Noreen Bullock and Russ Stone
Rooms: 10 (6 PB; 4 SB) $70-135
Full Breakfast
Credit Cards: A, B, C, F
Notes: 2, 5, 7, 9, 11, 12, 13, 14

CONCORD

Apple Mountain Lodge

1301 Upper City Road, Pittsfield, 03263
(800) 435-8241; (603) 435-7641

This converted apple barn is in the center
of a 400-acre orchard, in the hills above
the Suncook River. It is convenient to the
state capital, Lake Winipisakie, seacoast,
and the White Mountains. All rooms have
private baths and beautiful views and are
furnished in the warm, friendly style of
New England countryside. Common areas
have cozy fireplaces. Full country breakfast. Afternoon tea includes a delicious
home-grown apple dessert. Walk or bike
to beautiful woodland trails or excellent
fishing streams.

Host: Kathy Williams
Rooms: 5 (PB) $55-130
Full Breakfast

NOTES: Credit cards accepted: A MasterCard; B Visa; C American Express; D Discover; E Diner's Club;
F Other; 2 Personal checks accepted; 3 Lunch available; 4 Dinner available; 5 Open all year; 6 Pets welcome;

Credit Cards: A, B, C, D
Notes: 2, 3, 4, 5, 6, 7, 8, 9, 10, 11, 12, 13, 14

CONWAY

Darby Field Inn

Bald Hill Road, P.O. Box D 03818
(603) 447-2181; (800) 426-4147
www.darbyfield.com

A charming, out-of-the-way country inn that offers excellent dining, a cozy atmosphere, and spectacular mountain views. An outdoor pool, cross-country ski trails, and a staff that is both friendly and courteous. Reservations recommended. Rate includes breakfast. Mid-week and off-season packages. Minimum stay on weekends is two nights and on holidays is two to three nights. Inquire about accommodations for children.

Hosts: Marc and Maria Donaldson
Rooms: 16 (14 PB; 2 SB) $90-160
Full Breakfast
Credit Cards: A, B
Notes: 2, 4, 9, 10, 11, 12, 13, 14

DURHAM

Bed and Breakfast Reservations North Shore, Greater Boston, Cape Cod

P.O. Box 600035, Greater Boston Branch,
    Newtonville, MA 02160-0001
(617) 964-1606; (800) 832-2632
FAX (617) 332-8572; e-mail: info@bbreserve.com
www.bbreserve.com

135. The Inn at Oyster River. Listed in the National Register of Historic Places, the inn is one of the oldest buildings in New Hampshire, dating back to 1649. The inn offers luxurious accommodations, private meeting space, an upscale restaurant, and a more casual tavern/pub with lighter fare. Guest rooms have four-poster canopied beds and private baths. Selected rooms offer working fireplaces. Jacuzzis and oversize tubs. In-room amenities include telephones, TVs, and data ports. Full gourmet breakfast. Very close to the University of New Hampshire in Durham. A short drive to the seacoast town of Portsmouth and the Kittery, Maine, outlets. No smoking. Open year-round. Children 12 and older are welcome. $149-189.

Three Chimneys Inn

17 Newmarket Road, 03824
(603) 868-7800; (888) 497-9777 (outside NH)
FAX (603) 868-5011
e-mail: chimney3@nh.ultranet.com

This 1649 three-and-one-half-acre estate overlooks, the Oyster River and Old Mill Falls on New Hampshire's seacoast A stone's throw from the University of New Hampshire, the inn provides an elegant alternative for New England fine dining, accommodation, and conference or private gathering space. The inn boasts 25 luxurious guest rooms with full private bath or Jacuzzi, color TV, business-size desk, and telephone with data port. A lavish complimentary breakfast is served in Coppers and guests may choose between upscale American cuisine in the inn's three-hearth dining rooms or casual fare and conversation in the ffrost Sawyer Tavern.

Hosts: Ron and Jane Peterson
Rooms: 24 (PB) $149-189
Full Breakfast
Credit Cards: A, B, C, D
Notes: 2, 3, 4, 5, 7, 9, 10, 11, 12, 14, 15

Three Chimneys Inn

EAST ANDOVER _____

Bed and Breakfast Reservations North Shore, Greater Boston, Cape Cod

P.O. Box 600035, Greater Boston Branch,
   Newtonville, MA 02160-0001
(617) 964-1606; (800) 832-2632
FAX (617) 332-8572; e-mail: info@bbreserve.com
www.bbreserve.com

66. The Lakeside Inn. This charming Colonial farmhouse inn, originally built in 1767 and enlarged in the 1800s, is nestled in a rural landscape, surrounded by fields, barns, stone walls, shady sugar maples, and century-old farmhouses. The inn has been completely and lovingly restored by its present owners to add modern amenities and additional space for guests' comfort and relaxation. The 10 spacious and beautifully appointed guest rooms include private baths, luxurious bedding, and fine linens. Several rooms have working fireplaces. Full country breakfast included. Children over eight are welcome. No smoking. $85-125.

Highland Lake Inn

32 Maple Street, P.O. Box 164, 03231
(603) 735-6426; FAX (603) 735-5355

Enjoy the perfect New England getaway—"New Hampshire at its most magical." Built in 1767, expanded in 1805, this classic building overlooks Highland Lake, Kearsarge, Tucker and Ragged Mountains. Beautifully decorated, the inn has been renovated to

Highland Lake Inn

include private baths en suite in the guest rooms. A sumptuous and different breakfast is served each morning. Cross-country and alpine trails, hiking, fishing, swimming, championship golf courses, country fairs, antiquing, outlet shopping all nearby. AAA three-diamond-rated. Barn gift/craft shop.

Hosts: The Peter Petras Family
Rooms: 10 (PB) $85-125
Full Breakfast
Credit Cards: A, B, C, D
Notes: 5, 7, 10, 12, 13

EAST MADISON _____

Purity Spring Resort

Purity Spring Resort

HC 63, Box 40, Route 153, 03849
(603) 367-8896 (business)
(800) 373-3754 (reservations)
FAX (603) 367-8664

For nearly 100 years the Hoyt family has been welcoming families to Purity Spring Resort, 1,000 private acres accented by pristine 150-acre Purity Lake and King Pine Ski area. It's the ideal destination resort for families in all seasons. Summer guests enjoy swimming in the lake, boating, canoeing, and water skiing. Winter families welcome the ease and affordability of King Pine Ski area. Enjoy the open hospitality of a traditional all-inclusive resort that offers the most value for the money.

Hosts: The Hoyt Family
Rooms: 48 (44 PB; 4 SB) $52-204
Full Breakfast
Credit Cards: A, B, C, D
Notes: 2, 3, 4, 5, 8, 9, 10, 11, 12, 13, 14, 15

NOTES: Credit cards accepted: A MasterCard; B Visa; C American Express; D Discover; E Diner's Club; F Other; 2 Personal checks accepted; 3 Lunch available; 4 Dinner available; 5 Open all year; 6 Pets welcome;

EATON CENTER

The Inn at Crystal Lake

Route 153, P.O. Box 12, 03832
(603) 447-2120; (800) 343-7336
FAX (603) 447-3599

Unwind in a restored 1884 country Victorian inn, in a quiet scenic corner of the Mount Washington Valley. Eleven guest rooms are furnished with antiques and have private baths. Relax in the living room with fireplace and large-screen TV or retreat to the antique parlor or library. Swim, fish, sail, canoe, ski, skate, or outlet shop. Smoking permitted in designated areas only. Children over 10 welcome.

Hosts: Richard and Janice Octeau
Rooms: 11 (PB) $60-130
Full Breakfast
Credit Cards: A, B, C, D, E
Notes: 2, 5, 9, 10, 11, 12, 13, 14

The Inn at Crystal Lake

ENFIELD

Boulder Cottage on Crystal Lake

Rural Route 1, Box 257, 03748
(603) 632-7355

A turn-of-the-century Victorian cottage owned by the host's family for 70 years. The inn, in the Dartmouth-Sunapee region, faces beautiful Crystal Lake. Hosts promise their guests an unspoiled environment with classic New Hampshire views of the lake and mountains. Many enjoy an extended stay with kitchen privileges. Open April through October.

Hosts: Barbara and Harry Reed
Rooms: 4 (2 PB; 2 SB) $40-65
Full Breakfast
Credit Cards: None
Notes: 2, 7, 8, 9, 10, 11, 12

Mary Keane House

Lower Shaker Village, Box 5, 03748
(603) 632-4241

Unusual late-Victorian-style bed and breakfast overlooking Mascoma Lake, with five spacious and light-filled one- and two-room suites combines for guests' pleasure elegance and whimsy, antiques and comfort, sunrise balconies and sunset porches. Complete with glider swing, warm fires, and great breakfasts. Summer wine or winter hot cider on porch or by the fire. Lawns and gardens for strolling, private beach for swimming and canoeing. Shaker Museum nearby. Just 20 minutes to Hanover.

Hosts: David and Sharon Carr
Rooms: 5 (PB) $89-129
Full Breakfast
Credit Cards: A, B, C
Notes: 2, 5, 6, 7, 8, 9, 11, 12, 13, 14

Mary Keane House

Shaker Farm Bed and Breakfast

Route 4-A, Mascoma Lake, 03748
(603) 632-7664; (603) 632-9290; (800) 613-7664

Historic Shaker residence, circa 1794, features gunstock corners, original pegboards, and Shaker cupboards. Extra-large rooms

---

7 No smoking; 8 Children welcome; 9 Social drinking allowed; 10 Tennis nearby; 11 Swimming nearby; 12 Golf nearby; 13 Skiing nearby; 14 May be booked through a travel agent; 15 Handicapped accessible.

with period wallpaper, tastefully furnished, king-size beds, fully carpeted, TV, air conditioning, lake and mountain views, hiking trails, winter sports, and lake sports. Fifteen minutes to Dartmouth College. Hearty country breakfast. Warm hospitality, lovely rooms, and great food.

Hosts: Hal and Charlotte Toms
Rooms: 6 (2 PB; 4 SB) $60-90
Full Breakfast
Credit Cards: A, B
Notes: 2, 10, 11, 12, 13

EPPING

Dow Farm Bed and Breakfast

336 North River Road, 03042
(603) 679-1612

The late-18th-century Colonial farmhouse on 160 acres, furnished with antiques, overlooks the gardens, swimming pool, and woodlands. There is a private entrance to the guest rooms. Relax on the open porch, patio, or in the pool. A gift shop in the post-and-beam barn is open May through December. A full country breakfast is served fireside in the dining room. Many year-round activities are offered in the seacoast area. Ten miles from UNH/Durham and 10 miles from Phillips Exeter Academy. Children 14 and older welcome. Cross-country skiing on property.

Hosts: Lois and Richard Straw
Rooms: 2 (PB) $75-80
Full Breakfast

Dow Farm

Credit Cards: None
Notes: 2, 5, 9, 11, 13

FITZWILLIAM

Fitzwilliam Inn

On the Common, 03447
(603) 585-9000; FAX (603) 585-3495

A *Yankee* magazine "Editor's Pick." An inn since 1796, the Fitzwilliam Inn is on one of the most picturesque town commons in New England. Two spacious parlors and a baby grand piano remind guests of visiting Gramma's. Relax and enjoy fireside dining in winter. Full breakfast, lunch, and dinner served daily in the renowned dining room. Local sights: Rhododendron State Park, Mount Monadnock, Pisgah State Park, Cathedral of the Pines. Antique shops abound. Cross-country skiing. Only the dining room is handicapped accessible.

Hosts: The McMahon Family
Rooms: 23 (12 PB; 11 SB)
Full Breakfast
Credit Cards: A, B, D
Notes: 3, 4, 5, 8, 9, 10, 11, 12, 13

FRANCONIA

Bungay Jar Bed and Breakfast

P.O. Box 15, Easton Valley Road, 03580
(603) 823-7775

Secluded woodlands with spectacular mountain views, brook, and gardens make this home built from an 18th-century barn memorable. King or queen suites, private balconies, skylights, six-foot soaking tub, sauna, canopied bed. Two-story common area with fireplace for reading, music, and talk. Mountain-gaze in the morning sun while breakfasting outside in summer. Small in scale; intimate. Owners are a landscape architect, a patent attorney, and their young son. New suite with fireplace and two-person Jacuzzi. Higher rates during foliage season. School-age children welcome.

Bungay Jar

Owners/Innkeepers: Kate Kerivan and Lee
  Strimbeck
Rooms: 7 (PB) $95-195
Cottage 1 (PB)
Full Breakfast
Credit Cards: A, B, C, D
Notes: 2, 5, 7, 9, 10, 11, 12, 13

Franconia Inn

Easton Road, 03580
(603) 823-5542; (800) 473-5299
FAX (603) 823-8078

A charming inn on 107 acres in the Easton
Valley, affording breathtaking views of the
White Mountains. The inn's 34 rooms are
decorated simply, yet beautifully. Elegant
American cuisine highlights the inn's quiet
country sophistication. Children are welcome. On Route 116. Closed April 1
through May 15. On-premises recreational
activities include: four clay tennis courts,
outdoor heated pool and Jacuzzi, mountain
bikes, horseback riding, glider rides on air-
field, sleigh rides, lighted ice skating, cross-
country ski center with 65K groomed trails.

Hosts: The Morris Family
Rooms: 34 (30 PB; 4 SB) $75-110
Full Breakfast

Franconia Inn

Credit Cards: A, B, C
Notes: 4, 8, 9, 10, 11, 12, 13, 14, 15

The Hilltop Inn

Main Street, Sugar Hill, 03585
(603) 823-5695; (800) 770-5695
FAX (603) 823-5518
e-mail: amcah@hilltopinn.com

A charming Victorian country inn, circa
1895. Antique furnishings throughout make
each of the guest rooms unique and the
common rooms cozy and inviting. All guest
rooms include English cotton sheets and
handmade quilts. Pets are welcome if they
can get along with the resident dogs. AAA-
rated three diamonds. Now available is a
two-bedroom cottage with full kitchen,
bath, and fireplaced living room. Featured
in *Outside*, *Yankee*, *Country Victorian*,
Country Almanac, and numerous travel
guides. Boxed lunches available for hikers.
Smoking in designated areas.

Hosts: Meri and Mike Hern
Rooms: 6 (PB) $70-150
Cottage: $175-250
Full Breakfast
Credit Cards: A, B, D
Notes: 2, 5, 6, 9, 10, 11, 12, 13

The Horse and Hound Inn

205 Wells Road, 03580
(603) 823-5501; (800) 450-5501

A beautiful inn on a quiet country road is
close to all activities. Full breakfast served
every morning. In the evening, enjoy a
quiet cocktail in our lounge and candlelight
dining. Main living room offers a quiet
place to read by the fire. Close to hiking,
biking, swimming, skating, glider rides,
horseback riding. Large covered patio and
lawn offer the perfect place for weddings,
receptions, and other parties. Closed April 1
through mid-May and late October until
late November.

Hosts: Bill Steele and Jim Cantlon
Rooms: 10 (8 PB; 2 SB) $79.95
Full Breakfast
Credit Cards: A, B, C, D, E
Notes: 2, 4, 6, 8, 9, 10, 11, 12, 13, 14

7 No smoking; 8 Children welcome; 9 Social drinking allowed; 10 Tennis nearby; 11 Swimming nearby;
12 Golf nearby; 13 Skiing nearby; 14 May be booked through a travel agent; 15 Handicapped accessible.

The Inn at Forest Hills

The Inn at Forest Hills

P.O. Box 783, Route 142, 03580
(603) 823-9550; (800) 280-9550 (reservations)
e-mail: amerbb@innfhills.com
www.innatforesthills.com

This charming, historic 18-room, more than 100-year-old Tudor manor house beguiles guests to enjoy the majestic scenery and year-round attractions of the White Mountains of New Hampshire. Enjoy gracious hospitality in seven comfortable guest rooms, all with private baths. Relax in country casualness in the sun-filled solarium or by the fireplaces in the living room and alpine room. Savor a gourmet New England breakfast by the fireplace in a fine old country inn!

Hosts: Joanne and Gordon Haym
Rooms: 7 (PB) $90-150
Full Breakfast
Credit Cards: A, B
Notes: 2, 5, 7, 9, 10, 11, 12, 13

FRANKLIN

The Atwood Inn

Route 3A, 03235
(603) 934-3666; e-mail: atwoodinn@cyberportal.net
www.atwoodinn.com

Nestled in the heart of the lakes region, the inn is convenient for all tourist attractions, restaurants, seasonal sports, and activities. This 1830 brick Federal home was restored in 1984 preserving the original features,

among them Indian shutters, Count Rumford fireplaces, and old turnkey locks. Hosts offer old-fashioned hospitality, scrumptious breakfasts, and comfortable accommodations. Let this be "your home away from home."

Hosts: Fred and Sandi Hoffmeister
Rooms: 7 (PB) $70-90
Full Breakfast
Credit Cards: A, B, C
Notes: 2, 5, 7, 8, 9, 10, 11, 12, 13

GLEN

The Bernerhof Inn

P.O. Box 240, 03838
(603) 383-9132; (800) 548-8007

Elegant small hotel in the foothills of the White Mountains. Victorian inn featuring nine nonsmoking rooms (two suites, one with sauna), most with two-person spas and brass beds, all with private baths and color cable TV. Black Bear pub and restaurant featuring European classics and creative Continental dishes. Host of A Taste of the Mountains Cooking School.

Hosts: Ted and Sharon Wroblewski
Rooms: 9 (PB) $75-150
Suites: 2
Full Breakfast
Credit Cards: A, B, C, D, E
Notes: 2, 3, 4, 5, 7, 8, 9, 10, 11, 12, 13

The Bernerhof Inn

NOTES: Credit cards accepted: A MasterCard; B Visa; C American Express; D Discover; E Diner's Club; F Other; 2 Personal checks accepted; 3 Lunch available; 4 Dinner available; 5 Open all year; 6 Pets welcome;

Covered Bridge House

Route 302, P.O. Box 989, 03838
(603) 383-9109; (800) 232-9109

Feel at home at this cozy bed and breakfast in the Mount Washington Valley next to an 1850s covered bridge. In warm weather, cool off in the Saco River at the private beach or explore all the valley has to offer—hiking, biking, golf, shops, restaurants, attractions, and more. In winter, five major downhill ski areas and six cross-country ski networks are nearby. Enjoy hot cocoa and freshly baked goodies after skiing. AAA three-diamond-rated.

Hosts: Dan and Nancy Wanek
Rooms: 6 (4 PB; 2 SB) $49-89
Full Breakfast
Credit Cards: A, B, C, D
Notes: 2, 5, 7, 8, 9, 11, 12, 13, 14

GREENFIELD

Greenfield Bed and Breakfast Inn

Junction Routes 136 and 31, Box 400, 03047
(603) 547-6327
e-mail: innkeeper@thegreenfieldinn.com
www.greenfieldinn.com

A romantic Victorian mansion on three acres of lawn in Greenfield, a mountain valley village between Keene and Manchester just 90 minutes from Boston. Enjoy the relaxing mountain view from the spacious veranda. A full hot breakfast is served with crystal, china, and Mozart. Very close to skiing, swimming, hiking, tennis, golf, biking, and bargain antique shopping (no sales tax). A favorite of Mr. and Mrs. Bob Hope and honeymooners of all ages. Senior citizen discount. Vacation suites and sleep-six cottage also available.

Hosts: Vic and Barbara Mangini
Rooms: 12 (8 PB; 4 SB) $49-119
Cottage: $139
Full Breakfast
Credit Cards: A, B, C
Notes: 2, 5, 8, 9, 10, 11, 12, 13, 14

HAMPTON BEACH

Oceanside Inn

365 Ocean Boulevard, 03842
(603) 926-3542

The Oceanside overlooks the Atlantic Ocean and its beautiful sandy beaches. Each of the 10 rooms is tastefully and individually decorated, many with period antiques and all with private modern baths. A complimentary Continental breakfast is served each day and features homemade bread and pastries. This gracious inn is in a less congested part of Hampton Beach within easy walking distance of restaurants, shops, and other attractions. Closed mid-October through mid-May.

Hosts: Skip and Debbie Windemiller
Rooms: 10 (PB) $95-145
Continental Breakfast
Credit Cards: A, B, C, D
Notes: 7, 9, 10, 11, 12

HAMPSTEAD

Stillmeadow Bed and Breakfast at Hampstead

545 Main Street, P.O. Box 565, 03841
(603) 329-8381

Southern New Hampshire's premier bed and breakfast, Stillmeadow, is an 1850 Greek Renaissance Italianate Colonial house accessible to both the mountains and

Stillmeadow

7 No smoking; 8 Children welcome; 9 Social drinking allowed; 10 Tennis nearby; 11 Swimming nearby; 12 Golf nearby; 13 Skiing nearby; 14 May be booked through a travel agent; 15 Handicapped accessible.

the seacoast. Four rooms with private bath and refrigerator are available, including one family suite with crib, changing table, and "secret stairs" that lead to a children's playroom and play yard. Attractions nearby include the Robert Frost Farm, America's Stonehenge, Kingston State Park, and Rockingham Race Track. Between Manchester and Boston. Antique hardwood floors and a cookie jar that is always full.

Hosts: Lori and Randy Offord
Rooms: 4 (PB) $65-90
Continental Breakfast
Credit Cards: A, B, C, D
Notes: 2, 5, 7, 8, 9, 10, 11, 12, 13

HENNIKER

Colby Hill Inn

3 The Oaks, P.O. B 779, 03242
(603) 428-3281; (800) 531-0330
FAX (603) 428-9218
e-mail: info@colbyhillinn.com
www.colbyhillinn.com

Congenial inn-dogs Bertha and Delilah await with a handshake, and the cookie jar beckons at this rambling 1789 inn, a complex of farmhouse, carriage house, and barns on five village  acres. Sixteen antique-filled guest rooms, some with working fireplace, all with private bath and telephone with data port and a private line. And the food is memorable—from the bountiful breakfasts to the acclaimed candlelit dinners served every night in the gardenside dining room.

Hosts: Ellie and John Day; Laurel Day Mack
Rooms: 16 (PB) $85-175
Full Breakfast
Credit Cards: A, B, C, D, E
Notes: 2, 4, 5, 7, 9, 10, 11, 12, 13, 14

Henniker House Bed and Breakfast

2 Ramsdell Road, P.O. Box 191, 03242
(603) 428-3198

Romantic 1859 Victorian Inn overlooking the Contoocook River. The town is nestled in the foothills of the White Mountains and provides guests with picturesque covered bridges, riverfront restaurants, and shops. Stretch out and relax on one of the porches, balconies, or riverfront deck. The area provides canoeing, kayaking, skiing, biking, and hiking on miles of wooded trails. Easy walk to New England College and facilities. A full country breakfast is served in the riverfront solarium.

Host: Anita Lavigne
Rooms: 4 (2 PB; 2 SB) $65-85
Full Breakfast
Credit Cards: A, B, D
Notes: 2, 5, 7, 8, 9, 10, 11, 12, 13, 14

Meeting House Inn

35 Flanders Road, 03242
(603) 428-3228
e-mail: meetinghouse@conknet.com
www.conknet.com/meetinghouse/

The Meeting House Inn is family owned and operated. It is a renovated country farmstead (established 1982). A relaxed and cozy atmosphere where special attention is paid to individual comfort. A nonsmoking inn. The restaurant serves a delicious selection of individually prepared entrées. Rooms are filled with family furnishings and antiques, and all have private baths. A

Meeting House Inn

NOTES: Credit cards accepted: A MasterCard; B Visa; C American Express; D Discover; E Diner's Club; F Other; 2 Personal checks accepted; 3 Lunch available; 4 Dinner available; 5 Open all year; 6 Pets welcome;

hot full breakfast is brought to the room in a country basket. Air conditioned. AAA-approved. Private hot tub and sauna are available. Inquire about accommodations for children.

Rooms: 6 (PB) $65-105
Full Breakfast
Credit Cards: A, B, C, D
Notes: 2, 4, 5, 7, 9, 10, 11, 12, 13, 14

HILLSBOROUGH

The Inn at Maplewood Farm

447 Center Road, P.O. Box 1478, 03244
(603) 464-4242; (800) 644-6695
www.conknet.com/maplewoodfarm/

Award-winning country lodgings in the heart of New Hampshire. Guest rooms are tastefully appointed with American and European antiques, an inviting bed, and unique amenities. The inn is a great starting point for a retreat of hiking, swimming, or golfing. In the heart of antique country and on 14 acres of foliage trees. The Inn at Maplewood Farm has its own vintage radio station. Homemade breakfast every day. The inn was named one of America's 25 favorite bed and breakfasts. An all-suites bed and breakfast. AAA-rated.

Hosts: Laura and Jayme Simoes
Rooms: 4 (PB) $75-125
Full Breakfast
Credit Cards: A, B, C, D, E
Notes: 2, 5, 7, 8, 9, 10, 11, 12, 13, 14

HOLDERNESS

The Inn on Golden Pond

Route 3, P.O. Box 680, 03245
(603) 968-7269

An 1879 Colonial home on 50 wooded acres. Bright and cheerful setting, breakfast, and game rooms. Close to major ski areas. Nearby is Squam Lake, the setting for the film *On Golden Pond*. Minimum stay on holidays. Children over 12 welcome.

The Inn on Golden Pond

Hosts: Bill and Bonnie Webb
Rooms: 9 (PB) $95-140
Full Breakfast
Credit Cards: A, B, C
Notes: 2, 5, 7, 9, 10, 11, 12, 13, 14

HOPKINTON

The Country Porch Bed and Breakfast

281 Moran Road, 03229
(603) 746-6391

On 15 peaceful acres of lawn, pasture, and forest, this bed and breakfast is a reproduction of an 18th-century Colonial. Sit on the wraparound porch and gaze out over the meadow, bask in the sun, and then cool off in the pool. The comfortably appointed rooms have a Colonial, Amish, or Shaker theme and have king- or twin-size beds. Summer and winter activities are plentiful, and fine country dining is a short drive away. "Come and sit a spell." No smoking permitted indoors.

Hosts: Tom and Wendy Solomon
Rooms: 3 (PB) $60-75
Full Breakfast
Credit Cards: A, B
Notes: 2, 5, 7, 9, 10, 11, 12, 13, 14

7 No smoking; 8 Children welcome; 9 Social drinking allowed; 10 Tennis nearby; 11 Swimming nearby; 12 Golf nearby; 13 Skiing nearby; 14 May be booked through a travel agent; 15 Handicapped accessible.

JACKSON

Christmas Farm Inn

Route 16 B, Box CC, 03846
(603) 383-4313; (800) HI-ELVES
FAX (603) 383-6495
www.christmasfarminn.com

The spirit of Christmas lives year-round at
this classic inn. From hillside setting to
hearty breakfasts and candlelit dinners,
the hosts' warm hospitality lives up to
their motto, "We make memories." There
are 34 rooms that include two-bedroom
cottages, family suites, and Jacuzzi rooms.
Enjoy the heated pool in the summer set
among the award-winning gardens. In
winter, cross-country ski from the door or
travel 15 minutes for downhill skiing.
Relax in the outdoor hot tub or at Mistle-
toe Pub. Rates include room, breakfast,
and full dinner. There are nonsmoking
rooms available.

Rooms: 34 (PB) $156-250
Full Breakfast
Credit Cards: A, B, C
Notes: 2, 3, 4, 5, 8, 9, 10, 11, 12, 13, 14, 15

Dana Place Inn

Box L, Pinkham Notch, 03846
(603) 383-6822; (800) 537-9276
e-mail: dpi@ncia.net
www.danaplace.com

Century-old inn at the base of Mount
Washington on 300 acres along the Ellis
River. Dana Place features cozy rooms,
fine dining, indoor heated pool, river
swimming, Jacuzzi, tennis, hiking, walking trails, fishing, and cross-country skiing
on the premises. Golf, outlet shopping,
downhill skiing, and White Mountain
attractions all are nearby. Inquire abouth
the easonal escape packages available.

Hosts: Harris and Mary Lou Levine
Rooms: 33 (29 PB; 4 SB) $95-135
Full Breakfast
Credit Cards: A, B, C, D, E
Notes: 2, 3, 4, 5, 6, 7, 8, 9, 10, 11, 12, 13, 14

Ellis River House

Ellis River House

Route 16, P.O. Box 656, 03846
(603) 383-9339; (800) 233-8309
FAX (603) 383-4142
e-mail: innkeeper@erhinn.com; www.erhinn.com

Offering romance and rejuvenation, this
enchanting small hotel is just a short stroll
from the village. The comfortable guest
rooms are decorated with Laura Ashley
prints, some with fireplaces and two-person
Jacuzzis, cable TV, telephones, scenic balconies, and period antiques and all with
individually controlled heat and air conditioning. Two-room suites, riverfront cottage, hot tub, sauna, heated pool, sitting and
game rooms, and sun deck overlooking the
pristine Ellis River. Enjoy a full country
breakfast with homemade breads or a
romantic candlelight dinner. Afterwards
relax with libations and billiards in the pub.
Seasonal rates available. Children 10 years
and older welcome.

Hosts: Barry and Barbara Lubao
Rooms: 18 (15 PB; 3 SB) $69-229
Full Breakfast
Credit Cards: A, B, C, D, E
Notes: 2, 4, 5, 7, 9, 10, 11, 12, 13, 14, 15

Inn at Thorn Hill

Thorn Hill Road, P.O. Box A, 03846
(603) 383-4242; (800) 289-8990
FAX (603) 383-8062; e-mail: thornhll@ncia.net

This romantic, smoke-free 1895 inn overlooking Jackson village is the perfect choice

NOTES: Credit cards accepted: A MasterCard; B Visa; C American Express; D Discover; E Diner's Club;
F Other; 2 Personal checks accepted; 3 Lunch available; 4 Dinner available; 5 Open all year; 6 Pets welcome;

for honeymooners, romantics, and those seeking an adult sanctuary. There are 19 uniquely decorated bed chambers in the main inn, carriage house, and cottages (all with their own fireplaces and Jacuzzis for two) where guests rest comfortably in the mountain quiet. The pub is intimate, the dining elegant with expertly prepared food and attentive service. One never wants for activities; the charming village and the White Mountains offer many diversions throughout the year. Recommended by many country inn guides, *Gourmet, Bon Appétit,* AAA (four-stars for accommodations), and Mobil. Children 10 and over welcome.

Hosts: Jim and Ibby Cooper
Rooms: 19 (PB) $150-300
Full Breakfast
Credit Cards: A, B, C, D, E
Notes: 2, 4, 5, 7, 9, 10, 11, 12, 13, 14

Nestlenook Farm Resort

Dinsmore Road, P.O. Box Q, 03846
(603) 383-9443; (800) 659-9443

Escape into a Victorian past on a 65-acre estate. Seven luxurious guest rooms, all of which have two-person Jacuzzis and some of which have parlor stoves, canopied beds, and fireplaces. Charming guest kitchen, antiques, and fireplaced gazebo. Horse-drawn sleighs, carriage rides, mountain bikes, rowboats, fishing, and Victorian pool. Savor the romance and step back in time at a gingerbread country inn.

Host: Robert Cyr
Rooms: 7 (PB) $125-320
Full Breakfast

Nestlenook Farm Resort

Credit Cards: A, B, D
Notes: 5, 7, 10, 11, 12, 13, 14

The Village House

The Village House

P.O. Box 359, 03846
(603) 383-6666

Just over the covered bridge in the village of Jackson is the Village House. The Village House has enjoyed more than 100 years of hospitality. The circa 1860 inn offers its visitors all the amenities of a large resort, with the charm and personality of a small bed and breakfast. The outdoor pool, Jacuzzi, tennis court, and wraparound porch are perfect for summer nights. In the winter, after a day of alpine or Nordic skiing, enjoy the fire or sit under the stars in the Jacuzzi. In any season, guests are welcome. Full breakfast served in the fall and winter; Continental breakfast served in the summer.

Host: Robin Crocker
Rooms: 13 (PB) $65-140
Full and Continental Breakfast
Credit Cards: A, B, D
Notes: 2, 5, 6, 8, 9, 10, 11, 12, 13, 14

Whitneys' Inn

P.O. Box 822, Route 16B, 03846-0822
(603) 383-8916; (800) 677-5737

A classic country inn nestled in a lovely pastoral setting in the heart of the White Mountains. Spacious, comfortable rooms

---

7 No smoking; 8 Children welcome; 9 Social drinking allowed; 10 Tennis nearby; 11 Swimming nearby; 12 Golf nearby; 13 Skiing nearby; 14 May be booked through a travel agent; 15 Handicapped accessible.

Whitneys' Inn

grace this restored New England farm-house, circa 1842. Adjacent to the main inn are cozy fireplace cottages and family suites. The dining room, featuring delicious full country breakfasts and country gourmet dinners, is open to the public. Seasonal on-site activities range from tennis, swimming, and hiking in the summer to cross-country and downhill skiing during the winter.

Rooms: 29 (PB) $64-124
Full Breakfast
Credit Cards: A, B, C, D
Notes: 2, 4, 5, 6, 7, 8, 9, 10, 11, 12, 13, 14

Windy Hill Bed and Breakfast

Black Mountain Road, Box 462, 03846
(603) 383-8917; FAX (603) 383-8917
e-mail: windyhill@compuserve.com

Quiet, secluded bed and breakfast at the end of a road two miles from the picturesque vil-lage of Jackson. Set in a high valley between two mountains with a panoramic view of several mountain ranges, the bed and break-fast provides a place to unwind, enjoy nature and relish a quiet not easily found. Favorite guest occupations are hiking, mountain biking, cross-country and downhill skiing (near four downhill areas), snow shoeing, porch-sitting, star gazing, and enjoying the village's great restaurants. Windy Hill is close to shopping, golfing, seven major attractions, and a large variety of eateries.

Host: Anne Peterson
Rooms: 3 (PB) $60-80
Full Breakfast
Credit Cards: A, B, C
Notes: 2, 5, 7, 10, 11, 12, 13

JAFFREY

Woodbound Inn and Lake Front Cabins

62 Woodbound Road, 03461
(603) 532-8341; (800) 688-7770
FAX (603) 532-8341 ext. 213
e-mail: woodbound@aol.com

Come enjoy a country inn resort. There is plenty to do on 165 acres, including free golf on a nine-hole course, tennis, private beach, hiking and cross-country ski trails, arcade, gift shop, restaurant, lounge, meeting/banquet facilites for 5 to 200 people, and more. Accommodations include 19 rooms in a 100-year-old bed and breakfast, 14 modern rooms, and 11 lakefront cabins with fireplaces. A perfect place in any season for an escape week-end, wedding, business meeting, or vaca-tion. Pets welcome in cabins only.

Rooms: 44 (39 PB; 5 SB) $60-135
Full Breakfast
Credit Cards: A, B, C
Notes: 2, 5, 8, 9, 10, 11,1 2, 13, 14

JEFFERSON

Applebrook Bed and Breakfast

Route 115A, 03583-0178
(603) 586-7713; (800) 545-6504

Taste the midsummer raspberries while enjoying spectacular mountain views from this old Victorian farmhouse. Bike, hike,

Applebrook

NOTES: Credit cards accepted: A MasterCard; B Visa; C American Express; D Discover; E Diner's Club;
F Other; 2 Personal checks accepted; 3 Lunch available; 4 Dinner available; 5 Open all year; 6 Pets welcome;

fish, ski, go antiquing, or just relax in the sitting room by the goldfish pool. Near Santa's Village and Six Gun City. Dormitory and family suite available in addition to private guest rooms. Brochure available. Try the hot tub under the stars!

Hosts: Sandra J. Conley and Martin M. Kelly
Rooms: 12 (7 PB; 5 SB) $50-75
Dorm Rooms: $25 per person
Full Breakfast
Credit Cards: A, B
Notes: 2, 6, 7, 8, 9, 10, 11, 12, 13, 14

The Jefferson Inn

The Jefferson Inn

Route 2, RR 1, Box 68A, 03583
(603) 586-7998; (800) 729-7908

A comfortably gracious 1896 Victorian nestled in the northern White Mountains near Mount Washington. Eleven unique accommodations with spectacular views, private baths, and sumptuous breakfasts. Guests are encouraged to bring their boots, binoculars, and bicycle. Three of New Hampshire's 50 best rides start here. Golf, hiking trails, swimming, ice-skating, antiques, and crafts within walking distance. Close to several restaurants, cross-country and downhill skiing, snowmobile trails, summer theater, and children's attractions. The perfect getaway for all ages. AAA-rated three diamonds.

Hosts: Marla Mason and Don Garretson
Rooms: 11 (PB) $80-175

Full Breakfast
Credit Cards: A, B, C, D
Notes: 2, 7, 8, 9, 10, 11, 12, 13, 15

KEENE

Carriage Barn

358 Main Street, 03431
(603) 357-3812
e-mail: carriagebarn@top.monad.net

Across the street from Keene State College, in the barn of a New England village home, guests can park their car and take an easy walk up Keene's residential Main Street to restaurants, theaters, museums, shopping, or a concert on Central Square where the movie *Jumanji* was filmed. Come to the "quiet corner" of New Hampshire, climb Mount Monadnock, ski, hike, golf, swim, fish, go antiquing, and enjoy the quiet atmosphere and true hospitality.

Hosts: Ellen and Peter Gammans
Rooms: 4 (PB) $60-70
Continental Breakfast
Credit Cards: A, B
Notes: 2, 5, 7, 8, 9, 10, 11, 12, 13

LINCOLN

Red Sleigh Inn

Pollard Road, P.O. Box 562, 03251
(603) 745-8517

Family-run inn with mountain views. Just off the scenic Kancamagus Highway. One mile to Loon Mountains. Waterville, Cannon, and Bretton Woods nearby. Many summer attractions and superb fall foliage. Shopping, dining, and theater are minutes away. Hiking, swimming, golf, and train rides are available. Children over 12 are welcome.

Hosts: Bill and Loretta Deppe
Rooms: 6 (2 PB; 4 SB) $65-85
Full Breakfast
Credit Cards: A, B
Notes: 2, 5, 7, 9, 10, 11, 12, 13, 14

7 No smoking; 8 Children welcome; 9 Social drinking allowed; 10 Tennis nearby; 11 Swimming nearby; 12 Golf nearby; 13 Skiing nearby; 14 May be booked through a travel agent; 15 Handicapped accessible.

LITTLETON

The Beal House Inn

2 West Main Street, 03561
(603) 444-2661; (888) 616-BEAL
e-mail:Beal.House.inn@connriver.net
www.musar.com/traveler/bealhs.html

Come enjoy the good things in life at this 1833 Main Street inn. Delight in the antiques, down comforters, and fireplaces. Escape to the romantic suite. Soak in the antique claw-foot tubs. Two common rooms with fireplaces. Read a book, chat, or watch TV and movies in the parlor. Watch the town of Littleton go by from the wicker-filled enclosed front porch. Ten rooms with private baths, whimsical beds, and some with TV/VCR. Sip a favorite beverage on the outdoor deck while viewing the mountains and star-filled skies. The jazzy bistro restaurant features a contemporary mix of classic cuisine, wood-grilled items, fine wines and spirits. Walk to town for shopping, movies, and dining after a day of exploring the White Mountains.

Hosts: Pat and Michael McGuin
Rooms: 10 (PB) $85-150
Full Breakfast
Credit Cards: A, B, C, D
Notes: 2, 4, 5, 7, 9, 11, 12, 13, 14

LONDONDERRY

Bed and Breakfast Reservations North Shore, Greater Boston, Cape Cod

P.O. Box 600035, Greater Boston Branch,
   Newtonville, MA 02160-0001
(617) 964-1606; (800) 832-2632
FAX (617) 332-8572; e-mail: info@bbreserve.com
www.bbreserve.com

134. Orchard Hill Bed and Breakfast. This quiet country farmhouse overlooks acres of "U-Pick" apple orchards. The hosts have made extensive renovations to the farmhouse, which was originally built in 1850. The cozy accommodations offer two comfortable guest rooms, sharing a bath when both rooms are occupied. The spacious common room offers guests a wonderful place to relax before or after a long day of travel or sightseeing. Full country breakfast. Local attractions include horse-drawn farm tours, Stoneyfield Yogurt Factory tours, Canobie Lake Amusement Park, horseback riding, golf, and even hot-air balloon rides. No smoking. $95-125.

LOUDON

Elaine's Bed and Breakfast Selections

4987 Kingston Road, Elbridge, NY 13060
(315) 689-2082 (after 10 A.M.)

This Georgian Colonial was built in 1790 and offers elegant accommodations in this house and also in the attached carriage house. All guest rooms have private baths, reading lights, and ceiling fans. The family room has games, TV, an extensive book collection, and a wood stove. Complimentary beverages and snacks are served here. A full hearty country breakfast is served. Hiking, mountain biking, cross-country skiing and snowmobiling, all accessible from the farm's doorway. Nearby is alpine skiing, canoeing, golfing, horseback riding, fishing, antiquing, and tax-free shopping. Well-traveled host is fluent in French and Spanish. Two suites have fireplaces and one has a sitting area and large modern bath. $115-125.

Lovejoy Farm Bed and Breakfast

268 Lovejoy Road, 03301
(888) 783-4007 (phone/FAX)

A 1790 Federal Colonial in a quiet rural setting. Seven rooms, all with private

---

NOTES: Credit cards accepted: A MasterCard; B Visa; C American Express; D Discover; E Diner's Club; F Other; 2 Personal checks accepted; 3 Lunch available; 4 Dinner available; 5 Open all year; 6 Pets welcome;

baths, ceiling fans, two with fireplaces are offered. Easy access to major highways, five miles from Canterbury Shaker Village, New Hampshire International Speedway, close to Lake Winnepesankee. The area offers cross-country skiing, hiking, snow shoeing, all from the bed and breakfast's doorway. A full country breakfast with the inn's own maple syrup and fresh fruit.

Hosts: Art Monty and Rena Simard
Rooms: 7 (PB) $57-92
Full Breakfast
Credit Cards: A, B, C
Notes: 2, 5, 6, 7, 8, 9, 10, 11, 12, 13

LYME

Alden Country Inn

On the Common, One Market Street, 03777
(603) 795-2222; (800) 794-2296

This historic inn (circa 1809), at the head of the town common in Lyme, has been recently renovated to its original charm. Enjoy romantic fireside dining in the country tavern or a cup of hot mulled cider by the roaring fire in guests' private room or in the charming lobby. Dine in one of the candlelit dining rooms and experience this inn's New England hospitality. Fifteen minutes from Hanover and Dartmouth College of the Ivy League. AAA-rated three diamonds and Mobil Travel Guide.

Rooms: 15 (PB) $95-160
Full Breakfast
Credit Cards: A, B, C, D, E, F
Notes: 2, 3, 4, 5, 7, 8, 10, 11, 12, 13, 15

Loch Lyme Lodge

70 Orford Road, 03768
(800) 423-2141; FAX (603) 795-2141
e-mail: loch.lyme.lodge@valley.net

Eleven miles north of Dartmouth College, the lakeside location has hosted family vacations since 1924. The 24 seasonal cabins and four rooms in the main lodge

Loch Lyme Lodge

are open for the enjoyment of summer vacationers. During the fall and winter, three rooms in the main lodge, a farmhouse built in 1784, are open for bed and breakfast guests. Children are welcome during any season and the emphasis is always on comfortable, informal hospitality. Brochure available. Lunch and dinner available in the summer. Inquire about accommodations for pets.

Hosts: Paul and Judy Barker
Rooms: 4 (SB) $56-94
Summer Cabins: 24
Full Breakfast
Credit Cards: None
Notes: 2, 5, 7, 8, 9, 10, 11, 12, 13

MADISON

Elaine's Bed and Breakfast Selections

4987 Kingston Road, Elbridge, NY 13060
(315) 689-2082 (after 10 A.M.)

This large rambling farmhouse is on 216 acres. The four guest rooms on the second floor have private baths, and a family suite on the third floor has two bedrooms, a sleeper-sofa, TV, and a table with chairs. Relax on the large open wraparound porch with a mountain view. There are two guest living rooms, one with a woodstove and the other with a keyboard. Full homemade country breakfast. Moderate rates.

7 No smoking; 8 Children welcome; 9 Social drinking allowed; 10 Tennis nearby; 11 Swimming nearby; 12 Golf nearby; 13 Skiing nearby; 14 May be booked through a travel agent; 15 Handicapped accessible.

MARLBOROUGH

Peep-Willow Farm

51 Bixby Street, 03455
(603) 876-3807

Peep-Willow Farm is a 20-acre working Thorough-bred horse farm that also caters to humans, with a view all the way to the Connecticut River valley. Guests are welcome to help with chores or watch the young horses frolic in the fields, but there is no riding. Flexibility and serenity are the key ingredients to enjoying the stay. Pets and children welcome by prior arrangement. Cross-country skiing.

Host: Noel Aderer
Rooms: 3 (SB) $35-55
Full Breakfast
Credit Cards: None
Notes: 2, 5, 7, 9, 10, 11, 12, 13

MEREDITH

The Inns at Mill Falls

312 Daniel Webster Highway #28, 03253
(603) 279-7006; (800) 622-MILL
FAX (603) 279-6797
e-mail: millfalls-baypoint@worldnet.att.net

The Inns at Mill Falls offer the best of the Lakes Region. A 40-foot waterfall is between the 54-room inn at Mill Falls and the market-place which has 18 shops and restaurants. Bay Point offers 24 luxury lake view rooms and the popular Boathouse Grille. The new Chase House offers 23-lakeview rooms and suites, plus a state-of-the-art 200-seat conference center. The Inns have rooms and rates for all.

Rooms: 101 (PB) $89-249
Credit Cards: A, B, C, D, E
Notes: 2, 5, 8, 10, 11, 12, 13, 14, 15

MOULTONBOROUGH

Olde Orchard Inn

Route 1, Box 256, 03254
(603) 476-5004; (800) 598-5845

This bed and breakfast features nine guest rooms, with private baths, in a beautifully

Old Orchard Inn

restored farmhouse. The inn is on 13 acres with a mountain brook and pond. Hosts offer guests a large country breakfast with home-baked goods and all the fixings. Only one mile from beautiful Lake Winnipesaukee and only minutes away from many other lakes, regional attractions, and activities. Within one hour's drive, guests will find five major ski areas, or guests may decide to take a cross-country ski tour from the inn's front door. The foliage is stunning in Autumn, but anytime is a delightful time to stay here.

Hosts: The Senner Family
Rooms: 9 (PB) $70-125
Full Breakfast
Credit Cards: A, B,
Notes: 2, 5, 7, 8, 9, 10, 11, 13, 14

NEWFOUND LAKE

The Inn on Newfound Lake

Route 3A, Bridgewater, 03222
(603) 744-9111; (800) 745-7990
FAX (603) 744-3894
e-mail: inonlk@cyberportal.net

Beautiful Victorian inn that has been welcoming guests since 1840. Resting on the shore of one of the most pristine lakes in

The Inn on Newfound Lake

NOTES: Credit cards accepted: A MasterCard; B Visa; C American Express; D Discover; E Diner's Club; F Other; 2 Personal checks accepted; 3 Lunch available; 4 Dinner available; 5 Open all year; 6 Pets welcome;

the country. Hiking, biking, skiing. Truly a four-season destination spot. Dine in the renowned restaurant, or just watch the beautiful sunsets from the 120-foot veranda. Return to a bygone era. One of New Hampshire's hidden secrets. Near Wellington State Park, the White Mountains, and tax-free outlet shopping.

Hosts: Larry Delangis and Phelps Boyce
Rooms: 31 (24 PB; 7 SB) $65-110
Continental Breakfast
Credit Cards: A, B, C, D
Notes: 2, 4, 5, 7, 9, 10, 11, 12, 13, 14

NEW LONDON

The Inn at Pleasant Lake

The Inn at Pleasant Lake

125 Pleasant Street, P.O. Box 1030, 03257
(603) 526-6271; (800) 626-4907
FAX (603) 526-4111
e-mail: bmackenz@kear.tds.net
www.innatpleasantlake.com

Descending 500 feet from Main Street, visitors will find the inn on the shore of Pleasant Lake with Mount Kearsarge as its backdrop. All rooms have beautiful views, private baths, and are furnished with antiques. Dining room serves a prix fixe five-course one-sitting dinner—reservations required. Five acres of woods, pastures, and gardens surround the inn. Hiking trails nearby. The lake provides swimming and fishing in summer; skiing and skating are equally popular in winter. Children are welcome.

Hosts: Linda and Brian Mackenzie
Rooms: 12 (PB) $95-155
Full Breakfast

Credit Cards: A, B, D
Notes: 2, 5, 7, 8, 9, 10, 11, 12, 13, 14

NEWPORT

The Eagle Inn at Coit Mountain

523 North Main Street, 03773
(603) 863-3583; (800) 367-2364

All four seasons provide nature's backdrop to this gracious, historic Georgian-Federal estate summer residence that was built for an aristocratic French family with unlimited income and a lifestyle to match. Enjoy a hearty full country breakfast. In the evening a nightcap and dessert are delivered to guests' rooms. Dinner is available in the Greene Room Restaurant. There are many outdoor activities year-round in the Lake Sunapee region. Numerous shops, parks, historic sites, and museums to enjoy in the surrounding area.

Hosts: Jim Forman and Georgia Hopkins
Rooms: 6 (3 PB; 3 SB) $79-129
Full Breakfast
Credit Cards: A, B, C
Notes: 2, 3, 4, 5, 6, 8, 9, 10, 11, 12, 13, 14

The Eagle Inn at Coit Mountain

NORTH CONWAY

The Buttonwood Inn

Mount Surprise Road, P.O. Box 1817, 03860
(603) 356-2625; (800) 258-2625 U.S. and Canada
FAX (603) 356-3140
e-mail: button_w@moose.ncia.net
www.buttonwoodinn.com

Nationally recognized for superior innkeeping. Visit this 1820s farmhouse on 17

7 No smoking; 8 Children welcome; 9 Social drinking allowed; 10 Tennis nearby; 11 Swimming nearby; 12 Golf nearby; 13 Skiing nearby; 14 May be booked through a travel agent; 15 Handicapped accessible.

The Buttonwood Inn

secluded acres, two miles from the village of North Conway. Guests enjoy a peaceful, rural setting, with the convenience of being close to everything. Decorated with Shaker furniture, stenciling, and antiques. Breakfasts are second to none. Three-time award-winning perennial gardens surround the inn. Hike or cross-country ski from the back door. Individually prepared daily intineraries. A memorable blend of hospitality, laughter, and kindness.

Hosts: Claudia and Peter Needham
Rooms: 10 (PB) $85-200
Full Breakfast
Credit Cards: A, B, C, D
Notes: 2, 5, 7, 8, 9, 10, 11, 12, 13, 14

Cabernet Inn

Box 489, 03860
(603) 356-4704; (800) 866-4704
www.cabentinn.com

Nestled in a grove of towering pines, this 1842 Victorian cottage was refurbished and enhanced into an elegant nonsmoking inn. Deluxe rooms have either Jacuzzis or gas fireplaces, queen-size beds, and air conditioning. Two guest living rooms with fireplaces open to shaded outdoor patios and provide relaxing ambiance. Period lighting and furnishings are found throughout the inn. When guests step into the large gourmet kitchen, the secrets behind the delicious, bountiful breakfasts are revealed.

Hosts: Chris and Bob Wyner
Rooms: 10 (PB) $69-169
Full Breakfast
Credit Cards: A, B, C, D
Notes: 2, 5, 7, 9, 10, 11, 12, 13, 14, 15

The Forest: A Country Inn

P.O. Box 37, Intervale, 03845
(603) 356-9772; (800) 448-3534
FAX (603) 356-5652

Step into an era of old-fashioned charm and hospitality at the beautifully maintained 1890 Victorian inn set on 25 quiet, wooded acres just minutes from North Conway. Eleven lovely rooms are furnished with antiques and some rooms have fireplaces. A romantic stone cottage with a fireplace and a cottage with a whirlpool tub are honeymoon hideaways. The guests-only dining room serves a country breakfast each morning. Enjoy the large screened veranda, outdoor pool, and 65K of cross-country ski trails at the back door. Seasonal variations. Packages available.

Rooms: 11 (PB) $79-169
Full Breakfast
Credit Cards: A, B, C, D
Notes: 2, 5, 7, 8, 9, 10, 11, 12, 13, 14

The Forest: A Country Inn

Isaac Merrill House

720 Kearsarge Road, P.O. Box 8, 03847-0008
(800) 328-9041; FAX (603) 356-9055
www.nhinns.com

This historic 225-year-old inn is in a country setting surrounded by spectacular views. With 20 rooms, the inn is complete with fireplaces and suites. View the inn and all its splendor on its web site. Bakery Café breakfast.

Hosts: The Levine Family
Rooms: 20 (PB) $68-168
Credit Cards: A, B, C, D
Notes: 3, 5, 6, 7, 8, 9, 10, 11, 12, 13, 14

Nereledge Inn

River Road (off Main Street, Route 16)
P.O. Box 547, 03860
(603) 356-2831

This small 1787 traditional bed and breakfast with views of Cathedral Ledge offers charm, hospitality, and relaxation. Daydream in a rocking chair on the front porch, relax by the fire, or enjoy a game of darts or backgammon. A friendly, informal atmosphere awaits guests. The country breakfast includes warm apple crumble with ice cream. Close to hiking, biking, rock and ice climbing, and skiing. Walk to the village for dining, theater, and shopping or to the river for swimming, fishing, and canoeing.

Hosts: Valerie and Dave Halpin
Rooms: 11 (6 PB; 5 SB) $60-110
Full Breakfast
Credit Cards: A, B, C, D
Notes: 2, 5, 7, 8, 9, 10, 11, 12, 13, 14

Scottish Lion Inn and Restaurant

P.O. Box 1527, 03860-1527
(888) 356-4945; FAX (603) 356-4802
e-mail: info@scottishlioninn.com

At the Scottish Lion, guests will find a genuine country inn atmosphere with eight lovely rooms, all with private baths and air conditioning. Splendid cuisine consisting of American, Scottish, and international fare with an award-winning wine list to complement each dish. The Black Watch Pub features a very large selection of single malts and also Scotch whiskies, ales, brandies and liqueurs.

Hosts: Michael and Janet Procopio
Rooms: 8 (PB) $59-110
Full Breakfast
Credit Cards: A, B, D, E, F
Notes: 3, 4, 5, 8, 9, 10, 11, 12, 13, 14

The 1785 Inn and Restaurant

3582 White Mountain Highway
P.O. Box 1785, 03860-1785
(603) 356-9025; (800) 421-1785 (reservations)
FAX (603) 356-6081; e-mail: the1785inn@aol.com

The 1785 Inn has a famous view of Mount Washington popularized by the White Mountain School of Art in the 1800s. The inn was completely refurbished by the current owners and offers romantic accommodations where guests can relax and savor the view while being pampered with fine dining and friendly service. On six pristine acres with swimming pool, skiing, nature trails, 210-year-old fireplaces, hiking, biking, fishing. Free color brochure.

Hosts: Becky and Charlie Mallar
Rooms: 17 (12 PB; 5 SB) $69-169
Full Breakfast
Credit Cards: A, B, C, D, E
Notes: 2, 4, 5, 7, 8, 9, 10, 11, 12, 13, 14

The Victorian Harvest Inn

28 Locust Lane, Box 1763, 03860
(603) 356-3548; (800) 642-0749
FAX (603) 356-3548

Nonsmokers will delight in this 1850s multigabled Victorian find. The inn is on a quiet side street, yet is within walking

The Victorian Harvest Inn

distance to quaint North Conway village shops and eateries. All rooms have antiques with modern bed and bath comforts in mind. Start a romantic adventure with a full country breakfast and hospitality of New England as it was meant to be. Fireplace, in-ground pool, and air conditioning. Great mountain views. Wonderful common areas and decks. Three-diamond rated. Listed in Frommer's *Guide to Best Bed & Breakfasts* (1997). Children over six are welcome.

Hosts: David and Judy Wooster
Rooms: 6 (5 PB) $75-140
Full Breakfast
Credit Cards: A, B, C, D
Notes: 5, 7, 9, 10, 11, 12, 13, 14

Wyatt House Country Inn

Main Street, Route 16, P.O. Box 777, 03860
(603) 356-7977; (800) 527-7978

Experience the charm of an elegant country Victorian inn with panoramic mountain and river views. New suite with two-person Jacuzzi bath and mountain views.

Gourmet multientrée breakfast is served with candlelight. Early morning coffee and muffins and Victorian tea time are served in the handsome study. Village location, and minutes to downhill and cross-country skiing. Stroll from the back yard to the Saco River for swimming or fishing. Tax-free outlet shopping. Air conditioning, color cable TV, optional breakfast in bed. Fresh flowers, fruits, and cookie baskets. AAA-rated. Smoking limited to Victorian wraparound porch and grounds. Children over seven welcome.

Hosts: Bill and Arlene Strickland
Rooms: 7 (5 PB; 2 SB) $65-95
Full Breakfast
Credit Cards: A, B, C, D
Notes: 3, 5, 7, 9, 10, 11, 12, 13, 14

NORTH CONWAY (INTERVALE) _____

Elaine's Bed and Breakfast Selections

4987 Kingston Road, Elbridge, NY 13060
(315) 689-2082 (after 10 A.M.)

This is a unique country lodge with resort amenities. Central to all activities in Mount Washington Valley, on the Intervale Resort Loop—just north of North Conway. All rooms have TV, refrigerators, and air conditioning. Two swimming pools, an outdoor Jacuzzi, tennis, fishing, and hiking on premises. Cross-country ski on groomed trails. Just five minutes away is excellent alpine skiing at either Cranmore or Attitash/Bear Peak. Open year-round. Continental breakfast. $55-220.

NORTH SUTTON _____

Follansbee Inn on Kezar Lake

P.O. Box 92, 03260
(603) 927-4221; (800) 626-4221
e-mail: follansbeeinn@conknet.com
www.follansbeeinn.com

An authentic 1840 New England inn with white clapboard and green trim. On peaceful Kezar Lake, with an old-fashioned porch, comfortable sitting rooms with fireplaces, and charming antique furnishings. Nestled in a small country village but convenient to all area activities (New London, 4 miles; Hanover/Dartmouth, 20 miles; Lake Sunapee,

Follansbee Inn on Kezar Lake

NOTES: Credit cards accepted: A MasterCard; B Visa; C American Express; D Discover; E Diner's Club; F Other; 2 Personal checks accepted; 3 Lunch available; 4 Dinner available; 5 Open all year; 6 Pets welcome;

8 miles). One and one-half hours from Boston and less than four hours from Montreal and Cape Cod. Private pier with rowboat, canoe, paddleboat, and windsurfer for guests. Beautiful walk around the lake during all seasons. Beer and wine license. Healthy nonsmoking inn. Closed parts of November and April. Children over eight welcome.

Hosts: Dick and Sandy Reilein
Rooms: 23 (11 PB; 12 SB) $80-110
Full Breakfast
Credit Cards: A, B
Notes: 2, 7, 9, 10, 11, 12, 13

NORTH WOODSTOCK

Wilderness Inn
Bed and Breakfast
Routes 3 and 112, RFD Box 69, 03262
(603) 745-3890; (800) 200-WILD
www.masar.com/wildernessinn/

Built in 1912, the Wilderness Inn is decorated with antiques and turn-of-the-century photographs. Guest rooms have views of Lost River or the mountains. Avid skiers, canoers, and hikers themselves, the owners are delighted to help guests explore the area. Breakfasts include fresh fruit and juice, home-baked muffins, a choice of apple or cranberry-walnut pancakes, crêpes with sour cream, applesauce, and chopped nuts, or vegetable omelets. Cottage with fireplace.

Hosts: Michael and Rosanna Yarnell
Rooms: 8 (6 PB; 2 SB) $40-115
Full Breakfast
Credit Cards: A, B, C
Notes: 2, 5, 7, 8, 9, 10, 11, 12, 13, 14

ORFORD

American Country Collection
1353 Union Street, Schenectady, NY 12308
(518) 370-4948; (800) 810-4948
FAX (518) 393-1637 (call first)
e-mail: carolbnbres@msn.com

178. This is a large country home surrounded by 125 acres of open fields and of woods and

wonderful views. It has a living room with fireplace, cozy sitting room with wood stove, and a screened veranda. A second-floor sitting room has TV/VCR. Bedrooms have individually controlled heating and are comfortably furnished with carpets or area rugs, reading lamps, sitting areas, and down pillows and comforters. Children are welcome; 14 and under stay free in the same room as parents; half-price for children under 18 staying in separate room. No resident pets. Smoking permitted outside. Continental breakfast served. $90-135.

PETERBOROUGH

Apple Gate Bed and Breakfast
199 Upland Farm Road, 03458
(603) 924-6543

The Apple Gate Bed and Breakfast is a charming 1832 Colonial home nestled among gardens, trees, and apple orchards. It is just two miles from downtown Peterborough, Thornton Wilder's *Our Town*, and the center for cultural and outdoor activities in the Monadnock Region. There are four guest rooms, all with Laura Ashley bed linens, stencil-decorated walls, and private baths. Here guests can relax in a house filled with country elegance and enjoy a full candlelight breakfast served by a crackling fire.

Apple Gate

Hosts: Ken and Dianne Legenhausen
Rooms: 4 (PB) $65-80
Full Breakfast
Credit Cards: A, B
Notes: 2, 5, 7, 11, 12, 13

PLYMOUTH

Colonel Spencer Inn

Rural Route 1, Box 206, 03264
(603) 536-3438; (603) 536-1944

The inn is a taste-fully restored 1764 Colonial home featuring hewn post-and-beam construction, Indian shutters, gunstock corners, wainscoting, paneling, and wide-pine floors. Seven antique-appointed bedrooms with private baths welcome guests with New England warmth and hospitality. A full country breakfast is served in a fireplaced dining room within view of the White Mountains and the Pemigewasset River. Convenient to lake and mountain attractions, at exit 27, off I-93, one-half mile south on Route 3.

Hosts: Carolyn and Alan Hill
Rooms: 7 (PB) $45-65
Full Breakfast
Credit Cards: None
Notes: 2, 5, 7, 8, 9, 10, 11, 12, 13, 14

RINDGE

Cathedral House

63 Cathedral Entrance, 03461
(603) 899-6790

The Cathedral House is on the grounds of the internationally renowned Cathedral of the Pines. Here guests and their families can enjoy the comforts of a tasteful 1850s farmhouse surrounded by meadows and mountain ranges. Marked trails lead to a

Cathedral House

grassy pond for fishing and canoeing or to the cathedral gardens and chapels where outdoor weddings, christenings, and services are conducted. Bring the family and step back to a time when traveling meant being welcomed into a stranger's house only to find a home away from home.

Hosts: Donald and Shirley Mahoney
Rooms: 5 (SB) $50-125
Full Breakfast
Credit Cards: A, B
Notes: 2, 5, 7, 8, 11, 12, 13

RYE

Rock Ledge Manor Bed and Breakfast

1413 Ocean Boulevard, Route 1A, 03870
(603) 431-1413

Gracious traditional seaside manor home (1840-80) with wraparound porch. All rooms have paddle fans, an ocean view, and queen-size beds. Six minutes to historic Portsmouth; 20 minutes to University of New Hampshire; 15 minutes to Hampton; 30 minutes to southern Maine's seacoast attractions. Two rooms with half baths, shared shower. Open year-round. Children over 15 welcome.

Hosts: Stan and Sandi Smith
Rooms: 4 (2 PB; 2 SB) $90-110
Full Breakfast
Credit Cards: None
Notes: 2, 7, 9, 10, 11, 12

NOTES: Credit cards accepted: A MasterCard; B Visa; C American Express; D Discover; E Diner's Club; F Other; 2 Personal checks accepted; 3 Lunch available; 4 Dinner available; 5 Open all year; 6 Pets welcome;

SUTTON MILLS

The Village House at Sutton Mills

14 Grist Mill Road, 03221
(603) 927-4765; e-mail: jm_paige@conknet.com
www.xcity.com/sutton/villahse.htm

The Village House is an 1857 country Victorian house on four private acres overlooking a quaint New England village in a four-season resort area. The rooms are comfortably appointed, each with its own unique charm. Jack operates a blacksmith shop in the barn, and Marilyn creates canvas floorcloths, popular in the 18th and 19th centuries in New England. Full country breakfast included. Picnic lunches on request.

Hosts: Marily and Jack Paige
Rooms: 3 (PB) $60-70
Full Breakfast
Credit Cards: None
Notes: 5, 7, 8, 9, 13

The Village House at Sutton Mills

TAMWORTH

Whispering Pines Bed and Breakfast

Route 113 A and Hemenway Road
9 Hemenway Road, 03886-5100 (mailing)
(603) 323-7337

Tucked into the hills between the White Mountains and the Lakes Region, Whispering Pines offers tall sheltering pines, sparkling starlight, and a wonderful, relax-

ing quiet. Settle into a comfortable chair on the porch, relax in the cozy sitting room, or let "your spirit move you"...to the hills for hiking, biking skiing...to the streams and lakes for swimming, canoeing...to quaint villages for unique shops, summer theater, country auctions, autumn fairs.

Hosts: Karen and Kim Erickson
Rooms: 4 (1 PB; 3 SB) $75-90
Full Breakfast
Credit Cards: A, B, D
Notes: 2, 5, 7, 9, 10, 11, 12, 13

TWIN MOUNTAIN

Northern Zermatt Inn and Motel

Route 3, P.O. Box 83, 03595
(603) 846-5533; (800) 535-3214
FAX (603) 846-5664

Clean and charming guest rooms have a private bath in country inn, five kitchenettes (fully equipped), cable TV in motel, and cottage suites. The inn is near Mount Washington, hiking trails, biking, fishing, skiing, golf, tennis. Outdoor swimming pool. Picnic area and playground. Relax in front of the fireplace; play a game of cards in the library/living room. Children stay free.

Hosts: Thomas and Kandy Lee
Rooms: 17 (PB) $20-79
Continental Breakfast
Credit Cards: A, B, D
Notes: 2, 5, 8, 10, 11, 12, 13, 14

WAKEFIELD

Elaine's Bed and Breakfast Selections

4987 Kingston Road, Elbridge, NY 13060
(315) 689-2082 (after 10 A.M.)

History buffs are enchanted with this 200-year-old inn. The seven guest rooms are individually decorated and have private baths and ceiling fans. The living room has a three-sided fireplace, TV, sofa, and comfortable chairs and shares the fireplace with

---

7 No smoking; 8 Children welcome; 9 Social drinking allowed; 10 Tennis nearby; 11 Swimming nearby; 12 Golf nearby; 13 Skiing nearby; 14 May be booked through a travel agent; 15 Handicapped accessible.

the dining room that has a large picture window overlooking the patio, garden, and yard where guests can watch the birds. A piano is set between the living room and dining room that guests may play. There are more than six acres of walking trails. The innkeeper also holds quilting weekends, mystery weekends, and small weddings and/or receptions. Moderate rates.

The Wakefield Inn

2723 Wakefield Road, 03872
(603) 522-8272; (800) 245-0841

Within the national historic district of Wakefield Corner, the inn and its surrounding homes are all 19th-century white wooden structures surrounded by gracious fence-encircled yards and historic landmarks, such as a hay scale, granite horse trough, and town pound. Built in 1804, the inn features a free-standing spiral staircase, a three-sided fireplace, Indian shutters, and a wraparound porch. Comfortable, immaculate guest rooms are large with attractive furnishings featuring Lou's handmade quilts.

Hosts: Harry and Lou Sisson
Rooms: 7 (PB) $70-80
Full Breakfast
Credit Cards: A, B
Notes: 2, 5, 9, 11, 12

WEST SWANZEY

The Loafer Inn at the 1792 Whitcomb House Bed and Breakfast

27 Main Street, 03469
(603) 357-6624; FAX (603) 357-6621
e-mail: loaferinn@monad.net

Five covered bridges and lovely English gardens cast a relaxing spell. Classic 22-room mansion. Loaf, swim, fish, bike, jog, golf, tennis, canoe, go antiquing, or "shop till you drop" in nearby Keene. Antique furnishings; "At your leisure" country breakfast buffet.

Hosts: Richard and Cheryl Munson
Rooms: 6 (2 PB; 4 SB) $55-65
Full Breakfast
Credit Cards: A, B
Notes: 2, 5, 7, 9, 10, 11, 12, 13

WHITEFIELD

The Spalding Inn

Mountain View Road, 03598
(603) 837-2572; (800) 368-VIEW

A White Mountain family destination since 1865. On 200 acres, among old-fashioned cottage gardens and apple orchards. Mountain views are spectacular and the hospitality warm. Family suites and cottage are popular with couples traveling with children. Amenities include four clay tennis courts, a heated swimming pool, adjoining golf course, and hiking trails. Breakfast and dinner are served daily. The food is excellent and abundant. There is a large living room with grand piano, lobby, lounge, card room, sun room, and other quiet nooks. Rooms are furnished with cottage antiques. Close to all area attractions. Pets in cottages only. Seasonal June through November. Canadian funds on par June through August.

Hosts: April and Diane Cockrell; Michael Flinder
Rooms: 24 (PB) $89 and up
Suites: 12
Cottages: 6
Full Breakfast
Credit Cards: A, B
Notes: 2, 4, 7, 8, 12, 14

NOTES: Credit cards accepted: A MasterCard; B Visa; C American Express; D Discover; E Diner's Club; F Other; 2 Personal checks accepted; 3 Lunch available; 4 Dinner available; 5 Open all year; 6 Pets welcome;

Rhode Island

The Atlantic Inn

High Street, P.O. Box 188, 02807
(401) 466-5883; (401) 466-2005
FAX (401) 466-5678

An elegant Victorian inn, built and first opened in 1876, occupies six acres of gently rolling slopes overlooking the Atlantic Ocean and Old Harbor Village. A gourmet restaurant for up to 85 guests is in the inn. Activities include a formal croquet court, two full-size tennis courts, a horseshoe pit, and landscaped gardens and paths. The unique location, extraordinary views, expansive grounds and gardens, conference facilities, and recreation options all come together with Victorian ambiance and charm to make the Atlantic Inn truly a unique property to Block Island and Rhode Island itself.

Hosts: Anne and Brad Marthens
Rooms: 21 (PB) $99-195
Suite: $210
Continental Breakfast
Credit Cards: A, B, C, D
Notes: 2, 4, 7, 8, 9, 10, 11

The Barrington Inn

Corner of Beach and Ocean Avenues,
    P.O. Box 397, 02807
(401) 466-5510; FAX (401) 466-5880
e-mail: barrington@block-island-ri.com

Known for its warmth and hospitality, the Barrington Inn is an 1886 farmhouse on a knoll overlooking the New Harbor area of Block Island. There are six individually decorated guest rooms with private baths, and two housekeeping apartments. A light breakfast is served each morning by the

The Barrington Inn

innkeepers. Amenities include two guest sitting rooms, guest refrigerator, ceiling fans, comfortable beds, front porch, back deck, and afternoon beverages. No smoking. Continental plus breakfast served. Children over 12 welcome.

Hosts: Joan and Howard Ballard
Rooms: 6 (PB) $60-158
Continental Breakfast
Credit Cards: A, B, D
Notes: 2, 7, 9, 10, 11

Old Town Inn

P.O. Box 351, 02807
(401) 466-5958

The Old Town Inn is at the junction of Old Town Road and Center Road, about one mile from the ferry landing. Ten guest rooms, four in the old section featuring antique furniture and six in the new east wing featuring queen-size beds, full baths, refrigerators. Continental breakfasts are served in the 19th-century dining rooms. On about four acres of landscaped area.

Hosts: Ralph, Monica, and David Gunter
Rooms: 10 (8 PB; 2 SB) $85-125
Full Breakfast
Credit Cards: A, B
Notes: 2, 7

7 No smoking; 8 Children welcome; 9 Social drinking allowed; 10 Tennis nearby; 11 Swimming nearby; 12 Golf nearby; 13 Skiing nearby; 14 May be booked through a travel agent; 15 Handicapped accessible.

6

Providence

Bristol

95

North Kingstown

Narragansett

Newport

South Kingstown

Westerly   Green Hill
Charlestown

Haversham

Watch Hill

Block Island   Block Island

Rhode Island

Rose Farm Inn

Roslyn Road, Box E, 02807
(401) 466-2021; (401) 466-2034

Experience the romance of the Victorian era. Guests may treat themselves to a romantic room beautifully furnished with antiques and king- or queen-size canopied bed. Enjoy the peaceful tranquility of the farm from shaded decks cooled by gentle ocean breezes. Gaze at the ocean from the window or share a whirlpool bath for two. Awaken to a light buffet breakfast served in a charming porch dining room with an ocean view. Bicycle rentals are available. Children over 12 welcome.

Hosts: Robert and Judith Rose
Rooms: 19 (17 PB; 2 SB) $89-195
Continental Breakfast
Credit Cards: A, B, C, D, F
Notes: 7, 9, 10, 11, 15

The Sheffield House Bed and Breakfast

High Street, P.O. Box C-2, 02807
(401) 466-2494; FAX (401) 466-8890
e-mail: info@sheffieldhouse.com

The Sheffield House, an 1888 Queen Anne Victorian, is set amidst perennial gardens, a

The Sheffield House

five-minute walk from beaches, shops, and restaurants. The seven guest rooms are individually decorated with antiques and family pieces for the comfort of the guests. Rocking chairs on the porch, a country kitchen, and quiet private garden ensure a tranquil getaway.

Hosts: Molly and Chris O'Neill
Rooms: 7 (5 PB; 2 SB) $40-160
Continental Breakfast
Credit Cards: A, B, C, D
Notes: 2, 5, 7, 9, 10, 11, 14, 15

The 1661 Inn & Hotel Manisses

Spring Street, 02807
(401) 466-2421; FAX (401) 466-3162
e-mail: biresorts@aol.com

Enjoy the New England decor of the 1661 Inn and the Victorian charm of the Hotel Manisses. Each room is individually decorated and many rooms feature whirlpool tubs, decks, ocean views, or fireplaces. Marvel at the spectacular views of the Atlantic Ocean from the covered porch while enjoying a complimentary full buffet breakfast. Enjoy fine dining in the casual elegance of the Manisses Dining Room as featured in *Gourmet* magazine. There are also a unique farm and garden with many exotic animals including llamas, emus, zebu, and more. All rates include breakfast, the wine and nibble hour, and a tour of the island. Rooms open year-round. Children welcome.

Hosts: Joan and Justin Abrams;
   Rita and Steve Draper
Rooms: 55 (51 PB: 4 SB) $50-335
Full Breakfast
Credit Cards: A, B
Notes: 2, 3, 4, 5, 7, 8, 9, 10, 11, 14

The White House

02807-0447
(401) 466-2653

Large island manor house with two bedrooms sharing two baths and opening onto balconies overlooking the ocean. French Provincial antique furnishings. Notable

NOTES: Credit cards accepted: A MasterCard; B Visa; C American Express; D Discover; E Diner's Club; F Other; 2 Personal checks accepted; 3 Lunch available; 4 Dinner available; 5 Open all year; 6 Pets welcome; 7 No smoking; 8 Children welcome; 9 Social drinking allowed; 10 Tennis nearby; 11 Swimming nearby; 12 Golf nearby; 13 Skiing nearby; 14 May be booked through a travel agent; 15 Handicapped accessible.

The White House

collection of presidential autographs and documents. Full breakfast. All kinds of in-house services and amenities. Inquire about accommodations for pets and children. Open year-round.

Host: Mrs. Joseph V. Connolly
Rooms: 2 (SB) $55-120
Full Breakfast
Credit Cards: A, B
Notes: 2, 5, 9, 10, 11

BRISTOL

William's Grant Inn

154 High Street, 02809
(401) 253-4222; (800) 596-4222

Just two blocks from Bristol's harbor is William's Grant Inn, circa 1808. The home of a sea captain, this five-bay Colonial Federal house is now a gracious inn for guests to enjoy. It is a showcase for traditional and whimsical artwork throughout. The eclectic full breakfasts

William's GrantrInn

are always a treat! A central location to Boston, Providence, and Newport. Seven museums and a 30-mile bike path within two miles of the inn. Excellent swimming beaches are within 30 minutes. Children over 12 welcome.

Hosts: Diane, Warren, Janet, and Matthew Poehler
Rooms: 5 (3 PB; 2 SB) $85-125
Full Breakfast
Credit Cards: A, B, C,D, E
Notes: 2, 5, 7, 9, 10, 11, 12, 14

CHARLESTOWN

One Willow by the Sea

1 Willow Road, 02813-4162
(401) 364-0802

A warm, inviting "kick your shoes off and relax" stay on the beautiful Atlantic South Coast. Enjoy delicious sun deck breakfasts in summer. Whatever season one chooses, there's lots to do: miles of sandy beaches, sea and land sports, fine dining, festivals, and entertainments. Visit historic New England villages and Narragansett Indian events. Easy drives to events in the capital city, Providence, Newport, Mystic, and Foxwoods and Mohegan Sun casinos. French spoken. Young children welcome.

Host: Denise Dillon Fuge
Rooms: 2 (SB) $70
Suite: 1 (PB) $80
Full Breakfast
Credit Cards: None
Notes: 2, 5, 7, 9, 10, 11, 12, 14

GREEN HILL

Green Shadows Bed and Breakfast

803 Green Hill Beach Road, Wakefield, 02879-6228
(401) 783-9752

This new home is in the beautiful Green Hill area of South Coast Rhode Island. Set on a wooded acre; the ocean and the beach are a

NOTES: Credit cards accepted: A MasterCard; B Visa; C American Express; D Discover; E Diner's Club; F Other; 2 Personal checks accepted; 3 Lunch available; 4 Dinner available; 5 Open all year; 6 Pets welcome;

10-minute walk away. Light-filled bedrooms with king-size beds and private baths, quiet lounge with cable TV, VCR, and screened porch for breakfast and relaxing with views of Green Hill Pond. First-floor accommodations, full breakfast. Within easy drive of Mystic Seaport, Foxwoods Casino, wildlife preserves, flea markets, antique shops, summer theater, and Newport.

Hosts: Don and Mercedes Kratz
Rooms: 2 (PB) $85-95
Full Breakfast
Credit Cards: None
Notes: 2, 5, 7, 9, 11, 12, 15

HAVERSHAM

Covered Bridge

69 Maple Avenue, Norfolk, CT 06058
(860) 542-5944; FAX (860) 542-5690

1HR1. Early 1900s beach home the artist/architect owner has redone to create a spectacular home in a secluded setting overlooking a saltwater pond with a view of the ocean. There are two guest rooms in the main house, one with a balcony, which are decorated with antiques and paintings done by the owner. There in one cottage on the grounds. A Continental plus breakfast is served in the dining room or on the terrace overlooking the water. $95-150.

NARRAGANSETT

Four Gables

12 South Pier Road, 02882
(401) 789-6948

Built by an architect in 1898, this charming Arts and Craft-style home has many interesting features. It is furnished with antiques and unique handcrafted items. Fishing equipment and advice available. Breakfast is served in the dining room overlooking the ocean, or guests may choose to enjoy the veranda with its spectacular views. Within walking distance of the beach,

restaurants, and shops, and within a short drive to many attractions.

Hosts: Terry and Barbara Higgins
Rooms: 2 (SB) $60-90
Full Breakfast
Credit Cards: A, B, C
Notes: 2, 5, 7, 9, 10, 11, 12, 14

1900 House

59 Kingston Road, 02882
(401) 789-7971

Restored Victorian, circa 1900, with antique furniture, quiet street, lavender front door, and pretty gardens. Each room is unique, but all include country antiques, wooden bed frames, canopied beds, thick oriental rugs, and small special touches, such as the original owners' marriage certificate. Beach is a five-minute walk. Guests have use of a porch, which has cool sea breezes. Full gourmet breakfast served.

Hosts: Bill and Sandra Panzeri
Rooms: 3 (1 PB; 2 SB) $55-85
Full Breakfast
Credit Cards: None
Notes: 2, 5, 7, 10, 9, 11, 12, 14

The Old Clerk House

49 Narrangansett Avenue, 02882-3386
(401) 783-8008; e-mail: plwat@aol.com

Enjoy English country comfort in this Victorian home. Queen-size bed and king-size suite with private baths, cable TV, VCR, and air conditioning. Full, home-cooked breakfast, all made from scratch—no mixes—is served in the plant-filled sunroom. Only one block from beautiful beach and fine restaurants. Kayaking, fishing, whale watching, bay cruises, water sports, Block Island ferry, and University of Rhode Island nearby. Eighteen miles from Newport. Foxwoods Casino is a half-hour drive. Off-street parking.

Host: Patricia Watkins
Rooms: 2 (PB) $65-125
Full Breakfast
Credit Cards: None
Notes: 2, 5, 7, 9, 10, 11, 12, 14

7 No smoking; 8 Children welcome; 9 Social drinking allowed; 10 Tennis nearby; 11 Swimming nearby; 12 Golf nearby; 13 Skiing nearby; 14 May be booked through a travel agent; 15 Handicapped accessible.

Pleasant Cottage

104 Robinson Street, 02882
(401) 783-6895

This charming cottage is on a half-acre of woods and gardens. A quiet, serene atmosphere awaits guests just blocks from lovely Narragansett Beach. Enclosed outdoor shower. Relax on large screened porch. Bedrooms with shared bath, or private bath and private entrance. Full breakfast served, including a treat for coffee lovers. Reservations and advance deposit required.

Hosts: Fred and Terry Sepp
Rooms: 2 (1 PB; 1 SB) $65-80
Full Breakfast
Credit Cards: None
Notes: 2, 7, 9, 10, 11, 12

The Richards

144 Gibson Avenue, 02882
(401) 789-7746

These gracious and elegant accommodations are in an 1884 historic manse. Relax by the crackling fire in the library or in the guest room with a fireplace. Enjoy a leisurely and delicious full breakfast, complete with homemade muffins, strudels, and blintzes. The hostess's special touches will spoil anyone—down comforters, canopied beds, and flowers fresh from the gardens. There are minimum-stay requirements for weekends and holidays. Special suite rates are available for couples who are traveling together.

Hosts: Steven and Nancy Richards
Rooms: 2 (1 PB; 1 SB) $90-100
Suite: 2 (PB) $125-180
Full Breakfast
Credit Cards: None
Notes: 2, 5, 7, 9, 10, 11, 12

White Rose

22 Cedar Street, 02882
(401) 789-0181

A classic Victorian in Narragansett-by-the-Sea, just a half-block from the beach. The upbeat atmosphere is simple and ele-

White Rose

gant. Walk to the beach, shops, and restaurants or drive to Newport, Mystic, and Foxwoods Casino. Bicycles, bocce, basketball, croquet, darts, and more are available or arrange a private charter aboard the sailing sloop *White Rose*. A gourmet breakfast buffet is served daily.

Hosts: Pat and Sylvan Vaicaitis
Rooms: 4 (SB) $50-85
Full Breakfast
Credit Cards: None
Notes: 2, 5, 7, 9, 10, 11, 12

NEWPORT

Artful Lodger Inn

503 Spring Street, 02840
(401) 847-3132; (800) 503-1850
FAX (401) 849-2147; e-mail: artfullodger@ids.net
www.artfullodger.com

Enjoy a magnificent harbor view over a leisurely gourmet breakfast at a beautiful Victorian bed and breakfast in Newport. It is tucked in amongst the famous robber baron mansions to visit; guests can walk to all other attractions. Four rooms plus a suite of rooms. Amenities plus reasonable rates. "You provide the romance, we provide the setting."

Hosts: Rose and Ric Ranucci
Rooms: 4 plus a suite (5 PB; 2 SB) $79-169
Full Breakfast
Credit Cards: A, B, C
Notes: 2, 5, 7, 9, 10, 11, 12, 14

NOTES: Credit cards accepted: A MasterCard; B Visa; C American Express; D Discover; E Diner's Club; F Other; 2 Personal checks accepted; 3 Lunch available; 4 Dinner available; 5 Open all year; 6 Pets welcome;

Bannister's Wharf Guest Rooms

Bannister's Wharf, 02840
(401) 846-4500; FAX (401) 849-8750

Rooms and suites with harborside decks. At the center of the best shopping, dining, and waterfront activities in Newport. Guests may watch the lobster and deep sea trawlers unload their catch as well as the arrival and departure of visiting yachtmen. Just off America's Cup Avenue guests will view all of Newport's magnificent harbor and enjoy its cool evening breezes. Rooms have private baths, air conditioning, TVs, telephones, refrigerators. Free parking.

Host: Jan Buchner
Rooms: 8 (PB) $75-200
Continental Breakfast
Credit Cards: A, B, C, D
Notes: 2, 3, 4, 5, 8, 9, 10, 11, 12

Bed and Breakfast on the Point

102 Third Street, 02840
(401) 846-8377

This bed and breakfast is in a century-old Victorian, furnished with a tasteful combination of antiques and contemporary furniture. The location is ideal: one block from Narragansett Bay and a short walk to the middle of Newport. Owners are interested in Newport history and have an extensive collection of early Newport prints and turn-of-the-century photos. Parking on premises; air conditioning; open year-round. Children over five welcome.

Hosts: Sheila and George Perry
Rooms: 4 (2 PB; 2 SB) $75-155
Continental Breakfast
Credit Cards: A, B, D
Notes: 5, 7, 9, 10, 11, 12, 14

Beech Tree Inn

34 Rhode Island Avenue, 02840
(401) 847-9794; (800) 748-6565
FAX (401) 847-6824

The Beech Tree Inn is a bed and breakfast offering the largest breakfast with the greatest variety of entrées in Newport. The inn was completely renovated in 1994, and all guest rooms are large with new bathrooms. Some rooms have fireplaces and Jacuzzis. Some have outside decks. A casual and relaxed atmosphere with charming Colonial decor. No smoking in guest rooms.

Hosts: Ed and Kathy Wudyka
Rooms: 8 (PB)
Full Breakfast
Credit Cards: A, B, C, D
Notes: 5, 8, 9, 10, 11, 12, 14

Bellevue House

14 Catherine Street, 02840
(401) 847-1828; (800) 820-1828
www.bellevuehouse.com

Built in 1774, Bellevue House was converted into the first summer hotel in Newport in 1828. On top of historic hill, off the famous Bellevue Avenue and three blocks from the harbor, the house retains a combination of ideal location, colonial history, economical rates, and a friendly host and hostess. All guest rooms have air conditioning and are nonsmoking. Children over 12 welcome.

Hosts: Joan and Vic Farmer
Rooms: 8 (6 PB; 2 SB) $75-150
Continental Breakfast
Credit Cards: None
Notes: 2, 7, 9, 10, 11, 12, 14

Black Duck Inn

29 Pelham Street, 02840
(401) 841-5548; (800) 206-5212
FAX (401) 846-4873
e-mail: mary@blackduckinn.com
www.blackduckinn.com

A charming inn in the waterfront area footsteps away from harborfront shops, restaurants, and sailing. A short stroll to the Cliff Walk and Newport mansions. For that romantic getaway, stay in one of the Jacuzzi and fireplace rooms where guests can relax in comfort. The inn has central air and each room has TV, telephone, and off-street parking. No smoking.

Host: Mary A. Rolando
Rooms: 8 (6 PB; 2 SB) $69-185

7 No smoking; 8 Children welcome; 9 Social drinking allowed; 10 Tennis nearby; 11 Swimming nearby; 12 Golf nearby; 13 Skiing nearby; 14 May be booked through a travel agent; 15 Handicapped accessible.

Continental Breakfast
Credit Cards: A, B, C
Notes: 5, 7, 8, 9, 10, 11

Brinley Victorian Inn

23 Brinley Street, 02840
(401) 849-7645; (800) 999-8523
FAX (401) 845-9634

Romantic year-round, the inn becomes a Victorian Christmas dream come true. Comfortable antiques and fresh flowers fill every room. Friendly, unpretentious service and attention to detail will make this inn a traveler's haven in Newport. Park and walk everywhere. AAA-approved. Minimum stay on weekends is two nights and on holidays is three nights. A suite with Jacuzzi and fireplace is available. Children over 12 welcome.

Hosts: John and Jennifer Sweetman
Rooms: 15 (13 PB; 2 SB) $69-199
Continental Breakfast
Credit Cards: A, B, C
Notes: 2, 5, 7, 9, 10, 11, 12, 14

Castle Hill Inn and Resort

Ocean Drive, 02840
(401) 849-3800; (888) 466-1355
FAX (401) 849-3838

On a 40-acre peninsula at the top of Newport's world-renowned Ocean Drive, Castle Hill offers guests the seclusion, beauty, and romance of a private oceanfront retreat. An elegant Victorian mansion with stunning water-view guest rooms and quaint beach cottages, Castle Hill provides an escape from daily routines and cares. Guests can do more than just imagine the splendor of Victorian seacoast life—they can experi-

Castle Hill Inn

ence it. Enjoy regional cooking with an international flair. Lunch, dinner, and Sunday brunch including outdoor dining and barbecue available. Open year-round.

Host: Len Panaggio
Rooms: 38 (33 PB; 5 SB) $115-325
Continental Breakfast
Credit Cards: A, B, C, D
Notes: 2, 3, 4, 5, 7, 9, 10, 11, 12, 15

Chambord Bed and Breakfast

25 Ayrault Street, 02840
(401) 849-9223; (800) 379-3244

An elegant Victorian built in 1863 in the heart of Newport. One-half mile to beaches, waterfront, and shops. Conveniently near mansions. Tastefully appointed rooms with private baths, fireplaces, air conditioning, roof decks, and private gardens. In the formal dining room with marble fireplace, a full breakfast is served. Complimentary bicycles and off-street parking are available. Gift certificates available.

Hosts: Regina and Robert Morrissey
Rooms: 5 (3 PB; 2 SB) $75-160
Full Breakfast
Credit Cards: A, B, C
Notes: 2, 5, 7, 10, 11, 12

The Clarkeston Inn

28 Clarke Street, 02840
(401) 849-7397; FAX (401) 847-7630
e-mail: innsofnewport.com

The Clarkeston, listed in the National Register of Historic Places, is one of the oldest inns in Newport. The inn was fully restored in 1993 with all modern luxuries and amenities of today while keeping the charm of a Colonial inn. Romantic fireplaces, canopied and sleigh beds of old, Jacuzzi tubs, and air conditioning for comfort. In the heart of the historic district just two blocks from the bustling shops and harbor.

Host: Rick Farrick
Rooms: 9 (PB) $95-175
Full Breakfast
Credit Cards: A, B, C
Notes: 2, 5, 7, 8, 9, 10, 11, 12, 14, 15

NOTES: Credit cards accepted: A MasterCard; B Visa; C American Express; D Discover; E Diner's Club; F Other; 2 Personal checks accepted; 3 Lunch available; 4 Dinner available; 5 Open all year; 6 Pets welcome;

Cliffside Inn

Cliffside Inn

2 Seaview Avenue, 02840
(401) 845-1811; (800) 845-1811
e-mail: cliff@wsii.com; www.cliffsideinn.com

An elegant Victorian inn near the beginning of Newport's famous Cliff Walk and the beach. Built in 1880 by Governor Thomas Swann of Maryland as a summer residence, the house became the first location of St. George's School in 1897 and was later owned by Newport artist Beatrice Turner. In addition to a full breakfast, host serves afternoon Victorian tea and a morning coffee room service. Guest rooms have private baths. Most rooms have whirlpool tubs or fireplaces. Seven suites available. Air conditioning, cable TV, and telephones. The inn has received a four-crown rating from the American Bed & Breakfast Association.

Host: Stephan Nicolas
Rooms: 15 (PB) $155-350
Full Breakfast
Credit Cards: A, B, C, D, E
Notes: 2, 5, 7, 9, 10, 11, 12, 14

Cliff View Guest House

4 Cliff Terrace, 02840
(401) 846-0885

A two-story 1870 Victorian on a quiet dead-end street leading to the beautiful Cliff Walk, a three-mile path bordering the ocean. Five-minute walk to beach; 15-minute walk to downtown harbor area. Ten-room house with four guest bedrooms; two share a bath and have view of ocean; two have private baths, but no ocean view. Three rooms have air conditioning. The hostess's French-speaking grandson is on the premises during school summer vacation.

Host: Pauline Shea
Rooms: 4 (2 PB; 2 SB) $65-75
Continental Breakfast
Credit Cards: A, B
Notes: 2, 9, 10, 11, 12, 14

1855 Marshall Slocum Guest House

29 Kay Street, 02840
(800) 372-5120; FAX (401) 846-3787
e-mail: marshallslocuminn@edgenet.net

This home has been meticulously restored to reflect the charm and beauty of its Victorian heritage. Breakfast is often served on the deck overlooking the expansive back yard. Refreshments served daily at 5:00 P.M. Guests staying three nights midweek enjoy a complimentary New England clambake. A 5-minute walk to downtown and a 10-minute walk to the beaches; plenty of off-street parking for guests.

Hosts: Joan and Julie Wilson
Rooms: 6 (PB) $110-150
Full Breakfast
Credit Cards: A, B, C
Notes: 2, 3, 4, 5, 7, 9, 10, 11, 12, 14

The Francis Malbone House

392 Thames Street, 02840
(401) 846-0392; (800) 846-0392
FAX (401) 848-5956; www.malbone.com

This historic inn was built in 1760 for Col. Francis Malbone, who made his fortune as a shipping merchant. The design of the house is attributed to Peter Harrison, the architect responsible for Touro Synagogue and the Redwood Library. Guests will enjoy the comfortable elegance of the Francis Malbone House, which is proudly listed in the National Register of Historic Places. The inn offers a downtown harbor location, private baths with Jacuzzis, full breakfast, fireplaces, corporate

The Francis Malbone House

packages, and gracious rooms and gardens for elegant entertaining.

Host: Will Dewey
Rooms: 18 (PB) $145-355
Full Breakfast
Credit Cards: A, B, C
Notes: 2, 5, 7, 11, 14, 15

Gardenview

8 Binney Street, 02840
(401) 849-5799

Gardenview is a cozy, quaint, countrified private home bed and breakfast. It is a short distance from the mansions, beaches, and famous Ocean Drive. The yard is filled with flowers, a fish pond with a waterfall, and many birds to view and enjoy. Hosts offer two quiet rooms for their guests: a cozy room that faces the gardens and a suite with a sitting area. Both rooms have private whirlpool baths, air conditioning, fireplaces, cable TVs, antiques, and handmade quilts.

A separate common room is available and the dining room has a fireplace.

Hosts: Mary and Andrew Fitzgerald
Rooms: 2 (PB) $75-165
Full Breakfast
Credit Cards: None
Notes: 2, 5, 7, 9, 10, 11, 12, 14

Halidon Hill Guest House

Halidon Avenue, 02840
(401) 847-8318

Halidon Hill is up the street from the Ida Lewis and the New York Yacht Clubs. Relax around the large in-ground pool and spacious deck. It is close to shopping, restaurants, mansions, and beaches. All rooms are beautifully decorated with air conditioning, small refrigerators, and TVs. Full breakfast served.

Hosts: Helen and Paul Burke
Rooms 2 $55
Apartments: 2 $250
Full Breakfast
Credit Cards: C, D, E
Notes: 2, 5, 8, 9, 11, 12

Harborside Inn

Christies Landing, 02840
(401) 846-6600; (800) 427-9444

A luxurious waterfront inn in downtown Newport with a lovely combination of suites and rooms overlooking scenic Newport Harbor. Parking and Continental breakfast included.

Harborside Inn

NOTES: Credit cards accepted: A MasterCard; B Visa; C American Express; D Discover; E Diner's Club; F Other; 2 Personal checks accepted; 3 Lunch available; 4 Dinner available; 5 Open all year; 6 Pets welcome;

Host: Carol Bamberry
Rooms: 15 (PB) $55-285
Continental Breakfast
Credit Cards: A, B, C, D
Notes: 5, 7, 8, 10, 11, 12

The Inn at Shadow Lawn

The Inn at Shadow Lawn

120 Miantonomi Avenue, Middletown, 02842
(401) 847-0902; (800) 352-3750
FAX (401) 848-6529

The Inn at Shadow Lawn, one of Newport County's finest bed and breakfast inns, is on two acres of beautifully landscaped lawns and gardens. This 1850s Victorian mansion, with its crystal chandeliers and stained-glass windows, has eight large bedrooms, each with private bath, cable TV with VCR, refrigerator, telephone, and air conditioning. Four rooms also have attached kitchens, and six rooms have working fireplaces. Complimentary shuttle to Newport Harbor district. Enjoy a complimentary bottle of wine and join the hosts daily for a glass of sherry.

Hosts: Randy and Selma Fabricant
Rooms: 8 (PB) $49-175
Full Breakfast
Credit Cards: A, B, C, D, E, F
Notes: 5, 7, 8, 9, 10, 11, 12, 14

The Inntowne Inn

6 Mary Street, 02840
(401) 846-9200; (800) 457-7803
FAX (401) 846-1534

An elegant traditional inn in the heart of downtown Newport offers some four-poster beds with canopies and a rooftop deck. Use of health club and pool within walking distance. Afternoon tea and gourmet Continental plus breakfast served daily. One mile from the Newport mansions. Take harbor cruises, shop for antiques, or just enjoy the bustle of the harbor.

Host: Carmella L. Gardner
Rooms: 25 (PB) $110-250
Continental Breakfast
Credit Cards: A, B, C
Notes: 2, 5, 8, 9, 11, 12

Jailhouse Inn

13 Marlborough Street, 02840
(401) 847-4638; (800) 427-9444

A restored 1700 Colonial landmark with fully modern conveniences. Centrally in the heart of Newport's shops, fine restaurants, and waterfront district. Parking and Continental breakfast included.

Host: Susan P. Mauro
Rooms: 22 (PB) $55-225
Continental Breakfast
Credit Cards: A, B, C, D,
Notes: 5, 7, 8, 10, 11, 12, 15

Jenkins Guest House

206 South Rhode Island Avenue, 02840
(401) 847-6801

The hosts built this Cape Cod when they were married. Since their eight children, who were raised in this house, are now grown and on their own, the hosts have been using the extra rooms for guests since 1978. Having lived in Newport all their lives, they have interesting stories to tell from a local viewpoint and can provide

Jenkins Guest House

7 No smoking; 8 Children welcome; 9 Social drinking allowed; 10 Tennis nearby; 11 Swimming nearby; 12 Golf nearby; 13 Skiing nearby; 14 May be booked through a travel agent; 15 Handicapped accessible.

helpful information about restaurants and places to visit. On a quiet little street just a 3-minute walk from the beach or a 10-minute walk to the mansions or the harbor, with plenty of parking on the grounds. Enjoy the homemade muffins for breakfast in a country-in-the-city atmosphere. Air conditioned. Smoking permitted on the deck only.

Hosts: David and Sally Jenkins
Rooms: 3 (1 PB; 2SB) $75
Continental Breakfast
Credit Cards: None
Notes: 2, 7, 8, 9, 10, 11, 12, 14

The Melville House

La Forge Cottage

96 Pelham Street, 02840-3130
(401) 847-4400
e-mail: info@laforgecottage.com
www.laforgecottage.com

A Victorian bed and breakfast in the heart of Newport's historic hill area. Close to beaches and downtown. All rooms have private baths, TVs, telephones, air conditioning, refrigerators, and complimentary breakfast. French, Spanish, and German spoken. Reservations suggested. Minimum stay on weekends is two nights and on holidays is three nights.

Hosts: Louis and Margot Droual
Rooms: 6 (PB) $67.20-162.40
Suites: 4 (PB) $89.60-190.40
Full Breakfast
Credit Cards: A, B, C, D
Notes: 2, 5, 7, 8, 9, 10, 11, 12

The Melville House

39 Clark Street, 02840
(401) 847-0640

Step back into the past and stay at a colonial inn, built circa 1750, "where the past is present." The Melville House is in the National Register of Historic Places and is in the heart of Newport's beautiful historic district. Walk around the corner to the Brick Market and the wharves. Enjoy a leisurely homemade breakfast in the morning, afternoon tea, and join the hosts for complimentary tea and sherry before dinner. Off-street parking.

Hosts: Vince DeRico and David Horan
Rooms: 7 (5 PB; 2 SB) $85-145
Suite: $165
Full Breakfast
Credit Cards: A, B, C, D
Notes: 2, 3, 5, 7, 9, 10, 11, 12, 14

Mount Vernon Inn

26 Mount Vernon Street, 02840
(401) 846-6314; (888) MT VERNON
FAX (401) 846-0530; e-mail: mtvernon@wsii.com
www.wsii.com/rhodeisl/users/mtvernon//

A charming 1850 Victorian bed and breakfast with lovely spacious rooms furnished with king-, queen-size, or twin beds, antiques and wicker. A six-minute walk to the harbor, town, restaurants, and more. Ideal for families, small weddings, and groups. On a lovely, quiet street. Off-street parking, air conditioning, and full breakfast.

Hosts: Marcia and Kevin Smith
Rooms: 5 (3 PB; 2 SB) $80-140
Full Breakfast
Credit Cards: A, B, C, D, E
Notes: 2, 5, 7, 8, 9, 10, 11, 12, 14

The Old Beach Inn

19 Old Beach Road, 02840
(401) 849-3479; (888) 303-5033
FAX (401) 847-1236
e-mail: info@oldbeachinn.com
www.oldbeachinn.com

Elegant Victorian bed and breakfast in one of Newport's most prestigious areas. Built

NOTES: Credit cards accepted: A MasterCard; B Visa; C American Express; D Discover; E Diner's Club; F Other; 2 Personal checks accepted; 3 Lunch available; 4 Dinner available; 5 Open all year; 6 Pets welcome;

in 1879, this inn was once the home of an affluent physician and commodore and is now listed in the Rhode Island historic register. The fabled mansions, Cliff Walk, beaches, and historic harborfront are only a short walk away. Each of the romantic guest rooms has a private bath, and several have fireplaces. Continental plus breakfast served Monday through Saturday. A full entrée is served as well on Sundays. Seasonal rates. Children over 12 welcome.

Hosts: Luke and Cynthia Murray
Rooms: 7 (PB) $85-165
Continental Breakfast
Credit Cards: A, B, C, D
Notes: 2, 5, 7, 9, 10, 11, 12

Pilgrim House Inn

123 Spring Street, 02840
(800) 525-8373; FAX (401) 848-0357

The Pilgrim House Inn is on Newport's historic hill and offers 11 spacious rooms with private baths. Each room is furnished in Victorian decor and is immaculate. Breakfast is served each morning and parking is conveniently behind the inn. In warmer weather guests enjoy a spectacular harbor view from the deck while eating breakfast and watching sailboats glide through Newport Harbor. During cooler months sherry and shortbread are served fireside. The inn is one block from Thames Street—a short stroll to Newport's restaurants and unique shops. Come and enjoy fresh flowers and the charm of a bygone era. Children over 12 welcome.

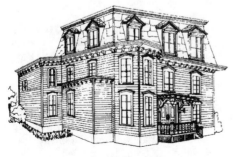

Pilgrim House Inn

Host: Donna Messerlian
Rooms: 11 (9 PB; 2 SB) $50-155
Continental Breakfast
Credit Cards: A, B
Notes: 2, 5, 7, 9, 10, 11, 12, 14

Polly's Place

349 Valley Road, Route 214, 02842
(401) 847-2160
www.bbonline.com/ri/pollysplace/

A quiet retreat one mile from Newport's harbor, historic homes, and sandy beaches. Polly is a long-time Newport resident willing to give helpful advice to travelers interested in the area. Rooms are large, clean, and very attractive. Breakfast is served in the dining room with a lovely view of wildlife and birds of the area. The hostess also offers a one-bedroom apartment that is available by the week and completely equipped. This bed and breakfast has been inspected and approved for cleanliness and quality. Children over 12 welcome.

Host: Polly Canning
Rooms: 4 (2 PB; 2 SB) $80-125
Apartment: 1
Full Breakfast
Credit Cards: None
Notes: 2, 5, 7, 9, 10, 11, 12, 14

Rhode Island House

77 Rhode Island Avenue, 02840
(401) 848-7787; FAX (401) 849-3104

Spacious, elegant, grand 1881 Victorian residence featuring unsurpassed sun-filled rooms, personalized decor, and relaxed ambiance. Each bedroom has a private bath, fine linens, queen-size bed, and air conditioning. Fireplaces, Jacuzzis, and private deck available. Easy walk to restaurants, shopping, beach, and tourism sites. A full gourmet breakfast is prepared by a renowned chef to the Newport summer colony.

Host: Michael Dupre
Rooms: 5 (PB) $95-225
Full Breakfast
Credit Cards: A, B, C
Notes: 2, 5, 7, 9, 10, 11, 12

7 No smoking; 8 Children welcome; 9 Social drinking allowed; 10 Tennis nearby; 11 Swimming nearby; 12 Golf nearby; 13 Skiing nearby; 14 May be booked through a travel agent; 15 Handicapped accessible.

Spring Street Inn

Spring Street Inn

Corner of Howard Street, 353 Spring Street, 02840
(401) 847-4767; e-mail: sprngstlinn@aol.com

Circa 1858 Empire Victorian, centrally in
downtown Newport on a residential street.
Open February through December. Cozy,
quaint, and romantic. The inn's amenities
include a gourmet full breakfast with choice
of hot entrées, afternoon refreshments in the
guest living room/library, on-site parking,
air conditioning, fresh flowers throughout
inn, and concierge services. No smoking.
AAA- and ABBA-approved. Five guest
rooms with private baths, one harbor-view
suite, one two-bedroom suite are offered.

Hosts: Patricia Golder and Jack Lang
Rooms: 5 (PB) $65-220
Suites: 2
Full Breakfast
Credit Cards: A, B
Notes: 2, 7, 9, 10, 11, 12, 14

Stella Maris Inn

91 Washington Street, 02840
(401) 849-2862

Elegant, romantic 1861 Victorian mansion
completely restored in 1990. Some rooms

with water views and fireplaces, all tastefully furnished with antiques. Large wraparound front porch with water view.
Spacious gardens. Hearty Continental
breakfast featuring homemade muffins and
breads. Walking distance to town. Parking
on premises.

Hosts: Dorothy and Ed Madden
Rooms: 8 (PB) $75-175
Continental Breakfast
Credit Cards: None
Notes: 2, 5, 7, 9, 10, 11, 12, 14

The Victorian Ladies Inn

63 Memorial Boulevard, 02840
(401) 849-9960

The inn is circa 1850s. Established and
totally refurbished in 1985. The inn is
appointed with period pieces. The rooms
have down quilts, lots of wonderful fabrics;
all rooms are light, airy, and fresh. There
are lovely courtyards, with a profusion of
flowers and plants. The inn is just three
blocks from the public beaches, shops, and
restaurants. The inn has been featured in
many popular publications, such as *Bride's*,
Glamour, *Country Inns*, etc.

Hosts: Don and Hélène O'Neill
Rooms: 11 (PB; $95-185
Full Breakfast
Credit Cards: A, B
Notes: 2, 7, 9, 10, 11, 12, 14

Villa Liberté

22 Liberty Street, 02840-3221
(401) 846-7444; (800) 392-3717
www.villaliberte.com

Neatly tucked away off historic Bellevue
Avenue, the Villa Liberté offers the charm
and romance of the City by the Sea. From
warm cherrywood furnishings to lush
imported bedding, the villa offers uniquely
appointed queen-size rooms, elegant master
suites, and comfortable apartment suites;
each with private bath, air conditioning,
telephone, TV, and parking. Dramatic black
and white tile baths feature pedestal sinks
and arched alcoves. Enjoy buffet Continen-

NOTES: Credit cards accepted: A MasterCard; B Visa; C American Express; D Discover; E Diner's Club;
F Other; 2 Personal checks accepted; 3 Lunch available; 4 Dinner available; 5 Open all year; 6 Pets welcome;

tal breakfast in the tea room or on the terrace sun deck. Walk to the mansions, Newport's beautiful beaches, Brick Marketplace, and the wharf area.

Host: Leigh Anne Mosco
Rooms: 15 (PB) $69-225
Continental Breakfast
Credit Cards: A, B, C
Notes: 7, 8, 10, 11, 12

The Willows of Newport, Romantic Inn and Garden

8 Willow Street, Historic Point, 02840-1927
(401) 846-5486
www.newportri.com/users/willows

In the historic section of Newport, the Willows pampers guests with secret gardens, handcrafted canopied beds, fresh flowers, mints on pillows, champagne glasses and silver ice bucket, and the lights on dim. Breakfast in bed on bone china and silver service. Three blocks from downtown/waterfront. Parking and air conditioning. A Continental plus breakfast served. Open year-round. Three-star rating from Mobil. Award of Excellence by American Bed & Breakfast Association. Awarded Best Garden in 1994, 1995, and 1996. America Online's Inn of the Week, February 1997.

Host: Patricia Murphy
Rooms: 5 (PB) $98-198
Continental Breakfast
Credit Cards: None
Notes: 2, 5, 7, 9, 10, 11, 12, 14

The Willows of Newport

Yankee Peddler Inn

113 Touro Street, 02840
(401) 846-1323; (800) 427-9444

An inn of rare charm and easy elegance centrally positioned only a few blocks from the waterfront on historic Touro Street. Parking and Continental breakfast included. Dinner and sailing packages available.

Host: Tobiann Quigg
Rooms: 19 (17 PB; 2 SB) $55-195
Continental Breakfast
Credit Cards: A, B, C
Notes: 5, 7, 8, 10, 11, 12

NEWPORT (MIDDLETOWN) _____

Lindsey's Guest House

6 James Street, Middletown, 02840
(401) 846-9386

One mile to Newport's famous mansions, Cliff Walk, and the Tennis Hall of Fame. Lindsey's is a split-level home with a large yard, deck, Continental plus breakfast, and off-street parking. Ten-minute walk to beaches and Norman Bird Sanctuary.

Host: Anne
Rooms: 3 (PB) $50-90
Continental Breakfast
Credit Cards: A, B, C
Notes: 2, 5, 7, 8, 9, 10, 11, 12, 14

NORTH KINGSTOWN _____

The Fifty Seven Bed and Breakfast

57 Thomas Street, 02852
(401) 294-7201

Enjoy a friendly stay at Fifty Seven—a comfortable contemporary Cape cottage, three minutes from Wickford's historic district, harbor, and shopping. Guest bedroom with private bath has access to a large outdoor pool and landscaped garden. Air conditioning and TV/VCR in room. Near South County beaches, sailing, golf, and bird watching. Home-cooked breakfasts are a special feature.

Host: Audrey Ebrahim
Rooms: 1 (PB) $65-75
Full Breakfast
Credit Cards: None
Notes: 2, 5, 7, 9, 10, 11, 12, 13

The John Updike House

19 Pleasant Street, Wickford Village, 02852-5019
(401) 294-4905; FAX (401) 295-2825

Built in 1745, this Georgian has retained its beauty and charm for over 250 years. Only bed and breakfast on shore of Narragansett Bay and Wickford Harbor with its own private sandy beach. Accommodations vary with individual needs: one of two bedrooms with common living room (shared bath); a suite of two bedrooms and common living room; an apartment that includes suite and full private kitchen. Excellent travel base to Newport, ocean beaches, Providence, Cape Cod, Boston. Smoking in designated areas only. In national historic register.

Hosts: Mary Anne and Bill Sabo
Rooms: Variable $100-200
Continental Breakfast
Credit Cards: None
Notes: 2, 5, 8, 9, 10, 11, 12, 13, 14

PROVIDENCE

Old Court Bed and Breakfast

144 Benefit Street, 02903
(401) 751-2002

In the heart of Providence's historic Benefit Street area, guests will find the Old Court, where tradition is combined with contemporary standards of luxury. The Old Court was built in 1863 and reflects early Victorian styles. In rooms that overlook downtown Providence and Brown University, visitors feel as if they have entered a more gracious era. Lunch and dinner available by request. Inquire about accommodations for children. Smoking permitted in designated areas only.

Host: David Dolbashian
Rooms: 11 (PB) $95-250
Full Breakfast
Credit Cards: A, B, C, D
Notes: 2, 5, 14

State House Inn

State House Inn

43 Jewett Street, 02908
(401) 351-6111

In the center of a quiet and quaint neighborhood, the State House Inn is a 100-year-old building newly restored and renovated into a country bed and breakfast. Minutes from downtown Providence and the many local colleges and universities. Brings country living to the big city.

Hosts: Frank and Monica Hopton
Rooms: 10 (PB) $79-109
Full Breakfast
Credit Cards: A, B, C, D
Notes: 5, 7, 8, 9, 10, 12, 13, 14

PROVIDENCE AREA

Historic Jacob Hill Farm Bed and Breakfast/Inn

120 Jacob Street, Seekonk, MA 02771
(508) 336-9165; (888) 336-9165
FAX (508) 336-0951

Casual elegance. Built in 1722, with a long history of hosting some of America's most affluent families, including the Vanderbilts. Recently updated rooms are spacious with queen- and king-size beds and private bathrooms or suites. Some with a Jacuzzi. Each room individually appointed with antiques and traditional wall coverings, some with fireplaces and whirlpool tubs.

Historic Jacob Hill Farm

In-ground pool, tennis, stable, and riding lessons available, or just relax in the gazebo. Ten minutes from Providence, Rhode Island. One hour from Boston, Cape Cod, or Newport.

Hosts: Bill and Eleonora Rezek
Rooms: 5 (PB) $95-225
Full Breakfast
Credit Cards: A, B, C, D
Notes: 5, 7, 9, 10, 11, 12, 13, 14, 15

SOUTH KINGSTOWN

The Kings' Rose

1747 Mooresfield Road, 02879
(401) 783-5222; (888) 230-ROSE

This mini-estate (1933) offers two acres of rose-filled gardens, tennis, sunny public rooms, easy access to a half-dozen ocean beaches. Just east of historic Kingston village and the University of Rhode Island, the inn is 30 minutes from Newport's mansions and Mystic (Connecticut) Seaport and Aquarium. Fine dining, antiquing, wildlife preserves, music, and theater nearby. On Rhode Island Route 138, three and one-half miles west of U.S. Route 1, two miles east of West Kingston (Amtrak) Railroad station. Inquire about accommodations for pets.

Hosts: Barbara and Perry Viles
Rooms: 5 (PB and SB) $75-120
Full Breakfast
Credit Cards: None
Notes: 2, 5, 7, 8, 9, 10, 11, 12, 13, 14

Larchwood Inn

521 Main Street, Wakefield, 02879
(401) 783-5454; (800) 275-5450
FAX (401) 783-1800

The Larchwood Inn is a family-run country inn that has kept pace with the 20th century without sacrificing its rural beauty. Most rooms have private baths, and all guests are encouraged to use the services of the main inn, which includes three dining rooms (all of which serve three meals daily) and a cocktail lounge (with lunch and happy hour daily and live music on the weekends). Near beaches, boating, hiking, horseback and bike riding, and skiing. Breakfast not included in rates.

Hosts: Francis and Diann Browning
Rooms: 20 (12 PB; 8 SB) $40-110
Credit Cards: A, B, C, D, E
Notes: 2, 3, 4, 5, 6, 8, 9, 10, 11, 12, 13, 14

WATCH HILL

Watch Hill Inn and Restaurant

38 Bay Street, 02891
(800) 356-9314; FAX (401) 596-9410
www.digiworld.com/watchhillinn

A romantic seaside inn overlooking the bay in historic Watch Hill village. Pleasant stroll to breathtaking beaches, quaint shops, famous carousel. Deck seaside restaurant serves fresh seafood, steaks, pastas, grilled pizzas. Relax with a favorite beverage on the outside deck and enjoy the most spectacular sunsets in the area. Well-suited for a romantic getaway, the Watch Hill Inn also specializes in wedding receptions, rehearsal dinners, private parties, and corporate meeting and seminars for up to 200 guests. Lunch and dinner available seasonally.

Hosts: Mark Szaco, general manager
Rooms: 16 (PB) $95-195
Continental Breakfast
Credit Cards: A, B
Notes: 5, 8, 9, 10, 11, 12

7 No smoking; 8 Children welcome; 9 Social drinking allowed; 10 Tennis nearby; 11 Swimming nearby; 12 Golf nearby; 13 Skiing nearby; 14 May be booked through a travel agent; 15 Handicapped accessible.

WESTERLY

Nutmeg Bed and Breakfast Agency

P.O. Box 1117, West Hartford, 06127-1117
(860) 236-6698; (800) 727-7592
FAX (860) 232-7680

504. Savor the splendid views from the wraparound stone porch of this turn-of-the-century bed and breakfast. There are 11 guest rooms, four with private baths. The home has a large family room equipped with a player piano, cable TV, games, and a variety of reading material. Pick-up available from local train station or airport. If guests love the beach, this home is a perfect base for enjoying the five Rhode Island beaches nearby. Only minutes from Mystic, Connecticut. Continental breakfast. Limited smoking. Children welcome. Pets in residence.

507. Five minutes from the beach, this renovated 1920 summer home is by a saltwater pond that looks out to the ocean. Originally a working farm, it provides the perfect quiet getaway. One guest room has two double beds, many windows, and a private bath with shower. The second guest room has a canopied double bed, private deck with a view of the water, and a private bath with a tub. For the family getaway, there are also two summer cottages available, one with three bedrooms and the other with six. Continental breakfast. No smoking. Children welcome. Pets in residence.

Woody Hill Bed and Breakfast

149 South Woody Hill Road, 02891
(401) 322-0452

The hostess, a high school English teacher, invites guests to share this reproduction Colonial home with antiques and gardens. Snuggle under quilts, relax on the porch swing, visit nearby Newport and Mystic, and swim in the pool or at beautiful ocean beaches. Westerly has it all!

Host: Dr. Ellen L. Madison
Rooms: 5 (4 PB or SB) $65-125
Full Breakfast
Credit Cards: None
Notes: 2, 5, 7, 8, 9, 10, 11, 12

Woody Hill

Vermont

ALBURG

Auberge Alburg

Rural Delivery 1, Box 3, 05440
(802) 796-3169; (514) 481-3922

Auberge Alburg has a view of Lake Champlain and is about halfway between Burlington and Montréal, Québec. The atmosphere is informal and Continental. The hosts speak a number of languages, including French. All of the rates include Continental breakfast but dinners can be arranged. Get ideas about touring Montréal as well as the Green Mountains and the Adirondacks from the hosts. There is one suite, completely private, with bath and deck with a lake view. The house has three upstairs guest rooms with shared common areas and bath. The barn has a loft with skylight and private bath in the barn proper. Dormitory space for small groups is also available. Inquire about accommodations for pets. Smoking is permitted on decks and designated areas only.

Hosts: Charles Stastny and Gabrielle Tyrnauer
Rooms: 6 (2 PB; 4 SB) $50-85
Continental Breakfast
Credit Cards: None
Notes: 2, 3, 5, 8, 9, 11, 12, 13

Thomas Mott Bed and Breakfast

Blue Rock Road, Route 2, Box 149B, 05440-9620
(802) 796-3736 (phone/FAX); (800) 348-0843
www.go-native.com/Inns/0162.html

Hosted by Patrick J. Schallert, a prominent importer and distributor of fine wines, retired, this pre-Civil War shoreline property offers a full view of the Green Mountains or the Adirondacks from all rooms in this beautifully restored bed and breakfast. One hour from Burlington or Montréal Island. Enjoy four-season lake activities; cross-country skiing, lawn games, complimentary canoes, private 75-foot dock, swimming, fishing, or sunning; 12 Ben & Jerry's ice creams (complimentary); AAA three diamonds; ABBA three crowns. Children over six are welcome.

Host: Patrick J. Schallert Sr.
Rooms: 5 (PB) $75-95
Full Breakfast
Credit Cards: A, B, C, D, E, F
Notes: 2, 5, 7, 9, 10, 11, 12, 13, 14

ANDOVER

Inn at HighView

Rural Route 1, Box 201A, 05143
(802) 875-2724

Vermont the way guests always dreamed it would be, but the way they've never found it. Secluded and relaxed elegance; breathtaking views of countryside from overlook gazebo and screened porch. Classically restored 18th-century farmhouse comfortably furnished. Warm conversation by a blazing fire, hearty breakfasts, and gourmet dinners. All guest rooms have private baths. Cross-country skiing-hiking trails on 72 acres. Rock garden and swimming pool. Ten minutes from Okemo Mountain, Weston, and Chester. Conference facilities and planning services available.

Hosts: Greg Bohan and Sal Massaro
Rooms: 8 (PB) $95-155
Full Breakfast
Credit Cards: A, B
Notes: 2, 4, 5, 6, 7, 8, 9, 10, 11, 12, 13, 14

7 No smoking; 8 Children welcome; 9 Social drinking allowed; 10 Tennis nearby; 11 Swimming nearby; 12 Golf nearby; 13 Skiing nearby; 14 May be booked through a travel agent; 15 Handicapped accessible.

Vermont

The Arlington Inn

ARLINGTON

The Arlington Inn

Historic Route 7A, P.O. Box 369, 05250
(800) 443-9442
e-mail: arlingtoninn@compuserve.com
www.arlingtoninn.com

A stately Greek Revival mansion set on lushly landscaped lawns offers elegantly appointed rooms filled with antiques and amenities. All rooms have private baths, air conditioning, and include breakfast. Between Bennington and Manchester. Antique shops, boutiques, museums, skiing, hiking, biking, canoeing, fly-fishing, golfing, and many other outdoor activities are nearby. Tennis on the private court. Outstanding cuisine is served by romantic candlelight in the fire-placed, award-winning dining room with superb service. AAA three-diamond rating, and Mobil three-star rating.

Hosts: Deborah and Mark Gagnon
Rooms: 19 (PB) $70-205
Full Breakfast
Credit Cards: A, B, C, D, E
Notes: 3, 4, 5, 7, 8, 9, 10, 11, 12, 13, 14, 15

Arlington Manor House Bed and Breakfast

Buck Hill Road, RR2-420-Antiques, 05250
(802) 375-6784; e-mail: kiboodle@Vtel.com
www.vermonter.net/~kiboodle

The Arlington Manor House is a charming, unusual Dutch Colonial home which was built in 1905 as a summer estate. In 1987 Al and Kit McAllister purchased the home. In August 1991 it was converted into a bed and breakfast with the added feature of many beautiful antiques for sale. Nutmeg, a golden retriever, known for her friendly greeting as well as a sad face when guests leave. Bring a camcorder for a bed and breakfast's "funniest home movies." Terrace char-grill (BYO). Tea social at 4 P.M.—ice (BYOB). Bikers' workshop. Bench stand. Beautiful views of lawns and four mountain peaks. River tubes. Garage parking for two available. Rates include a full breakfast and brunch. Children 10 and older welcome.

Hosts: Kit and Al McAllister
Rooms: 5 (3 PB; 2 SB) $65-130
Full Breakfast
Credit Cards: A, B, C
Notes: 2, 3, 5, 7, 10, 11, 12, 13, 14

Country Willows

East Arlington Road, RR 2, Box 40, 05250
(802) 375-0019; (800) 796-2585
FAX (802) 375-8302
www.cimarron.net/usa/vt/cw.html

Country Willows, a gracious 1860s Victorian with a wraparound porch and is a village historic landmark on spacious parklike lawns in the heart of this village's picturesque historic district. The town of Arlington is hugged by the Green Mountains and meanders along the pristine waters of the famed Battenkill River. Choose from one of the individually appointed, antique-filled spacious rooms. Victorian and country decor. All rooms have queen-size beds, handmade quilts, some with fireplaces and claw-foot tubs.

Hosts: Craig and Kathleen Yanez
Rooms: 3 (PB) $65-145
Full Breakfast
Credit Cards: None
Notes: 2, 5, 7, 8, 10, 11, 12, 13, 14

Hill Farm Inn

Rural Route 2, Box 2015, 05250
(802) 375-2269; (800) 882-2545
www.hillfarminn.com

Take a step back in time and experience the quiet, comfortable nature of this historic inn

NOTES: Credit cards accepted: A MasterCard; B Visa; C American Express; D Discover; E Diner's Club; F Other; 2 Personal checks accepted; 3 Lunch available; 4 Dinner available; 5 Open all year; 6 Pets welcome; 7 No smoking; 8 Children welcome; 9 Social drinking allowed; 10 Tennis nearby; 11 Swimming nearby; 12 Golf nearby; 13 Skiing nearby; 14 May be booked through a travel agent; 15 Handicapped accessible.

Hill Farm Inn

on 50 acres of farmland, with a mile of frontage on the Battenkill River. Guests will enjoy magnificent mountain views in every direction. Full country breakfast, cooked to order. Four-course dinner available. Complimentary jar of homemade jam. Make Hill Farm Inn your place in the country and be surrounded with caring comfort. Four seasonal cabins (May through October) with baths also available. Pets welcome in cabins (May through October) and Lilac Suite only.

Hosts: George and Joanne Hardy
Rooms: 13 (8 PB; 5 SB) $70-125
Full Breakfast
Credit Cards: A, B, C, D
Notes: 2, 4, 5, 6, 8, 10, 11, 12, 13, 14

Shenandoah Farm

Route 313, 05250
(802) 375-6372

This Colonial home near the Battenkill River is five miles from Route 7A on Route 313. Close to Norman Rockwell Museum and recreational activities. Five antique-filled guest rooms are offered with private baths.

Rooms: 5 (PB) $70-80
Full Breakfast
Credit Cards: A, B
Notes: 2, 3, 5, 7, 8, 9, 10, 11, 12, 13, 14, 15

BENNINGTON

American Country Collection

1353 Union Street, Schenectady, NY 12308
(518) 370-4948; (800) 810-4948
FAX (518) 393-1634 (call first)
e-mail: carolbnbres@mon.com

041. This carefully landscaped Victorian has a stream on the back property and a large front porch for rocking. There's a wood-burning stove on the brick hearth in the first-floor common room. Braided rugs cover wide-plank pine floors. Five guest rooms, all with private baths, and one cottage with king-size bed and private bath with Jacuzzi. Full gourmet breakfast includes pancakes, French toast, eggs, Belgian waffles, blintzes, or quiche. Smoking outdoors only. Children over 11 welcome. Ten percent gratuity. $85-145.

Molly Stark Inn

1067 East Main Street, 05201
(800) 356-3076
e-mail: mollyinn@vermontel.com
www.mollystarkinn.com

A true country inn with an intimate atmosphere, this 1890 Victorian home is on the main road through a historic town in southwestern Vermont and welcomes visitors year-round. Decorated and tastefully furnished with antiques, country collectibles, braided rugs on gleaming hardwood floors, and patchwork quilts on the beds. Private guest cottage with brass bed, Jacuzzi, and woodstove. Guests are invited to use the wraparound front porch with rocking chairs, and the den and parlor with wood-burning stoves are most inviting on those cool Vermont nights. Clean, affordable. Champagne dinner packages available.

Hosts: Cammi and Reed Fendler
Rooms: 7 (PB) $65-95
Cottage: $145
Full Breakfast
Credit Cards: A, B, C, D
Notes: 2, 4, 5, 7, 8, 9, 12, 13, 14

NOTES: Credit cards accepted: A MasterCard; B Visa; C American Express; D Discover; E Diner's Club; F Other; 2 Personal checks accepted; 3 Lunch available; 4 Dinner available; 5 Open all year; 6 Pets welcome;

BETHEL

Greenhurst Inn

Rural Route 2, Box 60, River Street, 05032-9404
(802) 234-9474; (800) 521-2553

Queen Anne Victorian mansion listed in
the National Register of Historic Places. In
central Vermont near I-89, halfway between
Boston and Montréal. Mints on the pillows
and a library of 3,000 volumes. The inn
was featured in the *New York Times* on
March 3, 1991. Inquire about accommodations for pets.

Host: Lyle Wolf
Rooms: 13 (7 PB; 6 SB) $50-100
Continental Breakfast
Credit Cards: A, B
Notes: 2, 5, 8, 9, 10, 11, 12, 13, 14

BOLTON VALLEY

Black Bear Inn

HC 33, Box 717, 05477 (mailing)
Bolton Access Road (location)
(802) 434-2126; (800) 395-6335
FAX (802) 434-5161; e-mail: blkbear@wcvt.com
www.blkbearinn.com

A true Vermont country inn 2,000 feet above
the valley floor with fantastic views of the
Green Mountain range or fall foliage. Minutes from Burlington, one hour from Canada,
antiquing, golfing, fishing, and 6,000 private

Black Bear Inn

acres for hiking, fishing, biking, and horseback riding. Twenty-four decorated rooms
with antiques, handmade quilts, telephones,
color TVs, fireplaces, and Vermont
firestoves. Relax poolside or soak in the hot
tubs. Enjoy gourmet dining in the evening
and a hearty Vermont breakfast.

Hosts: The Richardson and Wallace Families
Rooms: 24 (PB) $69-109
Full and Continental Breakfast
Credit Cards: A, B
Notes: 4, 5, 7, 8, 9, 10, 11, 12, 13, 14, 15

BRANDON

American Country Collection

1353 Union Street, Schenectady, NY 12308
(518) 370-4948; (800) 810-4948
FAX (518) 393-1634 (call first)
e-mail: carolbnbres@mon.com

177. This restored 1860s three-story manor
offers travelers a truly Victorian experience.
The owners painstakingly gathered authentic Victorian furnishings that make the intimacy of the inn more than just a notion.
The elegant breakfast and common rooms
are comfortably arranged for socializing or
just relaxing before the fireplace with a
good book. Guests may enjoy the wicker
rockers on the porch, or stroll through the
gardens. Four guest rooms with private and
shared baths are on the second floor. Two
additional guest rooms with private baths
are on the third floor. Full breakfast served.
Children 12 and over welcome. Smoking
permitted outside only. $75-95.

The Brandon Inn

20 Park Street, 05733
(802) 247-5766; (800) 639-8485
FAX (802) 247-5768
www.brandoninn.com

Restored 1786 inn in the national historic
register, on the village green. Individually
decorated guest rooms have private baths.
Beautifully appointed spacious public
rooms. Secluded pool. Fine award-winning

7 No smoking; 8 Children welcome; 9 Social drinking allowed; 10 Tennis nearby; 11 Swimming nearby;
12 Golf nearby; 13 Skiing nearby; 14 May be booked through a travel agent; 15 Handicapped accessible.

dining. Lunch and dinner. Terrace. Ask about family rates—children welcome. Weddings are a speciality.

Hosts: Sarah and Louis Pattis
Rooms: 35 (PB) $90-155
Full Breakfast
Credit Cards: A, B, C, D
Notes: 2, 3, 4, 5, 8, 10, 11, 12, 13, 14, 15

Churchill House Inn
Rural Route 3, Box 3115, 05733
(802) 247-3078; FAX (802) 247-6851
e-mail: rciatt@sover.net; www.inntoinn.com

40 Putney Road

A century-old inn at the edge of the Green Mountain National Forest is a center for outdoor activities with extensive hiking, biking, and cross-country skiing available. Outdoor pool and rental bikes. The inn's casual atmosphere, award-winning cuisine, and comfortable, antique-appointed accommodations complement an active day. All eight rooms have private baths, some with Jacuzzis. The sky-lit porch and two sitting rooms provide a homey setting. A candle-lit, four-course dinner served around an antique oak table completes the house-party atmosphere. Picnic lunches available.

Hosts: The Jackson Family
Rooms: 8 (PB)
Full Breakfast
Credit Cards: A, B, C
Notes: 2, 4, 7, 8, 9, 10, 11, 12, 13, 14

BRATTLEBORO

40 Putney Road Bed and Breakfast
40 Putney Road, 05301
(802) 254-6268; (800) 941-2413
FAX (802) 258-2673; e-mail: frtyptny@sover.net

One of Brattleboro's finest architectural landmarks, this antique-filled estate is nestled along the West River yet is within walking distance to downtown. The grounds feature classically landscaped gardens, mature trees, and fountains. Four individually decorated guest rooms, two with gas fireplaces, offer queen-size beds,

telephone with modem, TV/VCR, Caswell-Massey toiletries, and fresh flowers. Other amenities include a full breakfast, turn-down service, self-serve selection of beverages and fresh fruit, port wine, a video library, and air conditioning. Featured in *Vermont* magazine.

Hosts: Pete and Joan Broderick
Rooms: 4 (PB) $105-175
Full Breakfast
Credit Cards: A, B, C, D
Notes: 2, 5, 7, 9, 10, 11, 12, 13, 14

The Tudor Bed and Breakfast and Culinary Retreat
76 Western Avenue, 05301
(802) 257-4983; FAX (802) 258-2632

Enjoy luxurious casual comfort and personalized service. The Tudor is an elegantly furnished brick mansion with striking formal gardens. All rooms have queen-size beds, private bathrooms and telephone lines, cable TVs, air conditioning, and fireplaces. A Yamaha grand piano awaits guests' tickling of her ivories. Savor a gourmet breakfast, customized private dining, and culinary classes. Convenient to four seasons' recreation, tourist destinations, fine restaurants, and shopping. "Welcome to your home!" Corporate welcome.

Hosts: Shelly Huber-Smith and William P. Smith
Rooms: 3 (PB) $69-165
Continental to Full Breakfast
Credit Cards: A, B, C, D, F
Notes: 3, 4, 5, 7, 8, 9, 10, 11, 12, 13, 14

NOTES: Credit cards accepted: A MasterCard; B Visa; C American Express; D Discover; E Diner's Club; F Other; 2 Personal checks accepted; 3 Lunch available; 4 Dinner available; 5 Open all year; 6 Pets welcome;

BROOKFIELD

Green Trails Inn

By the Floating Bridge, 05036
(802) 276-3412; (800) 243-3412

Comfortably elegant 14-room historic inn—relax and be pampered! Suites with Jacuzzis or fireplaces, lake-view rooms. Thirty-five-kilometer cross-county skiing from the front door. Ice skating, snowshoeing, sledding, and horse-drawn sleigh rides available in winter. Fishing, swimming, canoeing, hiking, and biking can be enjoyed summer and fall. An antique clock collection is displayed throughout the inn; clocks repaired and sold on premises. Bed and breakfast year-round. Wonderful dining just across the road.

Hosts: Sue and Mark Erwin
Rooms: 14 (8 PB; 6 SB) $75-125
Credit Cards: A, B, D
Notes: 2, 5, 7, 9, 10, 11, 12, 13, 14

BURLINGTON

Burlington Redstone Bed and Breakfast

497 South Willard Street, Route 7, 05401
(802) 862-0508

In the national historic register. This lovingly restored home offers warm hospitality and gracious accommodations with art and

Burlington Redstone

antiques from around the world. Begin the day with coffee in the solarium overlooking Lake Champlain and the Adirondacks, followed by a country breakfast in the formal dining room. Guests are invited to wander about the patio and porches or stroll the flower-filled gardens. Walk to Church Street Marketplace, shopping, restaurants, theater, and the university. Discount tickets to Shelburne Museum and local restaurants.

Host: Helen Sellstedt
Room: 3 (SB) $75-95
Full Breakfast
Credit Cards: None
Notes: 2, 5, 7, 9, 10, 11, 12, 13

Hartwell House Bed and Breakfast

170 Ferguson Avenue, 05401
(888) 658-9242
www.members.aol.com/hartwellbb

Hartwell House offers a warm homelike atmosphere in a quiet Burlington neighborhood. Easy access to downtown shopping and activities or short walks to nearby lake, beach, bike path, and shopping centers. Convenient location provides guests varied options—restaurants, theaters, museums, boat rides, colleges, churches, hiking, skiing, swimming. Continental breakfast, fireplaced living room, large deck, and pool provide families, couples, singles comforts of home. Hartwell House welcomes everyone!

Host: Linda Hartwell
Rooms: 2-3 (SB) $45-65
Continental Breakfast
Credit Cards: None
Notes: 2, 5, 7, 8, 9, 10, 11, 12, 13

CABOT

Creamery Inn Bed and Breakfast

P.O. Box 187, 05647
(802) 563-2819

This spacious and comfortable home, circa 1835, is picturesquely set only a mile from

---

7 No smoking; 8 Children welcome; 9 Social drinking allowed; 10 Tennis nearby; 11 Swimming nearby; 12 Golf nearby; 13 Skiing nearby; 14 May be booked through a travel agent; 15 Handicapped accessible.

Cabot Creamery, with new lambs each spring. Guests may walk the country roads, enjoy ponds and waterfalls, drive to Burke Mountain or Stowe for skiing, or just relax. Sitting room, original stenciling. Enjoy the full, homemade breakfasts, featuring fruit, baked dish, and sweet breads. Special rates for stays of more than two nights. Candlelight dinners by advance reservation.

Host: Dan Lloyd
Rooms: 3 (PB) $55-75
Full Breakfast
Credit Cards: None
Notes: 2, 4, 5, 7, 8, 9, 11, 13, 15

CHELSEA

Shire Inn

Main Street, 05038
(802) 685-3031; e-mail: J&K@shireinn.com
www.shireinn.com

Vermont before factory outlets and ski resorts? Come to Chelsea! In an 1832 brick mansion, bright, antique-furnished guest rooms with canopied beds, wood-burning fireplaces, 10-foot ceilings, and tall windows await guests. On 23 acres with gardens, a river, farm bridge, and hiking trails. Candlelight gourmet dinners. A romantic respite in a historic, unspoiled village. Ideal central location for exploring the best of Vermont. Come see!

Hosts: Jay and Karen Keller
Rooms: 6 (PB) $95-205
Cottage: 1
Full Breakfast
Credit Cards: A, B, D
Notes: 2, 4, 5, 7, 9, 10, 11, 12, 13, 14

CHESTER

Greenleaf Inn

Depot Street, Box 188, 05143
(802) 875-3171

A gracious 1860s home, now an elegant, yet comfortable, village bed and breakfast. Five charming rooms furnished with antiques and country quilts. All with full private baths.

Walk to antiques, restaurants, and village green attractions. A hearty Vermont breakfast is served each morning in the sunny dining room. Fully air conditioned.

Hosts: Jerry and Robin Szawerda
Rooms: 5 (PB) $85-110
Full Breakfast
Credit Cards: A, B, C, D
Notes: 2, 4, 5, 7, 9, 10, 11, 12, 13

Henry Farm Inn

Henry Farm Inn

Green Mountain Turnpike, P.O. Box 646, 05143
(802) 875-2674; (800) 723-8213

The Henry Farm Inn provides the beauty of Vermont with old-time simplicity. Nestled on 50 acres of rolling hills and meadows, it assures peace and quiet. Spacious rooms, private baths, country sitting rooms, kitchen, and sunny dining room guarantee a feeling of home. Come visit for a day or more.

Host: B. M. Bowman
Rooms: 7 (PB) $50-90
Full Breakfast
Credit Cards: A, B, C
Notes: 2, 5, 7, 8, 9, 10, 11, 12, 13, 14

The Hugging Bear Inn and Shoppe

244 Main Street, 05143
(802) 875-2412; (800) 325-0519
www.vbvonline.com/huggingbear.com

Bed, breakfast, and bears. Charming Victorian home on the village green. The shop has

NOTES: Credit cards accepted: A MasterCard; B Visa; C American Express; D Discover; E Diner's Club; F Other; 2 Personal checks accepted; 3 Lunch available; 4 Dinner available; 5 Open all year; 6 Pets welcome;

The Hugging Bear

more than 6,000 teddy bears, and guests may "adopt" a bear for the night as long as he is back to work in the shop by 9:00 A.M. Puppet show often performed at breakfast; breakfast music provided by an 1890 music box. Two lovable cats in residence. A magical place to visit! Two-night minimum stay required for holidays and high season weekends.

Hosts: The Thomases
Rooms: 6 (PB) $85-115
Full Breakfast
Credit Cards: A, B, C, D
Notes: 2, 5, 7, 8, 9, 10, 11, 12, 13

Inn Victoria

333 Main Street, P.O. Box 788, 05143
(802) 875-4288; (800)732-4288

Victorian elegance in a village setting. Rooms feature fireplaces Jacuzzi tubs, and the occasional TV. Enjoy tea in front of the fireplace in the parlor or on one of the

Inn Victoria

porches. Top off a strenuous day with a soak in the hot tub. Outside the inn, snow sports abound in winter. Summer brings theater, music, cycling, hiking, and museums. Shopping and antiques are available year-round. There is a suite with full kitchen and living room. Space is available for workshops and weddings.

Hosts: Norbert Gauthier and Cathy Hasbroock
     with Rusty and Gabe, the watch cats
Rooms: 9 (8 PB; 1 SB) $85-150
Full Breakfast
Credit Cards: A, B, C, D
Notes: 2, 5, 7, 8, 9, 11, 12, 13, 15

Night with a Native Bed and Breakfast

P.O. Box 327, 05143-0327
(802) 875-2616

Feel at home at this bed and breakfast. Enjoy the warm ambiance of hand-stenciled rooms, family-made rugs, antiques, collectibles, and wood stoves. TV in living room. The host, a sixth-generation Vermonter, offers true Vermont hospitality. Complimentary refreshments. Delicious breakfast served in dining room which was originally a one-room schoolhouse. Walking distance to restaurants and shops.

Host: Doris Hastings
Rooms: 2 (PB) $60-95
Full Breakfast
Credit Cards: None
Notes: 2, 5, 7, 9, 10, 11, 12, 13

CHESTER (ROCKINGHAM)

The Madrigal Inn and Fine Arts Center

61 Williams River Road, 05143
(802) 463-1339; (800) 854-2208
FAX (802) 463-8169; madrigal@sover.net
www.sover.net/~madrigal

The Madrigal Inn is a harmony of natural beauty inside and out, amid hundreds of acres of mountain meadows and forest. Five kilometer trails, pond. New post-and-beam

7 No smoking; 8 Children welcome; 9 Social drinking allowed; 10 Tennis nearby; 11 Swimming nearby; 12 Golf nearby; 13 Skiing nearby; 14 May be booked through a travel agent; 15 Handicapped accessible.

has 11 guest rooms, all with private baths, library, three-storied living room, Palladian windows, three fireplaces. Craft and gift shop. Candlelight breakfast buffet and hot entrée of blueberry pancakes and sausage or French toast and bacon—all served with local maple syrup.

Hosts: Ray and Nancy Dressler
Rooms: 11 (PB) $90-110
Full Breakfast
Credit Cards: A, B, D, E
Notes: 2, 4, 5, 7, 9, 10, 11, 12, 13, 14, 15

CUTTINGSVILLE (SHREWSBURY)

Maple Crest Farm

Lincoln Hill Road, Box 120, 05738
(802) 492-3367

High in the Green Mountains, 10 miles south of Rutland and 12 miles north of Ludlow, this beautiful 1808 27-room historic home has been lovingly preserved for five generations. Cross-country skiing and hiking are offered on the farm. Close to many major ski areas, Rutland, and places of historic interest. A real taste of old Vermont hospitality. Maple syrup made on the premises.

Hosts: William and Donna Smith
Rooms: 6 (1 PB; 5 SB) $54-75
Full Breakfast
Credit Cards: None
Notes: 2, 5, 8, 9, 10, 11, 12, 13, 14

DANBY

Silas Griffith Inn

South Main Street, Rural Route 1, Box 66 F, 05739
(800) 545-1509

Built in 1891 by Vermont's first millionaire, a lovingly restored gracious Victorian mansion and carriage house. Relax in a quiet 19th-century village and walk to antique and gift shops. Full hearty breakfast and elegant dining in the carriage house. "Come, enjoy our beautiful views."

Hosts: Paul and Lois Dansereau
Rooms: 17 (14 PB; 3 SB) $70-91

Full Breakfast
Credit Cards: A, B
Notes: 2, 4, 7, 8, 9, 10, 11, 12, 13, 14

DERBY LINE

The Birchwood Bed and Breakfast

48 Main Street, P.O. Box 550, 05830
(802) 873-9104; FAX (802) 873-9121
e-mail: birchwd@together.net
www.together.net/~birchwd

A 1920 lovingly restored home in a charming village in the Northeast Kingdom at the Canadian border. Three individually decorated, antique-filled bedrooms include private bathrooms. A full breakfast is served each morning in the sunlit dining room. The region offers miles of unspoiled scenery. Enjoy the beauty of the area as well as the comfort and spaciousness of this home. A warm welcome awaits guests at the Birchwood Bed and Breakfast.

Hosts: Betty and Dick Fletcher
Rooms: 3 (PB) $70
Full Breakfast
Credit Cards: None
Notes: 2, 5, 7, 9, 10, 11, 12, 13

The Birchwood

Derby Village Inn

46 Main Street, P.O. Box 1085, 05830
(802) 873-3604; FAX (802) 873-3047

Neoclassical elegance in a circa 1902 home on the Canadian border. Five lovely bedrooms, each with its own individual personality and private bath. Enjoy beautiful sunsets, golfing, downhill and cross-country skiing, hiking, water sports, cycling, snowmobiling, fishing, sleigh rides, antiquing, and most of all—peace and tranquility. Within walking distance of the world's only international library and opera house. Delicious home cooking.

Hosts: Catherine McCormick and Sheila Steplar
Rooms: 5 (PB) $75-100
Credit Cards: A, B, C, D
Notes: 2, 5, 7, 8, 9, 10, 11, 12, 13

EAST BURKE

The Village Inn of East Burke

Route 114, P.O. Box 186, 05832
(802) 626-3161
e-mail: villginn@plainfield.bypass.com
www.discover-vermont.com/banner/villageinn/
   welcome.htm

A cozy and comfortable bed and breakfast in a small rural village. In winter curl up in the sitting area in front of the wood stove with a good book, or in summer tickle one's toes in the cool back yard stream. A guest kitchen available for use. Perfect location for all outdoor activities. Stores, restaurant, laundromat, post office, and church all within walking distance. A perfect getaway for all seasons. Inquire about accommodations for pets.

Hosts: George and Lorraine Willy
Rooms: 4 (PB) $55
Continental Breakfast
Credit Cards: A, B
Notes: 2, 5, 7, 8, 9, 10, 11, 12, 13

EAST DOVER

Cooper Hill Inn

Cooper Hill Road, Box 146, 05341
(802) 348-6333; (800) 783-3229

Informal and cozy hilltop inn with "one of the most spectacular mountain panoramas in all New England." Quiet country road location. Hearty home-cooked meals. Five double rooms, three two-bedroom

family suites, and two large family rooms, all with private baths. Close to area activities. Direct access from inn to mountain biking, hiking, snowmobiling, and cross-country skiing. Just 12 minutes to downhill skiing. Closed for one week in April and November.

Hosts: Pat and Marilyn Hunt
Rooms: 10 (PB) $72-120
Full Breakfast
Credit Cards: A, B, D
Notes: 2, 4, 7, 8, 9, 10, 11, 12, 13, 14

EAST MIDDLEBURY

Waybury Inn

Route 125, 05753
(802) 388-4015; (800) 348-1810

Built in 1810, the Waybury Inn has 14 individually appointed guest rooms, all with private baths. Known to many as the inn featured on *The Bob Newhart Show*, the inn offers dinner daily and Sunday brunch. The Pub opens at 4:00 P.M. No smoking.

Hosts: Marty and Marcia Schuppert
Rooms: 14 (PB) $80-115
Credit Cards: A, B, D, E
Notes: 2, 4, 5, 7, 8, 10, 11, 12, 13, 14

ENOSBURG FALLS

Berkson Farms

RR #1, Box 850, Route 108, 05450
(802) 933-2522

Berkson Farms is a full working dairy farm sitting on a picture-postcard 600 acres up near the Canadian border. The inn offers homey and comfortable lodging in a century-old restored farmhouse where guests can relax and enjoy all the simple, wonderful joys of nature, people, and of life itself. The hosts serve home-cooked country-style meals and warm, friendly Vermont hospitality.

Hosts: Dick and Joanne Keesler
Rooms: 4 (1 PB; 3 SB) $55-65
Full Breakfast

7 No smoking; 8 Children welcome; 9 Social drinking allowed; 10 Tennis nearby; 11 Swimming nearby; 12 Golf nearby; 13 Skiing nearby; 14 May be booked through a travel agent; 15 Handicapped accessible.

Berkson Farms

Credit Cards: None
Notes: 2, 3, 4, 5, 6, 7, 8, 10, 11, 12, 13

ESSEX (BURLINGTON)

The Inn at Essex

70 Essex Way, 05452
(802) 878-1100; (800) 727-4295 (reservations)
FAX (802) 878-0063
e-mail: innessex@together.net
www.innatessex.com

A beautiful 97-room Colonial-style inn, no two rooms alike; 30 rooms have wood-burning fireplaces. Enjoy the library, the art gallery, or watching the chefs in the pastry shop. The most outstanding feature is the food service, which is operated by the acclaimed New England Culinary Institute. There are more than 140 student chefs and 18 chef instructors. Two restaurants offer country, casual, or more formal dining experiences. Enjoy the patio, the outdoor pool, and the gardens. Hiking, snowshoeing. Nearby upscale outlet shopping at Essex Outlet Fair. Ten minutes from Burlington International Airport via complimentary shuttle service. Just minutes from Lake Champlain, the Vermont Teddy Bear Company, Ben & Jerry's Ice Cream Factory, Shelburne Museum, and the University of Vermont. Nonsmoking rooms are available.

Hosts: Jim and Judi Lamberti
Rooms: 97 (PB) $139-199
Continental Breakfast
Credit Cards: A, B, C, D, E
Notes: 2, 3, 4, 5, 8, 9, 10, 11, 12, 13, 14, 15

FAIRFAX

American Country Collection

1353 Union Street, Schenectady, NY 12308
(518) 370-4948; (800) 810-4948
FAX (518) 393-1634 (call first)
e-mail: carolbnbres@mon.com

149. Imagine being in a completely renovated New England carriage house in the year 1790, and begin the journey through this inn with original exposed beams and wood-burning stove. Four rooms are available for guests. Two rooms on the second floor share a bath, and two rooms on the first floor share another bath and a whirlpool tub. Snacks, wine, beer, and soft drinks available, and a fax machine, Macintosh computer, copier, and antique and gift shop are on premises. In the spring, enjoy watching maple syrup being made. Full breakfast. $48-78.

FAIR HAVEN

American Country Collection

1353 Union Street, Schenectady, NY 12308
(518) 370-4948; (800) 810-4948
FAX (518) 393-1634 (call first)
e-mail: carolbnbres@mon.com

077. This circa 1843 Greek Revival home is on three and one-half acres of lawn and gardens and features beautiful moldings and wide-plank pine and maple parquet floors. The five guest rooms, with private baths, have picture-perfect farm and mountain views and are individually decorated in period styles; four have fireplaces. Each room has extra pillows and blankets, quilts, extra-thick towels, reading lamps, TVs, telephones (if requested), candies, and wine glasses. Suites have decanter of sherry. Either mix with other guests or find a quiet corner to curl up with a book. The keeping room has a fireplace and TV. There is also a BYOB tavern. Bike rentals available. Full breakfast served. Smoking permitted in designated areas only. $70-105.

NOTES: Credit cards accepted: A MasterCard; B Visa; C American Express; D Discover; E Diner's Club; F Other; 2 Personal checks accepted; 3 Lunch available; 4 Dinner available; 5 Open all year; 6 Pets welcome;

Maplewood Inn

Maplewood Inn

Route 22A South, 05743
(802) 265-8039; (800) 253-7729 (reservations only)
e-mail: maplewd@sover.net
www.sover.net/~maplewd

Romantic 1843 Greek Revival listed in the National Register of Historic Places offering exquisitely appointed guest rooms and suites with private baths, antiques, working fireplaces, in-room color cable TVs, radios, telephones, and air conditioning. Common rooms include gathering room/library, breakfast room with hot beverage bar, and parlor with games and complimentary cordial bar. Near lakes, skiing, restaurants, and many other attractions. Area's only three-star Mobil-, three-diamond AAA-rated inn. Hearty Continental plus breakfast. Innkeeper/Realtor.

Hosts: Cindy and Doug Baird
Rooms: 5 (PB) $80-135
Continental Breakfast
Credit Cards: A, B, C, D
Notes: 2, 5, 9, 10, 11, 12, 13, 14

FAIRLEE

Elaine's Bed and Breakfast Selections

4987 Kingston Road, Elbridge, NY 13060
(315) 689-2082 (after 10 A.M.)

There are eight guest rooms in the main house, which is more than 200 years old, and three duplex cottages plus a single cottage for a total of 15 rooms. Six rooms in the main house have private baths and two share one. All cottages have private baths,

three have fireplaces, and two have kitchenettes. Main house is nonsmoking. All outdoor activities nearby as well as Quechee Gorge, Maple Grove Maple Museum, Ben & Jerry's Ice Cream Factory, the Cabot Farmer's Cooperative Creamery, Calvin Coolidge homestead, and many other historic sites. Continental breakfast is served in the dining room. Extra person in room six dollars. $54-79.

Silver Maple Lodge and Cottages

Route 5, 05045
(802) 333-4326; (800) 666-1946

Historic bed and breakfast country inn. Cozy rooms with antiques or knotty pine cottages, some with fireplaces. Enjoy the beach, boating, fishing, and swimming at Lake Morey, one mile away. Golf, tennis, skiing, and hot-air balloon rides are nearby. Dartmouth College is 17 miles away. Walk to restaurants. Two-night minimum stay required for holidays. Closed Christmas Eve.

Hosts: Scott and Sharon Wright
Rooms: 16 (14 PB; 2 SB) $56-82
Continental Breakfast
Credit Cards: A, B, C, D
Notes: 2, 6, 8, 9, 10, 11, 12, 13, 14, 15

GAYSVILLE

Laolke Lodge

P.O. Box 107, 05746
(802) 234-9205; e-mail: laolke@juno.com

Just one-half mile off Vermont Route 107, this authentic log house was built in 1964 especially to be an inn. Guests enjoy its cozy, informal, and relaxing atmosphere. Easy access to major ski areas as well as scenic day trips. Every season is special.

Host: Ms. Olive Pratt
Rooms: 5 (5 SB) $25-45
Full Breakfast
Credit Cards: None
Notes: 2, 4, 5, 6, 7, 8, 9, 10, 11, 12, 13, 14

7 No smoking; 8 Children welcome; 9 Social drinking allowed; 10 Tennis nearby; 11 Swimming nearby; 12 Golf nearby; 13 Skiing nearby; 14 May be booked through a travel agent; 15 Handicapped accessible.

GOSHEN

Judith's Garden

Judith's Garden Bed and Breakfast

Goshen-Ripton Road, 05733
(802) 247-4707; e-mail: gardenbb@together.net

Spectacular mountain setting with broad lawns and abundant perennial gardens. Spacious guest rooms and antique-filled living room. Praise-winning breakfasts served in the large country kitchen, featuring delicious home baking. Walking and hiking on quiet country roads and numerous mountain trails in the Green Mountain National Forest. Cross-country skiing and snowshoeing from the front door on Blueberry Hill's renowned 40-mile trail system. Thirty minutes to interesting shops and fine restaurants in Middlebury.

Hosts: Judith Irven and Dick Conrad
Rooms: 3 (PB) $75-95
Full Breakfast
Credit Cards: None
Notes: 2, 3, 5, 7, 9, 11, 12, 13, 14

GRAFTON

The Old Tavern at Grafton

Main Street, 05146
(802) 843-2231; (800) 843-1801
FAX (802) 843-2245

Centerpiece of picturesque and historic Grafton village since 1801, this inn offers 65 guest rooms, six guest cottages with four to seven rooms, and a honeymoon cottage secluded on a hilltop meadow. Rates include breakfast and afternoon tea. Award-winning dining and live music in Phelps Barn Pub. Freshwater swimming pond, bicycles, and hiking are available on property. The 30K cross-country ski area offers snowmaking, snowshoeing, ice skating, rentals for all activities, and professional instruction. Member of Historic Hotels of America. No smoking in public areas except the bar and no smoking in guest rooms. Inquire about availability of lunch. Inquire about accommodations for children.

Host: Kevin O'Donnell
Rooms: 66 (PB) $125-185
Full Breakfast
Credit Cards: A, B
Notes: 2, 4, 7, 10, 12, 13, 14, 15

GREENSBORO

Highland Lodge

Rural Route 1, Box 1290, Craftsbury Road, 05841
(802) 533-2647; FAX (802) 533-7494
e-mail: hlodge@connriver.net
www.pbpub.com/vermont/hiland.htm

Highland Lodge is a family-owned country inn and resort in a turn-of-the-century summer community on Caspian Lake. The lodge has a clay tennis court, lawn games, and a private beach for swimming and boating. Dirt roads for biking and hiking lead

Highland Lodge

NOTES: Credit cards accepted: A MasterCard; B Visa; C American Express; D Discover; E Diner's Club; F Other; 2 Personal checks accepted; 3 Lunch available; 4 Dinner available; 5 Open all year; 6 Pets welcome;

through farm country and a nature preserve. Golf is nearby in the village. Children love the play program. The delicious food is complimented by all. Admire the breathtaking vistas at fall foliage time and from the lodge's own cross-country ski trails. Dinner and breakfast are both included in the rates per person per night.

Hosts: David and Wilhelmina Smith
Rooms: 11 (PB) $95-125 MAP
Cottages: 10
Full breakfast
Credit Cards: A, B, D
Notes: 2, 3, 4, 5, 8, 9, 10, 11, 12, 13, 14, 15

HARDWICK

American Country Collection
1353 Union Street, Schenectady, NY 12308
(518) 370-4948; (800) 810-4948
FAX (518) 393-1634 (call first)
e-mail: carolbnbres@mon.com

215. Victorian home, circa 1899, in the heart of Vermont's Northeast Kingdom with porch, large lawn, and perennial gardens. Heirloom and antique furniture. Three rooms share two full baths. One room with private bath. Smoking outside. Full breakfast. Children welcome. No pets. $69.

HARTLAND

American Country Collection
1353 Union Street, Schenectady, NY 12308
(518) 370-4948; (800) 810-4948
FAX (518) 393-1634 (call first)
e-mail: carolbnbres@mon.com

163. Contemporary home in a rural farm setting with a spectacular view. Guests have the privacy of the entire first floor, including private entrance, if desired. Soft country decor with handmade quilts. Continental breakfast. Two rooms, one with twin beds and one with a double bed; each has a private bath. Common room with fireplace and TV. Resident cat. Children welcome. No smoking. $65-75.

JACKSONVILLE

American Country Collection
1353 Union Street, Schenectady, NY 12308
(518) 370-4948; (800) 810-4948
FAX (518) 393-1634 (call first)
e-mail: carolbnbres@mon.com

165. Victorian country home built in 1840. Queen Anne Colonial furnishings and country accessories. Dining room with fireplace, living room, and sitting room with TV. Four guest rooms with private and shared baths. In-ground swimming pool. Twenty minutes from Mount Snow. Full breakfast. Children welcome. Smoking outside. $50-65.

JAMAICA

Three Mountain Inn
P.O. Box 180 A, 05343
(802) 874-4140

Small, romantic 1780s authentic country inn. Fine food and comfortable rooms. Many original details can be found, including three wood-burning fireplaces on the main floor, and several guest rooms also boast original fireplaces. In a historic village, just four blocks to hiking in the state park and cross-country skiing. Swimming pool on premises. Ten minutes to Stratton. The innkeepers plan special day trips with detailed local maps of the area. Special midweek rates. Honeymoon suites available. Small weddings, reunions, meetings.

Three Mountain Inn

---

7 No smoking; 8 Children welcome; 9 Social drinking allowed; 10 Tennis nearby; 11 Swimming nearby; 12 Golf nearby; 13 Skiing nearby; 14 May be booked through a travel agent; 15 Handicapped accessible.

Bed and breakfast and modified American plan available.

Hosts: Charles and Elaine Murray
Rooms: 16 (14 PB; 2 SB) $75-180
Full Breakfast
Credit Cards: A, B, C, D
Notes: 2, 4, 8, 9, 10, 11, 12, 13, 14

JAY

Jay Village Inn

Route 242, Box 138, 05859
(802) 988-2306; (800) 565-5641

A nice country inn in the village of Jay, three miles from Jay Peak Ski Resort. Snowmobile trails across the street. Close to area restaurants. Beautiful, rural setting in the Northeast Kingdom of Vermont. Full breakfast served in winter; Continental breakfast served in the spring, summer, and fall.

Hosts: Jane and Bob Angliss
Rooms: 15 (PB) $79-99
Full or Continental Breakfast
Credit Cards: A, B
Notes: 8, 9, 10, 11, 12, 13, 14

JEFFERSONVILLE

Jefferson House Bed and Breakfast

Main Street, P.O. Box 288, 05464
(802) 644-2030; (800) 253-9630
e-mail: jeffhouse@pwshift.com
www.pbpub.com/smugglers/jeffhouse.htm

Enjoy the picturesque beauty of this turn-of-the-century Victorian home in historic Jeffersonville. It features a large wraparound porch; a warm, friendly atmosphere; attractive, comfortable rooms; and a hearty, home-cooked breakfast. In spring and summer bike the country roads, hike the Long Trail or Mount Mansfield. Autumn's foliage is a sight to behold. In the winter, nearby Smugglers' Notch offers great skiing while other activities are only minutes away.

Hosts: Dick and Joan Walker
Rooms: 3 (1 PB; 2 SB) $50-65

Full Breakfast
Credit Cards: A, B, D
Notes: 2, 5, 7, 8, 9, 12, 13

Mannsview Inn

Rural Route 2, Box 4319, 05464
(802) 644-8321; (888) 937-6266
FAX (802) 644-2006
e-mail:r.s.v.p.@mannsview.com
www.mannsview.com

Set on a plateau on 10 acres on Route 108, Vermont's most scenic highway. Fifteen minutes from Stowe. The inn is superbly decorated with antiques from the 10,000-square-foot antique center next door. Queen-size high poster beds, billiard room, library, sunroom, parlor, whirlpool bath, and outdoor spa. Sumptuous full country breakfast in the sunroom with window views of Smugglers' Notch and Mount Mansfield. The inn is also Smugglers' Notch Canoe Touring. Canoe vacation packages from $99. Children over 10 welcome.

Host: Kelley and Bette Mann
Rooms: 6 (2 PB; 4 SB) $65-95
Full Breakfast
Credit Cards: A, B, C
Notes: 2, 5, 7, 9, 10, 11, 12, 13

Smugglers' Notch Inn

Church Street, 05464
(802) 644-2412; (800) 845-3101
e-mail: smuginn@pwshift.com
www.smugglers-notch-inn.com

Escape to a warm, friendly, 200-year-old, Vermont country inn in an authentic rural village of Jeffersonville. Eleven guest rooms with private baths, one with a Jacuzzi and

Smuggler's Notch Inn

one with gas fireplace. Lounge, fireplace, great restaurant, outdoor hot tub, pool. See why generations of artists return here again and again. Wide variety of activities, from casual to vigorous. Great road or mountain biking, fly-fishing, ice or rock climbing, canoeing, skiing, golf, hiking, antiquing.

Hosts: Cynthia Barber and Jon Day
Rooms: 11 (PB) $60-125
Full Breakfast
Credit Cards: A, B, C
Notes: 2, 3, 4, 5, 8, 9, 10, 11, 12, 13

JERICHO

Homeplace

P.O. Box 96, 05465
(802) 899-4694

A quiet spot in a 100-acre wood. The spacious house is filled with European and American antiques. The living room has a large fireplace and looks out on Mount Mansfield. The house is surrounded by perennial gardens, and there are many wooded trails on the property. Friendly house and barn animals complete the picture.

Host: Mariot Huessy
Rooms: 3 (1 PB; 2 SB) $55-65
Full Breakfast
Credit Cards: None
Notes: 2, 5, 7, 8, 9, 10, 11, 12, 13, 14

Sinclair Inn Bed and Breakfast

389 Vermont Route 15, 05465
(802) 899-2234; (800) 433-4658

A showcase of builder Edmund Sinclair's craftsmanship, fully restored in 1993, this 1890 Victorian "painted lady" has been described as "a study in architectural styles, incorporating features such as turrets, colored glass, and an intricately carved fretwork across the living room and stairway." Halfway between Burlington and Smugglers' Notch. Enjoy the nearby hiking, boating, sailing, biking, festivals, and shows. Discount ski lift tickets available. One room, fireplace. One, handicapped accessible. Children over 12

welcome. Social drinking permitted in rooms. Garden weddings available on property.

Hosts: Jeanne and Andy Buchanan
Rooms: 6 (PB) $80-115
Full Breakfast
Credit Cards: A, B, D
Notes: 2, 5, 7, 10, 11, 12, 13, 14, 15

KILLINGTON

Elaine's Bed and Breakfast Selections

4987 Kingston Road, Elbridge, NY 13060
(315) 689-2082 (after 10 A.M.)

This lodge, open year-round, has 6 suites, 11 nonsmoking rooms, and 35 smoking rooms. All the rooms have modern private baths and TVs. There is a pool, hot tub, sauna, exercise room, adjoining lounge for games or cards. Full breakfast. Inquire about accommodations for pets. Children welcome and babysitters can be arranged. Killington Mountain is near great hiking and biking trails, fishing streams, rafting rivers, native craft shops, antiquing. Several golf courses are nearby. There is also a restaurant on the premises. $109-269.

Mountain Meadows Lodge

Rural Route 1, Box 4080, 05751
(802) 775-1010; (800) 370-4567
e-mail: havefun@mtmeadowslodge.com
www.mtmeadowslodge.com

An unspoiled lakeside farm setting on the Appalachian Trail. Outdoor, indoor, and lake activities abundantly available. On-site cross-country ski center. Fireside dining with regional and country fare and full vegetarian menu. Complete breakfasts with granola, fresh fruit, and griddle cakes. All-day snacks. Boxed lunches. Cheese, wine available. On-site children's farm and adventure program.

Hosts: Mark and Michelle Werle
Rooms: 19 (PB) $105-250
Full Breakfast
Credit Cards: A, B, C
Notes: 2, 3, 4, 5, 7, 8, 10, 11, 12, 13, 14, 15

7 No smoking; 8 Children welcome; 9 Social drinking allowed; 10 Tennis nearby; 11 Swimming nearby; 12 Golf nearby; 13 Skiing nearby; 14 May be booked through a travel agent; 15 Handicapped accessible.

The Peak Chalet

The Peak Chalet

South View Path, P.O. Box 511, 05751
(802) 422-4278; e-mail: home@thepeakchalet.com
www.thepeakchalet.com

The Peak Chalet is a four-room bed and breakfast within the beautiful Green Mountains of Vermont. The exterior is authentically European alpine. The interior is furnished with a fine country inn flavor and reflects high quality with attention to detail. The bed and breakfast offers panoramic mountain views with a cozy stone fireplace to unwind by. All rooms have queen-size beds and private baths. Within the Killington Ski Resort, this is a truly relaxing experience. Mobil and AAA three-diamond-rated. Children over 12 welcome.

Hosts: Diane and Greg Becker
Rooms: 4 (PB) $50-110
Continental Breakfast
Credit Cards: A, B, C, E
Notes: 2, 5, 7, 9, 10, 11, 12, 13, 14

Red Clover Inn

7 Woodward Road, Mendon, 05701
(802) 775-2290; (800) 752-0571
e-mail: redclovr@vermontel.com
www.redcloverinn.com

Down a winding country road, nestled on 13 acres, this 1840s lovingly restored farmhouse estate offers guests warmth, pampering, and an award-winning wine list to complement the exquisite cuisine. From enticing rooms with private baths, antiques, some with double whirlpools and gas fireplaces, to sumptuous breakfasts and candle-light dining, the atmosphere is relaxed and peaceful. Hiking and biking. Knoll-top pool. AAA three-diamond-rated. Mobil three-star-rated. Selected as a romantic hideaway by the *Discerning* Traveler.

Hosts: Sue and Harris Zuckerman
Rooms: 14 (PB) $100-325
Full Breakfast
Credit Cards: A, B, D
Notes: 2, 4, 7, 9, 10, 11, 12, 13, 14

Snowed Inn

Miller Brook Road, RD #1, Box 2336, 05751
(802) 422-3407; (800) 311-5406
FAX (802) 422-8126; e-mail: snowdinn@sover.net
www.snowedinn.com

A gracious bed and breakfast inn in the heart of Vermont's picturesque mountains. Distinctive design and casual hospitality warmly welcome guests. Nineteen lovely contemporary country rooms and luxury fireplace/kitchenette/Jacuzzi suites, all with private bath, color cable TV, telephone. Fieldstone fireplace lounge, greenhouse breakfast room, game room, outdoor hot tub overlooking wooded, babbling brook. An intimate setting, yet walk to restaurants, night spots, shops. One and one-half miles to Killington Resort's winter and summer activities.

Hosts: Manfred and Jeanne Karlhuber
Rooms: 19 (PB) $60-240
Continental Breakfast
Credit Cards: A, B, C, D
Notes: 8, 9, 10, 11, 12, 13, 14, 15

Snowed Inn

NOTES: Credit cards accepted: A MasterCard; B Visa; C American Express; D Discover; E Diner's Club; F Other; 2 Personal checks accepted; 3 Lunch available; 4 Dinner available; 5 Open all year; 6 Pets welcome;

The Vermont Inn

The Vermont Inn

Route 4, 05701
(802) 775-0708; (800) 541-7795
FAX (802) 773-2440; e-mail: vtinn@aol.com

Built as a farmhouse in 1840, the Vermont Inn has been known for many years for its fine dining and lodging. The original wood beams are exposed in the living room, the lounge has a wood stove, and there is an old-fashioned game room. The rooms are individually decorated and some have fireplaces. Outdoor pool and tennis. Indoor hot tub and sauna. Screened porch and extensive gardens.

Hosts: Megan and Greg Smith
Rooms: 18 (PB) $50-185
Full Breakfast
Credit Cards: A, B, C, E
Notes: 2, 4, 5, 7, 8, 9, 10, 11, 12, 13, 14, 15

LONDONDERRY

The Blue Gentian Lodge

Magic Mountain Road, Rural Route 1
Box 29, 05148
(802) 824-5908; (800) 456-2405
FAX (802) 824-3531

In scenic south central Vermont, the lodge has 13 comfortable rooms and an outstanding view of Magic Mountain. All rooms have private baths, most have cable TVs, one is completely handicapped accessible. Lovely lounge with fireplace; dining area can accommodate 40 guests. Outdoor pool on premises. Centrally located between many must-see attractions, such as outlet shopping, museums, summer theaters, hiking, and skiing.

Hosts: The Alberti Family
Rooms: 13 (PB) $50-80

Full Breakfast
Credit Cards: A, B
Notes: 2, 5, 7, 8, 10, 11, 12, 13, 15

Swiss Inn

Route 11, Rural Route 1, Box 140, 05148
(802) 824-3442; (800) 847-9477

The Swiss Inn is in the heart of the Green Mountains with spectacular views of the surrounding area. These cozy, comfortable rooms all feature cable TVs, telephones, and private baths. Full Vermont breakfast is served daily. Two fireside sitting rooms and library are available. Restaurant on premises features Swiss specialties. Both downhill and cross-country skiing nearby in the winter. Shopping, antiques, golf, summer theater, and fall foliage at its best.

Hosts: Joe and Pat Donahue
Rooms: 18 (PB) $49-89
Full Breakfast
Credit Cards: A, B
Notes: 2, 4, 5, 8, 9, 10, 11, 12, 13

LOWER WATERFORD

Rabbit Hill Inn

1 Pucker Street, 05848
FAX (802) 748-8342 ; (800) 76-BUNNY
  (reservations)
e-mail: Rabbit.Hill.Inn@ConRiver.net
www.RabbitHillInn.com

It is here that guests will find that romantic departure from their hectic world. This 200-year-old classic country inn is set on 15 acres above the Connecticut River. Enjoy pampering service, adventurous gourmet dining, and truly heartfelt hospitality unlike anything ever experienced. Enchanting candlelit guest rooms and suites—some with fireplaces, whirlpool tubs for two, and private porches. Repeatedly chosen one of American's Ten Best Inns. Rated four-diamonds by AAA and four-stars by Mobil.

Hosts: Brian and Leslie Mulcahy
Rooms: 21 (PB)
Full Breakfast
Credit Cards: A, B, C
Notes: 2, 4, 5, 7, 9, 10, 11, 12, 13, 14, 15

7 No smoking; 8 Children welcome; 9 Social drinking allowed; 10 Tennis nearby; 11 Swimming nearby; 12 Golf nearby; 13 Skiing nearby; 14 May be booked through a travel agent; 15 Handicapped accessible.

LUDLOW

The Combes Family Inn

953 East Lake Road, 05149
(802) 228-8799; (800) 822-8799
e-mail: billcfi@aol.com
www.combesfamilyinn.com

Bring the family to the Combes Family Inn in Vermont. The inn, a century-old farmhouse on a country back road, offers a quiet respite from the hustle and bustle of today's hectic lifestyle. Relax and socialize (BYOB) in the Vermont barnboard keeping room, furnished with turn-of-the-century oak. Sample Bill's country breakfasts and Ruth's delicious home cooking. Lush Green Mountains invite a relaxing, casual vacation. Eleven cozy, country-inspired guest rooms—all with private baths. Minimum-stay requirements for fall and winter weekends and for holidays. Closed April 15 through May 15.

Hosts: Ruth and Bill Combes
Rooms: 11 (PB) $55-124
Full Breakfast
Credit Cards: A, B, C, D
Notes: 2, 4, 6, 8, 9, 10, 11, 12, 13, 14

MANCHESTER

1811 House

Box 39, 05254
(802) 362-1811; (800) 432-1811
FAX (802) 362-2443

This classic Vermont inn offers guests the warmth and comfort of their own home. Built in the 1770s, the house has operated as an inn since 1811 except for one brief period when it was the residence of Abraham Lincoln's granddaughter. All guest rooms have private baths; some have fireplaces, oriental rugs, fine paintings, and canopied beds. More than seven acres of lawn contain flower gardens and a pond and offer an exceptional view of the Green Mountains. Walk to golf and tennis, near skiing, fishing, canoeing, and all sports. Young people over 16 welcome.

1811 House

Hosts: Marnie and Bruce Duff
Rooms: 14 (PB) $120-220
Full Breakfast
Credit Cards: A, B, C, D
Notes: 2, 5, 7, 9, 10, 11, 12, 13, 14

The Inn at Manchester

Historic Route 7A, Box 41, 05254-0041
(802) 362-1793

Beautifully restored turn-of-the-century Victorian set on four acres in the picture-book village of Manchester. Elegant rooms with bay windows, brass beds, antiques, and an extensive art collection. Luscious full country breakfast. Secluded pool. Skiing, shops, and theater in the area. Come for peace, pancakes, and pampering. Guests can choose among 14 rooms and 4 suites with fireplaces. Smoking outside only. Children over eight welcome.

Hosts: Stan and Harriet Rosenberg
Rooms: 18 (PB) $95-130
Suites: 4
Full Breakfast
Credit Cards: A, B, C, D, E
Notes: 2, 5, 7, 9, 10, 12, 13, 14

Manchester Highlands Inn

Box 1754 AD, Highland Avenue, 05255
(802) 362-4565; (800) 743-4565
FAX (802) 362-4028
e-mail: relax@highlandsinn.com
www.highlandsinn.com

Discover Manchester's first "painted lady," a graceful Queen Anne Victorian inn on a hilltop overlooking town. Front porch with

NOTES: Credit cards accepted: A MasterCard; B Visa; C American Express; D Discover; E Diner's Club; F Other; 2 Personal checks accepted; 3 Lunch available; 4 Dinner available; 5 Open all year; 6 Pets welcome;

Manchester Highlands Inn

rocking chairs, large outdoor pool, game room, and pub with stone fireplace. Rooms individually decorated with feather beds, down comforters, and lace curtains; many with canopied beds. Gourmet country breakfasts and afternoon snacks are served. Air conditioned.

Hosts: Robert and Patricia Eichorn
Rooms: 15 (PB) $95-135
Full Breakfast
Credit Cards: A, B, C
Notes: 2, 5, 7, 8, 9, 10, 11, 12, 13, 14

MANCHESTER CENTER

The Inn at Ormsby Hill

Historic Route 7A, Rural Route 2
P.O. Box 3264, 05255
(800) 362-1163; www.ormsbyhill.com

This splendid restored manor house is on two and one-half acres overlooking the Green Mountains. Listed in Vermont register of historic places, the inn offers 10 luxurious bed chambers, all with private baths, fireplaces and two-person whirlpools. The inn is known for its exceptional dining in the conservatory. Manchester is a four-season resort community with a full assortment of sports and cultural activities.

Hosts: Ted and Chris Sprague
Rooms: 10 (PB) $115-290

Full Breakfast
Credit Cards: A, B, D
Notes: 2, 4, 5, 7, 9, 10, 11, 12, 13, 14, 15

River Meadow Farm

P.O. Box 822, 05255
(802) 362-1602

Secluded farm at the end of a country lane with beautiful views of the surrounding countryside. The remodeled farmhouse was built just prior to 1800. Five guest bedrooms sharing two and one-half baths, large country kitchen with a fireplace and adjoining screened-in, glassed-in porch, pleasant dining room, living room with baby grand piano, and den with TV. Ninety acres to hike or cross-country ski, bordered by the famous Battenkill River. Swimming is available 15 miles away.

Host: Patricia J. Dupree
Rooms: 5 (SB) $60
Full Breakfast
Credit Cards: None
Notes: 2, 5, 7, 8, 9, 10, 11, 12, 13

MCINDOE FALLS

McIndoe Falls Inne

P.O. Box 18, 05050
(802) 633-2240

This historic landmark, some 200 years old, stands in the center of a Scottish-settled village. Its feather bed and eclectic antiques make it very inviting. The host, Gloria LaBorie, is a lecturing nutritionist who enjoys creating lovely gourmet meals from her organic vegetable and herb gardens. Owned for more than a quarter of a century by the LaBorie family with their wealth of information, the inn offers guests the makings of a great stay in the Northeast Kingdom of Vermont.

Rooms: 7 (2 PB; 5 SB) $45-75
Full Breakfast
Credit Cards: A, B, C, D, E, F
Notes: 2, 3, 4, 5, 7, 8, 9, 10, 11, 12, 13, 14

7 No smoking; 8 Children welcome; 9 Social drinking allowed; 10 Tennis nearby; 11 Swimming nearby; 12 Golf nearby; 13 Skiing nearby; 14 May be booked through a travel agent; 15 Handicapped accessible.

MIDDLEBURY

The Annex

Route 125, 05740
(802) 388-3233

This 1830 Greek Revival home was originally built as an annex to the Bob Newhart "Stratford Inn." The annex features six rooms decorated in a blend of country, antiques, and homemade quilts. The nearby national forest provides hiking, skiing, and biking trails. Visit the UVM Morgan Horse Farm and the Shelburne Museum while in the area. Please inquire about accommodations for children.

Host: T. D. Hutchins
Rooms: 6 (4 PB; 2 SB) $50-75
Continental Breakfast
Credit Cards: None
Notes: 2, 5, 7, 9, 10, 11, 12, 13

The Annex

Brookside Meadows Country Bed and Breakfast

Rural Delivery #3, Box 2460, 05753-8751
(802) 388-6429; (800) 442-9887
FAX (802) 388-1706
e-mail: rcole@brooksmeadow.com
www.brooksmeadow.com

Offering special hospitality since 1982. Gracious residence three miles from center of lovely college town. Set well off a country road; no traffic noise. Spectacular Green Mountain views. Quiet central air

conditioning. Two-bedroom apartment-style suite with living room and private entrance. All private baths. Two-night minimum stay preferred, one-night visits accommodated if possible. Breakfast included, served in attractive dining room. A nonsmoking establishment.

Hosts: Linda and Roger Cole
Rooms: 5 (PB) $85-135
Full Breakfast
Credit Cards: A, B
Notes: 2, 5, 7, 9, 10, 11, 12, 13, 14

The Middlebury Inn

Courthouse Square, P.O. Box 631, 05753
(802) 388-4961; (800) 842-4666

Traditional 1827 New England inn within scenic college town enhanced by a legion of historical, cultural, and entertaining attractions. Walking distance to museums, boutique shops, magnificent waterfall. Elegantly restored rooms in the main house, Porter Mansion and contemporary motel. All rooms provide cable color TVs, direct-dial telephones, private bathrooms with amenities, telephones, and hair dryers. Fine dining, afternoon tea, Sunday brunch, special packages. Gift shop. AAA three-diamond-rated. Member of Historic Hotels of America. Inquire about accommodations for pets. Smoking permitted in designated areas only.

Hosts: Frank and Jane Emanuel
Rooms: 75 (PB) $80-260
Continental Breakfast
Credit Cards: A, B, C, D, E
Notes: 2, 3, 4, 5, 8, 10, 11, 12, 13, 14, 15

MIDDLETOWN SPRINGS

American Country Collection

1353 Union Street, Schenectady, NY 12308
(518) 370-4948; (800) 810-4948
FAX (518) 393-1634 (call first)
e-mail: carolbnbres@mon.com

147. There is a treat waiting for guests as they step back 100 years in time to an age of elegance in this rural New England vil-

---

NOTES: Credit cards accepted: A MasterCard; B Visa; C American Express; D Discover; E Diner's Club; F Other; 2 Personal checks accepted; 3 Lunch available; 4 Dinner available; 5 Open all year; 6 Pets welcome;

lage. Listed in the National Register of Historic Places, this historic home is filled with antiques and a large music box collection. Near Lake St. Catherine for boating and picnicking. Fishermen will love the trout that can be caught in a stream bordering the property. Six guest rooms are available, all with private baths, and a full breakfast. Dinner available nightly. $78-85.

MONTGOMERY CENTER

The Inn on Trout River

P.O. Box 76, The Main Street, 05471
(802) 326-4391; (800) 338-7049
FAX (802) 326-3194; e-mail: troutinn@sover.net
www.pbpubicom/trout.htm

Surrounded by magnificent mountain ranges in a quaint Currier and Ives-style village, this 100-year-old country Victorian inn features private baths, queen-size beds, down comforters, feather pillows, flannel sheets, cozy fireplaces, antiques, gourmet restaurant, a pub, and game room. Close to summer and winter sports, covered bridges, and shopping. A full menu at breakfast is always included. AAA three-diamond Historic Country Inn and AAA three-diamond restaurant.

Hosts: Michael and Lee Forman
Rooms: 10 (PB) $86-103
Full Breakfast
Credit Cards: A, B, C, D
Notes: 4, 5, 7, 8, 9, 10, 11, 12, 13, 14

The Inn on Trout River

Phineas Swann Bed and Breakfast

The Main Street, P.O. Box 43, 05471
(802) 326-4306

Phineas Swann is a classic intimate Vermont country bed and breakfast. Written about recently in *Country Living* magazine, the *Boston Phoenix*, and *Out* magazine. The main house is a 100-year-old gingerbread Victorian with hardwood floors, two fireplaces, and canopied and carved-wood beds. The Carriage House suites have upscale accommodations with in-room Jacuzzis, fireplaces, and queen-size beds. The inn is at the base of Jay Peak Ski resort and one mile from world-class cross-country skiing; rentals available.

Hosts: Michael Bindler and Glen Bartolomeo
Rooms: 4 (2 PB; 2 SB) $69-89
Suites: 2 (PB) $125-145
Full Breakfast
Credit Cards: A, B, D
Notes: 2, 5, 7, 8, 9, 10, 11, 12, 13, 14

MONTPELIER

Betsy's Bed and Breakfast

74 East State Street, 05602
(802) 229-0466; FAX (802) 229-5412
e-mail: betsybb@plainfield.bypass.com
www.central-vt.com/business/betsybb

Betsy's Bed and Breakfast is a warm and inviting Queen Anne home in the nation's smallest capital. The rooms are furnished with period antiques. Guests are invited to linger over a cup of coffee in the sun-filled dining room, chat with the owners by a crackling fire in the formal parlor, lift weights or cycle in the exercise room, rock on the front porch, or hide away in their room and enjoy the peace and quiet.

Hosts: Jon and Betsy Anderson
Rooms: 12 (PB) $55-115
Full Breakfast
Credit Cards: A, B, C, D
Notes: 2, 5, 7, 8, 9, 11, 12, 13, 14

7 No smoking; 8 Children welcome; 9 Social drinking allowed; 10 Tennis nearby; 11 Swimming nearby; 12 Golf nearby; 13 Skiing nearby; 14 May be booked through a travel agent; 15 Handicapped accessible.

MORGAN

Hunts Hideaway

Rural Route 1, Box 570, West Charleston, 05872
(802) 895-4432; (802) 334-8322

Contemporary split-level on 100 acres:
brook, pond, and a 44-foot in-ground pool.
In Morgan, six miles from I-91, near the
Canadian border. Guests may use kitchen
and laundry facilities. Lake Seymour is two
miles away; 18-hole golf courses at Newport and Orleans; bicycling, jogging, skiing
at Jay Peak and Burke Mountain, antiquing,
bird watching, and fishing.

Host: Pat Hunt
Rooms: 3 (SB) $40
Full Breakfast
Credit Cards: None
Notes: 2, 5, 6, 8, 9, 10, 11, 12, 13

MOUNT SNOW

The Inn at Quail Run

106 Smith Road, Wilmington, 05363
(802) 464-3362; (800) 34 ESCAPE
www.bbonline.com/vt/quailrun/

Enjoy pristine mountain views, recently renovated rooms all with private baths, several
with fireplaces, a full country breakfast, and
après-ski snacks. On a quiet country road
away from traffic, the inn is on 15 beautiful
wooded acres. In winter, enjoy cross-country
and snowmobile trails, and in the summer,
enjoy the heated pool. Large sauna, eight-
person outdoor year-round Jacuzzi, TV room,
BYOB lounge, sitting room, and dining room
with spectacular views of the valley. A
charming and romantic getaway. A three-
bedroom cottage complete with living room,
kitchen, and cable TV, as well as a two-room
fireplace suite are also available. Children
and well-behaved pets are welcome.

Hosts: Robert and Lorin Streim
Rooms: 9 (PB) $100-175
Full Breakfast
Credit Cards: A, B, C, D
Notes: 2, 5, 6, 7, 8, 9, 10, 11, 12, 13, 14

MOUNT SNOW VALLEY

Shield Inn

Route 100, P.O. Box 366, West Dover, 05356
(802) 464-3984; FAX (802) 464-5322
e-mail: shieldinn@aol.com
www.sover.net/~dvalnews/shieldinn.html

Romantic and relaxing nonsmoking country inn set back from Route 100 on a
three-acre wooded lot. Relax in one of 12
beautifully decorated rooms, each with
private bath and TV. Half have Jacuzzis
and wood-burning fireplaces. Full breakfast served each morning and dinner
during ski season. A Steinway grand piano
enhances the living room. Chamber music
and jazz series, planned and impromptu.
Near Mount Snow/Haystack and Marlboro
Music Festival. Children 10 and older
welcome. Bed and breakfast and MAP
rates available.

Hosts: Phyllis and Lou Isaacson
Rooms: 12 (PB) $90-240
Full Breakfast
Credit Cards: A, B
Notes: 2, 5, 7, 9, 10, 11, 12, 13, 14

NEWBURY

Peach Brook Inn Bed and Breakfast

Doe Hill, 05051
(802) 866-3389

A 1780s manse on
a country lane
just off Route
5 overlooking
the Connecti-
cut River and
Valley view-
ing   fields,
farms, village,
and majestic
mountains. Plenty of farm animals and
places to walk. Breakfast on the veranda to
enjoy the view. French toast or pancakes

NOTES: Credit cards accepted: A MasterCard; B Visa; C American Express; D Discover; E Diner's Club;
F Other; 2 Personal checks accepted; 3 Lunch available; 4 Dinner available; 5 Open all year; 6 Pets welcome;

with Vermont maple syrup. Children over 10 welcome. Cross-country skiing nearby.

Hosts: Joyce and Raoul Emery
Rooms: 3 (1 PB; 2 SB) $50-70
Full Breakfast
Credit Cards: None
Notes: 2, 5, 7, 9, 10, 11, 12, 13

NORTHFIELD

Northfield Inn
27 Highland Avenue, 05663
(802) 485-8558

Turn-of-the-century mansion, restored to its original Victorian elegance with magnificent panoramic views of the Green Mountains and the Northfield Valley. Graceful porches, gardens, gentle breezes, golden sunsets, romantic ambiance. Rated three-diamond by AAA, three-star by Mobil, and three-crown by ABBA. Dinner available for groups only.

Host: Aglaia Stalb
Rooms: 8 (PB) $85-130
Full Breakfast
Credit Cards: A, B
Notes: 2, 5, 7, 9, 10, 11, 12, 13, 14

NORTH HERO ISLAND

Charlie's Northland Lodge
3829 US Route 2, 05474-9713
(802) 372-8822

Early 1800s guest house in a quiet village setting on North Hero Island in Lake Champlain. Two guest rooms furnished with country antiques share a modern bath, private entrance, and living room. A place to fish, sail, canoe, kayak, bike, or just plain relax. In winter, guests may ice fish and cross-country ski. Guest cottages available upon request.

Hosts: Dorice and Charlie Clark
Rooms: 2 (SB) $60-65
Continental Breakfast
Credit Cards: A, B
Notes: 2, 5, 9, 10, 11, 12, 13, 14

NORTH THETFORD

Stone House Inn
Route 5, P.O. Box 47, 05054
(802) 333-9124

An 1835 stone farmhouse on the banks of the Connecticut River in eastern central Vermont. Enclosed porches and a sitting room with fireplace. Central location and proximity to Dartmouth College make this a good base for touring. Nearby lakes, Fairlee and Mobey, and the White Mountains offer opportunities for boating and hiking.

Hosts: Art and Dianne Sharkey
Rooms: 5 (5 SB) $55
Continental Breakfast
Credit Cards: A, B
Notes: 2, 5, 7, 9, 10, 11, 12, 13

NORTH TROY

Bed and Breakfast North Shore, Greater Boston, Cape Cod
P.O. Box 600035, Greater Boston Branch,
    Newtonville, 02160-0001
(617) 964-1606; (800) 832-2632
FAX (617) 332-8572; e-mail: info@bbreserve.com
www.bbreserve.com

39. Canadian Border Farmhouse. In northern Vermont, close to the Canadian border, this wonderful old farmhouse sits on 52 acres, offering panoramic views of the Sutton Range and Jay Peak. Acres of woodlands and fields provide the outdoor enthusiast with options for hiking, cross-country and downhill skiing, fishing, and horseback riding. The location is a photographer's paradise for capturing the colors of fall foliage. Guest accommodations include two rooms with shared bath, one room with private bath, a cozy living room with parlor stove, TV, and piano. A country breakfast is included. Farm-made items of maple syrup, jams, jellies, honey, and homespun yarn are for sale. Twenty dollars for extra person in room. $65-80.

7 No smoking; 8 Children welcome; 9 Social drinking allowed; 10 Tennis nearby; 11 Swimming nearby; 12 Golf nearby; 13 Skiing nearby; 14 May be booked through a travel agent; 15 Handicapped accessible.

OLD BENNINGTON

The Four Chimneys

21 West Road, 05201
(802) 447-3500; FAX (802) 447-3692

This Georgian Revival mansion, on an 11-acre parklike setting, combines elegance with comfort and relaxation. The full service restaurant is considered one of the finest in the state. All rooms have been renovated and provide all the modern amenities, yet retain the Old World charm that makes this inn so unique. The inn provides a respite from the hectic pace of everyday life. Rated three diamonds by AAA and three stars by Mobil. Continental plus breakfast served.

Hosts: Ron and Judy Schefkind
Rooms: 11 (PB) $125-185
Continental Breakfast
Credit Cards: A, B, C, D, E, F
Notes: 2, 3, 4, 5, 7, 9, 10, 11, 12, 13, 14, 15

ORWELL

Historic Brookside Farms— A Four Season Country Inn

Route 22A, 05760
(802) 948-2727; FAX (802) 948-2015

This 1789-1843 historic register Greek Revival mansion is on 300 acres. All rooms are furnished in period antiques. Enjoy a full country breakfast, afternoon tea, and romantic candlelit gourmet dinner. Cross-country ski on miles of trails through 78 acres of magnificent forest. Hiking, lawn games, boating, and fishing on a 20-acre lake. There is a lovely antique shop on the premises. Family-owned and -operated. Limited smoking allowed. Suite and all common rooms are handicapped accessible.

Rooms: 7 (4 PB; 3 SB) $85-150
Full Breakfast
Credit Cards: F
Notes: 2, 3, 4, 5, 8, 9, 10, 11, 12, 13, 14

PERU

The Wiley Inn

Route 11, P.O. Box 37, 05152
(888) 843-6600; FAX (802) 824-4195
e-mail: wileyinn@sover.net
www.wileyinn.com

Romantic rooms for couples plus fireplaces and Jacuzzis. Spacious family rooms and suites and a great lounge to relax in. Special packages and group rates available. Summer/fall: enjoy the pool, the hot tub, the trout ponds plus golf, tennis, and hiking nearby. Winter: Ski Bromley, Stratton, Okemo, and cross-country plus sleigh rides, skating, and snowmobile rides nearby. Unique dining experience year-round. Long-stay discounts available.

Hosts: Judy and Jerry Goodman
Rooms: 10 (PB) $60-185
Suites: 6
Full Breakfast
Credit Cards: A, B, C, D
Notes: 2, 4, 5, 7, 8, 9, 10, 11, 12, 13, 14

PITTSFIELD

Pittsfield Inn

Route 100, Box 685, 05762
(802) 746-8943; e-mail: escapert@vermontel.com

On a quintessential New England village green. The inn's central location on Route 100, one of America's most scenic highways, is a perfect base to explore the magic of Vermont and to ski Killington and Sugarbush ski areas. It is filled with antiques, has bright country decor, and a friendly fun-loving atmosphere. Delicious dinners and breakfasts, always made with fresh and healthy ingredients, are offered. Free historic towns. Escape Routes, an outdoor adventure company, is based at the inn. It offers guided and self-guided hiking, mountain biking, snowshoeing, and back-country skiing.

Host: Tom Yennerell
Rooms: 9 (PB) $60-100

NOTES: Credit cards accepted: A MasterCard; B Visa; C American Express; D Discover; E Diner's Club; F Other; 2 Personal checks accepted; 3 Lunch available; 4 Dinner available; 5 Open all year; 6 Pets welcome;

Full Breakfast
Credit Cards: A, B
Notes: 2, 4, 5, 6, 8, 9, 10, 11, 12, 13, 14

Swiss Farm Lodge

Route 100, P.O. Box 630, 05762
(802) 746-8341; (800) 245-5126
www.mediausa.com/vt/swissfarmlodge/

A homey, comfortable, and attractive
lodge nestled in a beautiful valley surrounded by mountains. Delight in the
ambiance of a working farm, producing
the hosts' own polled Hereford beef.
Maple syrup is made from the trees on the
farm. Convenient to major downhill and
cross-country ski areas. Anything guests
may desire is nearby. All meals are home
cooked and served in a large, pleasant
dining room. Dinner available December 1
through April 1.

Hosts: Mark and Sandy Begin and Family
Rooms: 17 (14 PB; 3 SB) $50-60
Full Breakfast
Credit Cards: A, B
Notes: 5, 7, 8, 9, 10, 11, 12, 13, 14

POULTNEY

Lake St. Catherine Inn

Cones Point Road, 05764
(802) 287-9347; (800) 626-LSCI (reservations)

Rural country resort on crystal-clear Lake
St. Catherine. Relaxation and wholesome
dining. Families welcome. AAA- and
Mobil-approved. Rates include use of alu-
minum boats, canoes, paddleboats, and
sailboats. Breakfast, five-course dinner,
and all gratuities are included in the daily
rate. One housekeeping cottage sleeps six
and is available with weekly rates. Many
specials available throughout the season.
Modified American plan is available. Open
mid-May through mid-October. Partially
handicapped accessible.

Hosts: Patricia and Raymond Endlich
Rooms: 35 (PB) $134-176
Full Breakfast

Credit Cards: None
Notes: 2, 4, 8, 9, 10, 11, 12, 14

Tower Hall

2 Bently Avenue, 05764
(800) 894-4004; e-mail: towerhal@sover.net
www.sover.net/~towerhal/

Enjoy the ambiance of this century-old
Queen Anne Victorian in Poultney, with
original woodwork, imposing staircase, and
wraparound porch. Large, bright guest
rooms decorated with the warmth and comfort of antique and period furnishings.
Adjacent to Green Mountain College and
near two lakes, ski resorts, and outlet shopping. Continental plus breakfast served.
Skiing is 30 miles away.

Host: Pat Perrine
Rooms: 4 (2 PB; 2 SB) $60-85
Continental Breakfast
Credit Cards: None
Notes: 2, 5, 7, 8, 10, 11, 12

PROCTORSVILLE

Golden Stage Inn

1 Depot Street, 05153
(802) 226-7744; (800) 253-8226
TTY (802) 226-7136; e-mail:gldstgin@ludl.tds.net

History galore: 1700s stagecoach stop;
Underground Railroad safe house; Otis
Skinner family residence. Full breakfasts
and five-course gourmet dinners
(optional) often feature inn's own harvest.
Homemade breads a speciality. Large,
sunny rooms reflect traditions of warm
hospitality. Abundant fishing in nearby
lakes and rivers. "You catch and clean
'em, we cook 'em (or freeze 'em) for
you." Swimming pool. Bicycles available
for leisurely exploring. Modified American plan available.

Hosts: Micki and Paul
Rooms: 8 (PB) $99-218
Suite: 1
Full Breakfast
Credit Cards: A, B, D
Notes: 2, 4, 5, 7, 8, 9, 11, 12, 13, 14, 15

7 No smoking; 8 Children welcome; 9 Social drinking allowed; 10 Tennis nearby; 11 Swimming nearby;
12 Golf nearby; 13 Skiing nearby; 14 May be booked through a travel agent; 15 Handicapped accessible.

PUTNEY

Hickory Ridge House Bed and Breakfast

Rural Delivery 3, Box 1410, 05346
(802) 387-5709; (800) 380-9218
FAX (802) 387-4328

Gracious 1808 Federal manor on eight beautiful acres in country setting. Large guest rooms with fireplaces, high ceilings, private baths, air conditioning, TV/VCRs, telephones, and robes. Full breakfast served. Great restaurants and shopping nearby. Hiking, biking, swimming, and cross-country skiing nearby. Theater and art galleries abound.

Hosts: Linda and Jack Bisbee
Rooms: 8 (PB) $105-145
Full Breakfast
Credit Cards: A, B, C
Notes: 2, 5, 7, 9, 10, 11, 12, 13, 14, 15

The Putney Inn

P.O. Box 181, 05346
(800) 653-5517; FAX (802) 387-5211

In the heart of southern Vermont. Nationally acclaimed cuisine. Concerts, theater, meandering strolls, and artisan studios. Voted area's best in lodging and dining. Small inn charm with the luxury of privacy. Incredible food; gracious friendliness. Chef Ann Cooper offers locally farmed New England fare, from wholesomely simple to extravagantly delightful. So bring bikes, canoes, hiking boots. Come to play, or to just enjoy exquisite food and quietude.

Host: Randi Ziter
Rooms: 25 (PB) $68-148
Full Breakfast
Credit Cards: A, B, C, D
Notes: 2, 3, 4, 5, 6, 7, 8, 9, 10, 11, 12, 13, 14, 15

RIPTON

The Chipman Inn

Route 125, 05766
(802) 388-2390; (800) 890-2390

A traditional Vermont inn built in 1828 in the Green Mountain National Forest. Fine food, wine, and spirits for guests. Eight rooms, all with private baths. Fully licensed bar and large fireplace. Closed November 15 to December 26 and April 1 to May 15. Children over 12 welcome.

Hosts: Joyce Henderson and Bill Pierce
Rooms: 8 (PB) $85-115
Full Breakfast
Credit Cards: A, B, C, D
Notes: 2, 4, 9, 11, 12, 13

ROCHESTER

The New Homestead

Route 100, 05767-0025
(802) 767-4751

Just a small village on a blue highway in a narrow winding valley of the Green Mountains. Delightfully seedy gardens surround the house. Hens cluck contentedly in the barn, providing the basis for memorable breakfasts. "We keep our price low to attract people like us." Sandy also practices law. David dabbles in domestic art/architecture. Ike and Tina are resident cats.

Putney Inn

The New Homestead

Hosts: Sandra Haas and David Marmor
Rooms: 5 (3 PB; 2 SB) $40
Full Breakfast
Credit Cards: None
Notes: 2, 5, 7, 8, 9, 10, 11, 12, 13

ROYALTON

Fox Stand Inn

Route 14, 05068
(802) 763-8437

Built in 1818 as a stagecoach stop on the banks of the White River. The dining room and tavern are open to the public and offer international creations. The inn's second floor has five comfortably furnished guest rooms. In the center of one of Vermont's acclaimed recreational regions. Swimming, canoeing, tubing, bicycling, hiking, and fishing are readily at hand. Antique shops, auctions, flea markets, and horse shows are found throughout the countryside.

Hosts: Jean and Gary Curley
Rooms: 5 (SB) $50-75
Full Breakfast
Credit Cards: A, B
Notes: 2, 4, 5, 7, 9, 10, 11, 12, 13

RUTLAND

The Inn at Rutland

70 North Main Street, Route 7, 05701
(802) 773-0575; (800) 808-0575

The Inn at Rutland is an 1890s Victorian mansion restored to its original condition.

Guest rooms have been tastefully decorated to re-create the past while maintaining modern comforts. All rooms have private bathrooms, telephones, and cable TVs, with some rooms having air conditioning and VCRs. A large breakfast is served. The common rooms offer a comfortable atmosphere for conversation, reading by the fireplace, or just relaxing. Carriage house for ski or bike storage, with some mountain bikes available for guests. AAA-, Mobil-, ABBA-rated.

Hosts: Bob and Tanya Liberman
Rooms: 10 (PB) $49-175
Full Breakfast
Credit Cards: A, B, C, D, E
Notes: 5, 7, 8, 9, 10, 11, 12, 13, 14

The Inn at Rutland

SANDGATE

Green River Inn

2480 Sandgate Road, 05250
(802) 375-2272

Tucked away on 450 acres, the Green River Inn offers guests a memorable Vermont vacation. Fourteen newly renovated, beautiful rooms with private baths, antiques, and handpainted furniture, some with whirlpools and fireplaces. Spacious sunroom and deck with mountain views. A perfect setting for romantic rendezvous, family getaways, or weeklong holidays. Seasonal outdoor activities begin right at the door or relax by the river and enjoy outstanding

---

7 No smoking; 8 Children welcome; 9 Social drinking allowed; 10 Tennis nearby; 11 Swimming nearby; 12 Golf nearby; 13 Skiing nearby; 14 May be booked through a travel agent; 15 Handicapped accessible.

service and gourmet dining. Modified American plan rates available.

Hosts: James and Betsy Gunn
Rooms: 14 (PB) $70-170
Full Breakfast
Credit Cards: A, B, C
Notes: 2, 3, 4, 5, 7, 8, 9, 10, 11, 12, 13, 15

SAXTONS RIVER

The Inn at Saxtons River

27 Main Street, 05154
(802) 869-2110; FAX (802) 869-3033

Lodging and dining in the casual elegance of an old Victorian setting. Fine European and American cuisine and 16 individually decorated Victorian rooms. Full Vermont breakfast included. There has been an inn on the present site since 1818. The current inn, built in 1903, features traditional Victorian styling. The Pub is open nightly and offers a lighter version of the inn's menu. Coffee and desserts are best enjoyed in the comfort of the sitting room by the fireplace. Inquire about accommodations for pets.

Hosts: Jeremy Burrell and Steven Griffiths
Rooms: 16 (PB) $108
Full Breakfast
Credit Cards: A, B
Notes: 2, 3, 4, 5, 7, 8, 9, 10, 11, 12, 13, 14

SHOREHAM

Shoreham Inn and Country Store

Route 74 West Inn Road, 05770
(802) 897-5081; (800) 255-5081
e-mail: shoreinn@together.net

This 200-year-old inn is in the beautiful and historic Champlain Valley. Whimsically furnished rooms in a comfortable country atmosphere. Private baths. Hearty breakfasts. Children welcome. No smoking,

Circa 1790

please. Great location for cycling and snowmobiles. Close to Lake Champlain, Fort Ticonderoga, Mount Independence, and the college town of Middlebury.

Hosts: Jim and Julie Ortuno
Rooms: 10 (PB) $85-95
Full Breakfast
Credit Cards: A, B
Notes: 2, 3, 5, 7, 8, 9, 12, 13, 14

SHREWSBURY

Crisanver House

Wiley Hill, P.O. Box 157, 05738
(802) 492-3589; (800) 492-8089
e-mail: M.Calotta@Mindspring.com
www.crisanver.com

Circa 1850. During the Revolutionary War, the road that runs in front of this inn was used as the main supply route between Boston Harbor and Fort Ticonderoga. Listed in Vermont's register of historic buildings, its location is ideal, boasting spectacular views of mountain/sunsets and surrounded by more than 100 acres. The guest rooms, decorated in an elegant country style, feature beds bedecked with luxury linens and topped with down comforters. Breakfasts are healthy and sumptuous, often featuring low-fat and low-cholesterol fare. Inquire about accommodations for pets.

Hosts: Michael and Carol Calotta
Rooms: 8 (6 PB; 2 SB) $90-135
Full Breakfast
Credit Cards: None
Notes: 2, 4, 5, 7, 9, 10, 11, 12, 13, 14

SOUTH LONDONDERRY

The Londonderry Inn

P.O. Box 301-70, 05155-0301
(802) 824-5226; FAX (802) 824-3146
e-mail: londinn@sover.net

An 1826 homestead that has been welcoming guests for 50 years overlooks the West River and the quiet village of South Londonderry in the Green Mountains of southern Vermont.

Special family accommodations. Living room with huge fireplace; billiard and Ping-Pong rooms. Dinner available on weekends and holidays.

Hosts: Jean and Jim Cavanagh
Rooms: 25 (20 PB; 5 SB) $41-116
Full Breakfast
Credit Cards: None
Notes: 2, 5, 8, 10, 11, 12, 13, 14

SOUTH NEWFANE

The Inn at South Newfane

HCR 63, Box 57, (Dover Road), 05351-7901
(802) 348-7191; e-mail: cullinn@sover.net
www.innatsouthnewfane.com

A charming turn-of-the-century country inn provides elegant relaxation, international cuisine, and warm hospitality. The incredible beauty and serenity of the more than 100 private acres surrounding the inn are ideal for any occasion. Three fireplaces. Guest rooms are delightfully distinctive— each with a private bath. Lunch (seasonal) and dinner served. Alfresco dining on the large porch. Fully licensed bar. Antique shops and many activities nearby. Children over 10 welcome.

Hosts: Neville and Dawn Cullen
Rooms: 6 (PB) $95-120
Full Breakfast
Credit Cards: A, B
Notes: 4, 5, 7, 10, 11, 12, 13, 14

SPRINGFIELD

Hartness House

30 Orchard Street, 05156
(802) 885-2115; (800) 732-4789

This beautiful 1903 inn is listed in the National Register of Historic Places. Once the home of Gov. James Hartness, this inn invites guests to step back in time to a setting of gracious living, with carved beams, majestic fireplaces, and a grand staircase leading up to 11 beautifully decorated rooms. Guests may also choose from 29 modern rooms in

Hartness House

the annex. Enjoy swimming, gracious poolside dining, and unique features: a 1910 tracking telescope and a small underground museum reached via a 240-foot tunnel. Lunch available Monday through Friday. Dinner available Monday through Saturday. Smoking restricted. Dining room is handicapped accessible.

Hosts: The Blair Family
Rooms: 40 (PB) $80-130
Full Breakfast
Credit Cards: A, B, C, D, E
Notes: 2, 3, 4, 5, 8, 9, 10, 12, 13, 14, 15

STOWE

American Country Collection

1353 Union Street, Schenectady, NY 12308
(518) 370-4948; (800) 810-4948
FAX (518) 393-1634 (call first)
e-mail: carolbnbres@mon.com

074. Drive over the wooden bridge that crosses the brook and up the long drive to the white Colonial set amid tall pine trees. The inn operates as a bed and breakfast from spring until the end of autumn. For the remainder of the year, the modified American plan is honored. The five guest rooms are large and sleep three or four people. Four rooms have private baths. Guests may use the living room/lounge with stone fireplace, game room, and workshop, where guests repair and sharpen skis. Easy access to antiquing, biking, hiking, canoeing, and leaf peeking. Smoking permitted. Full breakfast is offered. $63-113.

7 No smoking; 8 Children welcome; 9 Social drinking allowed; 10 Tennis nearby; 11 Swimming nearby; 12 Golf nearby; 13 Skiing nearby; 14 May be booked through a travel agent; 15 Handicapped accessible.

Andersen Lodge— an Austrian Inn

3430 Mountain Road, 05672
(802) 253-7336; (800) 336-7336

A small Tyrolean inn ideal for the gourmet who appreciates European delights. Open grounds with swimming pool and tennis courts. Exercise room with Jacuzzi and sauna, recreation path. Open seasonal. Some rooms are nonsmoking.

Hosts: Dietmar and Gertrude Heiss
Rooms: 18 (PB) $68-120
Full Breakfast
Credit Cards: A, B, C, D
Notes: 2, 4, 5, 6, 8, 9, 10, 11, 12, 13, 14, 15

Brass Lantern Inn

717 Maple Street, 05672
(802) 253-2229; (800) 729-2980
FAX (802) 753-7425; e-mail: brasslntrn@aol.com
www.stoweinfo.com/saa/brasslantern

A traditional Vermont bed and breakfast inn in the heart of Stowe. Award-winning restoration of an 1810 farmhouse and carriage barn overlooking Mount Mansfield, Vermont's most prominent mountain. The inn features period antiques, air conditioning, handmade quilts, and planked floors. Some rooms have whirlpools and/or fireplaces and most have views. Award-winning breakfast. An intimate spot for house guests only. AAA three-diamond inn. Special packages include honeymoon, adventure, skiing, golf, air travel, sleigh and surrey rides, and more.

Host: Andy Aldrich
Rooms: 9 (PB) $80-225
Full Breakfast
Credit Cards: A, B, C
Notes: 2, 5, 7, 9, 10, 11, 12, 13, 14

Fitch Hill Inn

258 Fitch Hill Road, Hyde Park, 05655
(802) 888-3834; (800) 639-2903
FAX (802) 888-7789

Friendly affordable elegance on a hilltop overlooking Vermont's highest mountains in the beautiful Lamoille River Valley. Ten miles north of Stowe, the historic Fitch Hill Inn, circa 1797, offers four guest rooms and two suites. There are three common living room areas and more than 300 video movies for guests to enjoy. Three porches offer spectacular views; rest and relax in the beautiful gardens. A full gourmet breakfast is served, and candlelit four-course dinners are available by reservation. Packages available. Seasonal rates. Minimum stays for holidays and most weekends. Some rooms have fireplaces, hot tub, and Jacuzzis.

Hosts: Richard A. Pugliese and Stanley E. Corklin
Rooms: 4 (PB) $85-175
Suites: 2 (PB)
Full Breakfast
Credit Cards: A, B, C
Notes: 2, 3, 4, 5, 7, 9, 10, 11, 12, 13, 14

Guest House Christel Horman

4583 Mountain Road, 05672
(802) 253-4846; (800) 821-7891 (U.S.)

Small, cozy bed and breakfast offers eight large double rooms with full private baths. Guest living room with fireplace, color TV, VCR, movies, and many books and magazines. Rates include choice menu breakfast. One and one-half miles to downhill and cross-country skiing. Ski week rate available. Children over 10 welcome.

Hosts: Christel and Jim Horman
Rooms: 8 (PB) $35-50
Full Breakfast
Credit Cards: A, B
Notes: 2, 5, 7, 9, 10, 11, 12, 13, 14

Miguel's Stowe Away Lodge

3148 Mountain Road, 05672
(802) 253-7574; (800) 245-1240
FAX (802) 253-5192

A quaint and cozy bed and breakfast on Mountain Road. Three miles from the base of Mount Mansfield and four miles from the village of Stowe. A full country-style breakfast offered to all guests. There is also an authentic Mexi-

---

NOTES: Credit cards accepted: A MasterCard; B Visa; C American Express; D Discover; E Diner's Club; F Other; 2 Personal checks accepted; 3 Lunch available; 4 Dinner available; 5 Open all year; 6 Pets welcome;

can restaurant and cantina, that's been serving the best Mexican cuisine in the area for 20 years.

Hosts: Michael and Adrienne Henzel
Rooms: 9 (6 PB; 3 SB) $40-100
Full Breakfast
Credit Cards: A, B, C, D, E
Notes: 2, 3, 4, 5, 6, 7, 8, 9, 10, 11, 12, 13, 14

Nichols Lodge

P.O. Box 1028, 05672
(802) 253-7683

Rustic farm house inn with assortment of rooms—dormitory rooms with baths in hall, connecting and private. Fireplaced lounge and recreation room. Some with air conditioning. Breakfast available during winter months. Walks through campground and uphill. Bike path one and one-half miles away, accessible from lodge. Brochure available.

Host: Kathryn K. Nichols
Rooms: 12 (2 PB; 8 SB) $16-62
Credit Cards: A, B, C
Notes: 2, 5, 6, 8, 10, 11, 12, 13, 14

The Raspberry Patch Bed and Breakfast

606 Randolph Road, 05672
(802) 253-4145; (800) 624-0639
e-mail: ljonesrpbb@aol.com
www.bizindex.com/raspberrypatch

"My home is your home!" After a busy day guests will enjoy relaxing in the peaceful atmosphere of this friendly country getaway. Lovely rooms with antiques and down comforters on the cozy beds. A large common area with fireplaces and lace curtains to frame the mountain view. Breakfast is always fresh and hearty. Air conditioned. Minutes to many fine restaurants. Resident cat Bronte.

Host: Linda Jones
Rooms: 4 (PB) $55-75
Full Breakfast
Credit Cards: A, B, C
Notes: 2, 5, 6, 7, 8, 9, 10, 11, 12, 13, 14

The Siebeness

3681 Mountain Road, 05672
(802) 253-8942; (800) 426-9001

A warm welcome awaits guests at this charming country inn. Antiques, private baths, homemade quilts, and air conditioning. Mountain-view suites, Jacuzzi, gas fireplace, views. Fireplace lounge, BYOB bar, hot tub, pool with beautiful mountain views. Famous for outstanding food. Adjacent to Stowe's famous recreation path. Honeymoon, golf, and ski packages available.

Hosts: Nils and Sue Andersen
Rooms: 12 (PB) $70-200
Full Breakfast
Credit Cards: A, B, C, D
Notes: 2, 5, 7, 8, 9, 10, 11, 12, 13, 14

Ski Inn

Route 108, 05672-4822
(802) 253-4050; www.ski-inn.com/bb

This comfortable inn, noted for good food and good conversation, is a great gathering place for interesting people. Guests enjoy themselves and others. Nearest lodge to all Stowe ski lifts, with miles of cross-country trails at the door. Cool and quiet in the summer. Rooms are large and colorful, each with a double and single bed. Evening meal available during ski season.

Host: Harriet Heyer
Rooms: 10 (5 PB; 5 SB) $45-60
Full or Continental Breakfast
Credit Cards: C
Notes: 2, 5, 7, 8, 9, 10, 11, 12, 13, 14

Ski Inn

Timberholm Inn

452 Cottage Club Road, 05672
(802) 253-7603; (800) 753-7603
FAX (802) 253-8559

Nestled in the woods, this 10-room bed and breakfast is friendly, romantic, and comfortable. The large, airy common room has a striking fieldstone fireplace. Enjoy beautiful mountain views from the deck. Guests are also invited to relax and enjoy the outdoor hot tub. The two-bedroom suites are ideal for families. Near skiing, golf, hiking, tennis, and bike trails. Feast on a Vermont country buffet breakfast. Game room. "The inn to return to."

Hosts: Louise and Pete Hunter
Rooms: 10 (PB) $80-150
Full Breakfast
Credit Cards: A, B, D
Notes: 2, 5, 7, 8, 9, 10, 11, 12, 13, 14

WalkAbout Creek Lodge

199 Edson Hill Road, 05672
(802) 253-7354; (800) 426-6697
FAX (802) 253-8429; e-mail: walkcreek@aol.com
www.walkaboutcreeklodge.com

Experience the authenticity of a classic mountain lodge and retreat to this secluded haven. WalkAbout Creek Lodge is nestled on five wooded acres beside a flowing mountainside creek and is a true historic gem, one of the oldest of its kind. Solidly built of hewn logs and fieldstone, this is the perfect place to relax with friends and family. Guests can look forward to the fieldstone fireplaces, expansive living areas, individually furnished rooms, outdoor hot tub, swimming pool, rustic Billabong Pub, hearty breakfasts, and on-site access to unlimited trails, for the hiker, biker, and cross-country skier alike. Let this season be yours to discover WalkAbout Creek Lodge, for it is a winter wonderland, a fall spectacular, and a summer haven, with all the attractions and activities of Stowe close at hand.

Hosts: Joni and crew
Rooms: 17 (PB) $90-150
Full Breakfast

Credit Cards: A, B, C
Notes: 2, 5, 6, 7, 8, 9, 10, 11, 12, 13, 14

TOWNSHEND

Boardman House Bed and Breakfast

Box 112, 05353
(802) 365-4086

A 19th-century farmhouse set on the village green next to the most photographed church in Vermont. This is a prime foliage and antiquing area. Direct access to State Routes 30 and 35 allows guests to pursue other interests from cross-country and downhill skiing to canoeing on the West River. Guests may choose among five rooms and one suite. Gourmet breakfasts feature pear pancakes, individual soufflés, hot fruit compotes, homemade muffins, and more. Inquire about restrictions concerning pets.

Hosts: Sarah Mesenger and Paul Weber
Rooms: 6 (5 PB; 1 SB) $65-85
Full Breakfast
Credit Cards: None
Notes: 2, 5, 7, 8, 11, 12, 13

VERGENNES

Emersons' Bed and Breakfast

82 Main Street, 05491-1155
(802) 877-3293

Experience fine Vermont hospitality in this 1850 Victorian home surrounded by spacious lawns and flowers. Enjoy roomy, comfortable accommodations in a home filled with antiques and collectibles. Enjoy a full breakfast which includes homemade breads and muffins. Visit the nearby Shelburne Museum, the Lake Champlain Maritime Museum, and Kennedy Brothers Marketplace. Area recreation includes fishing, boating, canoeing, hiking, and bicycling. Walk to fine restaurants.

Hosts: Jeannette and Don Michalets
Rooms: 6 (2 PB; 4 SB) $58-90

NOTES: Credit cards accepted: A MasterCard; B Visa; C American Express; D Discover; E Diner's Club; F Other; 2 Personal checks accepted; 3 Lunch available; 4 Dinner available; 5 Open all year; 6 Pets welcome;

Emerson's

Full Breakfast
Credit Cards: A, B
Notes: 2, 5, 7, 8, 9, 10, 11, 12, 14

WAITSFIELD

1824 House Inn

Route 100, Box 159, 05673
(802) 496-7555

Enjoy a home away from home in an atmosphere of relaxed elegance. Seven beautiful guest rooms, each with private bath. Appetizers are offered each evening and a three-course gourmet breakfast each morning. The kitchen is the focal point and guests are welcome to come in, sit with the owners to sip wine, drink coffee, or sample goodies. Recreational activities are abundant in the Mad River Valley and the inn has its own swimming hole. Rated two diamonds by AAA and two stars by Mobil. Seasonal rates. Children over 10 welcome.

Hosts: Carol Davis and Jack Rodie
Rooms: 7 (PB) $85-140
Full Breakfast
Credit Cards: A, B, C
Notes: 2, 4, 5, 7, 9, 11, 12, 13, 14

Hyde Away Inn

Route 17, Rural Route 1, Box 65, 05673
(802) 496-2322; (800) 777-HYDE

A comfortable, casual, circa 1820 inn less than five minutes from Sugarbush and Mad River Glen ski areas, hiking and biking trails, and historic Waitsfield Village. Twelve rooms, common area with TV, children's toy area. Unpretentious and friendly atmosphere. Hearty breakfast each morning. Public restaurant with outstanding, affordable American cuisine. Rustic tavern with pub fare and summer deck dining. Some rooms where pets may be allowed. Smoking permitted in designated areas only.

Hosts: Bruce and Margaret
Rooms: 12 (4 PB; 8 SB) $49-89
Full Breakfast
Credit Cards: A, B, C
Notes: 4, 5, 8, 9, 10, 11, 12, 13, 14

Lareau Farm Country Inn

Box 563, Route 100, 05673
(802) 496-4949

In an open meadow near the Mad River, this 1832 Greek Revival farmhouse is only minutes from skiing, shopping, dining, soaring, and golf. Sleigh rides, cross-country skiing, and swimming on the premises. When guests come, they feel at home and relaxed. Hospitality is the inn's specialty. "One of the top 50 inns in America"—*Inn Times.*

Hosts: Dan and Susan Easley
Rooms: 13 (11 PB; 2 SB) $60-125
Full Breakfast
Credit Cards: A, B
Notes: 2, 5, 7, 8, 10, 11, 12, 13, 14

The Mad River Inn Bed and Breakfast

Tremblay Road, P.O. Box 75, 05673
(802) 496-7900; (800) TEA-TART

A romantic 1860s country Victorian inn nestled alongside the Mad River with picturesque mountain views. Nine unique guest rooms with feather beds and private baths. Gourmet breakfast and afternoon tea included daily. Porches, gardens, gazebo, Jacuzzi, and swimming hole. Fireplace, library, BYOB lounge. Catered weddings.

7 No smoking; 8 Children welcome; 9 Social drinking allowed; 10 Tennis nearby; 11 Swimming nearby; 12 Golf nearby; 13 Skiing nearby; 14 May be booked through a travel agent; 15 Handicapped accessible.

Midweek specials. Families and groups welcome. Walk to new recreation path.

Hosts: Luc and Rita Maranda
Rooms: 9 (PB) $59-125
Full Breakfast
Credit Cards: A, B, C
Notes: 2, 5, 7, 8, 9, 10, 11, 12, 13, 14

Millbrook Inn

Route 17, Rural Free Delivery, Box 62, 05673
(802) 496-2405; (800) 477-2809 (reservations)

Relax in the friendly, unhurried atmosphere of this cozy 1850s inn. Seven guest rooms are decorated with hand stenciling, antique bedsteads, and handmade quilts. Breakfast and dinner included in the daily rate. Dine in the romantic small restaurant that features hand-rolled pasta, fresh fish, veal, shrimp, and homemade desserts from a varied menu. Bed and breakfast rates are available during the summer only, Modified American plan during winter and fall. Two-day minimum stay required for weekends, three-nights for holidays. Closed from April 1 to June 15 and October 20 to mid-December. Inquire about accommodations for pets. Children over six are welcome.

Hosts: Joan and Thom Gorman
Rooms: 7 (PB) $68-140
Credit Cards: A, B, C
Notes: 2, 4, 7, 9, 10, 11, 12, 13

Mountain View Inn

Route 17, Rural Free Delivery, Box 69, 05673
(802) 496-2426

This small country inn (circa 1826) has seven guest rooms, each with private bath, accommodating two people. The rooms are decorated with stenciling, quilts, braided rugs, and antique furniture. Meals are served family style around an antique harvest table. Good fellowship is enjoyed around the wood-burning fireplace in the living room. Two-night minimum stay required on weekends.

Hosts: Fred and Susan Spencer
Rooms: 7 (PB) $43.60-70.85

Mountain View Inn

Full Breakfast
Credit Cards: None
Notes: 2, 5, 7, 8, 9, 10, 11, 12, 13, 14

Tucker Hill D Lodge

Marble Hill Road, RD #1, Box 147, 05673
(802) 496-3983; (800) 543-7841
FAX (802) 496-3203
e-mail: tuckhill@madriver.com
www.tuckerhill.com

Tucker Hill Lodge has 21 cozy guest rooms, a bar and game room, and a great restaurant. There are two tennis courts, an outdoor pool, a hiking trail, and 14 acres of wooded land. Some rooms have balconies. There is a suite with a fireplace and a three-bedroom restored 1810 Vermont farmhouse. All rates include a full country breakfast. The restaurant offers a delicious and varied menu. Vegetarian dishes and children's menu always available. Inquire about accommodations for pets.

Rooms: 21 (17 PB; 4 SB) $60-115
Full Breakfast
Credit Cards: A, B, C
Notes: 4, 7, 8, 10, 11, 12, 13, 14

The Waitsfield Inn

Route 100, Box 969, 05673
(802) 496-3979; (800) 758-3801
FAX (802) 496-3970; e-mail: W8FLDN@aol.com
www.site-works.com/waitsfield

This gracious 1820s restored Colonial inn is in the heart of the beautiful Mad River Valley. The inn, just minutes from Sugar-

NOTES: Credit cards accepted: A MasterCard; B Visa; C American Express; D Discover; E Diner's Club; F Other; 2 Personal checks accepted; 3 Lunch available; 4 Dinner available; 5 Open all year; 6 Pets welcome;

bush, is convenient to spectacular skiing and wonderful hiking, shopping, antiquing, and much more. Relax in one of the 14 rooms, all of which are beautifully appointed with antiques, quilts, and private baths. Enjoy a delicious full breakfast and let the "innspired" hosts make every stay a memorable one.

Hosts: Steve and Ruth Lacey
Rooms: 14 (PB) $69-119
Full Breakfast
Credit Cards: A, B, C, D
Notes: 2, 5, 7, 8, 9, 10, 11, 12, 13, 14

WALLINGFORD

American Country Collection

1353 Union Street, Schenectady, NY 12308
(518) 370-4948; (800) 810-4948
FAX (518) 393-1634 (call first)
e-mail: carolbnbres@mon.com

241. The Victorian warmth and Italian architectural motifs carry through to the individually decorated rooms. Antique furnishings and special touches make this bed and breakfast a true country pleasure. North of Manchester, near Killington and Pico and a short drive to the Appalachian Trail, this bed and breakfast is in the heart of Vermont. Claw-foot tubs, canopied beds, wicker on the porch complete the scene. Seven rooms with private baths. Children over 12 welcome. $100-160.

I. B. Munson House Bed and Breakfast Inn

7 South Main Street, P.O. Box 427, 05773
(802) 446-2860; FAX (802) 446-3336

Elegant 1856 Italianate Victorian inn, in the national historic register. Exquisitely restored to former glory. Seven guest rooms with private baths, some with claw-foot tubs and wood-burning fireplaces. Full breakfast by fireside or on deck overlooking garden (seasonal). Beautiful large common rooms with stunning chandeliers. In a quaint his-

toric village. Dining nearby. Boyhood home of Paul P. Harris, founder of Rotary International. Children 12 and older welcome.

Hosts: Karen and Phillip Pimental
Rooms: 7 (PB) $85-160
Full Breakfast
Credit Cards: A, B, C, D
Notes: 2, 7, 9, 10, 11, 12, 13, 14

WARREN

Beaver Pond Farm Inn

Rural Delivery Box 306, Golf Course Road, 05674
(802) 583-2861; FAX (802) 583-2860

Beaver Pond Farm, an elegantly restored Vermont farmhouse in a country meadow. Spectacular views of nearby Green Mountains. Adjacent to the Sugarbush Golf Course and 40K of groomed cross-country ski trails. One mile from downhill trails of Sugarbush. Hiking, fishing, cycling, fine restaurants, charming villages, swimming holes nearby. Hearty breakfasts, snacks, hors d'oeuvres, setups. Prix fixe dinners are available Tuesday, Thursday, and Saturday during winter. Ski and golf packages available. Closed April 15 to May 25. Children over seven welcome.

Hosts: Bob and Betty Hansen
Rooms: 5 (PB) $82-118
Full Breakfast
Credit Cards: A, B
Notes: 2, 7, 9, 10, 11, 12, 13, 14

The Powder Hound

Route 100, P.O. Box 369, 05674
(802) 496-5100; (800) 548-4022
FAX (802) 496-5163

Enjoy the charm of a country inn with the privacy of own condo. Two-room suites include kitchenette, cable TV, and deck. Outdoor hot tub, pool, and tennis court. Hearty breakfasts available at the inn, dinners available to groups of 20 or more. Inn features pub with full bar, pool table, and fun. Close to Sugarbush in the scenic Mad River Valley. Lots to see and do year-round. Pets always welcome for a small fee.

7 No smoking; 8 Children welcome; 9 Social drinking allowed; 10 Tennis nearby; 11 Swimming nearby; 12 Golf nearby; 13 Skiing nearby; 14 May be booked through a travel agent; 15 Handicapped accessible.

Hosts: Robin and Cindy Lehman
Rooms: 44 (PB) $70-164
Full Breakfast
Credit Cards: A, B, C, D
Notes: 2, 5, 8, 9, 10, 11, 12, 13, 14

Sugartree Inn

Rural Route 1, Box 38
Sugarbush Access Road, 05674
(802) 583-3211; (800) 666-8907
FAX (802) 583-3203
e-mail: sugartree@madriver.com

An intimate mountainside inn at Sugarbush. Nine guest rooms furnished with antiques, brass or canopied beds, and one fireplaced suite. In summer, flowers abound. Relax in the gingerbread gazebo. Golf, tennis, hiking, and swimming holes nearby. Winter brings cross-country and downhill skiing just a quarter-mile away. Warm up with hot cider by the parlor fireplace. Hearty country breakfasts. Picnic lunches available. Dinner is available for groups.

Hosts: Frank and Kathy Partsch
Rooms: 9 (PB) 80-135
Full Breakfast
Credit Cards: A, B, C, D
Notes: 2, 5, 7, 9, 10, 11, 12, 13, 14

West Hill House
Bed and Breakfast

West Hill Road, Rural Route 1, Box 292, 05674
(802) 496-7162; (800) 898-1427
FAX (802) 496-6443
e-mail: westhill@madriver.com
www.westhillhouse.com

Up a quiet country lane, nine acres with gardens, pond, views, this 1850s farmhouse is just one mile from Sugarbush Ski Resort, adjacent to championship golf course and cross-country ski trails. Extraordinary hiking, cycling, canoeing, fishing. Near fine restaurants, quaint villages, covered bridges. Enjoy comfortable porches, fireplaces, library, great room, sunroom. Guest rooms—three with fireplace and/or Jacuzzi tub—offer premium linens, down comforters, good reading lights. Dinner available by reservation with six-guest minimum. Children over 10 welcome.

West Hill House

Hosts: Dotty Kyle and Eric Brattstrom
Rooms: 7 (PB) $85-145
Full Breakfast
Credit Cards: A, B, C
Notes: 2, 5, 7, 9, 10, 11, 12, 13, 14

WATERBURY

American Country Collection

1353 Union Street, Schenectady, NY 12308
(518) 370-4948; (800) 810-4948
FAX (518) 393-1634 (call first)
e-mail: carolbnbres@mon.com

039. This 1790 Cape Cod was once a stagecoach stop and is now a haven for modern-day travelers seeking country comfort and hospitality. The six guest rooms are filled with country antiques. One room has a working fireplace. All have private baths. The inn has a library, living room, dining room, large porch, and country kitchen, where a full breakfast is served at the long trestle table next to the brick hearth. Smoking in common areas only. Children over six are welcome. Three-night minimum stay over holiday weekends. $85-140.

Grünberg Haus
Bed and Breakfast

Rural Route 2, Box 1595 AD, Route 100 S, 05676
(802) 244-7726; (800) 800-7760
e-mail: grunhaus@aol.com
www.bestinns.net/usa/vt/grun.html

Romantic Austrian chalet on a quiet mountainside, hand-built of native timber and

---

NOTES: Credit cards accepted: A MasterCard; B Visa; C American Express; D Discover; E Diner's Club; F Other; 2 Personal checks accepted; 3 Lunch available; 4 Dinner available; 5 Open all year; 6 Pets welcome;

fieldstone. Gorgeous guest rooms, secluded cabins, and spectacular carriage house suite. Warm-weather Jacuzzi, cold-weather sauna, cross-country ski and walking trails, tennis court, year-round fireplace, and BYOB pub. Savor memorable breakfast feasts. In Ben & Jerry's hometown, between Stowe and Sugarbush ski resorts. "Home of hospitable innkeepers, chickens, and teddy bears." Central to Stowe, Burlington, Montpelier, covered bridges, and waterfalls.

Hosts: Christopher Sellers and Mark Frohman
Rooms: 14 (9 PB; 5 SB) $59-145
Full Breakfast
Credit Cards: A, B, D
Notes: 2, 5, 7, 8, 9, 10, 11, 12, 13, 14

Inn at Blush Hill

Blush Hill Road, Box 1266, 05676
(802) 244-7529; (800) 736-7522
www.blushhill.com

Waterbury's oldest inn, a circa 1790 restored Cape on five acres with beautiful mountain views. The inn has four fireplaces, a large sitting room, fireplaced guest room, canopied bed, down comforters, and lots of antiques. One room has a Jacuzzi bath. Across from a golf course, and all summer sports are nearby. Enjoy skiing at Stowe, Sugarbush, and Bolton Valley. Back-to-back to Ben and Jerry's Ice Cream Factory. Packages available. AAA- and Mobil-rated. Children over six welcome.

Hosts: Gary and Pam Gosselin
Rooms: 5 (PB) $59-130
Full Breakfast
Credit Cards: A, B, C, D
Notes: 2, 5, 7, 9, 10, 11, 12, 13, 14

Old Stagecoach Inn

18 North Main Street, 05676
(802) 244-5056; (800) 262-2206

Experience the charm of a bygone era in the heart of Vermont's premier recreational area. Beautiful rooms, antiques throughout, listed in the National Register of Historic

Places. Minutes to world-class skiing, hiking, biking, water sports, and unmatched sightseeing. Complimentary full breakfast. Just one-half mile south of I-89 on scenic Route 100 in the village of Waterbury. AAA-approved.

Hosts: Jack and John Barwick
Rooms: 11 (8 PB; 3 SB) $45-125
Full Breakfast
Credit Cards: A, B, C, D
Notes: 2, 5, 6, 7, 8, 9, 10, 11, 12, 13, 14

Thatcher Brook Inn

Route 100 North, P.O. Box 490, 05676
(802) 244-5911; (800) 292-5911

This faithfully restored Victorian mansion is listed in the Vermont Register of Historic Buildings. The guest rooms all have private baths; some have fireplaces and others, whirlpool tubs. Enjoy French country cuisine in the main restaurant or light fare in Victoria's Bar and Grill. Near Ben & Jerry's Ice Cream Factory, Cold Hollow Cider Mill, and Shelburne Museum. No smoking in guest rooms.

Hosts: Kelly and Peter Varty
Rooms: 24 (PB) $75-185
Full Breakfast
Credit Cards: A, B, C, D, E
Notes: 2, 4, 5, 8, 9, 10, 11, 12, 13, 14, 15

WATERBURY CENTER

The Black Locust Inn

Route 100, Box 715, 05677
(802) 244-7490; (800) 366-5592 (reservations only)
FAX (802) 244-8473; www.blacklocustinn.com

Amid glorious black locust trees, the elegantly restored 1832 farmhouse is an unspoiled retreat from the world. Spend tranquil days and nights savoring relaxed conversation or sit back and reflect on life's delights. All rooms have guest-controlled heat and air conditioning and ceiling fans. The hosts take great pride in making each room an enchanting place to be. Scrumptious country breakfasts and evening wine

7 No smoking; 8 Children welcome; 9 Social drinking allowed; 10 Tennis nearby; 11 Swimming nearby; 12 Golf nearby; 13 Skiing nearby; 14 May be booked through a travel agent; 15 Handicapped accessible.

The Black Locust Inn

and appetizers. Activities year-round in nearby Stowe and Waterbury. Easy access to Montpelier, Burlington, and the Northeast Kingdom. Exit 10 from I-89, five miles on route 100. Rated three diamonds by AAA and two stars by Mobil.

Hosts: Len, Nancy, and Valerie Vignola
Rooms: 6 (PB) $89-135
Full Breakfast
Credit Cards: A, B, C, D, E
Notes: 2, 5, 7, 8, 10, 11, 12, 13, 15

WEATHERSFIELD

The Inn at Weathersfield

Route 106, Box 165, 05151-0165
(802) 263-9217; (800) 477-4828
FAX (802) 263-9219

A 204-year-old estate nestled on 21 peaceful acres with guest chambers and suites presenting settings inspired by the grandest love stories of all time. Enjoy canopied beds, working fireplaces, and Victorian claw-foot tubs. Creative cuisine by candlelight and hearth is offered nightly with grand piano entertainment. Dinner, afternoon tea, and full breakfast included in the rate. Inn also offers exercise room, sauna, and spring-fed pond with many areas of interest nearby.

Hosts: Mary and Terry Carter
Rooms: 12 (PB) $195-250
Full Breakfast
Credit Cards: A, B, C, D
Notes: 2, 4, 5, 7, 9, 10, 11, 12, 13, 14

WEST DOVER

Deerhill Inn and Restaurant

P.O. Box 136, Valleyview Road, 05356-0136
(802) 464-3100; (800) 99-DEER-9
e-mail: deehill@sover.net; www.deerhill.com

A friendly English-style country house with mountain views, candlelight dining, superb cuisine, spacious sitting rooms, fine antiques, art gallery, a licensed lounge, private baths, some rooms with fireplaces, lovely grounds, swimming pool. In Mount Snow area. Alpine and Nordic skiing, mountain biking, two championship golf courses, golf school, airport, walking, fishing, boating, antiquing, shopping, craft fairs, Marlboro Music Festival, and just plain relaxing. Weddings a specialty. Children over eight welcome.

Hosts: Michael and Linda Anelli
Rooms: 15 (PB) $95-220
Full Breakfast
Credit Cards: A, B, C
Notes: 2, 4, 5, 9, 10, 11, 12, 13

The Gray Ghost Inn

Route 100, P.O. Box 938, 05356
(802) 464-2474; (800) 745-3215

The guest book is filled with comments saying "super," "lovely," "warm and comfy," "better than home!" Of course it is; hosts cook breakfast, make the bed, even bake cookies for guests. Very clean rooms, nicely decorated, all with private baths. Guests are welcomed by caring, gracious host and hostess who live at the inn. They are happy to assist guests with information regarding dining, entertainment, sports, or whatever their needs are. A rural area with beautiful villages. Personal checks accepted for reservations only. Sixteen rooms are nonsmoking rooms and five rooms are handicapped accessible.

Hosts: John and Kaye Collingwood
Rooms: 25 (PB) $30-50
Full Breakfast
Credit Cards: A, B, C, D
Notes: 5, 8, 9, 10, 11, 12, 13, 14

NOTES: Credit cards accepted: A MasterCard; B Visa; C American Express; D Discover; E Diner's Club;
F Other; 2 Personal checks accepted; 3 Lunch available; 4 Dinner available; 5 Open all year; 6 Pets welcome;

West Dover Inn

West Dover Inn

Route 100, P.O. Box 1208, 05356
(802) 464-5207; FAX (802) 464-2173
e-mail: wdvrinn@sover.net
www.westdoverinn.com

Continuously operating for more than 150 years, this beautifully restored historic inn features individually appointed guest rooms, all with private baths, as well as luxurious fireplace suites with whirlpool tubs. Memorable dining at Gregory's Restaurant, featuring innovative country gourmet fare, relaxed ambiance, and an extensive wine list as well as a pub-like cocktail lounge. Within minutes of golf, skiing, mountain biking, tennis, and swimming. AAA three-diamond-rated. Closed late April through mid-May. Children over eight welcome.

Hosts: Greg Gramas and Monique Phelan
Rooms: 12 (PB) $90-200
Full Breakfast
Credit Cards: A, B, C, D
Notes: 2, 4, 9, 10, 11, 12, 13, 14

WESTON

Inn at Weston

Route 100, P.O. Box 56, 05161
(802) 824-6789

Enjoy beautifully appointed guest rooms and continental cuisine served in gracious style in this historic country inn. Set on the Green Mountains in the heart of the picture-book village of Weston, the inn was recently featured in *Gourmet* magazine. A pleasant walk to the Weston Playhouse, shops, and galleries. Dining rooms open to the public for dinner. Golf, tennis, downhill and cross-country skiing, and other activities nearby.

Hosts: Jeanne and Bob Wilder
Rooms: 19 (12 PB; 7 SB) $68-110
Full Breakfast
Credit Cards: A, B, C, D
Notes: 2, 4, 5, 9, 10, 11, 12, 13

The Wilder Homestead Inn and 1827 Craft Shoppe

25 Lawrence Hill Road, 05161
(802) 824-8172; FAX (802) 824-5054

An 1827 brick home listed in the National Register of Historic Places. Walk to shops, museums, and summer theater. Crackling fires in common rooms, canopied beds, and down comforters. Rooms have original Moses Eaton stenciling and are furnished with antiques and reproductions. Weston Priory nearby. Some holidays and weekends may require minimum stays. Children over six welcome.

Hosts: Peggy and Roy Varner
Rooms: 7 (5 PB; 2 SB) $65-125
Full Breakfast
Credit Cards: A, B
Notes: 2, 5, 7, 9, 10, 11, 12, 13

The Wilder Homestead Inn

7 No smoking; 8 Children welcome; 9 Social drinking allowed; 10 Tennis nearby; 11 Swimming nearby; 12 Golf nearby; 13 Skiing nearby; 14 May be booked through a travel agent; 15 Handicapped accessible.

WILMINGTON

The Hermitage Inn

Coldbrook Road, P.O. Box 457, 05363
(802) 464-3511; FAX (802) 464-2688
e-mail: hermitag@sover.net
www.hermitageinn.com

Fifteen individually decorated guest
rooms each with working fireplace, private bath, telephone, and cable TV. Fourteen guest rooms at nearby Brookbound.
Award-winning restaurant serving Continental cuisine, and featuring home-raised
gamebirds and venison. *Wine* Spectator's
Grand Awardwinner yearly since 1983.
More than 2,000 labels and 35,000 bottles
in stock to complement every meal. Sporting clays course and hunting preserve on-
site. A 55K ski touring center with
equipment rentals and lessons. Wine and
Gift shop offers homemade maple syrup,
jams, and jellies.

Host: James McGovern
Rooms: 29 (25 PB; 4 SB)
Credit Cards: A, B, C, E
Notes: 2, 4, 5, 8, 10, 11, 12, 13, 14, 15

Misty Mountain Lodge

326 Stowe Hill Road, 05363
(802) 464-3961; e-mail: mistymtn@together.net

A circa 1803 farmhouse inn on 150 acres.
All rooms have a beautiful view of the
Green Mountains. Two guest rooms with
private baths and TVs, two deluxe rooms
with private baths and TVs (one with
whirlpool tub), and four rooms with shared
baths. Home-cooked meals (dinner by
reservation) are prepared by owners. Cozy
living room with fireplace for reading, visiting, or joining in a sing-along with hosts.
Close to skiing, hiking, boating, golf, and
Marlboro Music Festival.

Hosts: Buzz and Elizabeth Cole
Rooms: 8 (4 PB; 4 SB) $55-125
Full Breakfast
Credit Cards: A, B, C, D
Notes: 2, 4, 5, 7, 8, 9, 10, 11, 12, 13, 14, 15

Nutmeg Inn

Nutmeg Inn

153 Route 9W (Molly Stark Trail), P.O. Box 818,
    Mount Snow Valley, 05363
(802) 464-3351; (800) 277-5402

Just as guests always imagined a New England country inn to be. Beautifully restored
circa 1777 Vermont farmhouse appointed
with period antiques. All rooms and suites
with private baths, central air conditioning,
and telephones; many with wood-burning
fireplaces and TVs. All have king- or
queen-size beds (four-poster, brass, and
wrought iron). Luxurious suites with
whirlpools, living rooms, wood-burning
fireplaces, TVs, and VCRs. Common area
with BYOB and fireplace. Full gourmet
country breakfast cooked to order.

Hosts: Dave and Pat Cerchio
Rooms: 14 (PB) $78-215
Full Breakfast
Credit Cards: A, B, C, D
Notes: 2, 5, 7, 9, 10, 11, 12, 13

The Red Shutter Inn

Route 9 West, Box 636, 05363
(802) 464-3768; (800) 845-7548

This 1894 nine-room Colonial inn with
fireplace suites sits on a hillside within
walking distance of the town of Wilmington. Tucked behind the inn is the renovated
carriage house with four rooms, one a
two-room fireplace suite with a two-person
whirlpool bath. A renowned restaurant
with candlelight dining (alfresco dining on
an awning-covered porch in the summer-
time). Championship golf (golf packages),

skiing at Mount Snow and Haystack, cross-country skiing, hiking, boating, and antiquing are minutes away. Experience the congenial atmosphere of country inn life. Closed April. No smoking in inn.

Hosts: Renée and Tad Lyon
Rooms: 9 (PB) $105-210
Full Breakfast
Credit Cards: A, B, C, D
Notes: 2, 4, 7, 9, 10, 11, 12, 13, 14

Shearer Hill Farm Bed and Breakfast

Shearer Hill Road, P.O. Box 1453, 05363
(802) 464-3253; (800) 437-3104
e-mail: ppuseySHF@sover.net

Enjoy the quiet setting of this small working farm with white-faced Hereford cows, on a pristine country road. The inn, just five miles from the center of Wilmington, has large rooms with private baths. The hosts serve a delicious Vermont breakfast. Near Mount Snow and Haystack ski areas, groomed cross-country skiing trails on property, connected to VAST trails, snowmobile rentals and sleigh rides nearby. Marlboro Music Festival just five miles away. Outstanding golf courses, swimming, hiking, boating, horseback riding, mountain biking, and many fine restaurants nearby.

Hosts: Bill and Patti Pusey
Rooms: 6 (PB) $90
Full Breakfast
Credit Cards: A, B, C
Notes: 2, 5, 7, 8, 9, 10, 11, 12, 13, 14, 15

Trail's End—A Country Inn

5 Trail's End Lane, 05363
(802) 464-2727; (800) 859-2585

A unique country inn tucked away on 10 acres with flower gardens, a clay tennis court, heated outdoor pool, and a large pond. Described as "irresistibly romantic" by the author of Best Places to Kiss in New England. Picture-perfect rooms, including fireplace rooms and fireplace suites with canopy beds and whirlpool tubs. Full break-

fast menu and afternoon tea. Warm hospitality and attention to detail are the hosts' specialties. Ski and golf packages available as well as dining discounts.

Hosts: Debby and Kevin Stephens
Rooms: 15 (PB) $95-155
Suites: $145-185
Full Breakfast
Credit Cards: A, B, C, D
Notes: 2, 5, 9, 10, 11, 12, 13, 14

The White House of Wilmington

Route 9, P.O. Box 757, 05363
(802) 464-2135; (800) 541-2135
FAX (802) 464-5222; e-mail: whitehse@sover.net
www.whitehouseinn.com

Set on the crest of a high rolling hill overlooking the Deerfield Valley, the White House of Wilmington is southern Vermont's premier landmark. Built in 1915 as a private summer home, the Victorian mansion now offers romantic accommodations amidst casual surroundings. It's easy to see why the inn was voted "one of the 10 most romantic inns" by both the New York Times and Boston Herald. Twenty-three guest rooms, 13 fireplaces, indoor and outdoor pools, whirlpool and sauna. Ski touring center.

Host: Robert Grinold
Rooms: 23 (PB) $108-195
Full Breakfast
Credit Cards: A, B, C, D
Notes: 2, 4, 10, 11, 12, 13, 14, 15

The White House of Wilmington

_____

Juniper Hill Inn

Rural Route 1, Box 79, 05089
(802) 674-5273; (800) 359-2541
www.juniperhillinn.com

This elegant but informal inn allows guests to pamper themselves. Antique-furnished guest rooms, many with working fireplaces. Marvelous views. Sumptuous candlelit dinners and hearty breakfasts. Cool off in the pool, canoe, bike, hike, or visit antique and craft shops, covered bridges, and museums. Twenty minutes from Woodstock and Quechee, and Hanover, New Hampshire. A perfectly romantic inn. Mobil- and AAA-rated. Closed April.

Hosts: Rob and Susanne Pearl
Rooms: 16 (PB) $90-150
Full Breakfast
Credit Cards: A, B, D
Notes: 2, 4, 7, 10, 11, 12, 13, 14

WOLCOTT _____

American Country Collection

1353 Union Street, Schenectady, NY 12308
(518) 370-4948; (800) 810-4948
FAX (518) 393-1634 (call first)
e-mail: carolbnbres@mon.com

130. Twelve miles north of Stowe, this Greek Revival-style three-bedroom inn is bordered by the LaMoille River and has authentically appointed rooms and spacious bedchambers. The three guest rooms with private baths are decorated according to themes. One room has a gas-fired wood stove. Full breakfast. Smoking outdoors only. Children 12 and older welcome. $64-79.

WOODSTOCK _____

Canterbury House

43 Pleasant Street, 05091
(802) 457-3077

A 115-year-old village townhome just east of the village green. This bed and breakfast,

Canterbury House

furnished with authentic Victorian antiques, has eight rooms with private baths. Living room with TV and VCR. Within walking distance of shops, the historic district, and restaurants. A full gourmet breakfast is served in the dining room. Guest rooms have air conditioning. Described as elegant but comfortable. Children over 12 welcome.

Hosts: The Frosts
Rooms: 8 (PB) $85-155
Full Breakfast
Credit Cards: A, B, C
Notes: 2, 5, 7, 9, 10, 11, 12, 13, 14

Deer Brook Inn

HCR 68, Box 443, Route 4 West, 05091
(802) 672-3713

Handmade quilts, original pine floors, and an immaculately maintained country decor are just a few of the charming features of this 1820 farmhouse. Five spacious guest rooms, one of which is a two-room suite, with private baths, and queen- or king-size beds. Enjoy a crackling fire in the winter or a view of the Ottauquechee River from the porch in the summer. A bountiful breakfast provides the perfect start for the day. Five minutes to Woodstock village and 15 minutes to Killington ski area. AAA-rated three diamonds.

Hosts: Brian and Rosemary McGinty
Rooms: 5 (PB) $70-125
Full Breakfast
Credit Cards: A, B, C
Notes: 2, 5, 7, 8, 9, 10, 11, 12, 13, 14

NOTES: Credit cards accepted: A MasterCard; B Visa; C American Express; D Discover; E Diner's Club; F Other; 2 Personal checks accepted; 3 Lunch available; 4 Dinner available; 5 Open all year; 6 Pets welcome;

Four Pillars at Taftsville, circa 1836

Happy Valley Road, P.O. Box 132, Taftsville, 05073
(802) 457-2797

Historic Greek Revival, circa 1836, restored home. Four huge hemlock trees were used to erect the "four pillars" on the front porch. Enjoy the splendor of Vermont all year, with everything from golfing to skiing. Each guest room is charming and unique with private baths. Delightful down comforters, lace curtains, wide-pine-board floors and lush towels are just a sampling of the amenities. Breakfasts may be candlelit and dinner served upon advanced notice. Enjoy country walks and wonderful bike paths. An authentic Russian stove graces the kitchen.

Innkeepers: Gail and Gui
Rooms: 5 (PB) $75-140
Credit Cards: A, B
Notes: 2, 5, 7, 9, 10, 11, 12, 13, 15

The Jackson House Inn

37 Old Route 4 West, 05091
(802) 457-2065; (800) 448-1890
FAX (802) 457-9290; www.jacksonhouse.com

"Vermont's hottest gourmet getaway,"— *Country Inns* magazine. Fine dining and luxurious accommodations in an 1890 Victorian mansion in the National Register of Historic Places. Fifteen guest rooms, including six suites, are furnished with

Jackson House Inn

fine period antiques in various gracious styles. Memorable gourmet breakfast and evening wine/champagne bar included. Five beautifully landscaped acres of formal gardens with stream and pond. Spa with steam room.

Host: Juan Florin
Rooms: 15 (PB) $170-260
Full Breakfast
Credit Cards: A, B, C
Notes: 2, 4, 5, 7, 9, 10, 11, 12, 13, 14, 15

Kedron Valley Inn

Kedron Valley Inn

Route 106, South Woodstock, 05071
(800) 836-1193; FAX (802) 457-4469
e-mail: kedroninn@aol.com
www.innformation.com/vt/kedron

Historic country inn, nestled seven minutes south of picturesque Woodstock. Private baths, Jacuzzis, in-room fireplaces, queen-size canopied beds, heirloom quilts, private decks. Award of Excellence wine list with cuisine that is tied for top honors in all Vermont. Swimming lake with two white-sand beaches. Surrounded by skiing, antiques, historic estates, and shopping. Featured in *Country Living*, *Country Home*, and *Yankee*. Voted Inn of the Year by *Inn-Goers*.

Hosts: Max and Merrily Comins
Rooms: 26 (PB) $120-205
Full Breakfast
Credit Cards: A, B, C, D
Notes: 2, 4, 9, 10, 11, 12, 13, 14

7 No smoking; 8 Children welcome; 9 Social drinking allowed; 10 Tennis nearby; 11 Swimming nearby; 12 Golf nearby; 13 Skiing nearby; 14 May be booked through a travel agent; 15 Handicapped accessible.

The Lincoln Inn at the Covered Bridge

Rural Route 2, Box 40, Route 4, 05091
(802) 457-3312; FAX (802) 457-5808
e-mail: lincon2@aol.com
www.pbpub.com/woodstock/lincoln.htm

A full service country inn set in a lovingly
restored farmhouse. Six cozy guest rooms
await, each with private bath, each unique
in style and character. Just three miles
west of the village, the inn sits on six
acres of beautiful riverfront grounds.
Dinner, available in the country-elegant
dining room, is prepared by Swiss
chef/owner for guests' delight. AAA
three-diamond-rated. Nonsmoking.

Hosts: Kurt and Lori Hildbrand
Rooms: 6 (PB) $99-139
Full Breakfast
Credit Cards: A, B, D
Notes: 2, 4, 5, 7, 8, 10, 11, 12, 13

Three Church Street

3 Church Street, 05091
(802) 457-1925; FAX (802) 457-9181

Built in the early 1800s, Three Church
Street is on the Ottauquechee River in the
heart of historic Woodstock, with its numerous restaurants, galleries, and shops. The
antique-filled Georgian mansion sits on two
acres of lawns, gardens, a large swimming
pool, and tennis court. Indoors, guests can
enjoy the classic 19th-century music room,
the cozy library, and the spacious porch
facing the river and the mountains.

Host: Eleanor C. Paine
Rooms: 11 (6 PB; 5 SB) $75-105
Full Breakfast
Credit Cards: A, B
Notes: 2, 5, 6, 7, 8, 9, 10, 11, 12, 13, 14

Woodstock House Bed and Breakfast

Route 106, P.O. Box 361, 05091
(802) 457-1758

Renovated old farmhouse with exposed
hand-hewn beams and lovely mellow old
floors. Three miles south of Woodstock on
Route 106. Open May through December.

Host: Mary Fraser
Rooms: 5 (3 PB; 2 SB) $60-75
Full Breakfast
Credit Cards: None
Notes: 2, 4, 7, 9, 10, 11, 12, 13

The Woodstocker Bed and Breakfast

Route 4, 61 River Street, 05091
(802) 457-3896; FAX (802) 457-3897
www.scenesofvermont.com/woodstocker/
index.html

Nestled at the foot of Mount Tom, this
charming 1830s Cape offers nine large,
tastefully appointed air-conditioned rooms
with private baths. Queen-size beds, full
kitchens, and private sitting areas are among
the many amenities available. Each morning begins with a sumptuous buffet breakfast, and complimentary refreshments are
served in the afternoon. Within the picturesque village of Woodstock, a short stroll
over a covered bridge brings guests to fine
dining and shopping.

Hosts: Tom and Nancy Blackford
Rooms: 9 (PB) $85-155
Full Breakfast
Credit Cards: A, B
Notes: 2, 5, 7, 8, 9, 10, 11, 12, 13, 14

NOTES: Credit cards accepted: A MasterCard; B Visa; C American Express; D Discover; E Diner's Club;
F Other; 2 Personal checks accepted; 3 Lunch available; 4 Dinner available; 5 Open all year; 6 Pets welcome;

Canada

New Brunswick

New Brunswick

ALBERT

Florentine Manor

Rural Route 2 (on Route 915 at Harvey), E0A 1A0
(506) 882-2271; (800) 665-2271
FAX (506) 882-2936

Sleep where the stars have slept. While visiting Canada's east coast, experience country living in a perfect natural setting in this 1860 manor. The rooms are decorated with antiques of the Victorian era. All nine rooms are nonsmoking with private baths. Prime opportunity for viewing waterfowl, woodland birds, Fundy National Park, Hopewell Rocks Provincial Park, and the spectacular shorebird migration, along with the highest tides in the world. Within walking distance of Mary's Point, Canada's first hemispheric shorebird preserve. Hospitality is hosts' way of life. Exceptional hiking opportunities. Accommodation grade under inns: three and one-half stars. Lunch and dinner available by reservation. Closed for the month of March.

Hosts: Mary and Cyril Tingley
Rooms: 9 (PB) $69-119
Full Breakfast
Credit Cards: A, B
Notes: 7, 9, 10, 11, 12, 13

Florentine Manor

Sandpipers' Rest Bed and Breakfast

Rural Route 2, E0A 1A0
(506) 882-2744

The bed and breakfast is at the corner of Mary's Point Road and the scenic Route 915; three kilometers from Riverside/Albert. The 135-year-old home is comfortably furnished with antiques and features a unique bottle collection. It is three kilometers from the bird sanctuary at Mary's Point with its thousands of migrating sandpipers, 20 minutes from the Rocks, Fundy National Park, and a pleasant walk to the salt marshes. Enjoy a peaceful walk, a ride across the marsh on the available bicycles, a hearty breakfast, and a comfortable night's rest.

Hosts: Stephen and Patricia Marshall
Rooms: 2 (2 SB) $45
Full Breakfast
Credit Cards: A, B
Notes: 2, 3, 4, 6, 7, 8, 9, 11, 12

BOUCTOUCHE

Domaine-sur-Mer

Box 1, Site 13, Rural Route 3, E0A 1G0
(506) 743-6582; FAX (506) 743-8397
e-mail: Domaine@auracom.com
www.sn2000.nb.ca/comp/domaine-sur-mer

If one is looking for a quiet beach, cleansing salt air, enchanting scenery, and tranquility, Domaine-sur-Mer, a four-star bed and breakfast, is the place. Each room has an ocean view and is near the Irvine Eco Center with 2K of boardwalk and 12K of sandy beach. Swim in waters warmer than

---

NOTES: Credit cards accepted: A MasterCard; B Visa; C American Express; D Discover; E Diner's Club; F Other; 2 Personal checks accepted; 3 Lunch available; 4 Dinner available; 5 Open all year; 6 Pets welcome; 7 No smoking; 8 Children welcome; 9 Social drinking allowed; 10 Tennis nearby; 11 Swimming nearby; 12 Golf nearby; 13 Skiing nearby; 14 May be booked through a travel agent; 15 Handicapped accessible.

any north of Virginia. For a free New Brunswick catalogue, call 1-800-561-0123.

Host: Eueline Haché
Rooms: 3 (PB) $55-65
Full Breakfast
Credit Cards: B
Notes: 5, 7, 9, 11, 12

CARAQUET

"Le Poirier" Bed and Breakfast

98 Boulevard St-Pierre Ouest, E1W 1B6
(506) 727-4359; FAX (506) 726-1209

Wonderful sunsets in a cozy seashore fishing town on the Acadian Peninsula. Minutes from the world-renowned Acadian Historical Village. Caraquet features the Acadian Festival August 6-16, one of the 10 best recommended festivals in North America, wind surfing, boating, deep-sea fishing, kayak renting, horseback riding. "Le Poirier" homestead, built in 1927, has been restored to its original splendor and offers Acadian hospitality in a restful atmosphere.

Hosts: Roland and Martina Froilet
Rooms: 5 (2 PB; 3 SB) $45-65 Canadian
Continental Breakfast
Credit Cards: None
Notes: 2, 4, 5, 7, 8, 9, 11, 12

La Poirier

EDMUNDSTON

Auberge Le Fief Inn Bed and Breakfast

87 Church Street, E3V 1J6
(506) 735-0400; FAX (506) 735-0402

A Heritage Canada estate with themed rooms showing the history of the legendary

Republic of Madawaska. All rooms have private (full) baths, air conditioning, telephones, TVs, and VCRs. Guests can borrow a book from hosts' private library or a movie from their collection of Academy Award-winners. The licensed dining room offers fine regional cuisine in a romantic Victorian setting and can help create a wonderful memory.

Hosts: Sharon and Philip Bélanger
Rooms: 8 (PB) $64.95-99.95
Full Breakfast
Credit Cards: A, B
Notes: 4, 5, 7, 8, 9, 10, 11, 12, 13

FREDERICTON

Fowler House Bed and Breakfast

2785 Woodstock Road, E3C 1R1
(506) 459-7766; FAX (506) 454-5405

Charming 1820s farmhouse on the St. John River in the middle of 23 private acres. Cozy, comfortable rooms with two twin or queen-size beds and private en suite baths. Full breakfast included. Large in-ground swimming pool; informal flower and vegetable gardens; hiking and biking path along the river; minutes away from downtown, close to Mactaquac provincial park, golf courses, and King's Landing Historical Settlement.

Hosts: Don and Rita Fowler
Rooms: 3 (PB) $75 Canadian
Full Breakfast
Credit Cards: B
Notes: 7, 8, 9, 10, 11, 12

GRAND MANAN

Manan Island Inn

Box 15 North Head, E0G 2M0
(506) 662-8624

In the restful setting of this inn, guests will enjoy the comfort of antique furnishing, a cozy wood-burning fireplace, and an intimate atmosphere. Private baths are limited because of its quaint 19th-century architecture. Several favorite attractions delight visitors, including whale watching, hiking, sea kayaking, shopping, or spying comic puffins among the island's rare birds. Conveniently across the way from the ferry boat dock.

Host: Elaine Greene
Rooms: 9 (1 PB; 8 SB) $65-110
Full and Continental Breakfast
Credit Cards: A, B, C
Notes: 4, 5, 7, 8, 10, 11, 12

GRAND MANAN ISLAND

Compass Rose

North Head, E0G 2M0
(506) 662-8570; (514) 458-2607 (winter)
FAX (514) 458-3119

Two small turn-of-the-century houses overlooking the fisherman's wharf at North Head. The bedrooms are made inviting with quilts and pine furnishings. Breathtaking views of the Bay of Fundy and the busy harbor make dining in the Compass Rose always a special occasion. The menu features island-grown produce, locally caught seafood, and baked goods fresh from the ovens.

Hosts: Nora and Ed Parker
Rooms: 8 (PB) $89
Full Breakfast
Credit Cards: A, B
Notes: 3, 4, 7, 8, 9, 10, 11, 12

McLaughlin's Wharf Inn

Seal Cove, E0G 3B0
(506) 662-8760; (506) 662-3672 (reservations)
FAX (506) 662-9998

Bed and breakfast with relaxed homey atmosphere in center of small fishing village and historic property. Six cozy shared-bathrooms, TV lounge, dining room, deck overlooking tides of Bay of Fundy. Dining room wheelchair accessible. Close to all island interests, local bird and whale watching, and boat tours.

Rooms: 6 (SB) $69
Continental Breakfast

Credit Cards: A, B, C
Notes: 3, 7, 8, 10, 11, 12

MONCTON

Bonaccord House

250, Bonaccord Street, E1C 5M6
(506) 388-1535; FAX (506) 853-7191

Visible from Mountain Road, at the corner of John and Bonaccord Streets in downtown Moncton. It is a lovely yellow, three-story turn-of-the-century residence. The double living room, complete with fireplace and bay window, offers a convivial atmosphere in which to meet fellow travelers or to just sit quietly and read. Enjoy a morning coffee or afternoon tea on the lovely front veranda.

Host: Jeremy Martin
Rooms: 5 (3 PB; 2 SB) $50-58
Full Breakfast
Credit Cards: B
Notes: 2, 5, 7, 8, 9, 10, 11, 12, 13

Bonaccord House

RIVERSIDE

Cailswick Babbling Brook

Route 114, E02 2R0
(506) 882-2079

Babbling Brook is a century-old Victorian home in the village of Riverside, Albert County, New Brunswick, overlooking the Shepody Bay. The home is surrounded by running books, trees, flowers, and spacious land where one may relax and enjoy the beauty of nature. Country-style breakfasts served every morning in the spacious kitchen. Come and explore the beauty of Albert County and the hospitality of its people. The Fundy National Park, bird sanctuary, Cape Enrage, Hopewell Rocks, and a selection of craft shops and galleries are all nearby.

Host: Eunice Cail
Rates: $45-50
Full Breakfast
Credit Cards: None
Notes: 2, 3, 5, 7, 8, 9, 14

ROTHESAY

Shadow Lawn Inn

3180 Rothesay Road, E2E 5V7
(800) 561-4166; e-mail: sli@nbnet.ca.com.

Historic Victorian mansion with four-star accommodations and dining. Nine guest rooms and three suites, all with private en suite baths, cable TVs, and telephones. In the affluent town of Rothesay, it is minutes away from airport and the historic city of St. John. "Come, relax, and let us pamper you." Smoking permitted in designated areas only.

Rooms: 12 (PB) $89-175
Continental Breakfast
Credit Cards: A, B, C, E
Notes: 2, 3, 4, 5, 6, 8, 9, 10, 11, 12

ST. ANDREWS

Harris Hatch Inn Bed and Breakfast

142 Queen Street, E0G 2X0
(506) 529-4713; FAX (506) 529-4448
e-mail: jurabob@nbnet.nb.ca

The Harris Hatch Inn is a stately red brick house built in 1840 with bricks baked on the site. Extensively restored, the house blends modern convenience with historical design and decor. The large living room provides a perfect place for conversation and reading. Each bedroom has a spacious en suite full bath and a working fireplace.

Amenities include iron with ironing board, coffee maker, individual heat control, cable remote-controlled color TV. The whole house is smokefree and has central air. The beautiful and historic English town of St. Andrews offers shops, galleries, museums, and Victorian churches within a short walk. The waterfront, a block away, offers whale watching trips, sea kayaking, canoeing, and sightseeing excursions.

Hosts: Jura Everett and Robert Estes
Rooms: 2 (PB) $85-95
Full Breakfast
Credit Cards: A, B
Notes: 7, 9, 10, 11, 12

Kingsbrae Arms Relais & Chateaux

219 King Street, E0G 2X0
(506) 529-1897 (reservations)
(506) 529-1187 (guest line)
FAX (506) 529-1197; e-mail: kingbrae@nbnet.nb.ca

Kingsbrae Arms is a sprawling manor house, first to earn a Canada Select five-star rating and now first in Atlantic Canada to become Relais et Chateaux. The estate serves guests as friends who have come to stay at a private country home. The cuisine changes daily and with the seasons. There is a heated pool in the private gardens. The house is filled with traditional art and antiques, yet is prepared for the 21st century with the latest communication devices and marble-appointed bathrooms in the guest quarters.

Hosts: Harry Chancey and David Oxford
Rooms: 9 (PB) $150-400 Canadian
Full Breakfast
Credit Cards: A, B
Notes: 2, 3, 4, 5, 7, 9, 10, 11, 12, 13, 14

ST. ANDREWS-BY-THE-SEA

Pansy Patch

59 Carleton Street, E0G 2X0
(506) 529-3834; (888) PANSY PATCH(726-7972)
FAX (506) 529-9042

Distinctively rated a four-star (Canada Select) and a three-diamond (AAA/CAA)

NOTES: Credit cards accepted: A MasterCard; B Visa; C American Express; D Discover; E Diner's Club; F Other; 2 Personal checks accepted; 3 Lunch available; 4 Dinner available; 5 Open all year; 6 Pets welcome;

destination for romance, relaxation, or business. "The most photographed home in New Brunswick"—*St. Croix Courier*. Featured in *New York Times, Canadian Homes, Bride's*. Designated a Canadian Heritage property. Renowned for its Canadian warmth and hospitality. Thoughtful, yet discreet, attention given to each guest's needs and tastes. Outstanding quality in furnishings, appointments, and amenities. Resort-class recreational facilities. Bike rentals. Full breakfasts, breakfast-in-bed, fine dining room service, picnic lunches, barbecue. Advance reservations suggested.

Host: Jeannie Foster
Rooms: 9 (PB) $185-230 Canadian
Full Breakfast
Credit Cards: A, B
Notes: 3, 4, 7, 8, 10, 11, 12, 14

ST. JOHN

Five Chimneys Bed and Breakfast

238 Charlotte Street, West, E2M 1Y3
(506) 635-1888; FAX (506) 635-8402
e-mail: ajdg@nbnet.nb.ca

In Canada's oldest incorporated city, this 1855 Greek Revival home is near the Reversing Falls and the Digby Ferry. Three guest rooms, all with private baths. The

Five Chimneys

bedrooms are warm, cozy, decorated with antique reproductions, plush linens, and treasures. The Italianate dormer is complemented by its stained-glass coats of arms. Wake up each morning to the aroma of freshly brewed coffee and homemade breads and muffins with freezer jams. Full breakfast includes whole-wheat and oatmeal pancakes, a cheesey egg dish, and oatmeal porridge, all from scratch. A warm welcome awaits guests. Enjoy 1850s atmosphere with 1990s comfort.

Host: Linda Gates
Rooms: 3 (PB) $60-70
Full Breakfast
Credit Cards: A, B, F
Notes: 2, 5, 7, 8, 9, 10, 11, 12, 13

Mahogany Manor

Mahogany Manor

220 Germain Street, E2L 2G4
(506) 636-8000; FAX (506) 636-8001
e-mail: leavittr@nbnet.nb.ca
www.stnow.com/mm/

The graceful elegance of a bygone era greets guests in this restored turn-of-the-century home. Each guest room is decorated with antique or heirloom furniture, has a private bathroom, and a queen- or king-size bed. On a quiet residential street in the midst of historic Saint John, within walking distance of tourist attractions, restaurants, shops, and entertainment. "Make yourself at home—your comfort is our pleasure!" One room is handicapped accessible.

7 No smoking; 8 Children welcome; 9 Social drinking allowed; 10 Tennis nearby; 11 Swimming nearby; 12 Golf nearby; 13 Skiing nearby; 14 May be booked through a travel agent; 15 Handicapped accessible.

Hosts: Wayne Harrison, Ross Leavitt
Rooms: 5 (PB) $60-65
Full Breakfast
Credit Cards: A, B
Notes: 5, 7, 9, 11, 12

SHEDIAC

Auberge Belcourt Inn

310 Main Street, E0A 3G0
(506) 532-6098; FAX (506) 532-9398
e-mail: belcourt@nbnet.nb.ca

Come and revisit a bygone era in an elegantly renovated Victorian-style house entirely furnished with period antiques. Seven uniquely furnished bedrooms are available (five with private baths). A full breakfast is served on antique china in an oval dining room. In the heart of Shediac

Auberge Belcort

within walking distance of shops and restaurants, and close to Parlee Beach, one of the finest beaches in New Brunswick. Dinner available September through April only.

Hosts: Pauline and Chris Pyke
Rooms: 7 (5 PB; 2 SB) $79-109 Canadian
Full Breakfast
Credit Cards: A, B, C, E
Notes: 5, 9, 11, 12

WOODSTOCK

Foot of the Hill

109 Sherwood Drive, E7M 2R3
(506) 328-3585; (888) 354-4444
FAX (506) 325-2899
e-mail: bridgeo@nbnet.nb.ca

On the banks of the Meduxnekeag River, which runs through the center of Woodstock, guests will find this bed and breakfast removed from the noise and rush of life. Sit on the decks and watch nature play in the quiet, comfortable surroundings. Guests will be at home in this home, which is often commended for its cleanliness by previous guests. Inquire about accommodations for children.

Hosts: Jeanne and Tom Bridgeo
Rooms: 3 (1 PB; 2 SB) $50 Canadian
Full Breakfast
Credit Cards: None
Notes: 2, 5, 7, 9, 10, 11, 12, 13

NOTES: Credit cards accepted: A MasterCard; B Visa; C American Express; D Discover; E Diner's Club;
F Other; 2 Personal checks accepted; 3 Lunch available; 4 Dinner available; 5 Open all year; 6 Pets welcome;

Nova Scotia

AMHERST

Breeze In Bed and Breakfast

P.O. Box 153, B4H 3Z2
(902) 667-5518; FAX (902) 667-4998

Panoramic view across a narrow arm of the
Bay of Fundy of the New Brunswick hills.
Renovated farmhouse (circa 1890) featuring original pine floors, rustic antiques,
quilts, and primitive Nova Scotia folk art.
Brick front courtyard surrounded by perennial flower beds. One housekeeping apartment, one skylit bed and breakfast suite.

Hosts: Lee and Gerald Freeman
Units: 2 (PB) $55-70 Canadian
Full Breakfast
Credit Cards: B
Notes: 2, 6, 7, 8, 9, 11, 12

ANNAPOLIS ROYAL

Hillsdale House

519 St. George Street, P.O. Box 148, B0S 1A0
(902) 532-2345; FAX (902) 532-7850

Built in 1849, the inn has been host to two
kings of England, many of Canada's gover-
nors general, and leading politicians. Guests
will find their rooms impressive, and the
private bath en suite a welcome relief from
the wearies of travel. Next door are the
Royal Historic Gardens with more than a
mile of meandering pathways. Within walking distance are historic Fort Anne, museums, art galleries, fine restaurants, and
many other places of interest.

Host: Leslie J. Langille
Rooms: 10 (PB) $65-95
Full Breakfast

Credit Cards: A, B
Notes: 7, 8, 9, 10, 11, 12

The King George Inn

548 Upper St. George Street, B0S 1A0
(902) 532-5286; (902) 425-5656 (off-season)
(888) 799-KING (5464)
e-mail: dms@ns.sympatico.ca
www3.ns.sympatico.ca/dms/king.htm

Grand Victorian sea captain's home, furnished completely in period antiques. In
historic Annapolis Royal (Canada's oldest
settlement). A short walk from all major
attractions. Inn features large, bright rooms
with tall ceilings, cove moldings, leaded
glass, fireplaces, parquet floors, and legendary Nova Scotian hospitality. Family
suites available. Free bicycles. Whale
watching arranged.

Hosts: Michael and Donna Susnick;
   Faye McStravick
Rooms: 6 (2 PB; 4 SB) $49-79
Full and Continental Breakfast
Credit Cards: A, B
Notes: 6, 7, 8, 9, 10, 11, 12, 14

The King George Inn

Nova Scotia

BADDECK

Castle Moffett

P.O. Box 678, B0E 1B0
(902) 756-9070; FAX (902) 756-3399
e-mail: castle@canadamail.com
www.castlemoffett.com

Castle Moffett spans a cascading brook on 185 mountainside acres overlooking the Bras d'Or Lake. Centrally positioned to the Cabot Trail, Bell Museum, Fortress Louisbourg, bird and whale cruises, and championship golfing. Each deluxe suite features a four-poster bed, large whirlpool bath, fireplace, antiques, and magnificent views. Enjoy the Great Hall with its grand piano and fireplace, a quiet walk, bird watching, and an alfresco champagne lobster supper in a five-star bed and breakfast. Two- to five-night honeymoon/adventure/golf packages available. Rates include a Continental buffet breakfast and are based on per couple per night. Guaranteed reservations on Visa and MasterCard. Dinner available with advance reservations. Fully licensed Dungeon Lounge.

Hosts: Mr. and Mrs. Desmond Moffett
Rooms: 3 (PB) $225-400
Continental Breakfast
Credit Cards: A, B
Notes: 7, 9, 11, 12, 13, 14

CANNING

The Farmhouse Inn

1057 Main Street, P.O. Box 38, B0P 1H0
(800) 928-4346; FAX (902) 582-7900
e-mail: farmhous@ns.sympatico.ca
www.valleyweb.com/farmhouseinn

Charming 200-year-old farmhouse in historic shipbuilding village. Quaint decor; noted for its full breakfasts. Close to Atlantic Theatre Festival, fine dining, excellent hiking, and bird watching (bald eagles). In the Annapolis Valley, famous for the Apple Blossom Festival in late May. Family and deluxe suites, some with whirlpool tub and/or fireplace. Canopied beds, private baths. Some rooms have TV/VCRs and air conditioning. Afternoon tea and full breakfast included. Recommended by AAA and Canada Select (four stars). Smoking allowed outside only.

Hosts: Doug and Ellen Bray
Rooms: 6 (PB) $39-119 Canadian
Full Breakfast
Credit Cards: A, B
Notes: 5, 7, 8, 9, 11, 12, 13, 14

CHESTER

Haddon Hall Inn

67 Haddon Hill Road, B0J 1J0
(902) 275-3577; FAX (902) 275-5159

Haddon Hall, one of Chester's renowned summer estates, was built in 1905 by Vernon Woolrich. On top of Haddon Hill, the residence offers a spectacular view of Mahone Bay and the town of Chester. This elegant country inn offers 10 beautiful guest rooms furnished in period furnishings, with private baths, TVs, and telephones. Guests are invited to swim in the outdoor pool or relax on the broad veranda. In the evening sit in front of a warm crackling fire in the Moose Room prior to dining in the elegant restaurant.

Host: Cynthia O'Connell
Rooms: 10 (PB) $150 and up
Continental Breakfast
Credit Cards: A, B
Notes: 4, 9, 10, 11, 12, 14, 15

Mecklenburgh Inn

78 Queen Street, B0J 1J0
(902) 275-4638; FAX (902) 275-4638

A welcoming bed and breakfast in the heart of the celebrated seaside village of Chester. Full gourmet breakfasts are served at the large dining table before a crackling wood fire. Each room is unique in decor but all enjoy downy duvets, designer sheets, fluffy towels, and comfy robes. The inn is the

NOTES: Credit cards accepted: A MasterCard; B Visa; C American Express; D Discover; E Diner's Club; F Other; 2 Personal checks accepted; 3 Lunch available; 4 Dinner available; 5 Open all year; 6 Pets welcome; 7 No smoking; 8 Children welcome; 9 Social drinking allowed; 10 Tennis nearby; 11 Swimming nearby; 12 Golf nearby; 13 Skiing nearby; 14 May be booked through a travel agent; 15 Handicapped accessible.

Mecklenburgh Inn

perfect home base from which to browse the shops, explore the area and islands, golf, sail, or just relax in the hammock on the covered balcony. In the evenings enjoy the theater, fine dining, or curl up with a book in front of the fire. Atmosphere is leisurely and casual.

Host: Sue Fraser
Rooms: 3 (SB) $50-65
Suite: 1 (PB) $115
Full Breakfast
Credit Cards: B, C
Notes: 3, 9, 10, 11, 12, 14

CHESTER BASIN

The Sword and Anchor

5306 Highway #3, B0J 1K0
(902) 275-2478; FAX (902) 275-5116
e-mail: janemc@tallships.istar.ca
www.atlanticonline.ns.ca/sword-anchor

Nestled in the heart of Chester Basin, minutes from Chester, experience the warmth and hospitality of the South Shore and embrace the breathtaking view of Nova Scotia's picturesque coastline. The Sword and Anchor claims a place of prominence from its hilltop site overlooking the waters of Mahone Bay. On the very scenic "Lighthouse Route," it is perfectly positioned for easy access to all the unique attractions that Nova Scotia has to offer.

Hosts: Jane and Arthur McLoughlin
Rooms: 8 (PB) $75
Full Breakfast

Credit Cards: A, B, D
Notes: 2, 5, 8, 9, 11, 12

DARTMOUTH

Autumn Leaves Bed and Breakfast

12 Evans Court, B2X 2T5
(902) 435-3980
e-mail: autumn.b-b@ns.sympatico.ca
www3.ns.sympatico.ca/autumn.b-b

At exit 6 on Route 111, take Route 318 north (Braemar, Waverley Road exit), 1K turn right to Evans Court. Well-manicured court. Very quiet. Designated smoking area. Open April 1 through October 31. Three rooms, hair dryer, clock radio, shared four-piece bath. Cable TV and VCR in living room. Full breakfast 8:30-9:30 A.M. (earlier on request). Near bus routes, lakes (canoeing, wind surfing, boating), beaches, golf courses, shopping malls, parks with walking trails, and restaurants.

Host: Audrey Joyce Brown
Rooms: 3 (SB) $49
Full Breakfast
Credit Cards: None
Notes: 2, 8, 10, 11, 12

D'ESCOUSSE

D'Escousse Bed and Breakfast

Rural Route 1, Box 510, B0E 1K0
(902) 226-2936

Early 1800s home overlooking picturesque harbor. Two and one-half baths, four rooms, TV in lounge. Kitchen facilities available. Plenty of privacy (owner resides in separate dwelling). Breakfast 7:00 A.M. to 12:00 P.M. A half-minute walk to private beach. Rowboats available. In Canada's choice of seven best villages.

Hosts: Sara and Al McDonald
Rooms: 4 (SB) $42
Full Breakfast
Credit Cards: None
Notes: 7, 8, 11, 12

NOTES: Credit cards accepted: A MasterCard; B Visa; C American Express; D Discover; E Diner's Club; F Other; 2 Personal checks accepted; 3 Lunch available; 4 Dinner available; 5 Open all year; 6 Pets welcome;

DIGBY

Thistle Down Country Inn

98 Montague Row, P.O. Box 508, B0V 1A0
(902) 245-4490; (800) 565-8081
FAX (902) 245-6717

Canada Select-rated three and one-half
stars. Historic 1904 home on Digby Har-
bour with spectacular view of the fishing
fleet and the Annapolis Basin. Delicious
candlelight dinners for guests only in the
Queen Alexandra dining room, at 6:30 P.M.;
reservations appreciated. Bicycle rentals,
public telephone in lobby gift shop. *On
parle français.* Twelve gracious rooms, all
with private bath. Six units directly on the
water with refrigerators. Cable TV and
VCR in lounge. Full breakfast served 7:30-
9:00 A.M. Open May 1 through October 31.
Inquire about accommodations for pets.
Children over six welcome.

Hosts: Ed Reid and Lester Bartson
Rooms: 12 (PB) $75-99 Canadian
Full Breakfast
Credit Cards: A, B, C, E
Notes: 4, 7, 9, 11, 12, 14

HALIFAX

Fresh Start Bed and Breakfast

2720 Gottingen Street, B3K 3C7
(902) 453-6616; (888) 453-6616
FAX (902) 456-6617

Victorian mansion with antique furnishings.
Informal atmosphere. Flexible check-in and
-out. Delicious breakfast with healthful
choices. Off-street parking. Free local calls.
Walking distance to museums, art galleries,
Citadel Hill, public gardens, and shopping.
Close to interesting and entertaining waterfront. Wide variety of restaurants, pubs,
cafés, and theaters nearby.

Hosts: Innis and Sheila MacDonald
Rooms: 8 (2 PB; 6 S21/2B) $55-75 Canadian
Full Breakfast
Credit Cards: A, B, C, E, F
Notes: 2, 5, 6, 7, 8, 9, 11, 14

Halifax's Waverley Inn

1266 Barrington Street, B3J 1Y5
(800) 565-9346; FAX (902) 425-0167
e-mail: welcome@waverleyinn.com

A stately Victorian property close to all
amenities in the bustling seaport city of Halifax. Since 1876, the Waverley has been
offering quality service and accommodations to pleasure and business travelers
alike. Each room is comfortably decorated
in the Victorian style but several special
rooms also offer a few added luxuries
including large Jacuzzi tubs. A stay at the
inn includes an all-morning Continental
breakfast, an evening offering of tea, coffee,
and treats plus ample on-site parking. Nonsmoking and smoking rooms available. Two
rooms are handicapped accessible.

Hosts: Abe and Elaine Leventhal
Rooms: 32 (PB) $79-139 Canadian
Continental Breakfast
Credit Cards: A, B, E
Notes: 5, 8, 9, 10, 11, 12, 14

Halliburton House Inn

5184 Morris Street, B3J 1B3
(902) 420-0658; FAX (902) 423-2324

Halliburton House Inn is a four-star registered Heritage property and is home to one
of Halifax's finest restaurants. The inn's
28 comfortable guest rooms are tastefully
furnished with period antiques. All have

Halliburton House Inn

7 No smoking; 8 Children welcome; 9 Social drinking allowed; 10 Tennis nearby; 11 Swimming nearby;
12 Golf nearby; 13 Skiing nearby; 14 May be booked through a travel agent; 15 Handicapped accessible.

private baths, as well as the modern amenities expected by today's guests. Two suites have working fireplaces. The restaurant offers a relaxed, elegant setting for dinners. The menu specializes in seafood and wild game. On-site parking.

Host: Robert B. Pretty
Rooms: 28 (PB) $110-160
Continental Breakfast
Credit Cards: A, B, C, E
Notes: 4, 5, 7, 8, 9, 10, 11, 12, 14

HALIFAX COUNTY

Salmon River House Country Inn

Head Jeddore, 9931 #7 Highway, B0J 1P0
(902) 889-3553; (800) 565-3353
FAX (902) 889-3653
e-mail: salmonrh@istar.ca
www.home.istar.ca/~salmonrh

Circa 1855 inn is nestled in a beautiful panorama of woods, hills, and water. Forty-five minutes from Dartmouth-Halifax Airport. Seven cozy but comfortable guest rooms, all with private baths. Wheelchair accessible. Romance room features whirlpool bath. Dining room, craft shop, and deck overlooking the water. Ask for the Romantic Getaway, Canoe or Kayak Adventure, or Sailboat Cruise packages.

Host: Adrien Blanchette
Rooms: 6 (PB) $68-99
Credit Cards: A, B, C, D, E
Notes: 2, 3, 4, 7, 8, 9, 11, 12, 14, 15

LUNENBURG

Kaulbach House Historic Inn

75 Pelham Street, B0J 2C0
(902) 634-8818 (phone/FAX); (800) 568-8818
(reservations)

Award-winning restoration of registered Heritage inn (circa 1880). In the heart of the United Nations-designated World Heritage town and overlooking the waterfront, this inn offers elegant accommodation in a gracious Victorian atmosphere. Each of the

seven beautifully appointed guest rooms has TV and private bath. A complimentary elaborate three-course breakfast includes specialities like Orange Soufflé with Strawberry Sauce, Apricot Glazed Pears, Peach 'n' Creme Crêpes, and Strawberry Crème Brulée. Off-street parking.

Hosts: Karen and Enzo Padovani
Rooms: 7 (PB) $65-110
Full Breakfast
Credit Cards: A, B, C
Notes: 7, 9, 10, 11, 12, 14

The Lunenburg Inn

26 Dufferin Street, P.O. Box 1407, B0J 2C0
(902) 634-3963; (800) 565-3963
FAX (902) 634-9419; e-mail: luninn@auracom.com
www.lunco.com/lunenburginn

The hosts take pride in providing their guests an at-home warmth during a stay at this beautifully restored, classic Victorian registered Heritage property (circa 1893). Breakfasts, featuring home-baking and preserves, are always a favorite with guests. On the edge of the UNESCO-designated World Heritage Site of Old Town Lunenburg. A short stroll brings guests to the waterfront and the living history that has made Lunenburg famous the world over.

Hosts: Gail and Don Wallace
Rooms: 7 (PB) $70-135 Canadian
Full Breakfast
Credit Cards: A, B, C, D
Notes: 7, 8, 9, 10, 11, 12, 14

MASSTOWN

Shady Maple Bed and Breakfast

1207 Highway #2, B0M 1G0
(902) 662-3565 (phone/FAX) (800) 493-5844

Welcome to this fully operating farm. Walk through fields and wooded trails, view the milking, pet the animals, swim in outdoor, heated pool; outdoor year-round spa. In the evening come and sit by the fireplace in this country home. Close proximity to the Tidal Bore, Truro, Ski Wentworth, only 45 minutes from Halifax

---

NOTES: Credit cards accepted: A MasterCard; B Visa; C American Express; D Discover; E Diner's Club; F Other; 2 Personal checks accepted; 3 Lunch available; 4 Dinner available; 5 Open all year; 6 Pets welcome;

airport. Hosts offer homemade jams, jellies, maple syrup, and farm fresh eggs. Full breakfast by candlelight, and evening snack. Cribs and cots available.

Hosts: James and Ellen Eisses
Rooms: 4 (S2B) $40-65
Full Breakfast
Credit Cards: None
Notes: 2, 6, 7, 8, 9, 11, 12, 13

MIDDLETON

Fairfield Farm Inn

10 Main Street (Route 1 West), B0S 1P0
(902) 825-6989 (phone/FAX); (800) 237-9896

Rated four stars, this 1886 Victorian farmhouse has been completely restored
and furnished in
period antiques
to enhance its
original charm.
Guest rooms fea-
ture king- and queen-

size beds, en suite private bathrooms, air conditioning, cable TV, clock radios, and hair dryers. The inn is on a 110-acre estate on the Annapolis River, with woodland, mountain, and meadow views. A historic church, museum, galleries, and shops are within walking distance, and a short drive will take guests to the Bay of Fundy, national parks, and historic sites.

Hosts: Richard and Shae Griffith
Rooms: 5 (PB) $50-75 Canadian
Full and Continental Breakfast
Credit Cards: A, B, C, D, E
Notes: 3, 4, 5, 7, 9, 10, 11, 12, 13, 14, 15

MUSQUODOBOIT HARBOUR

Wayward Goose Inn Bed and Breakfast

343 West Petpeswick Road, B0J 2L0
(902) 889-3654; (888) 790-1777

The Wayward Inn is a quiet inn where deer and loons visit regularly. Thirty minutes

from Halifax-Dartmouth, the Goose blends the best of urbic nience with rural charm. The are the best of crafts, museums, and breathing scenery. Hike the trails, swim off the dock, sail in the daysailer, paddle a canoe, row a rowboat, relax in the private living room with fireplace, stereo, cable TV, and VCR. Rooms are tastefully appointed with private baths and other features. Honeymoon suite features a whirlpool bath for two. Packages are available. Open May through October 1. Canada Select three-star rating.

Hosts: Randy and Judy Skaling
Rooms: 3 (PB) $56-81
Full Breakfast
Credit Cards: A, B
Notes: 2, 7, 8, 9, 11, 12, 14

PEGGY'S COVE

Peggy's Cove Bed and Breakfast

19 Church Road, B0J 2N0
(902) 823-2265; (888) 726-8322

Bright, spacious accommodations overlooking beautiful Peggy's Cove. Large, comfortable rooms. Friendly, informal atmosphere. Spectacular view. Four rooms feature patio doors opening onto large shared balconies overlooking the cove. Fifth room offers a view of the mouth of the cove, the church, and the Barrens. One private, two shared baths. Small art gallery on premises. Resident artist. Fine display of work by local artists and craftsmen. Ocean (cold) swimming. Whale watching, fishing and sailing charters available.

Host: Audry O'Leary
Rooms: 5 (1 PB; 4 S2B) $70-85 Canadian

Peggy's Cove

7 No smoking; 8 Children welcome; 9 Social drinking allowed; 10 Tennis nearby; 11 Swimming nearby; 12 Golf nearby; 13 Skiing nearby; 14 May be booked through a travel agent; 15 Handicapped accessible.

...eakfast
...t Cards: A, B, C
...es: 7, 9, 11, 14

PICTOU

Walker Inn

34 Coleraine Street, P.O Box 629, B0K 1H0
(902) 485-1433; (800) 370-5553
FAX (902) 485-1109
e-mail: walkerinn@ns.sympatico.ca

Ten-minute drive from Prince Edward
Island ferry. One-minute walk to Hector
Heritage Quay, marina, and shops. Registered Heritage property in the heart of
beautiful, historic Pictou. Fully licensed
dining room (reservations required);
dinner at 7:00 P.M. Continental breakfast
included. View of the sea from most
rooms. Cable TV.

Hosts: Larry and Jacqueline LaFleche
Rooms: 10 (PB) $65-82
Continental Breakfast
Credit Cards: A, B, C
Notes: 4, 5, 7, 9, 11, 12, 13, 14

PORT WILLIAMS

The Old Rectory Bed and Breakfast

1519 Highway 358, Rural Route 1, B0P 1T0
(902) 542-1815

Four miles from Wolfville. Recently renovated Victorian home with sunroom, gardens, and orchard. (U-Pick and
cidermaking in season.) Evening tea
served. Geology field trips can be
arranged. Hike to Cape Split, visit historic
Prescott House and Grand-Pré National
Historic Site. Enjoy the many local art
galleries and cultural events available in a
university town.

Hosts: Ron and Carol Buckley
Rooms: 3 (1 PB; 2 SB) $55-60
Full Breakfast
Credit Cards: B
Notes: 7, 8, 11, 12, 14

PUBNICO

Yesteryear's Bed and Breakfast

P.O. Box 16, B0W 2W0
(902) 762-2969 (phone/FAX)
www.auracom.com/~yesteryr/

A majestic 90-year-old Victorian country
home, restored in keeping with yesteryear,
but with all the modern conveniences. An
ideal getaway providing peace and quiet in
the countryside. Spacious bedrooms, with
queen-size beds, tastefully furnished with
antiques and collectibles. Enjoy an evening
of friendly conversation on local history or
learn about the local lobster fishing industry
from the host, Richard, who is the captain
of a lobster fishing vessel. Twenty-five
miles from the Yarmouth Ferry and a great
seafood restaurant is nearby.

Hosts: Richard and Deborah Donaldson
Rooms: 3 (1 PB; 2 SB) $45-50
Full Breakfast
Credit Cards: A, B
Notes: 5, 7, 8, 12

QUEENSLAND

Surfside Inn

Rural Route 2 Hubbards, 9609 St. Margarets Bay
   Road, B0J 1T0
(902) 857-2417; (800) 373-2417
www.bbcanada.com/524.html

The inn overlooks Queensland Beach and
is 30 minutes away from Halifax, Peggy's

Surfside Inn

NOTES: Credit cards accepted: A MasterCard; B Visa; C American Express; D Discover; E Diner's Club;
F Other; 2 Personal checks accepted; 3 Lunch available; 4 Dinner available; 5 Open all year; 6 Pets welcome;

Cove, and Lunenburg. This sea captain's home, circa 1880, has been restored, keeping Victorian elegance, with all but modern amenities. Rooms feature color TVs, whirlpools, and special luxuries for guests' enjoyment. Guests will feel like royalty sleeping in one of the massive antique mahogany beds which come complete with Beautyrest mattress and cozy duvet. There is also an in-ground pool. Off-season rates available. Canada Select three and one-half-star rating. AAA three-diamond rating.

Hosts: Michelle and Bill Batcules
Rooms: 4 (PB) $75-110
Full Breakfast
Credit cards: A, B, C, D
Notes: 5, 7, 9, 10, 11, 12, 13, 14

SYDNEY

Park Place Bed and Breakfast

169 Park Street, B1P 4W7
(902) 562-3518

Victorian-style house built for the steel plant, circa 1901. Unique feature is curved walls in the living room and hall. Downtown Sydney and its many attractions are nearby. Enjoy close proximity to Louisbourg and the Miners' Museum.

Host: Ev McEwen and Lloyd McEwen
Rooms: 3 (SB) $40-50

Park Place

Full Breakfast
Credit Cards: A, B
Notes: 7, 8, 9, 10, 11, 12, 13, 14

SYDNEY MINES

Annandale Bed and Breakfast

157 Shore Road, B1V 1A9
(902) 736-0727; FAX (902) 736-0810

Annandale Bed and Breakfast is on Route 305 in Sydney Mines; five minutes from the Newfoundland Ferries. Centrally positioned (30-40 minutes) to Fortress of Louisbourg, scenic Cabot Trail, and Bell Museum. Enjoy one of three finely appointed rooms, two with ocean view. Full hearty breakfast. TV/media. Large Victorian veranda. Take Highway 105, exit 21 to Route 305 north two miles. This Queen Anne Revival with commanding view offers relaxation and affordable rates.

Rooms: 3 (SB) $45-68
Full Breakfast
Credit Cards: B
Notes: 5, 7, 9, 11, 12, 13

Gowrie House Country Inn

139 Shore Road, B1V 1A6
(902) 544-1050; (800) 372-1115
FAX (902) 736-0077
e-mail: gowriehouse@ns.sympatico.ca

Built circa 1820 in the Georgian style, Gowrie House has been redecorated and elegantly furnished with fine antiques and works of art. The inn offers 10 rooms with en suite bath, air conditioning, fireplaces, and a private caretaker's cottage for deluxe accommodation. Renowned for comfortable rooms, friendly people, and superb food. Dinner is served daily at 7:30 P.M. with advance reservations required. Pets welcome with prior arrangements. No smoking in rooms.

Hosts: Ken Tutty and Cliff Matthews
Rooms: 10 (PB) $99-189 Canadian
Full Breakfast
Credit Cards: A, B, C
Notes: 4, 5, 9, 11, 12, 14

7 No smoking; 8 Children welcome; 9 Social drinking allowed; 10 Tennis nearby; 11 Swimming nearby; 12 Golf nearby; 13 Skiing nearby; 14 May be booked through a travel agent; 15 Handicapped accessible.

TIVERTON

Bed and Breakfast by-the-Sea

Box 719, B0V 1G0
(902) 839-2417; FAX (902) 839-2182
e-mail: oceanexp@atcon.com
www.bbcanada.com/514.html
www.cottagelink.com/cottlink/novascotia/
ns10025.html

This bed and breakfast offers very simple
accommodations in a small "outport" fishing
village in the center of one of the best whale
and bird watching areas in the Northeast.
The house is across the street from scenic
fishing port and features skylights and new
breakfast solarium overlooking harbor.
Housekeeping cottage also available. World-
famous Balancing Rock nearby. Ocean
Explorations (Zodiac) Whale/Seabird adven-
tures depart here, with packages available.
Digby is 35 minutes away.

Host: Biologist Tom Goodwin
Rooms: 2 (SB) $40-45 Canadian
Credit Cards: A, B
Notes: 2, 6, 7, 8, 9

WOLFVILLE

Victoria's Historic Inn and Carriage House Bed and Breakfast

416 Main Street, P.O. Box 308, B0P 1X0
(902) 542-5744; (800) 556-5744 (reservations only)
www.valleyweb.com/victoriasinn

This circa 1893 Victorian mansion sits only
a short drive from the Bay of Fundy, where
the highest tides in the world can be seen.
Wingback chairs, lofty ceilings, and plush
down duvets accent the guest rooms. New
World luxuries such as cable TV, telephones,
and en suite baths will enhance guests' stay.
The deluxe air-conditioned suites offer
Jacuzzi bath and/or fireplace. Ground level
accommodations are available in the quaint
and comfortable Carriage House. All within
walking distance of beautiful Wolfville.
Breakfast is included. Open year-round.

Hosts: The Cryan Family
Rooms: 15 (PB) $89-175
Full Breakfast
Credit Cards: A, B, C, E
Notes: 5, 7, 10, 11, 12, 13, 14

YARMOUTH

Murray Manor Bed and Breakfast

225 Main Street, B5A 1C6
(902) 742-9625 (phone/FAX)
e-mail: m.manor@auracom.com
www.auracom.com/cts/mmanor

Beautiful three-star Heritage home (circa
1820s) with spacious garden and 100-year-old
rhododendrons tucked behind greenhouse.
Three attractive bedrooms decorated in period
furnishings. Close to ferry, bus, airport, shops,
and museums. On garden tour and historic
walking tour. English and French (Acadian)
spoken. Canadian personal checks accepted.
Pets welcome with prior arrangements.

Hosts: George and Joan Semple
Rooms: 3 (SB) $65
Full Breakfast
Credit Cards: B
Notes: 5, 7, 8, 9, 10, 11, 12, 14

Victorian Vogue Bed and Breakfast

109 Brunswick Street, B5A 2H2
(902) 742-6398

Built in 1872, this historic Queen Anne
Revival has all the richness and charm
guests will enjoy. Fireplaces, pocket doors,
wainscoting, and stained-glass windows are
just a few of the features gracing this beautiful sea captain's home. Complimentary
tea/coffee and desserts for guests are available in the parlor each evening. Yarmouth is
a wonderful historic seaport to explore.
Magnificent homes and scenic locations
abound. Home-cooked breakfast included.

Host: Dawn-Marie Skjelmose
Rooms: 6 (1PB; 5 SB) $38-60
Credit Cards: A, B
Notes: 5, 6, 7, 8, 9, 10, 11, 12, 14

NOTES: Credit cards accepted: A MasterCard; B Visa; C American Express; D Discover; E Diner's Club;
F Other; 2 Personal checks accepted; 3 Lunch available; 4 Dinner available; 5 Open all year; 6 Pets welcome;

Prince Edward Island

Alberta's Gem Reservation Agency

11216-48 Avenue, Edmonton, AB T6H 0C7
(403) 434-6098 (phone/FAX)

A network of host homes covering many areas in Alberta. Some cities listed are: Edmonton, Calgary, Red Deer, Lethbridge, Peace River, Grande Prairie, Edson, Hinton, Pincher Creek, and southern Alberta. Additional homes in other parts of Canada, United States, Northwest Territories, Yukon, and Alaska. Full, homestyle breakfast. From $50.

ALBANY

Carleton Cove Farm Tourist Home

Rural Route 2, C0B 1A0
(902) 855-2795

A warm welcome awaits guests on this beautiful island. This farm home overlooks the Northumberland Strait and the new Confederation Bridge. Trees and flowers surround the house and the lawn includes chairs, a picnic table, and barbecue to enjoy food or a relaxing moment. Two rooms with private bath. Two rooms with shared bath. Cable TV in each room. Join the hosts for a chat and complimentary snack. Full breakfasts are included in price.

Hosts: Gordon and Carol Myers
Rooms: 4 (2 PB; 2 SB) $35-45
Full Breakfast
Credit Cards: B
Notes: 4, 6, 7, 8, 11

CAVENDISH

Kindrezd Spirits Country Inn and Cottages

Memory Lane, Route 6, C0A 1N0
(902) 963-2434 (phone/FAX)
e-mail: ajames@peinet.pe.ca

A "decidedly country but intentionally quaint" inn that is family owned and specializes in warm hospitality. Spacious rooms and suites are beautifully furnished in country antiques and crafts. Twin, double, queen-, and king-size beds available. Evening tea is served in the cozy parlor-lobby and complimentary breakfast is served in the dining room. Large heated pool; whirlpool. Fireplaces. Air conditioned. Housekeeping cottages available.

Hosts: Al and Sharon James
Rooms: 27 (PB) $60-160
Continental Breakfast
Credit Cards: A, B
Notes: 7, 8, 9, 10, 11, 12, 15

CHARLOTTETOWN

Woodmere Bed and Breakfast

Route 2 East, C1A 7J7
(902) 628-1783; (800) 747-1783

Colonial home built with the guest in mind. Standardbred horses grazing in the fields, with fragrant roses blooming in the gardens. Each spacious room offers a view of the surrounding countryside and features private bath en suite, color TV, individually controlled heat, and attractive interiors. Close to airport, harness racing, theater, fine dining, and central to all

7 No smoking; 8 Children welcome; 9 Social drinking allowed; 10 Tennis nearby; 11 Swimming nearby; 12 Golf nearby; 13 Skiing nearby; 14 May be booked through a travel agent; 15 Handicapped accessible.

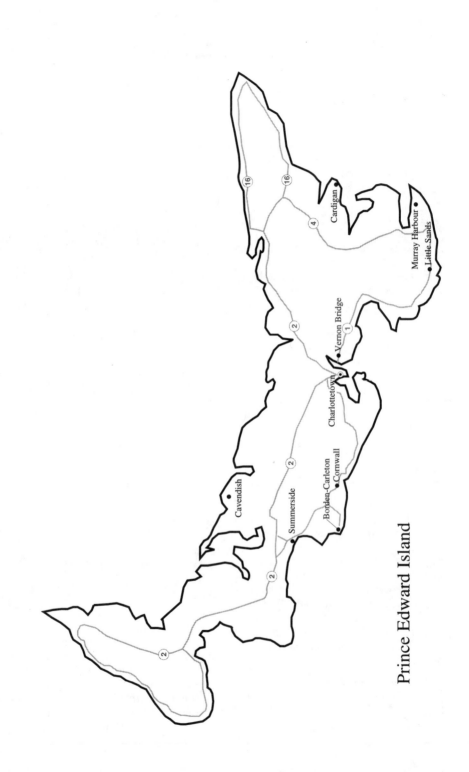

Prince Edward Island

Woodmere

attractions. National park beaches and Crow Bush golf course just a short drive of 15 minutes.

Hosts: Doris and Wallace Wood
Rooms: 4 (PB) $65-75
Full Breakfast
Credit Cards: A, B
Notes: 2, 5, 7, 8, 9, 11, 12

CORNWALL

The Unicorn Inn

Nine Mile Creek, C0A 1H0
(902) 675-3247; FAX (902) 675-2367
e-mail: unicorn@pei.sympatico.ca
www3.pei.sympatico.ca/unicorn

The inn offers comfort with class in this updated Victorian farmhouse overlooking St. Peters Island and Hillsborough Bay, only 15 minutes from Charlottetown and central to all attractions. Two guest rooms with ocean view, third with garden view and private deck, all with en suite baths. Tastefully decorated with unicorn accessories and antiques. Pub night on request with food and entertainment in pub-style games room plus second sitting area with library and TV.

Hosts: Joan and Ken Taylor
Rooms: 3 (PB) $65-75
Full Breakfast
Credit Cards: B
Notes: 2, 5, 7, 9, 11, 12

LITTLE SANDS

Bayberry Cliff Inn Bed and Breakfast

Rural Route 4, C0A 1W0
(902) 962-3395

On the edge of a 40-foot cliff on Northumberland Strait. Turn right at Wood Island Ferry Terminal, 8K on Route 4. Two uniquely decorated post-and-beam barns. Antiques and marine art. Four rooms with private baths and showers. Swimming, seal watching, craft stores, winery, air flights, restaurants handy. Open May 15 through September 30. Fifteen dollars per additional person. Breakfast included. All reservations, one night's deposit. No smoking.

Hosts: Nancy and Don Perkins
Rooms: 4 (PB) $85-125
Full Breakfast
Credit Cards: A, B
Notes: 4, 7, 8, 9, 11, 12, 14

NOTES: Credit cards accepted: A MasterCard; B Visa; C American Express; D Discover; E Diner's Club; F Other; 2 Personal checks accepted; 3 Lunch available; 4 Dinner available; 5 Open all year; 6 Pets welcome; 7 No smoking; 8 Children welcome; 9 Social drinking allowed; 10 Tennis nearby; 11 Swimming nearby; 12 Golf nearby; 13 Skiing nearby; 14 May be booked through a travel agent; 15 Handicapped accessible.

SUMMERSIDE

Silver Fox Inn

61 Granville Street, C1N 2Z3
(902) 436-4033; (800) 565-4033
e-mail: silver.fox.inn@pei.sympatico.ca
www.bbcanada.com/362.html

For more than a century, proud owners have carefully preserved the beauty of these spacious rooms with their fireplaces and fine woodwork. Combining modern comfort with the cherished past, the Silver Fox Inn

Silver Fox Inn

offers accommodations for 12 guests. Its six bedrooms, each with private bath, feature period furnishings.

Hosts: Zamborin Family—Mario, Susan,
   Jessica, and Matthew
Rooms: 6 (PB) $80-130
Full Breakfast
Credit Cards: A, B, C
Notes: 5, 7, 8, 9, 10, 11, 12, 13, 14

VERNON BRIDGE

Rainbow Lodge

Station Main, C0A 2E0
(902) 651-2202 (phone/FAX); (800) 268-7005

Rainbow Lodge is an old converted general store 15 minutes east of Charlottetown. Close to lobster suppers, beach, historic sites, golf. Relax in great room or cozy up in a suite and watch the setting sun after a fun-filled day. Take a ride in the 1931 Chevy or sit in guests' private garden area. King- or queen-size rooms. Ask about our lobster supper.

Rooms: 2 (PB) $80-125
Full Breakfast
Credit Cards: B
Notes: 4, 7, 9, 11, 12

Québec

AYER'S CLIFF

Auberge Ripplecove Inn
700 Ripplecove Road, J0B 1C0
(819) 838-4296; FAX (819) 838-5541

On the shores of Lake Massawippi, Ripple-cove Inn offers designer-appointed rooms and suites, many with fireplaces, whirlpool baths, and private balconies. One of only 10 hotels in the province awarded AAA four-diamond classification for both food and lodging. Called a "Club Med of the North" by Fodor's, Ripplecove Inn also offers year-round recreational activities, from skiing to sailing, on-site. No smoking allowed in suites.

Hosts: Jeffrey and Debra Stafford
Rooms: 26 (PB) $128-358 Canadian
Full Breakfast
Credit Cards: A, B, C
Notes: 3, 4, 5, 7, 8, 10, 11, 12, 13, 14

BATISCAN

Au Bois Dormant
1521 Rue Principale, G0X 1A0
(418) 362-3182

Au Bois Dormant is on Le Chemin du Roi Road, 90-minutes' drive from Montréal or 50 minutes from Québec City, and is a bed and breakfast, an antique and art shop, and a charming rural home from yesteryear which offers a warm welcome to guests year-round. The home is surrounded by silver maples and apple trees and includes a prom-enade that leads to the Batiscan River where is joins the St. Lawrence Seaway.

Hosts: Pierre and Ginette Lajoie
Rooms: 4 (4 SB) $40-45 U.S.

Full Breakfast
Credit Cards: B
Notes: 5, 7, 8, 10, 11

BONAVENTURE

Bay View Manor
395, Route 132, Bonaventure East, Box 21
New Carlisle, G0C 1Z0
(418) 752-2725; (418) 752-6718

Seaside home beside 18-hole Fauvel golf course, near Bonaventure East lighthouse, on the ruggedly beautiful Gaspé Peninsula of eastern coastal Québec. Once a country store and rural post office, this home now welcomes worldwide guests to this spectacular location. Fresh eggs, fruit, produce from the farm, freshly baked goods, homemade jams at breakfast. Hear the waves, view sunsets, visit museums, caves, bird sanctuary, national parks. Play tennis, canoe, fish, hike, swim, and golf.

Host: Helen Sawyer
Rooms: 5 (1 PB; 4 SB) $35
Full Breakfast
Credit Cards: None
Notes: 5, 7, 8, 10, 11, 12, 13

DESCHAMBAULT

Auberge Chemin Du Roy
106 St. Laurent, G0A 1S0
(418) 286-6958

First stop in Québec region, Deschambault invites guests to discover its historic past by staying at this Victorian inn. The antiques evoke a feeling of serenity and romance near the fireplace. Guests can also relax with the murmuring waterfall

7 No smoking; 8 Children welcome; 9 Social drinking allowed; 10 Tennis nearby; 11 Swimming nearby; 12 Golf nearby; 13 Skiing nearby; 14 May be booked through a travel agent; 15 Handicapped accessible.

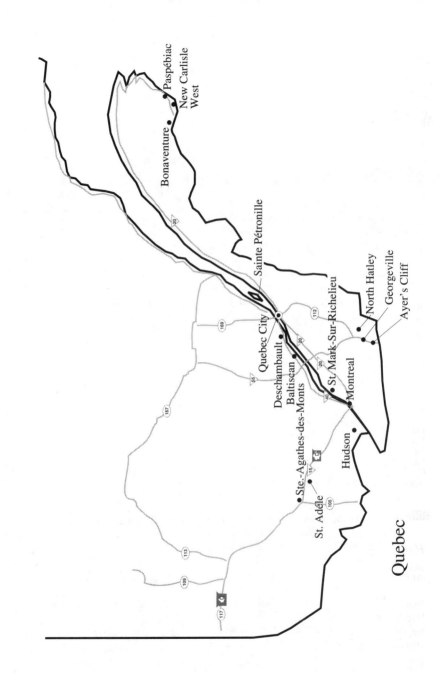

Quebec

and the St. Lawrence River breezes in front of the house.

Hosts: Francine Bouthat and Gilles Laberge
Rooms: 8 (6 PB; 2 SB) $64-99
Full Breakfast
Credit Cards: A, B
Notes: 4, 5, 9, 11, 12

GEORGEVILLE

Auberge Georgeville

71 chemin Channel, J0B 1T0
(819) 843-8683; FAX (819) 843-5045
www.fortune1000.ca/georgeville

A stately Victorian inn, Québec's oldest hotel sits majestically overlooking Lake Memphremagog, only 75 minutes east of Montréal. Guests enjoy award-winning cuisine with afternoon tea and sherry service, a wine-tasting cellar, and many on-site activities. Visit the quaint village or stroll to the lake. Theaters, museums, art galleries, and craft shops nearby. Recipient: AAA/CAA four-diamond culinary award, Fodor's *Great Country Inns*, Chamber of Commerce award of excellence. Rates include a full breakfast and a five-service gourmet dinner.

Hosts: Steven Beyrouty and Megan Seline
Rooms: 12 (8 PB; 4 SB) $170-250 Canadian
Suite: 1
Full Breakfast
Credit Cards: A, B, C
Notes: 4, 5, 7, 9, 10, 12, 13, 14

HUDSON

Riversmead

245 Main Road, J0P 1H0
(514) 458-5053

Exit 22 or 2, off Highway 40 (Trans-Canada Highway), north on Côte St. Charles or Bellevue Boulevard to Main Road. Fine 19th-century Georgian home set in large grounds with swimming pool. The quiet

and beautiful village on the shores of the Ottawa River offers fine restaurants, elegant shops, antiques, flea market, designer outlets, excellent bicycle routes, summer theatre, easy access to Montréal. Hosts offer English breakfast in the Victorian dining room or sun porch. Hosts take a warm interest in their guests.

Hosts: Naomi and Fred Henshaw
Rooms: 5 (5 S3B) $65
Full Breakfast
Credit Cards: None
Notes: 2, 7, 10, 11, 12, 13

MONTRÉAL

Armor Manoir Sherbrooke

157 Sherbrooke Est, H2X 1C7
(514) 845-0915

Armor Manoir Sherbrooke is a small inn with typical European character. In the heart of Montréal, it offers its guests a warm family atmosphere. The area contains a great many of Montréal's most fashionable shops and is central to the city's historic district. Three rooms newly renovated with Jacuzzi. Cancellation 48-hour notice.

Host: Annicu Moruan
Rooms: 30 (20 PB; 10 SB) $45-99 Canadian
Continental Breakfast
Credit Cards: A, B
Notes: 5, 7, 8, 10, 11, 13, 14

Auberge de la Fontaine

1301 East Rachel Street, H2J 2K1
(514) 597-0166; (800) 597-0597

Nice stone house where guests will be warmly welcomed in this charming bed and breakfast inn in front of Parc la Fontaine, an 84-acre park close to the downtown area. The 21 air-conditioned rooms and suites, some with whirlpool bath, others with terrace or balcony, are beautiful, comfortable, and will make guests feel at home. Enjoy a generous

NOTES: Credit cards accepted: A MasterCard; B Visa; C American Express; D Discover; E Diner's Club; F Other; 2 Personal checks accepted; 3 Lunch available; 4 Dinner available; 5 Open all year; 6 Pets welcome; 7 No smoking; 8 Children welcome; 9 Social drinking allowed; 10 Tennis nearby; 11 Swimming nearby; 12 Golf nearby; 13 Skiing nearby; 14 May be booked through a travel agent; 15 Handicapped accessible.

Continental buffet and free access to the kitchen for snacks. Parking is free as well behind the inn and in nearby streets.

Hosts: Céline Boudreau and Jean Lamothe
Rooms: 21 (PB) $99-175
Continental Breakfast
Credit Cards: A, B, C, E, F
Notes: 5, 8, 10, 11, 14, 15

Bed & Breakfast à Montréal: A City-wide Network

P.O. Box 575, Snowdon Station, H3X 3T8
(514) 738-9410; (800) 738-4338
FAX (514) 735-7493; e-mail: bbmtlnet@total.net
www.total.net/~bbntlnet

In the finest private homes and condo apartments, carefully selected for comfort, cleanliness, and location. Many are within walking distance of Vieux Montréal and the convention center. All of the hosts are fluent in English and will enhance any visit with suggestions, outgoing personalities, and delicious breakfasts. Stay long enough to visit Vieux Montréal, the lively Latin Quarter, the Underground Montréal, Botanical Gardens, Mont-Royal Park, and St. Joseph's Oratory, among others. Visits can also be arranged to Québec City. Coordinator: Marian Kahn.

Belvedere Bed and Breakfast. Five large guest rooms, each with private bath, await guests in this sprawling property, adjacent to downtown Montréal. This mansion features beautiful woodwork, a solarium, large grounds for easy parking and views. The real estate agent/hostess lives here with her two children and Blacky, the dog.

Brigette's Bed and Breakfast. Brigette's love of art and antiques is obvious in this fabulous three-story townhouse. Fireplace, cozy living room, and a view of the city's most historic park all add to the charm of this home. One double with brass bed, duvet, antique pieces, and guests' own bathroom. Experience nearby "bring your own wine" restaurants. $85 Canadian.

Jacky's Bed and Breakfast. This interior designer-hostess has created warmth and charm in this elegant downtown condo, with treasures collected from India and New Mexico. The guest room has a queen-size bed and private bathroom facilities. Sherbrooke Street, the Montréal Museum of Fine Arts, and the city's best shopping are all just two minutes away. $95 Canadian.

Johanna's Bed and Breakfast. This elegant hostess invites guests to this bright, airy, two-story home filled with European style. An avid gardener, she is pleased to share the joys of the garden with guests. This Westmount home is just five minutes from downtown. One double with a private bathroom is offered. $85 Canadian.

Marian's Bed and Breakfast. Stay in this 14th-floor apartment and enjoy magnificent views of St. Joseph's Oratory and Mont-Royal Park. Guests delight in the host's special pelican collection and the textile hangings collected during international travels. One charming double room with private bath is available. Downtown is just five minutes away. $70 Canadian.

Nelson Street Bed and Breakfast. This 15-room Victorian home with three double guest rooms is a real delight. The fashion designer-hostess has brought her artistic flair to the decoration of the house. On a quiet street in a chic neighborhood, where guests can enjoy cafés, restaurants, and elegant shops. Downtown is only 10-15 minutes away. $85-110 Canadian.

Manoir Ambrose

3422 Stanley, H3A 1R8
(514) 288-6922; FAX (514) 288-5757

A small Victorian-style mansion. Comfortable and quiet at reasonable rates. Right in the heart of the action.

Host: Lucie Gagnon
Rooms: 22 (15 PB; 7 SB) $40-70

NOTES: Credit cards accepted: A MasterCard; B Visa; C American Express; D Discover; E Diner's Club; F Other; 2 Personal checks accepted; 3 Lunch available; 4 Dinner available; 5 Open all year; 6 Pets welcome;

Continental Breakfast
Credit Cards: A, B
Notes: 5, 8, 11, 14

A Montréal Oasis
Bed and Breakfast

3000 chemin de Breslay, H3Y 2G7
(514) 935-2312

This spacious home is in downtown's select
West End, close to the Montréal Museum of
Fine Arts, Crescent and St. Catherine
Streets. It is decorated with Québec and
Swedish furniture, African, Asian, and
Swedish art. Breakfast is gourmet. Swedish
hostess, in Montréal by choice, has lived in
many parts of the world; she also operates a
quality bed and breakfast network of homes
in downtown, the Latin Quarter, and the
Old City. MasterCard and Visa accepted
only for reservations.

Host: Lena Blondel
Rooms: 30 (5 PB; 25 SB) $40-90
Full Breakfast
Credit Cards: None
Notes: 5, 7, 9, 13, 14

NEW CARLISLE WEST

Bay View Farm

Box 21, 337 Main Highway, Route 132, G0C 1Z0
(418) 752-2725; (418) 752-6718

Between New Carlisle and Bonaventure on
the rugged and beautiful Baie des Chaleurs
coastline of Québec's Gaspé Peninsula on
Route 132. Seaside accommodations include
five comfortable guest rooms. Full country
breakfast is made from fresh farm and garden
products. Handicrafts on display. Museums,
historic sites, Fauvel Golf Course, beaches,
lighthouse, hiking, bird watching. Breath-
takingly beautiful panoramic seascapes.
Tranquil and restful environment. Also available is a fully equipped seaside country house
for $350 per week.

Host: Helen Sawyer
Rooms: 5 (1 PB; 4 SB) $35
Country House: $350

Bay View Farm

Full Breakfast
Credit Cards: None
Notes: 5, 7, 8, 10, 11, 12, 13

NORTH HATLEY

Cedar Gables

4080 Magog Road, Box 355, J0B 2C0
(819) 842-4120

Established in 1985 as the area's premier
bed and breakfast, Cedar Gables is a large,
tastefully decorated home, circa 1890s, at
the lakeside on Lake Massawippi in the
heart of Québec's eastern townships.
Easily accessible, the inn is 10 minutes
from the U.S./Canada I-91/Autoroute 55
northeast corridor. The five guest rooms
have private baths en suite. Four rooms
have king-size beds and the fifth, a

Cedar Gables

7 No smoking; 8 Children welcome; 9 Social drinking allowed; 10 Tennis nearby; 11 Swimming nearby;
12 Golf nearby; 13 Skiing nearby; 14 May be booked through a travel agent; 15 Handicapped accessible.

canopied double. It is a five-minute walk to a unique resort village with shopping, browsing, and a full range of dining. Detailed brochure available. Limited smoking. Children over 12 welcome.

Hosts: Ann and Don Fleischer
Rooms: 5 (PB) $80-104
Full Breakfast
Credit Cards: A, B, C
Notes: 2, 5, 6, 9, 10, 11, 12, 13, 14, 15

PASPÉBIAC

Gîte à la ferme MACDALE

365 Route 132, Hope, P.O. Box 803, G0C 2K0
(418) 752-5270

For a relaxing holiday, visit the Gaspé Peninsula and MACDALE bed and breakfast. Overlooking Chaleur Bay on an active, fifth-generation beef farm, this spacious three-story home offers two family rooms and a variety of guest accommodations. The aroma of fresh coffee and assorted muffins and pastries will awaken guests and whet their appetite for an old-fashioned home-baked breakfast using farm-fresh eggs. Thanks to MACDALE's central location, tourist attractions such as world-famous Percé Rock and Forillon Park are well within daytrip driving distance. A seawater therapy resort is just minutes away, as are many museums, points of historical interest, and sports facilities. Pets welcome outdoors only.

Hosts: Anne and Gordon MacWhirter
Rooms: 5 (1 PB; 4 SB) $45-55
Full Breakfast
Credit Cards: None
Notes: 2, 3, 4, 5, 7, 8, 9, 10, 11, 12, 13, 14

QUÉBEC CITY

A L'étoile de Rosie

66 Lockwell, G1R 1V7
(418) 648-1044

Upon guests' arrival at this row house dated 1920, they will feel its energy. Guests will enjoy a splendid view of the Laurentian Mountains, as well as of the park near at hand, where squirrels can be watched. This home is in the Montcalm quarter, which is much sought after for its quietness, its ready access to social-cultural activities, and its tourist attractions, such as the Centre de congrés, the Musée du Québec, the Plaines d'Abraham, Vieux Québec, and the Château Frontenac. Grande Allée, Saint-Jean, and Cartier Streets are almost at the home's doorstep, as well as the parking. Complimentary breakfast is included in the rates.

Host: Marie-Denise Saint-Gelais
Rooms: 3 (3 SB) $50-75
Credit Cards: None
Notes: 5, 7, 10, 11, 12, 13

Au Petit Hôtel

3 ruelle des Ursulines, G1R 3Y6
(418) 694-0965; FAX (418) 692-4320

In the heart of Old Québec, Au Petit Hôtel offers quiet surroundings with a warm and hospitable atmosphere. Near major attractions such as the Ursulines convent, the Citadel, and Le Château Frontenac. Discriminating gourmets will have no trouble finding neighborhood restaurants, smart boutiques, and all kinds of entertainment.

Hosts: The Tim Family
Rooms: 16 (PB) $45–70
Continental Breakfast
Credit Cards: A, B
Notes: 5, 8, 9, 11, 13, 14

Bed & Breakfast à Montréal: A City-wide Network

P.O. Box 575, Snowdon Station, H3X 3T8
(514) 738-9410; (800) 738-4338
FAX (514) 735-7493; e-mail: bbmtlnet@total.net
www.total.net/~bbntlnet

A Québec City Choice. Delight in this restored 17th-century home in Old Québec offering three guest rooms with private bathrooms. Many special architectural features and antique furnishings. This bilingual

---

NOTES: Credit cards accepted: A MasterCard; B Visa; C American Express; D Discover; E Diner's Club; F Other; 2 Personal checks accepted; 3 Lunch available; 4 Dinner available; 5 Open all year; 6 Pets welcome;

host couple and their dog welcome guests. $95-110 Canadian.

Hayden's Wexford House

450 rue Champlain, G1K 4J3
(418) 524-0524; FAX (418) 648-8995

Ancestral Irish home built in the beginning of the 18th century at the heart of the Heritage and near Old Québec City. Near many points of interest. In summer, relax in the little flower garden and in winter by the fireside. Enjoy breakfast in a warm decor and relaxed atmosphere. Spectacular river view from guest rooms. Open year-round. Apartment also available; please call for rates.

Hosts: Jean and Louise
Rooms: 30 (SB) $65-70 Canadian
Full Breakfast
Credit Cards: A, B, C, E
Notes: 5, 8, 9, 10, 11, 12, 13, 14

Hôtel Château de la Terrasse, Inc.

6 Place Terrasse Dufferin, G1R 4N5
(418) 694-9472; FAX (418) 694-0055

Built in 1830, this stately residence is in between the Citadel and Château Frontenac, on the famous Dufferin Terrace overlooking the St. Lawrence River. Its unique inner architecture has been kept with a beautifully sculpted wooden staircase and a few authentic stained-glass windows. The ideal restover to feel the pulse of the oldest city in North America, amid a myriad of activities offered on the boardwalk.

Host: Christiane-Marie Bès
Rooms: 30 (16 PB; 2 SB) $75-120
Continental Breakfast
Credit Cards: A, B, C, E
Notes: 5, 8, 9, 10, 11, 12, 13, 14

Hôtel Marie Rollet

81 rue Sainte-Anne, G1R 3X4
(418) 694-9271; (800) 275-0338

Built in 1876 by the Ursulines order, the Marie Rollet offers the ancestral charm of a

turn-of-the-century European manor. Guests will be captivated by its warm woodwork and its tranquility and serenity. All area attractions can be reached by foot. Two rooms offer a functional fireplace and most have air conditioning. A rooftop terrace with a garden view gives guests an opportunity to relax in a calm and serene environment.

Hosts: Gerald Giroux and Diane Chouinard
Rooms: 10 (PB) $59-125
No Breakfast
Credit Cards: A, B
Notes: 5, 8, 10, 11, 12, 13, 14

La Maison Lafleur

2, re de Laval, G1R 3T9
(418) 692-0685; FAX (418) 694-0551
www.presentix.com/com/lafleur/

A peaceful, residential location in the heart of the old Latin quarter, Old Québec. Surrounded by an exceptional view of 17th-and 18th-century architecture. While this row house was rebuilt in 1950, portions still remain from the 18th century. All of the tourist attractions and services are right at the doorstep. Ten-minute walk to bus and train station. As a long-time resident of Old Québec, the host will gladly suggest many unforgettable places to visit. Cross-country skiing within walking distance. Maximum capacity is eight persons.

Host: Gilles Lafleur
Rooms: 3 (1 PB; 2 SB) $55-85
Full Breakfast
Credit Cards: B
Notes: 5, 7, 8, 10, 11, 13

7 No smoking; 8 Children welcome; 9 Social drinking allowed; 10 Tennis nearby; 11 Swimming nearby; 12 Golf nearby; 13 Skiing nearby; 14 May be booked through a travel agent; 15 Handicapped accessible.

SAINTE-ADELE

Auberge Beaux Rêves (Sweet Dreams Inn)

2310, boul. Ste-Adèle, J0R 1L0
(514) 229-9226; FAX (514) 229-2999
e-mail: welcome@beauxreves.com
www.Beauxreves.com

In Sainte-Adèle midway between Montréal and Mont-Tremblant in the heart of the Laurentians. A unique spa concept with outdoor hot tub, sauna, and relaxation pavilion, open year-round. A riverside nature path brings guests to dozens of natural whirlpools. All rooms have private bathrooms; some overlook the river. A full country breakfast is served fresh every morning. Close to snowmobiling, skiing, golf, cycling, nature walks, etc.

Host: Hannes Lamothe
Rooms: 4 (PB) $75-90 Canadian
Full Breakfast
Credit Cards: B
Notes: 5, 7, 8, 9, 10, 11, 12, 13, 14

SAINTE-AGATHE-DES-MONTS

Auberge du Lac des Sables

230 St-Venant, J8C 2Z7
(819) 326-3994; (800) 567-8329
FAX (819) 326-9159
e-mail: info@aubergedulac.com
www.aubergedulac.com

One hour north of Montréal, in the heart of the Laurentians, between St-Sauveur and Mont Tremblant. The warm welcome and the charm of an authentic country inn in an exceptional scenic site on the shores of Lac des Sables. Each of the 19 cozy rooms is equipped with a private bathroom and whirlpool, color TV, and air conditioning. Outside heated whirlpool and conference room also available. At walking distance from the village and a wide range of summer and winter activities. Many packages available.

Auberge du Lac des Sables

Hosts: Dominique Lessard and Luc Menard
Rooms: 19 (PB) $76-112 Canadian
   (approx. $54-80 U.S.)
Full Breakfast
Credit Cards: A, B, C
Notes: 4, 5, 8, 10, 11, 12, 13, 14

SAINT-MARC-SUR-RICHELIEU

Hostellerie Les Trois Tilleuls

290 rue Richelieu, J0L 2E0
(514) 856-7787; FAX (514) 584-3146
e-mail: host.3tilleuls@sympatico.ca

A stay at Les Trois Tilleuls means being an eagerly awaited guest in a century-old home. It's an opportunity to discover a multitude of artworks, acquired over the past 100 years, andto enjoy the labors of craftsmen from bygone days to the present, who put their hearts into creating an incomparable inn. At Les Trois Tilleuls a colorful garden, sparkling in the morning dew warm oneself in the early morning sun, and contemplate the Richelieu River, one of Québec's beautiful and historic rivers. A modern wing containing 24 charming rooms with every modern convenience.

Host: Mr. Michel Aubriot
Rooms: 24 (PB) $115-390 Canadian w/ room only
   $225-530 Candian w/ American plan
Full Breakfast
Credit Cards: A, B, C, D, E
Notes: 3, 4, 5, 8, 9, 10, 11, 12, 13, 14, 15

NOTES: Credit cards accepted: A MasterCard; B Visa; C American Express; D Discover; E Diner's Club; F Other; 2 Personal checks accepted; 3 Lunch available; 4 Dinner available; 5 Open all year; 6 Pets welcome;